Is This Reality?

D J Macleod

Is This Reality?

To my sister Kathleen

Sonny

Vanguard Press

VANGUARD PAPERBACK

© Copyright 2016
D J Macleod

The right of D J Macleod to be identified as author of
this work has been asserted by him in accordance with the
Copyright, Designs and Patents Act 1988.

A CIP catalogue record for this title is
available from the British Library.

ISBN 978 178465 103 9

Vanguard Press is an imprint of
Pegasus Elliot MacKenzie Publishers Ltd.

www.pegasuspublishers.com

First Published in 2016

Vanguard Press
Sheraton House Castle Park
Cambridge England

Printed & Bound in Great Britain

Acknowledgements

I would like to take this opportunity of thanking my wife Audrey, and our family for their encouragement and support in bringing my style of writing to be published.

I would also like to thank the staff of Pegasus Publishers for their professionalism and patience in keeping me on the right track. I would also like to share the observation that like so many other jobs and professions, 'Publishing' is not a half-hour task. Many people (including myself) have a tendency not to appreciate the skill and dedication needed for other professions to carry out their respective duties, and I am pleased once more to be reminded of this insight.

I would also like to thank the many wonderful people that I had the pleasure and privilege of meeting and getting to know over the years, they have been a constant inspiration. Also perhaps the not so wonderful people who also inspired emotions I never knew I had, and the awareness that although we are all in the same boat in this world, we are all unique. While it may be politically correct and even poetic to say we are all brothers and sisters, and even wish we were all like-minded. Yet I do not see this ever being possible, and perhaps for very good reasons. Instead, it may be a good idea to accept the fact that true reality is possibly out-with our comprehension, and should bear that in mind while we put up with our own perceptions.

Contents

RAMBLINGS 1   51

THE SALMON   53

FREEDOM   53

TAX RECEIPT   53

A MIRACLE   54

THE PARTY   54

GOOD SENSE   55

ALL THE SAME   55

WOMEN'S SENSE   56

THE MASON   56

DYING ROTTI   56

SNEAKS   57

SEMI-SOBER   57

LIBIDO   57

NEW NEIGHBOUR   57

THE BEECH TREE   58

TEMPTATION   58

THE EGO TRIP   58

MY SCONES   59

TRIER   59

LESSONS   59

SUSSED IT OUT   60

THE RESERVE   60

BLESSINGS   60

ACCOUNTANTS   61

NEW THINGS   61

RED INDIANS   61

LOGIC   62

IGNORANCE   62

PATIENCE	62
NEW NEIGHBOURS	63
PASSING OF TIME	63
TELL TALE	64
LOTTERY WINNER	64
FALSE MEMORY	64
UNDERSTANDING	65
REALITY	65
THE BUILDER	65
HAIRCUT	66
AN ANSWER	66
MECHANICS	66
CUT DOWN TO SIZE	67
MAD COW DISEASE	67
THE SAME	67
BRAVERY	68
GREED	68
THE BIG SHOT	69
WASTED	69
Z OR X	69
BE AWARE	69
THE GOOD THAT I DO	70
PRIDE	70
WHO TO TELL	71
BELIEF	71
MORE DEPRESSION	71
THE POOR	71
FAIRIES	72
KEEPING GOING	72
URI THE BRICKIE	72
ONCE BITTEN	73
ODDS	73

READING MINDS	**73**
BUDGET	**74**
RECIPES	**74**
WAITING	**74**
TIME TRAVEL	**75**
THE SCRAPPIE	**75**
BANK ON IT	**75**
THE VISION	**76**
HATE	**76**
FORGOTTEN	**77**
THE KEY	**77**
EVERYONE TO THEIR OWN JOB	**77**
NORMAL REACTION	**78**
WHY SOME	**79**
COMING BACK	**79**
AFFECTED	**80**
QUEEN	**80**
HEROES	**80**
LEFT HANDERS	**80**
CHOOSY	**81**
ANOTHER INVITATION	**81**
WAITING	**81**
DRY FLIES	**82**
SINISTER	**82**
THE AUTHOR	**83**
NATURE	**83**
DOUBT	**83**
CATCHING A SALMON	**84**
DEEP FROZEN	**84**
THE WILL	**85**
DIVINE GUIDANCE	**85**
MEDITATION AGAIN	**85**

ACT NOW   86

SPEED OF TIME   86

FORGOT   86

MOTIVE   87

NUTTER   87

BASIC INSTINCT   87

DAY DREAMING   88

GUILTY   88

RAN OFF   88

DAMN POACHERS   89

INVESTMENT   89

DOWNHILL   90

HAPPIEST TIMES   90

TWO SURE THINGS   90

OLD AGE   91

PAIN   91

THE ALCOHOLIC   92

HUMAN   92

SHOPPING   93

FISHING FLIES   93

EYES OPENED   94

THE REGISTER   94

DELETE   94

TRAGIC   95

TRAINING   95

FLITTING   95

READING   95

PERFECTION   96

MY HERO   96

THE ONE THAT GOT AWAY   96

CONTRARY NATURE   97

HUMANS   97

SENSE	98
REAL REALITY	98
DREAM WORLD	98
REVENGE	99
THE BALLET DANCER	99
WAIT FOR IT	99
THE FERRET	99
SMART GUY	100
A FOOL	100
SIMPLE	100
NO RESPECT	100
THE FINAL RESPONSE	101
THE MASSES	101
SO SURE	101
THE STUPID THIEF	102
THE PLAYING FIELDS OF ETON	102
THE MINER	102
HEAVEN	103
OLD BUILDINGS	103
RESPONSE TO BANK	103
ADVICE TO A YOUTH	104
A WEE DOWNER	104
DEEP THOUGHT	104
CONFIDENCE	104
HAPPINESS	105
IN THE PLAYGROUND	105
UNDERSTANDING	105
HUMAN	106
POSITIVE THINKING	106
NO NECESSITY	106
WHY CHANGE	107
THE OLD JERSEY	107

BIG MAN   107

A PRICK   107

HUMAN   108

INDIFFERENCE   108

THE PORTFOLIO   108

THE BIRD   109

SHOPPING   109

POPULARITY   109

COURT OF SESSION   110

THE GENE   110

THE TYCOON   110

AUTONOMY   111

MADONNA'S BOTTOM   111

REPEATS   112

LIFE   112

TOO MUCH   113

THE CURE   113

AGAIN AND AGAIN   113

BOREDOM   113

A CHILDHOOD DREAM   114

MORE PANIC   114

RAMBLINGS 2   116

HORMONES AGAIN   117

THE SLIPPERY SLOPE   117

THE INVENTION   117

LONELY   118

OUT OF PROPORTION   118

JUMPING OFF THE MANTELPIECE   119

BUILDING BRICKS   119

IT WILL BE BETTER   119

THE LEGACY   120

NEVER TOO OLD   120

HOPE	120
SICK JOKE	120
THE UPBRINGING	121
THE ARTIST	121
LOVE AFFAIR	121
LINDA	121
THE NEW AGE	122
ANOTHER DEAD FLY	122
LUCKY DOG	122
WHO KNOWS	122
MORE EXPERIENCE	123
TWISTERS	123
THE PLAN	123
FIGHTING DIRTY AGAIN	123
A GREAT LOSS	124
THE DRINKERS MEMORY	124
THE RULES	124
THE BARBI	124
NOT UP TO IT	125
QUITE SMART	126
WORKERS	126
HOLIDAYS	126
MYSTERIOUS	127
A VISIT TO THE DOC	127
MORE DRAMS	127
SUCCESS	127
IN DEFENCE	128
POOR CLEG	128
OPPORTUNITY	128
THANKFUL	128
A CHANGE OF HEART	129
WON'T BE EASY	129

SICKENING 129

KNOWLEDGE 129

CLOTHES 130

IT DOESN'T COST MUCH 130

LAST WILL 130

CATS AND DOGS 130

TARRING THE DRIVE 131

WONDER 131

THE PHONE CALL 131

INSIGHT 131

PRIORITIES 132

TRUE 132

THE SPACE 132

A LITTLE UNDERSTANDING 133

THE HERMIT 133

THE CAUSE 133

DRUNKARD 134

ANOTHER DRUNKARD 134

MY BUILDING LINE 134

BRAINWASHING AGAIN 135

A BILL 135

A WEE WORRY RESOLVED 135

BREAKDOWN 136

AGGRO 136

PERFECTION 136

FRESH START 136

OWNERSHIP 137

THE SPELL 137

PRIDE 138

THE HIGH RISE 139

THE HOLS' 139

THE OPPOSITE 139

THE BIG THREE	140
NO REASON	140
UTOPIA	140
THE NEW ROAD	140
ANOTHER FUNERAL	141
THE LIGHT	141
NO REPLACEMENT	141
THEM AND US	142
WISHING	142
GRAY'S ANATOMY	142
SOCIAL GAFFE	143
THE DEMON AGAIN	143
CHANGE FOR THE BETTER	143
HAPPINESS	144
MEANING WELL	144
THE INSULT	145
ERRING	145
THE BARKING DOG	146
REMEMBERED	146
THE HOUSEWIFE	146
IMPETUS	147
SHOPPING	147
SURE OF YOURSELF	147
IT'S NOT FREE	148
ADDICTED	148
IDLE HANDS	148
GOOD FOOD	149
PRIORITIES	149
NEW NEIGHBOURS	149
SUING	150
THE FINAL SOLUTION	150
A RELAPSE	150

GOOD ADVICE	151
TWELVE STEPS	151
ANOTHER FREUDIAN SLIP	151
THE ROBIN	152
PRETTY SMART	152
MIDGES	152
JEALOUSY	152
CAUGHT	153
PRIDE	153
CHEERED UP	153
THE MISSING SAW	154
ALL HIDDEN	154
HAPPINESS	154
RAMBLINGS 3	156
IS THERE MORE THAN ONE	157
MODERN ART	157
DOUBT	157
ONE SMILE	158
IT DIDN'T WORK	158
TELL TALE	158
ROYALTY	158
STUCK IN THE MUD	159
NOT STUPID	159
THE PRESENT	159
THIRST	159
A DIFFERENT DIRECTION	160
NOT IMPROVED	160
BAD TRAINING	160
DEPRESSED AGAIN	161
DO YOU KNOW	161
ANTICIPATION	161
CONTENTMENT	161

INNOCENCE 162

FLASHERS 162

ENJOYMENT 162

BITTER REGRET 162

COMPETITION 163

THE WEATHER 163

BULL BARS 163

IMPOSSIBLE 164

NO EXCUSE 164

LOVE 164

SPITE 164

THE WITNESS 164

PRIDE 165

LADS OF THE NORTH 165

HYPERACTIVE 165

SEXUAL HARASSMENT 166

CIVILISATION 166

BE TRUE 167

RANK 167

OTHER JOBS 167

NEW BAR 167

NO CUSTOMERS 168

WONDER 168

BLAMED 168

SINS 169

WEAKNESS 169

QUIET DAY IN THE SHOP 169

IN THE WAY 170

THE BARBER 170

INSTINCTS 170

SELFISH 171

TRAINING 171

SPOT THE BALL   171

STOLEN DRINK   171

THE MAN TRAP   172

LIAR   172

MEN   172

THE IDIOT   172

MODERATION   173

A LOST BUTTON   173

A GURNY MAN   174

COMMON SENSE   174

NAMES   174

MORE REGRET   174

A PAIN   175

PROGRAMMED   175

QUITE HAPPY   175

FIGURE IT OUT   176

FLY   176

SKI PANTS   176

CRAFTIER STILL   177

TYPICAL MAN   177

THE GREEN GRASS   177

A POOR CHAP   177

UNLUCKY THIEF   178

WOULD YOU   178

GET UP AND GO   178

THE TOOL FOR THE JOB   178

REAL YOU   179

PASSING THE TIME   179

EXCUSES   179

MORE EXCUSES   180

A QUIET DAY IN THE SHOP   180

GETTING BY   180

MY GARDEN WALL 181

RETURN 181

HELL 181

MORE FATE 182

THE SHAKE 182

NO SMILE 182

SOBER DAY 182

BROKE 183

WAS I RIGHT 183

SPITE 183

SO COMMON 184

DECISIONS 184

THE END 185

CAN IT GET WORSE 185

PARTY TIME 186

TRY THIS 186

HURT 186

WINNING 186

NO REWARD 186

GOOD SENSE 187

IT'S THERE 187

THE RACE 187

ADDICTION 187

THE WIDOWS PENSION 188

GROW UP 188

TOO LATE 189

DAYDREAM 189

TIME 190

WINTER 190

DIGNITY 190

BASIC 191

THE KILLER 191

THE RAT 191

TONIC 191

TEA TIME 192

PRIORITIES 192

OUT OF SIGHT 193

THE SAME 193

SATURDAY NIGHT 193

ALTERNATIVE 194

A MOOD 194

THE ULTIMATE 194

INBUILT 195

WATERTIGHT 195

ABSTINENCE 195

CIVILIZED 196

I WONDER 196

BE PREPARED 196

FORMS 197

YOU 197

BETTER 197

INSTINCT 198

INEVITABLE 198

THE THIEF 198

JUSTICE 198

DARK DAYS 199

NOT GOOD ENOUGH 199

MORE DEPRESSION 199

SOBRIETY 199

MORE TO COME 200

JUST YOUR LUCK 200

LIES 200

FATE MAYBE 201

RIGHT AFTER ALL 201

NOT ME	201
CONNED	201
IN PROPORTION	202
THE MISTAKE	202
A CHEAP JOB	202
CHANGE	202
NICE PEOPLE	203
CAN YOU	203
CONSEQUENCES	203
FOOD	204
THE SECRETARY	204
PRIDE	204
MYSTERY	204
LOGIE	205
TRY IT	205
AGREED	205
WAS THERE A PLAN	205
THE EXPERTS	206
COULD BE	206
A COMPLIMENT	206
A LITTLE ERROR	206
COMPARISON	207
THE REJECT	207
MAKING MONEY	207
LAST AMBITION	208
MY LETTER	208
VERY TRUE	208
THAT'S LIFE	209
ALCOHOL	209
THE TRANCE	209
THE GENERAL	210
PROPRIETARY	210

A WANT	210
SADNESS	211
REVENGE	211
DARWIN	211
CIRCUMSTANCES	212
RAMBLINGS 4	213
THE TEMPTATION	214
THEY ARE EVERYWHERE	214
DISCLOSED	214
YES I KNEW	214
WHAT YOU DO WITH IT	215
TRUE NATURE	215
HEALING	215
AMBITION	215
NOT OBVIOUS	216
I'M ALL RIGHT	216
TACT	216
NOTHING IS FAIR	217
ONE OF THE LAWS	217
TAX EVASION	217
QUALIFICATIONS	218
D I Y	218
I STILL WONDER	218
THE CREAM	218
LIVING ON YOUR WITS	219
IMAGINATION	219
TRAGIC	219
LESSON IN LENDING	220
BE EXOTIC	220
THE BEST BITS	220
FORBIDDEN FRUIT	220
DISTINCTION	221

ACCURATE SOUNDS   221

TOP OF MY LEAGUE   221

FALSE GUILT   222

NOT PREPARED   222

CERTAINTY   222

TRUSTY   222

MY DIET   222

THERE IS MORE   223

GET OUT THE SCALPEL   223

FAIR PLAY   223

KNOWLEDGE   223

ARE YOU SURE   223

WATCHING   224

LUCK   224

THE FUTURE   224

BASIC RULE   225

THE SYSTEM   225

CHANGING   225

CLEVER   226

THE BEST SO FAR   226

OLD SAYINGS   226

OWNERSHIP   226

THE EMPLOYER   227

THE URGE   227

FAILED   227

IN COMPARISON   228

MORE URGES   228

WAITING   228

NOT SO BAD   228

HONESTY   229

FAULTLESS   229

THE OPERATOR   229

INTOXICATION   230

CLARITY   230

BELIEF   230

CHOICES   231

LEFT IT TOO LATE   231

ASHAMED   231

SOBER AGAIN   231

EDUCATION   232

THE RAT   232

WHY NOT   232

IN THE LAP OF THE GODS   233

MUST HAVE   233

FIRST LESSON   233

IT WAS ALWAYS A STORY   233

A DIFFERENT PERSON   234

VALUES   234

EASY LEARNED   234

YOUR DIVISION   235

WHO IS WHO   235

TINS   235

MIND POWER   235

REVENGE   236

ALL THE SAME   236

HOW DO THEY DO IT   236

NO JUSTICE   237

GROWN UP   237

OLD SYSTEM   237

DOESN'T HURT YOU   237

MIRROR IMAGE   237

MUST BE   238

EGO   238

TOO MUCH IMAGINATION   239

THE HONEST TRUTH	239
BORN LUCKY	239
A GOOD TAX MAN	239
SMILE	240
ALL CHANGE	240
MAM	241
CULTURE	241
THE GREATEST SIN	241
COMMON BELIEF	242
YES WE ARE RIGHT	242
SPOILED	242
IN PROPORTION	243
WELL TRAINED	243
SURVIVAL INSTINCT	243
RAMBLINGS 5	245
THE PERFECT FRIEND	246
TWINS	246
ARE YOU POOR	246
WEIGH THE ODDS	247
EXCUSES	247
PATIENCE	247
ANOTHER LOST DOG	248
THE FUTURE	248
NEED	248
MORE TO THE EYE	248
GAMES	249
NEW THEORIES	249
A GOOD INSTINCT	249
FALSE CONFIDENCE	249
PRESSURE	250
EVOLUTION	250
GREED	250

BULLIES 250

DAY DREAMING 250

TENS AGAIN 251

CRACKED IT 251

FASHION DESIGNER 251

TEDDY BEAR 252

BE PREPARED 252

HAND IN POCKET 252

EASY WAY OUT 252

BEING SMART 253

PROGRAMMED 253

NO SMOKING 253

PARADISE LOST 254

GETTING YOUR OWN BACK 254

THE WORKER 254

THE BIG TEAM 254

ANOTHER CLAN 255

KNOWING 255

ABILITY 255

THE BUILDERS 255

TALENT 256

DAVE THE FISHMAN 256

THE WORST 256

BE FAIR 257

THE NOVEL 257

WHO'S CRAFTY 257

A DREAM 258

NEXT 258

THE ADULT 258

SMALL DEPRESSION 258

SAFETY 259

THE NURDS 259

THE VOLUNTEER WHO DOESN'T KNOW 259

I UNDERSTAND 260

THE FIGHT 260

PLAYING AT IT 261

IGNORED 261

A DREAMER 261

THE BOSS 261

GETTING ALONG 262

TRIPPED 262

NATURAL 263

UNDERSTANDING 263

THE RIGHT THEORY 263

TRUE ABILITY 264

NEVER TOO LATE 264

WHO KNOWS 264

IRRESISTIBLE 265

THE RECEPTION COMMITTEE 265

MOULDED 265

MAKING SURE 266

THE REAL REASON 266

AT THE END OF THE BATTLE 266

SPOILED 266

NO REASON 267

A TURN ON 267

KEPT BACK 267

LEARNING 268

ANOTHER MYSTERY 268

LUCKY 268

NOT TODAY 268

REALITY? 269

DO YOUR BEST 269

EASY WAY OUT AGAIN 269

NOSEY   269

CRACKING POINT   270

IS THERE ANYBODY THERE   270

THE ORIGIN   270

A CHANGE   270

FAIR PLAY   271

GRANNY   271

THE ANSWER   271

THE SYSTEM   271

A WANT   272

MOUSE TRAP   272

HOSPITAL   272

NERVE   273

WILL OF IRON   273

A THIEF   273

FATE   273

SHARED EXPERIENCES   274

NICE MAN   274

THE ANSWER   274

HORSE BEFORE THE CART   274

AN INSTANT DISLIKE   275

DIVINE AMBUSH   275

ANOTHER REGRET   275

INNATE WEAKNESS   276

WHAT TURNS YOU ON   276

TECHNICALLY TRUE   276

BE WISE   276

INSTINCTIVE   277

SUPPORTER   277

IT TAKES BRAINS   277

PRESSURE   277

WOULD YOU BELIEVE ME   278

MISS TIMED	278
APPRECIATION	278
TOO CLEVER	278
YOUR JOB	279
THE STATEMENT	279
TYPICAL SHOPPING DAY	279
THE SEDUCER	280
SECOND HAND	280
BASIC INSTINCT	281
IN JAIL	281
TEACH THE CHILD MEDITATION	281
HOLY JOE'S	282
THE CIRCUS	282
GOING ROUND IN CIRCLES	282
ARE WE SAFE	283
THE FLIRT	283
DISAPPOINTMENT	283
PRIORITIES	283
ON YOUR TOES	284
A CALLING	284
TELL ALL	284
BODY LANGUAGE	284
THE POLITICIAN	284
OLD PHILOSOPHY	285
KEEPING IT GOING	285
CONFIDENCE	285
OWNERSHIP	285
GETTING A WINNER	286
TOP OF THE PYRAMID	286
DISCOVER	286
UNIQUE	286
RAMBLINGS 6	287

VAMPIRE 288

TAX MAN AGAIN 288

THE CHEMISTS SHOP 288

DESERVE IT 288

HIDDEN VIRTUE 289

PRIDE 289

FOUND OUT 289

IMPROVEMENT 290

THE LIGHT 290

INEVITABLE 291

BENEVOLENT 291

ALTERNATIVE THERAPY 291

INSTINCT 292

UFOS 292

ENVY 292

HUMAN 292

FAUX PAS 293

DOES IT MATTER? 293

FAITH HEALER 294

NEW TYRES 294

NOT SPEAKING AGAIN 295

MANS CHIEF END 295

A LEGEND 295

A PAIN 296

SUPERSTITIOUS 296

THE LAST RESORT 297

YOU'LL REMEMBER 297

ASK THE QUESTION 297

ANOTHER FAITH HEALER 297

MISSED THE POINT 298

NATURAL EMOTION 299

WRONG PLACE 299

A GIFTED GIRL   299

THE PLAN   299

ALONE   300

IT'S FREE   300

HOMO   300

THE REQUEST   301

LAST STRAW   301

COMPARISON   301

NO HOPE   302

BEAR FRUIT   302

WHAT NAME   302

LOST   303

THE PROTECTION   303

CAN'T RESIST   304

THE BAT   304

LECTURED   304

HERMIT   304

THE RESULT OF DRUGS?   305

PLAYING A PART   305

TAX MAN YET AGAIN   306

THE BEGINNING   306

THINKING   306

MORE JEALOUSY   307

NO CHOICE   307

LOVE   307

PUT BY   307

NO GUARANTEE   308

ROBIN HOOD   308

ZOMBIE   308

SOMETHING MISSING   308

GOT IT   309

GUARDIAN ANGEL   309

SOBER   309

THE INEVITABLE   309

JUST TRY   310

THE COMPLEX BRAIN   310

BAD HABITS   310

THE HARE AND THE TORTOISE   311

AULD ACQUAINTANCE   311

BIGOTED   311

A LITTLE CLUE   311

THE JOY OF BEING RICH   312

THE QUALITY   312

A CHOICE   312

THE SPELL AGAIN   313

UNION   313

THE LETTER   313

THE LIONS AGAIN   314

NEVER FORGOT   314

THE URGE   314

PARADOX   315

THE GENE   315

EYE FOR AN EYE   315

A CUT ABOVE   316

LAZY   316

A NIGHTMARE JOB   316

STAND THE PACE   317

PROPAGANDA   317

FORETOLD   317

CLEVER DOG   318

DIFFERENT HEALERS   318

NAÏVE   319

GET REAL   319

SECTS   319

THE SAME STONES	320
MERCENARY	320
GUARDIAN ANGEL AGAIN	320
DEPRESSED	321
FREUD	321
BLAME	321
RAMBLINGS 7	323
REALITY	324
A LONG WAY TO GO	324
MEMORY	324
THE QUEEN	324
STARK TRUTH	325
THE ONLY ONES	325
INSTINCT	325
THE SEA SAW	326
INDIFFERENT	326
LOSE THE HEAD	326
THE BOTTOM	326
THE VAT MAN	327
GOD	327
JUST YOUR LUCK	327
NEAR IT	328
COMRADES	328
HEAVEN	328
STREET MARKET	328
ALWAYS ONE	329
LUCK	329
THE BOOK OF LIFE	329
WORKERS	330
THE WOLF	330
ACHILLES HEEL	330
POPULARITY	330

HUNTING 331

SNOOKER 331

LOCAL 331

PRETTY NICE 332

SOCIAL WORK 332

CONFORM 332

THE OPEN FIRE 333

UNEMPLOYED 333

ROAD RAGE 333

HANGING 334

AIDS 334

CHANGE 334

HANG ON 334

THE GUN 335

THE LOST GOOSE 335

THE GARDEN 335

HARLING 335

SNOBBISH 336

NIGHTMARE 336

PARIS & HELEN 336

THE SCHOOLBOY 336

MY OLD LORRY 337

THE CORNER SHOP 337

HOLE IN THE HEART 337

TALENT 338

USELESS 338

HOPE 338

JUSTICE 339

THE REPLACEMENT 339

PATIENCE 340

PESSIMISTIC 340

PRACTICE 340

CAN'T HELP IT	341
A CRAVING	341
NIGHTMARE	341
A TALL STORY?	341
TRUE	342
THE REAL URGES	343
NO DIFFERENCE	343
THE WIDE ROAD	343
DIFFICULTIES	343
PARTY MEMBER	344
JUSTICE	344
PUT OFF	344
GETTING DONE	345
ANOTHER LORRY	345
REMOVING A GALVANISED TANK	345
A SNARE	346
THE PUB	346
FORNICATE	347
MY LORRY	347
LOVE POEM	347
ROBIN HOOD	348
REVENGE	348
WHAT NEXT	348
HORROR STORY	349
REGRETS	349
LOVE	349
V FORMATION	350
IN CHARGE	350
PAY THE BILLS	350
THE TRICK	351
THE HAPPIEST	351
EVOLVE	351

ROAD MEN   352

ONE CURE   352

FORMS   352

PRINCIPLES   352

HAPPY PILLS   353

SUNSET   353

REWARD   353

DOG LOVER   354

ANOTHER REWARD   354

BORING   354

BE KIND   354

DRUNKEN GLASSES   355

THE LAIRD   355

MEMORY BLANKS   355

PLANNING   356

CHAOS   356

RETIRE IN SPAIN   357

IMPORTANT   357

HEAVEN   357

THE PART   357

ECONOMICS   358

WISDOM   358

ORDINARY   358

HOLIDAY   359

SUCCESSFUL JOINER   359

BUREAUCRACY   359

MILLIONAIRE   360

LEARNED WHAT   360

PAINTING   360

IN THE PEW   361

MORE LUCK   361

WHEN THINGS ARE GOOD   361

MAN	**362**
LIFE STYLE	**362**
THE MAGNIFICENT SEVEN	**362**
TOURETTES	**362**
MAM AGAIN	**363**
MIXER	**363**
THE ARREST	**363**
LOVE BIRD	**364**
SCAFFOLD	**364**
LATE HOME	**364**
NOSEY	**365**
IT HAPPENS	**365**
DON'T CARE	**366**
BIG LESSON	**366**
DO IT NOW	**367**
SPELLING	**367**
WAIT AND SEE	**367**
PERVERSION	**368**
THE ANSWER TO PRAYER	**368**
GETTING SORTED	**368**
MORE HAPPY PILLS	**369**
POKER	**369**
EXPORT ALE	**370**
HEAVEN	**370**
DOWN THE HILL	**371**
RAMBLINGS 8	**372**
SUCCESS	**373**
A TASTE OF HELL	**373**
A WEED	**373**
LOOKING AHEAD	**373**
GETTING OLDER	**374**
FAILURE	**374**

WE CAN'T HELP IT   374

NOT SURE   375

BASICS   375

WHO'S THE BOSS   375

PACIFISTS   376

WE SEE   376

THE BULLY   376

APPRECIATION   376

GETTING PAID   377

SLEEP TIME   377

THE STAG   377

SWEET TONGUE   378

BOYS   378

ONE ANSWER   378

ANOTHER TURN   378

SETTING OUT A RIG   379

OLD HABITS DIE HARD   379

TAXES   379

LESSON FROM BONE   380

COMPLEX   380

SEX MANUAL   380

IDEA SHARED   381

YOUNG LOVE   381

THE AGING TEDDY BOY   381

A COMPLETE BLANK   382

FALLEN ANGEL   383

EFFECTS   383

INSURANCE EXCESS   383

RAIN   384

OVER THE TOP AGAIN   384

JUST TO BE SURE   384

ALL IS DONE   385

THE IMPRESSIONIST	385
ESCAPE	385
HARD	385
VIOLENCE	386
GUILD OUTING	386
THE HIGHLAND SEER	386
THE ATTRACTION	387
LIES	387
HIDDEN TRUTH	387
WHITE SETTLERS	387
JUSTICE	388
SENT OFF	388
GUARANTEED BEHAVIOUR	388
THE QUALITY	389
A BIT OVER THE TOP	389
HIDDEN FACTOR	389
SYMPTOMS	389
EXPLAINED MAYBE	390
DIFFERENT RULES	390
THE ALTERNATIVE	390
THE EFFECTIVE TOOL	391
THE TWO SHE BEARS	391
NEAR	391
AMBITIONS	391
ANIMAL FARM	392
A DULL LIFE	392
OUTLOOK	393
REVENGE OF THE ROBIN	393
MURDERED	393
THE PLAN FOR A RENOVATION	393
ADJUST	394
THE GENERAL	394

THE BUILDERS 394

COMPENSATION 395

GUILT 395

GUARDIAN ANGEL 395

GIVE TO THE RICH 396

THE VIRUS 396

BUILDER 396

TELL THE TRUTH 396

WHITE MAN'S TREASURE 397

THE REASON 397

A GOOD IDEA 397

MANNERS 398

CONVENIENT 398

NO CHOICE 398

ENLIGHTENMENT 399

SEEING IS BELIEVING 399

FEELING GOOD 399

THE SHAKE 399

BE PREPARED 400

KNOWING THE LAWS 400

A LEGEND 400

THE ELECT 401

ADDING UP 401

DECREED 401

GENESIS 402

DOUBT 402

CHANGE OF HEART 402

FIRST EXPERIENCE (NEARLY) 403

PLANNING 403

CON MAN 403

D.I.Y. 404

WRONG 404

BIG ODDS	**404**
PLANNING DEPARTMENT	**404**
ROUSED	**405**
RESULTS	**405**
CIRCLES	**405**
THE THEORY OF EVERYTHING	**405**
IN PROPORTION	**406**
BOOMERANG	**406**
TOMORROW	**406**
EXPERIENCES TEACHES	**406**
HATE	**407**
SCARED	**407**
SNAPPED	**407**
FUTILITY	**407**
THE START	**408**
THE WAY YOU ARE	**408**
A HAPPY MAN	**408**
SUPERSTUD	**408**
THE SEER AGAIN	**409**
TRAVEL	**409**
LAST FLING	**409**
LIVE AND LEARN	**410**
LATE LEARNER	**410**
TOUGH	**410**
REGRET	**410**
VIDEO	**411**
MORE RULES	**411**
REALISATION	**411**
A BITCH	**411**
INHERITED	**412**
NO SATISFACTION	**412**
BEING POOR	**412**

REGRET 413

THE WORKERS 413

TIME 413

SLEEPING 414

JUSTICE 414

LOYALTY 414

NEXT PLEASE 415

DAY DREAMING 415

CONTEMPT 415

OLD PHILOSOPHY 415

OTHER FACTS 416

TIT FOR TAT 416

THE PUNCTURE 416

STRENGTH 417

BOMBS 417

OLD SOLDIERS 417

MY CAT 418

DEPRESSED 418

THE FOX 419

JUST YOUR LUCK 419

WIN 419

A MISTAKE 419

IS RICH THE BEST 420

MY DESIRE 421

DELAYED REACTION 421

READ AND WRITE 421

NO LIES 422

AWAY FROM HOME 422

THE TEST 423

RAMBLINGS 9 424

EDUCATION 425

INVERGORDON SMELTER 425

PENSIONS	425
YOUNG	426
HOLIDAYS AGAIN	426
TRUE STORY	427
A BIRD	427
SMART	427
THE JONES'S	428
HARD WORK	428
GETTING OLDER	428
DEATH DUTIES	429
ADVICE	429
RUINED	430
M.O.T.	430
PLEASURE	431
HIT BY A KINDLER	431
INVERNESS	431
OUTLOOK	432
BE A PUNK	432
GLADIATOR	432
THE MASON	433
MY BOLSTER	434
THE GALA QUEEN	434
WORKING HORSES	435
TWO PHEASANTS	435
SIR WALTER	435
NICE FLOWERS	436
THE TEMPTATION	436
DIESEL	436
THE NEGATIVE	436
LOST TRIBE	437
THE BURGLAR	437
BAMBI	437

SORRY   438

THE CREEPER   438

THE BRUTE   438

NICE   439

MY BEST FRIEND   439

PADDY   439

OLD LEGEND   440

NEAR PERFECTION   440

DONALD'S TUP   440

ANOTHER HAND   441

LIFE   441

THE LIST   442

LIONS   442

LORRY AGAIN   443

NO DREAM   443

LIES   444

NAVY   444

OUTSIDE CRAIG DUNAIN HOSPITAL   444

BIG BIRD   445

MOUSE TRAP   445

WEDDING   446

GREED   446

MEMORIES   447

GUARDIAN ANGEL   447

TOO LATE   448

OLD AGE AGAIN   448

EGYPTIANS   449

DRIVERS   449

MORE ANGRY DRIVERS   450

THE JEEP   451

SUCCESS   451

ARE YOU HAPPY   451

JACK THE LAD	451
THE SOLUTION TO THE SPARROW HAWK	452
HARD DISC	452
TESCO	453
A PIPE LINE	453
HATE	453
RECIPE FOR HAPPINESS	454
SENSE	454
SCHOOL DAYS	455
COLD WINTER	456
THE WORST	456
FRUSTRATED BUILDER	456
ANOTHER FACT	457
BIRDS	457
DOG BRAINS	458
SENSE	458
SUNDAY MORNING	459
THE FINAL CURTAIN	459
ANOTHER NOVEL	460
WOULD YOU	460
THE GALA	460
DEPRESSION	461
ANOTHER RANT	462
RAMBLINGS 10	464
ROAD RAGE	465
LAUGHTER	465
GULLIBLE	466
A TALENT	466
LOST	467
PARANOID	467
INSIGHT	468
IDENTICAL	468

THE INDUCTION	468
FIRST BOOK	469
KARMA	469
MEN	470
LAST CHANCE	470
INSTINCT	471
BLIND	472
FAUX PAS	472
UNFAIR	472
NATURE	473
MILD FANTASY	474
A GUARD	474
BRAIN CELLS	474
GODS	475
THE SHOOTING	475
RUDE ON THE ROAD	476
RUSTY CARS	476
NEW MINISTER	476
HERO'S	477
HAVE A PRICE	477
FOR BURNING	478
THE TATTIE	479
MOOD SWING	479
LEARNING	479
SPARROW HAWK	480
PUNISHMENT	480
SOMEWHERE	481
RULES	481
FISH	482
GOVERNMENT	482
THE SLAP	482
CULLODEN MOOR	483

THE ECONOMY   **483**

THE SHARPENER   **484**

DECISIONS   **484**

INSTINCT   **485**

A TOOL   **486**

REALITY   **486**

THE INTERNET FORM   **486**

UNIVERSITY CHALLENGE   **487**

SPORT   **487**

DEBT   **488**

Ramblings 1

The Salmon

I caught a salmon on the Averon river
and I won't forget that day in a hurry
when I got home the wife was gone
and do you know, I didn't worry.
All that I could do was gaze at the salmon
and check it's weight just once again
measure the length and also the girth
just like other normal men.
A note in front of the clock says she's had enough
the cupboard is empty too, not a cup or a dish
but I didn't care the cupboard was bare
I had only eyes for the fish.
Then I kind o' noticed the furniture was gone
also the lot of her clothes
why women don't get things into perspective
it's only God that knows.
I turned to my silver beauty once again
he was reclining there in the sink
I would have toasted the creature with whisky
But there wasn't a drop left to drink.
Now as you know anglers are sensitive folk
and to-day I didn't deserve sorrow
You'd think she would wait and celebrate to-night
then she could leave to-morrow.

....

Freedom

The limits of freedom is ignorance
now doesn't that sound good
If nobody had ever said that before
by now somebody should
Ignorance governs, ignorance rules
ignorance dictates obeyed by fools
Wide eyed ignorance can't see the truth
shut eyed ignorance demands some proof
Let's have some more laws somebody said
yet when we live by rules, reason is dead.

....

Tax Receipt

I got my receipt from the tax man
with not even a 'thank you' or 'please'
well I got to thinking
what kind of people are these.
surely their mothers told them a thing or two
about manners and things of that ilk
asking guests if they like tea or coffee
and if they take sugar and milk.
It didn't seem very likely
when I got that bald receipt

so I just phoned them up
which was a bit of a cheek.
And after a bit of 'getting to know ya'
and a fair amount of chit-chat
I asked them why they didn't say 'thank you'
and they told me computers didn't work like that.
....

A Miracle

I wonder what happened to my goldfish
yes, we had a death in the pond last night
this morning it was floating belly up
and it's wee face looked pale and white
I'm quite sure it didn't starve to death
for a fish it was quite porky
and they all enjoyed flakes for their dinner
and for a sweet a bit of Yorky.
No, it certainly wasn't starvation
and old age is also ruled out
could be some yob walking the road
ran in and gave it a clout.
But, that is a ridiculous thought
I better just get the vet
to see if he can figure out
what happened to my pet.
Now you may laugh at my concern
but where did it's wee life go
a miracle happened in the pond last night
and I just want to know
....

The Party

I went to a party in the Manse last Saturday
yes, I told you that I would go
remember, I said I had a problem
and how I would behave I didn't know.
Well to be quite honest, I'm proud
on a sliding scale I'd give me ten
for I out talked all of the women
and out drank all of the men.
Yes, of course I am joking
even I can exercise restriction
I was like a priest that night
or else a born again Christian.
The wine and juice flowed free of course
it was a pity it was juice most were drinking
albeit there were boxes of wine
which of course set me thinking.
There was a buffet, like a free for all
and as back and fore you pass
you were told to help yourself
and to replenish your glass.
Now as I passed back and fore

supposedly taking wee drops at a time
I kept filling up my glass
there's nothing wrong with a nice white wine.
After a couple of hours of this
it's only logical that the wine went to my head
then the minister came over and enquired 'What's yours?'
'Oh Perrior water' I smiled 'but I'll try a white wine instead!'
Now just to compound my little treachery
well, men like us have to grab their chances
an old elder started dozing in the chair
so I looked at the minister and exchanged knowing glances.
Then as I tottered of to my bed that night
I had drunk a box of wine there was no doubt
and as I cuddled beneath the clothes
I thanked the Lord I wasn't found out.

....

Good Sense

Have you noticed that when a human shuts their eyes
they don't go to sleep like other creatures
the only similarity that there is
is the vacant look on their features.
What men do, and women too
is they start bleating, asking and whinging
if it's not a lottery win it's Heaven they ask
terrified of being poor and of singeing.
It's hard to believe we lack the sense of beasts
every situation has to be dissected
while animals change what they can change
and for the rest it's just accepted.

....

All the Same

It doesn't take a mind reader
to know what you are thinking
this truth is so surprising
it could leave you dazed and blinking.
What you need to remember
is that all humans think the same
not all at the same time of course
that would be just a pain.
No, we all have our lusts and passions
and dreams of flying higher
the man that claims to be pure and true
then that man is nothing but a liar.
This could be some compensation I suppose
when you consider the beautiful and the frumpy
but when you are chatting to a priest
does it not make you kind o' jumpy.

....

Women's Sense

I'm really into psychology just now
well, I do that now and then
try and figure out the ways of the world
just like other normal men.
Then after months of study
the dark clouds begin to part
and I knew that I wasted my time again
for a woman knows all that at the start.

....

The Mason

I'm proud to be a mason you know
to be a fellow of craft
though some people think it ridiculous
and others' say it's a wee bit daft.
'The secrets' they screech 'the secrets'
that's unhealthy in modern days
why don't you divulge the mysteries
and disclose your wiles and your ways.
Now I have to laugh at this plea
for there are some things impossible to tell
and those who have tried came to naught
when it's free there's nothing to sell
Yes, there is a paradox all right
and there is mysteries that is true
but the ones that wish to publish
there is an enigma they never knew.

....

Dying Rotti

I knew the minute you bought me
you didn't want me to be kind and gentle
instead you wanted me to grow big and strong
and act, well, kind o' mental.
You frowned if ever I wagged my tail
albeit you cut it down to a stump
and yes, I have felt ridiculous
with that peg of a thing at my rump.
My ears too you would have clipped
instead you polished my coat
then just to make me look more evil
you put a studded collar round my throat.
But never the less I made you happy
I could feel the vibrations down my chain
you scoffed at the collie with Abel
you were happier to walk with Cain.
And now as I gaze behind this crafted face
I realize it's you that is the disgrace
genetically engineered, that's me all right
but your work was in vain,
I'll be a Spaniel tonight.

....

Sneaks

Have you ever noticed that sneaky folk
are rarely or never found out
while the rest of us scratch our heads
and our ethics and principles doubt.
'Of course they'll never get on like that'
we've all, heard the words of that song
but do you know it's an awful pity
that it's us and the song that is wrong.

....

Semi-Sober

Some folk may say that I'm half drunk
not always, but some of the time
and I take full responsibility
because the decision is always mine.
Yet these two words reveal a lot
not exactly subtle or even profound
you see my friends say 'semi-sober'
now isn't that a lovely sound.

....

Libido

They say that the kind of car you have
reveals a lot about you
I'm not really into that side of psychology
however it could be true.
The bigger the car the bigger your libido
that is the essence of what they say
but I wouldn't bet my life on that
there must be a better way.
But just in case I will give it a polish
and scrape some rust of the Jag
in case the wee blonde down the road sees it
and if she knows the theory her jaw will sag.
'Aye' I thought isn't psychology wonderful
deep down everyone knows I'm great
but I better keep an eye on that minister
because he drives a Volvo Estate.

....

New Neighbour

Our new neighbour moved in at last
and it would make your poor heart sink
another demented gardener
you know, it's no wonder that I drink.
There he's at it on Monday morning
singing and whistling, and not one cuss
oh! why can't he be a normal man

and have a hangover like the rest of us.
'Oh warlocks' I thought philosophically
Is this more than coincidence or chance
I'll just have to accept my doom and do it soon
when you're next door to the Church of Scotland Manse.

....

The Beech Tree

A beech tree towered in my garden
and beside it a little one grew
this was a mother and son of nature
it was obvious and everyone knew
Alas I chopped down the big one
for safety and also for light
at the time it never crossed my mind
if I was doing the wrong or the right.
Now sadly the little one died later that year
and this is only my own belief
it wasn't the lack of protection or the water table
if it were human, we'd call it 'grief'.

....

Temptation

I knew a very virtuous man once
didn't lie and would never steal
never fornicated or got drunk
for others it is sorrow that he'd feel.
Now this saint of a man was pretty wise
for in his righteousness he never basked
because he told me he was never tempted
and for adultery was never asked.

....

The Ego Trip

I thought that I'd go on an ego trip
that is when you're feeling smart
the very first thing in the morning
on the milkman I'd make a start.
'Young man' I said with dignity
(I really sounded a toff)
'Take these bottles round to the back door'
well his reply was 'something' off.
Now, as my nose was in the air I didn't quite catch him
no I thought 'enough time on the dross'
I'll just wait for Jock the coalman
and he'll understand who's boss.
Well perversely enough, the same thing happened
the riff-raff just wouldn't cower
and here was me in a state of bliss
exuding and perspiring power.
Now after a day of total failure

not even a mister but a 'here you' or 'mate'
I realized that it was all a mistake
and that I'd left it twenty years late.

....

My Scones

The wife was away so I'd make a scone
the kind you make on a girdle
I put a drop of Rennet in the milk
to see if it would curdle.
Next the ingredients, that was easy
I just followed the plan
yes, you ladies say, 'recipe'
but that's not a word for a working man.
Now when I was finished, the scones were perfect
they could win prizes at the WRI
do you know it is amazing what you can do
when you really try
As I gazed with rapture at my creation
and watched as the beauties began to cool
I heard the wife, so I dumped them
well, I may be an idiot, but not a fool.

....

Trier

I'm not going to take any more risks
you get fed up with getting things wrong
the other night at a party I'd thought I'd sing
and forgot all the words of the song.
I tried to be a businessman once or twice
and planned it all to perfection
the business took off at ninety miles an hour
but unfortunately in the wrong direction.
Then there is love, I failed at that too
five marriages and five in divorce
with the alimony I pay I'm starving today
and my wages are deducted at source.
Yes to be a trier can be traumatic
there can be a lot of shakes and nail biting
and I would pack the whole thing in today
if it wasn't so damn exciting.

....

Lessons

I was top of the class once you know
it was on a Friday after the test
when the teacher corrected the sums
it was mine that was the best.
Now I had visions of sitting at the back
and I really thought it a cheek
instead of taking my rightful place

teacher decided not to change places that week.
Now to be honest I wasn't bitter at all
that is just the way we were taught
yet the lessons I learned when I was seven
are lessons I never forgot.

....

Sussed it Out

I wish that Ian the chemist would stop it
he keeps writing 'avoid alcohol' on my pills
how would he like it if I built a wall for him
and then wrote that on my bills.
No he wouldn't like it at all
but maybe it's doctor Philpott's fault
just because my nose is a wee bit blue
he decided to call a halt.
Or else it could be the manufacturers
now I thought there were something wrong
they're just doing it to please the Buddha's
where they make them in Hong Kong.
Yes, that's probably the answer
and it's not Ian or Dr Philpott at all
so I'll just send an ordinary bill
when I build his wall.

....

The Reserve

I've only got a miniature left
and it is only Wednesday night
the wife reckoned that I'd had enough
and sometimes she is right.
But what if someone calls I pleaded
'Could you no' take home a bottle o' Grouse'
I feel so poor and naked
with only that titchy bottle in the house.
Well, as usual she relented
so on the phone I didn't linger
you know when I put my mind to it
I can twist her round my little finger.
Now when she came home I took the bottle
and poured myself a double
aye sometimes on a Wednesday
I can do that without any trouble.
Anyway she said 'I thought that was for the visitors'
and I gazed and gave a wee sigh
'Oh' I said 'don't worry about them'
I've still got a miniature of White and Mackay.

....

Blessings

Do you ever count your blessings
I sometimes do just for the crack

and do you know I can't complain
there is little that I lack.
I haven't a yacht or plane of course
or a villa out in Spain
I don't even look a bit like Tarzan
and the wife doesn't look like Jane.
Come to think of it I'm pretty deprived
it can be a bad thing, too much thought
maybe it's not a good idea to count
or you'd be aware of what you haven't got.

....

Accountants

Accountants try to confuse us you know
they complicate simple sums
then they compound the con trick
by treating us just like chums.
What they really do is make jobs for themselves
develop a language all of their own
write a wee book every year
where the profit and loss is shown.
Now I was thinking, I know this is simple
and no doubt the idea is not new
but when it comes to profit and loss
the only columns of figures you need, is two.

....

New Things

Did you ever notice how neat you write
when you get a new jotter or pen
not that I dwell on the subject a lot
but I think of it now and then.
Even new shoes, you walk so much better
and with new sandshoes you can run like a stag
when you buy a new suit or fancy shirt
the old one feels like a rag.
Well, I was thinking new friends are exciting
and a new wife to the death you'd guard her
but do you know the old things didn't change
it's just that you are trying harder.

....

Red Indians

Pocahontas is all the rage now
in my day it was Sitting Bull
he would race around the Black Hills
making the white man look a fool.
Geronimo too was popular
so was the big man Cochice
and as we saw in the 'Broken Arrow'
he was the one that wanted peace.

But things are not so simple now
we know the pesky injuns weren't so bad
and when we see it through adult eyes
no wonder Crazy Horse was mad.
Yes, I'm glad we now see the difference
the truth will be disclosed at last
and then we can all keep on hating
because we cannot change the past.
....

Logic

After her breakfast of porridge and eggs
I asked the wife what she'd like for dinner
'Oh' she said 'a salad's enough'
'Then the two of us will be slimmer.'
Some more toast, a cup of tea
then off to work delighted
I thought to myself 'no cooking tonight'
it really made me excited.
Anyway later on I prepared the lettuce
and the tomatoes to stick in your teeth
I had just cut up the cucumber when she came in
and she said 'I'm starving, where's the beef.'
No, there's no' sussing out women
their mystery goes to the bone
and when they can't think of a logical answer
the standard sentence is 'well, you might have known.'
....

Ignorance

That wee scruff of a terrier is in my garden again
and I know full well what he is thinking
every time I look out of the window
there he is, sitting and winking.
Now my dog is a haughty bitch
and normally wouldn't entertain a runt with no tact
but desperation can be a terrible thing
and we all know that is a fact.
So I will keep her inside of the house
then I'll throw stones at the little flirt
and my Great Dane will never know
then she won't get hurt.
....

Patience

Do you ever think when you see folk get lucky
'when is it going to be my shot'
maybe you never think of that
but do you know, it's worth a thought.
Everything else goes round in circles
the earth, the seasons, the moon

I suppose it could be worth a prayer
to see if it's your turn soon.
But have you considered the size of your circle
the wee ones gets lots of good and bad
but the big ones take you to the pinnacle of ecstasy
then to the depths of despair, and you're sad.
So round and round the wheelies turn
and no, you can't get off it
if you did, you might land on a worse one
so tell me where is the profit.
No, the answer is to hang on to your wheel
the very same as me
and it will turn to better times
now just you wait and see.
....

New Neighbours

They're buzzing around the manse like bees today
I think a new ministers visit is imminent
so I'd better sort myself out for a while
and give my back a rub with liniment.
It looks to me like a young couple
and I really think it sweet
seeing them stride out on the straight road
when the rest of us are battered and beat.
So I hope I won't disillusion them
or very soon they'd be out of favour
and that can happen to a priest or a saint
When they have me for a neighbour.
What I'll do, I think, is pace myself
and try and avoid the shot
but likely when it comes to Saturday
that idea will be forgot.
Or else maybe I could fox them
a man can always pretend
but there again that's no use
for I'll be found out in the end.
No, what I'll do is be myself
slouch about in jeans and bomber jacket
and if I lose the place again
then we will see if they can hack it!
....

Passing of time

If we could command the past and the present
and have control over the passing of time
we could press 'hold' when enjoying ourselves
and press 'pause' when things are going fine.
Rewind back to the juicy bits
or fast forward to something new
but eventually all would be static
and that would never do.
....

Tell Tale

We were on holiday in Cyprus once
for a blissful couple of weeks
one night we all went to a party
and fell in with a family of Greeks.
There were mother and father and sister in law
and I think there were one or two brothers
in fact there were a lot at the party
so I won't bother to mention the others.
Now during the course of the evening
the relationships were easy to spot
but no one else seemed to notice
so sometimes maybe it's not.
Well I don't consider myself a suspicious man
and if called cynical I would feel hurt
but one man's wife's sister divulged so much
when she brushed a speck off his shirt.

....

Lottery Winner

You're talking to a lottery winner now
(I know what you're thinking, ten pound)
well if that is your immediate thought
your judgement is pretty sound.
But as I checked the numbers
and as you know I got the three
the strangest thoughts I started thinking
which is not unusual for me.
I thought when I picked the digits
(now this may make you laugh)
maybe I didn't give it the full attention
and that is why I got half.
So this week I'm going to furrow my brow
and I hope they will give the balls a good mix
because now that I've figured it out
next week I'll have the six

....

False Memory

Another invitation to a party
well I was quite delighted
because the last time I was at their house
I got a bit over excited.
'Forgiven' I exclaimed 'forgiven'
and as usual the wife put me right
'Oh' she said 'you weren't that bad
'you were sleeping for most of the night.'

....

Understanding

This is a right cultural shock for me
doing nothing all day but the cooking
I'm creeping along like a man of ninety
it's no wonder the folk are all looking.
On a bad day I sometimes ponder and think
'is this the reward you get'
mind' if it wasn't for a damn puncture
I would be working away yet.
But no use crying or bleating I suppose
yet it's hard to be cheery and witty
anyway I like a good moan now and then
and nothing wrong with a bit of pity.
But you have to be positive
and be aware of what you've got
then you can understand what others go through
and that's what helps a lot

....

Reality

Do you ever think you could be a Lionheart
and battle for justice, truth and right
chivalry and virtue you will pursue
for duty and honour you'd fight.
Yes, that is a noble thought indeed
and I wish that it was the way
but when most of us get what we want
unfortunately we forget and walk away.

....

The Builder

Have you ever had your head examined
well I had mine done twice
the first time was no bother at all
but the second time wasn't so nice.
They asked me lots of stupid questions
and to be honest I hadn't a clue
but don't you think that they would stick to building
or something else that I knew.
Instead they rambled on about rubbish
in fact I think that psychiatrist was a chancer
if I quizzed him about facing brick
I'll bet he wouldn't have an answer.
It's not my fault I didn't like jigsaws either
and I was sensible to refuse electric shocks
what ten thousand volts does to your extremities
well the effects are similar to pox.
Mind you, I think that is what convinced them
also at the last test I was good
when the rest of them built their wee house
I made a mansion out of the wee blocks of wood.

....

Haircut

I paid thirteen pounds for a haircut once
it'll make a huge difference the young guy said
but when I think of all that money
I must have been off my head.
When the initial shock had left me
I thought I shouldn't have refused the wash
because the price was probably inclusive
bound to be, for that kind of dosh.
So the next time into the city
I went again and cunningly took the lot
a shampoo, massage and singe
I thought, the hell, why not.
A cup of coffee while waiting
and another one half way through
but I near fainted when I got the bill
for this time it was twenty two.
Well everyone learns their lessons
and me, I'll never go back
because Brenda in Alness only charges a pound
and you also get all of the crack.
....

An Answer

Well I've solved the mystery once again
though I've called it another name
albeit it is the same question
the answer is never the same.
Indeed it is the state of happiness
the utopian level of bliss
although you can forego pleasure
there is no need to miss out on this.
No sin involved, neither crime
the effort is almost minimal
and oh, the rewards of success
surely must be subliminal.
Now here is the formula for a triumph
the key to happiness health and wealth
it'd been staring you in the face for years
simply forget about yourself.
....

Mechanics

Did you ever notice luck goes in three's
but conversely the bad does too
well, that's what usually happens to me
so likely the same goes for you.
Well I was thinking why in three's
why not in a two or a four
mind you if it was only a one
some would be whinging for more.

A five or a six would be handy at times
but what if the luck was bad
then you would regret that you wanted that
and it would likely make you mad.
No, the magic figure has evolved
it's not a fluke or a guess
you see it puts you back on the same foot
or you'd be lopsided more or less.

....

Cut Down to Size

Have you ever heard of anything so ridiculous
as before the 'big bang' there was no time
yes I know there were no watches or clocks
we all know that perfectly fine.
I wish scientists would have some common sense
or at least a little bit more
because if time did not exist
how can they say 'before.'
I'm not convinced anyway of the theory
easy to believe because it's dramatic
and we humans think we are so special
so unique it leaves us ecstatic.
No such thoughts as growing like a fungus
or a spot scratched of a dinosaurs back
we will never know our origins
when it's humility that we lack.
Now I'm not saying that I know all the answers
only an idea I can proffer
we could be a flea upon a flea on a flea
and that's the best I can offer.

....

Mad Cow Disease

I was thinking I would make some cauliflower
and maybe a sauce with cheese
then we could be sure
we wouldn't get Mad Cow disease.
Then I thought, something's not right
no wonder the cow is mad if it's diseased
and the way we treat our cauliflower
it too can't be pleased.
So what do we eat, you may ask
nature must be sorely vexed
and undoubtedly trying to tell us
that the annoyed cauliflower will be next.

....

The Same

Women and men are so similar at times
and sometimes their brains work the same

just think when everything is going wrong
we all look for someone to blame.
....

Bravery

I got a right turn recently
the dog started barking in the middle of the night
and I heard strange noises too
which gave me a terrible fright.
I tried to push the wife out
then pretended that I was asleep
'Did you hear that noise' she said
and I whimpered 'No, not a peep.'
'Get out' she said, 'you're the man'
so shakily I put on my goon
'Are you no' off yet' she bawled
'Aye' I said 'soon.'
I picked up my twelve bore in the lobby
just to be on my guard
then the coward of a dog ran back in the house
and left me alone in the yard.
And then I saw it, as plain as day
it was a ghost I was pretty sure
but I couldn't quite make out the shape
because the light was pretty poor.
then suddenly on came the automatic bulb
just as I was about to fire
and do you know it wasn't a ghost at all
but a bag hanging on the fence wire.
Into the house then shaking with relief
the wife praised me and said I was plucky
I just sneered and drawled
'Yup, and that tattie bag sure was lucky.'
....

Greed

I dreamt last night I built a wall
just like any normal man would
and when you worked the same as me
it's bound to look pretty good.
All through the night I toiled and strained
enjoying every minute and second
my labourer said we made fifty pounds
that is the amount he reckoned.
Now, I was quite chuffed with that
so when tonight on the scaffold I'll sing
I'll try hard to make the sixty
you know greed is a terrible thing.
....

The Big Shot

He shot me dead in the courtyard
an inoffensive collie dog
my only crime was, that I got lost
in the snow the rain and the fog.
Why he did it, does he know?
perhaps it made him feel big
but no use now to wonder why
when I'm sniffed by a sheep and a pig.
My only regret now is about my master
he is a lord of high degree
and I was a faithful friend to him
and he thought the world of me.
now in my dying moments I thought
in the minutes before I was dead
if he knew who my master was
I'd be taken in to the house and fed.
Yet I know my master can be a vengeful man
and we'll see if my murderer is bigger
but I have a funny feeling
he will regret that he pulled the trigger.

....

Wasted

I've probably never told you this before
but to hell, it takes only a line
the worst feeling a person can have
is to feel they are wasting time.

....

Z or X

I wonder who decided to put the X in Xerox
when you pronounce it with a Z
to me it looks so crazy
because with an X it can't be said.
Yes, there must be a smart ass somewhere
and this guy doesn't know how to talk
but why do the rest of us listen
instead of telling him to stop.

....

Be Aware

Well we are going to a dance tonight
so I will try and behave myself once again
but I'll still keep my eye on the wife
in case she chats up other men.
Oh yes, you ladies may say, 'that's not nice'
and the attitude is pretty low
but that is the way women act

ask any man that you know.
Now while I keep one eye on the wife
I'll keep the other one on the kitty
because if anyone missed a turn
that would be an awful pity.
Conversely then I'll have to watch the young bucks
and the old stags when they get a dram
because I don't blame the wife a hundred per cent
well, that's the kind of guy I am.
Aye the duties of a man is immense indeed
a woman wouldn't know where to begin
mind you if we men get a bit legless
then that's where she comes in.
……………………………………..

The Good That I Do

Did you know that yesterday was Thursday
and I did not take one drop to drink
mind you I feel totally knackered today
for last night I never slept a wink.
That is what's called a withdrawal symptom
the very same as the shakes
or when you try to add two and two
and you make mistakes.
Yes, the mind can be a strange contraption
a very complicated device
but why doesn't it let you do good instead of bad
at least more than once or twice.
……………………………………..

Pride

My body is totally alcohol free today
I feel I deserve a bunch of flowers
albeit I know what the doctors say
that it only takes twenty four hours.
Never-the-less I'm feeling chuffed
when all is said and done
so today I can take the car out
and go for a nice wee run.
Well off I went in my old Cortina
you couldn't see my wheels for dust
it's only a pity she's a bit noisy now
the mechanic put it down to the rust.
Now I hadn't gone past Dingwall
when the white car drew in behind
now it didn't bother me, I was alcohol free
so I put on a spurt to be unkind.
Eventually my taunting worked, they stopped me
and I grinned as they came over with the bag
so I put on my innocent face
and nonchalantly lit a fag.
'Yes constable, is it the breathalyser' I said
(and I admit with a bit of a cheek)

'Oh no, have you no' heard
it's check your tyres and exhausts this week.

....

Who to Tell

Acts of courage, mercy and honour
that was once the measure of man
now it is money, money, money
and grab every penny you can.
Then in the end at glory time
you can tell about the cash you made
but there is no one there to listen
except for the pick and the spade.

....

Belief

One statement that always makes me jealous
is when someone says they believe in God
I don't say anything to them of course
but I think 'you lucky sod.'
Usually then they spoil the whole effect
by talking through their hat
and that's the time I thank their God
that I don't believe in that.

....

More Depression

Have you ever really been up against it
and you feel you just can't go on
confidence and faith have disappeared
and even hope is gone.
Then that is the time for the smart asses
when you are fit to tether
they appear with pearls of wisdom
like 'Pull your damn self together.'
Or else it's 'Why don't you try this'
because they know the cure
and yes there are so many ways
but their one is so sure.
And when you politely decline the advice
they look up and give a wee sigh
when the remedy is so simple
and when you don't take it they ask you why.

....

The Poor

Being poor has its compensations you know
we're not so frightened of the grim reaper
we don't squeal for tons of granite on top

or plead to make the hole deeper.
Now that's a good bonus isn't it
and no doubt there must be many
I only wish someone would tell me more
because honestly I can't think of any.
....

Fairies

Did you read about the girls who saw fairies
and the little people danced before their eyes
the girls are seventy years old now
and kind of admit it was all lies.
The fairies were pictures cut out of a book
laid on the grass and propped up with a stick
then they took some photographs
now isn't that a clever trick?
But one little thing spoils the explanation
the ladies said they were all dressed in pink
and they won't admit to the wee white one in the corner
now doesn't that make you think.
....

Keeping Going

Have you ever been asked the question
'What was the happiest day of your life?'
you might say your wedding day
maybe just to please the wife.
But when you give it serious thought
it's really difficult to think of one
now I'm not suggesting you have hundreds
or either implying you have none.
You see nature has devised a plan
and it is really a bit of a con
because if you have reached a pinnacle before
maybe you won't carry on.
....

Uri the Brickie

I wonder if I could lift a concrete block
and do it all by positive suggestion
or maybe I could try a brick for a start
but I suppose a bag of cement is out of the question.
Well I sat down in front of the brick
and concentrated my efforts on staring
in fifteen minutes that kindly look
turned into vicious glaring.
Still I persisted with my mind lifting act
if Uri Gellor could bend forks I could lift a brick
if it works I'll start a squad
and teach them this brand new trick.
I can imagine it now, my squad and me

on no more guttery sites we'd be sinking
when all the rest are slaving away
we'd all be sitting and thinking.
Yes indeed the idea was a good one
and to dream it up gave me satisfaction
but as usual there was one wee problem
I couldn't move the wee brick a fraction.

....

Once Bitten

Did I tell you I was in a casino
and the game was the same as pontoon
they don't start until eleven o'clock
so I went to bed in the afternoon.
Now there I was at two in the morning
kidding on that I was James Bond the spy
the man beside me was losing like mad
and to be honest, so was I
Now it's easy to be suave when you're winning
I know, because twice I got twenty one
but when you get a fifteen
that isn't quite so much fun.
So anyway as expected I lost all my cash
and me near licensed to kill
well, James Bond may go back to the casino
but I tell you I never will.

....

Odds

The strangest thing I've seen for sale
is numbers for the football pools
the digits were for an eight from ten
so no need to explain the rules.
Now this numbers came guaranteed
in twenty five years never won
no, not even your money back
not like some.
Now I could see the ploy all right
but it's losing numbers that you get
if he had said they won twenty times before
I would say that's a better bet.

....

Reading Minds

I'm glad that we can't read each other's minds
well, most of us can't anyway
it could be right handy at times I suppose
I was just thinking that today.
But then I thought, better not
we might read something not very nice
and like everything else we get in life
there always is a price.

....

Budget

I must listen to the budget today
yes, it's that time once again
mind you I suppose it is a change
from watching Bill and Ben.
The chancellor will be excited I'm sure
like the wife on a Thursday night
when we get the giro in the post
and the two of us starts to fight.
'We'll spend it on this, and not on that'
cut down a bit on the meals
yes when it comes to spinning it out
I know exactly how the chancellor feels.

....

Recipes

Men in the building trade are pretty tough
and that is no exaggeration
they would say 'not bad' instead of 'good'
and never 'a delightful little creation.'
Well I was thinking when I was making pancakes
the ingredients were very like a concrete mix
now it is quite irrelevant
that mine turned out like bricks.
Anyway I thought of the boys on the building site
exchanging recipes for concrete and mortar
instead of grabbing a shovel and screaming
'Let me in there and I will sort 'er.'
No, there are some things that will never happen
and the words 'concrete and recipe won't rhyme'
but I happen to know they exchange recipes all right
and they do it all of the time.

....

Waiting

The wife is making the Christmas pud again
all the ingredients are in a big dish
we all take turns to stir it around
and then that is the time to wish.
Now every year I plead for the same things
and likely the family does as well
but of course I do not know
because it's unlucky to tell.
Anyway this year I added an extra wish
although really you're only allowed three
so maybe my wishes are null and void
yet with luck there's no guarantee.
Now after the wishing comes the hard bit
which desire are you going to get first
is it number one, or in my case four
yes, waiting is definitely the worst.

....

Time Travel

The scientists now say that light can bend
now isn't that quite fantastic
instead of being like a rod of iron
it's variable and elastic.
Well I was thinking, if it bends
eventually a circle it will create
that is only logical
albeit at a terrible rate.
Then taking my equation one step further
and I hope that I don't go too far
but when you apply the theory to a planet
or to a far off star.
What happens is, millions of light years away
you can see a twinkling that is true
but if the light went round in a circle
the star could be right behind you.

....

The Scrappie

If I had to live my life again
and the priority was to be happy
this may take you by surprise
because I'd like to be a scrappie.
I just love to rake about in piles of junk
or anything else that's thrown away
the time would pass like lightening
I'd be delighted every day.
It's very like searching for treasure
the big thrill of discovery
oh yes I know it doesn't sound so grand
when you call it recovery.
But never the less that's what excites me
I'd spend blissful days on the dump
just imagine the delight of finding an old sewing machine
or a transit van without a bump.
Then there's all that lovely bits of metal also
far too valuable to disregard
well I'd take them home in my pick-up
and stack them neatly in the yard.
There is always one wee problem of course
and it could spoil a blissful day
I know that once I picked a thing up
it's not in my nature to throw it away.

....

Bank on It

I got a puncture repaired today
and I paid for it by cheque
but there is no money in the bank
so that's what's called a brass neck.

Never the less it will all work out
it's like a tightrope that I'm walking
me and the banker dodging each other
and it is him that's doing the stalking.
Mind you I'm not so worried because it's Saturday
and I personally don't think the lottery is sin
but I get a wee bit suspicious
when you 'rely' on getting a win.

....

The Vision

I stayed in bed a long time today
and no, I won't even mention 'pain'
if I did you'd put your hands to your ears
'oh not that old song again.'
But anyway I was going to tell you
I somehow slipped off into a deep trance
now don't think this was a normal dream
and I put it entirely down to chance.
Anyway, I drifted off quite slowly at first
and I consciously noticed the duvet getting lighter
although my eyes were closed by then
there were a sensation of it getting brighter.
All was peaceful and harmonious
the mists before my eyes cleared
I seemed to leave my whole body then
and through some holes I peered.
Now what I saw was a revelation
I was blessed with a glimpse of future time
everyone was there I ever loved
but alas the 'Rangers' were down to nine.
All were there the living and the dead
it was heaven all right it's true
but although I searched for hours
I couldn't find me or you.
Now don't be alarmed, because I am not
far more was revealed to me
because I saw our names on gate one
and the vision I had was of gate three

....

Hate

Did you know when you call up the emotion of love
the nearest relative to that is hate
in fact sometimes they are so close together
the two of them alternate.
Now you would think that they would be far apart
and not a next door neighbour
like going to the Tory conference
and they are all holding hands with Labour.
Yes, it is a strange phenomena indeed
yet nature has mysteries a plenty
but when you call up 'hate' on its own
that's when you're running on 'empty.'

....

Forgotten

Have you ever been pushed to the limit
your good times all forgotten
you know it's not the end of the world
but you still feel pretty rotten.
Then just when you think you're over the hump
and you stop for a moment to curse
you realise that the wheel has not turned at all
and things are getting worse.
Then at last when the end is in sight
and happiness stares you in the face
all the misery magically vanishes
and disappears without a trace.

....

The Key

The biggest shop in Dingwall now
is called the West End Stores
we used to call the owner 'Steptoe'
because he sold furniture round the doors.
But thirty years later things are different
and who would ever guess
not only has he a shop in Dingwall
he's got one also in Inverness.
Now isn't that a good success story
the trick is to give value, then you get
because I bought a chest o' drawers from Steptoe
and it's sitting in my bedroom yet.

....

Everyone to Their Own Job

I thought I'd fry some fish in batter yesterday
so I followed the directions on the packet
but when I lifted it by the tail
the batter fell of like a wee jacket.
I looked at the recipe once again
as any normal man would do
and no, there wasn't a mention
of any type of glue.
That is very strange I thought
as I rolled the pastry with a bottle of lemonade
to think they never devised a glue for the chef
in all the advances they made.
You realize I decided to make a pie by then
I was off the idea of frying the fish
and when I clapped the pastry on it
it looked such a lovely dish.
But one little thing caught my eye
it was the pastry now that wouldn't stick
now then I thought, there is an opening here
a special glue would do the trick.

Well I started thinking of edible adhesives
something that wouldn't smell
a formula that would stick batter to fish
and pastry to the pie as well.
I pondered for ages over the dilemma
then rang up Arildite
but the wifie on the other end wouldn't stop laughing
well personally I don't think that right.
I was only a chef with a wee practical problem
and after a bit of advice
there was no need for all that screeching
that just wasn't very nice.
Well to cut a long story short
as usual it was the wife, who told me all
and as I stomped off in the huff I shouted
'I'd like to see you set out and build a wall'
....

Normal Reaction

My car broke down again yesterday
it cut out and glided to a halt
I feverishly thought who had a shot of it
to see if it was their fault.
Reluctantly I had to admit it was only me
so I just buried my head in my hands
the heartless traffic screamed off by
yes, nobody understands.
After what seemed an eternity
the wee yellow van pulled up alongside
and by this time I was nearly sobbing
deep down I felt so vulnerable
wide open for a robbing.
Well the AA man did his best I know
he tried both screwdriver and a spanner
and I could see his frustration
when I saw him eyeing up a hammer.
Eventually he told me that he was defeated
and that a garage was the answer
he would tow me if I would drive
so I said I would chance her.
By this time of course expense again crossed my mind
for I couldn't pay another bill
my god I only finished paying the last one
and my bank balance now was nil.
'Oh no I screamed' when at last I got home
then straight to the bedroom to sob
is there no' a rich relative about at all
or even anybody that I could rob.
Well I was still sobbing when the wife got home
and she instinctively knew that I'd had enough
maybe it was the way I hurled abuse
and then went off to bed in the huff.
All night long I tossed and turned
well, you know yourself the garage prices

I woke up screaming 'I'm being ripped off'
to be honest that's one of my vices.
Anyway the next day, a phone call
'It's the garage' the wife peeped
so I put on my dressing gown
and out of the bedroom creeped.
'Yes' I said in a shaky voice
near fainting where I sat
'Oh' the mannie said' just a loose wire'
and we never charge for that.
....

Why Some

You know the town of Dingwall
well, can you guess what I was thinking
half of it is built on solid ground
while the other half is sinking.
Lintels are off the level by a mile
putting the building off the plumb
now, I'm not saying all of them
but certainly more than some.
I wonder who the builders were
it's probably too late to sue
but they didn't know as much as us
and likely of concrete they never knew.
Now that could be one excuse
and the bad foundations were never meant
but why did it not happen to the lot
instead of the fifty per cent.
....

Coming Back

I get fed up with being a human at times
if ever I come back I'd be an ape
a chimpanzee or even a gorilla
just to sit in the sun and gape.
But there again I could be a tiger
maybe even eat a Hindu or two
but some of the old Indians look pretty tough
and likely would be hard to chew.
No, I think I'll stick to the ape
and scratch away at my tum
oh, but when I think of it
I'd be too embarrassed to show my bum.
You know it's not easy to choose is it
and I better not tempt fate
in case she says 'do you see that warthog'
'well she's looking for a mate.'
....

Affected

Do you know what the word 'procrastinate' means
well all it really means is 'delay'
I was just thinking if you use words like that
you tell much more than you say.

....

Queen

It's really sad the way our monarchy is going
they seem no longer able to play their part
sooking toes and adulterous affairs
and that's just for a start.
Of course they may justly argue
they always did that but never got caught
but if you think that that is an excuse
well I'll tell you now it's not
To err is human, you might sympathise
they still do their duty, clearly seen
but I tell you this in days of darkness
I thank God for our Queen.

....

Heroes

There are both heroes and cowards
the same as there are day and night
yet the hero can be brave in darkness
and the coward be brave in the light.

....

Left Handers

Being a left hander is awkward at times
even doing simple things like writing
then sometimes you get called silly names
like a southpaw when you are fighting.
Superstition has it we're all witches of course
malevolent magic is our hobby
a black cat lying in the kitchen
and a broom stick in the lobby.
Doctors say our brains are back to front
or else they're upside down
that is why when you see us smile
it really is a frown.
Yes, we left handers are treated unjustly
definitely in the minority
but nature sometimes give special gifts
and they are never to the majority.

....

Choosy

I have a wee bit of a hangover today
and also I'm full of guilt
it's no wonder the wife nags me about money
when I think of the drink I spilt.
You know whisky and brandy are all the same to me
I've even been known to drink wine
if I go to a house and they offer me a drink
I'd say what ever you've got is just fine.
Mind you it could be construed as a talent
as through social circles we pass
for there is nothing worse than a choosy woman
and a man's just a pain in the ass.
....

Another Invitation

We are invited again to a party on Saturday
over the road at the manse
but they don't know my record
so they're taking a terrible chance.
They are my new neighbours of course
and really are very nice
but likely after Saturday
they'll never ask me twice.
Yet, on the other hand, they might not drink
or maybe just titchy nips they'll pour
oh but when I think of it
that never stopped me before.
'You're always the same' the wife would say
you cannot see a bottle pass
'There you'd be at full stretch,
holding out an empty glass.'
Oh yes I cringe when I think of it
the last time I was over there
I really lost control of my movements
and fell between the couch and the chair.
That was our old neighbours of course
you remember Margaret and Roddy
yes, they were real patient with me
when I was on the toddy.
Yet when all's said and done isn't it exciting
when you know what life's about
and if my new neighbours don't know already
on Saturday they will find out.
....

Waiting

I waited in all day for a delivery man
and all day the man was missing
do you know it would make no difference
if I had planned a day fishing.

There I was stuck there waiting
not one lorry stopped at the house
by five o'clock I was a bag of nerves
it's no wonder I took to the Grouse.
....

Dry Flies

I must make some more fishing flies
this time the kind that float
you see I can't get any more hair now
since the wife locked up her coat.
Now the floating kind are simple
they are made to represent flies
you can make them any colour
and also any size.
Well I had made about a dozen
and laid them to dry in the sun
now honestly this is perfectly true
when I turned a bluebottle was tackling one.
I know that most anglers would want that fly
and likely I could name my price
now I don't mean to be a prude or anything
but I didn't think it was very nice.
Anyway I made another dozen
(the fish will think the loch is infested)
and I'll need to mind to get a permit this year
or with my luck I'd get arrested.
Then when putting the flies away, a brainwave
and I don't care what you say
if I made a randy ugly fly for my hat
that would keep the midgies away
....

Sinister

When I think of all the brainwashing that goes on
albeit 'training' is what it's called
I just sit astonished
and yes, I am appalled.
Could it be part of a some big plan
or even a sinister plot
perhaps it's only evolution
on the other hand maybe it's not.
Does somebody else form our attitudes
and have power over you and me
then glibly they will tell you
'but of course you're free.'
So take a minute and ponder
it doesn't matter if you are rich or poor
do you really make your own mind up
'you do' but are you sure!
....

The Author

I thought I'd write a book again
and this time I'd do it right
but I couldn't think of a plot
so I was waken for half the night.
Then it came to me in a flash
yes, a romantic novel
I'd make the hero a real man
the kind that wouldn't grovel.
So out came the pencil and jotter
and really got wired in
but oh, the way the story developed
you know it was tantamount to sin.
Instead of being beautiful and curvy
my heroine turned out porky
and instead of calling my hero 'Darin' or something
I can hardly believe it but I called him 'Korky.'
it's a pity too I made him so short
that will need some adjusting
and oh, dash it the love scenes
they are just disgusting.
Mind you, I thought the location romantic
the wee church where they would marry
and I don't care what you say
they're nothing wrong with Clach-na-harrie
Well anyway I posted it off to the publishers
but the idiots never got the gist
mind you all we great authors get rejected at first
I heard that about Oliver Twist.

....

Nature

Now I was a wee brown mouse
quite happy to be alone
lived in a nice sandstone semi
that is where I made my home.
What a peaceful life I had then
until this visiting mouse wanted sex
of course I didn't know the consequences
Now we've both got a trap round our necks
Well as I gasped my last breath
I admitted regret, and she agreed
but as she smiled her last smile
she said 'Yes but there was a greater need.'

....

Doubt

Another wee lassie murdered
our sense of normality numb
will Christian values triumph
and love will overcome.
Will evil eventually be conquered

the wicked gene erased
surely God will do it now
and then he will be praised.
But alas alas that's not the way
good people must patience renew
yet I want you to destroy the murderers God
yes, that's what I want you to do.
....

Catching a Salmon

Oh what a dream I had last night
I dreamed again that I was fishing
this time it was on the Conon river
albeit for the Beauly I was wishing.
Well I was onto a salmon right away
the excitement was really great
mind you I was using the fly of course
because I'm not too keen on the bait.
I played the beauty for ages
it must have been twenty minutes at least
and when at last I saw him tire
I groped in the bag for the priest.
Now as I had no gaff or net that day
my plan was to pull it up on the shore
this is quite a safe method if done carefully
if you take a foot and then another foot more.
Eventually I had him in the recommended yard
by now I was trembling like a leaf
when I think of it now what happened then
you know it was beyond belief.
The silver beauty flapped its tail
now I didn't make any mistake
but if I didn't do something soon
the fish would make an escape.
So like every normal angler I leapt
my fingers tightly round its throat
grabbed the priest and gave it a tap
to see if it would croak.
But no such luck it struggled on
and this is the first time I heard it speak
'Wake up, wake up, let go of my neck'
now the wife won't speak for a week.
....

Deep Frozen

Did you see that guy in America who made a will
when he wasn't feeling very well
then he got himself frozen stiff
and left the lot to himsel'.
But here we come to the bitter bit
and I don't think it right
they put the company that froze him, bankrupt
because they never paid the light.
....

The Will

I thought at my age I'd better write a will
mind you, I'm in perfect health
now me being a practical man
no solicitors, I'd write it myself.
So let me think, what have I got
what possessions can I leave behind
not a lot of valuables left I fear
perhaps I have been far too kind.
A house, a car, a grand big dog
no cash, now isn't that tough
mind you the pension doesn't go far
when you have a piece of fluff.
Some planks and scaffolding
and a concrete mixer
I'll leave that to the wife
now that will fix her.
My rods and guns
these will have to go
but who will I leave them to
well I just don't know.
On and on I thought it was just like a flitting
the only difference is of course
I'm still here sitting.
Well after a couple of worrying hours
writing a list of what I've got
I suddenly saw the light at last
I'll sell it all and spend the lot.

....

Divine Guidance

God called him to his service he said
and was guided through intricate life
was given his tasks and labours
and even was picked out a wife.
Now to me this sounds so grand and holy
quite exceptional to the rest of us
but could God not have given that bairn a shout
before she was killed by a bus.

....

Meditation Again

Now that it's winter I'm into the meditation
yes I'm all enthusiastic once again
last year I tried 'transcendental'
so this time I'll try the Zen.
Oh Buddha sure would be proud of me
if he could see me in my trance
mind you if I do it in the front porch
they can see me over at the manse.
Yes, mental freedom and liberty of mind

that is the name of the game
but I'll close the curtains just in case
for thinking I was drunk would be a shame.
Now some people sit when they are doing their thing
and others we' their feet round their necks
but to be honest if it was a warmish day
I'd just sit there with a bottle of Becks.
Then in no time at all I'm in another dimension
you can tell by my vacant look
aye when it comes to Zen meditation
I surely should write a book.
But there again I remember why I stopped it
you would hardly believe that I'd forgot
but last January I got in so deep
I woke up frozen to the spot.

....

Act Now

Do you ever think our country has gone mad
with all this rape and child abuse
you try to be kind and forgiving
and then say 'What the hell's the use.'
Christ said 'Suffer little children'
and that they are safe in his arms somehow
but honestly Christ I do not blaspheme
the help they are needing is 'now.'
Genes of evil multiply
double up in each generation
Lord isn't it time for some engineering
and a total eradication.
Patience could be a virtue most times
but impatience at times is right
why toy with Satan and his demons
when you could win the fight tonight.

....

Speed of Time

The speed of light is a constant they say
one of the few things in physics that is stable
everything else fluctuates
as much as they are able.
Now I was thinking if speed varied at all
time itself would feel shorter or long
and we all know the truth of that
so therefore the scientists are wrong.

....

Forgot

My dog was barking late last night
so I got up and gave her a row
I told her that she was a noisy bitch

but it is me that is sorry now.
For during the night a thief was about
and stole near half my tools
while me and the wife scolded the dog
just like a couple of fools.
Now as usual we learned a lesson
when the thief he came to rob
I had forgot why I had trained that bitch
but she never forgot her job.

....

Motive

Well I better have another go at filling in that form
it's the one from the DSS
but the questions are so confusing
what they mean I can only guess.
'Are you fit to do this, are you fit to do that'
'is climbing a ladder out of the question'
and there is a blank space for comments
or anything else you'd care to mention.
Now when it comes to the bit 'how far can you walk'
I immediately thought of the yards so few
but if Kim Bassinger was beckoning a mile away
it would be amazing what a man could do.

....

Nutter

I've told you that flies must be pretty smart
when they can dodge a rolled up paper
then they came back and give you another shot
they must think it all a caper.
But the other day I swatted one
I saw it eyeing up the butter
and do you know it didn't even move half an inch
yes, in all walks of life there's a nutter.

....

Basic Instinct

We went off on a long weekend
unfortunately I forgot my pills
these are the ones that kill the pain
with no side effects or frills.
Now me being tough as usual
thought I'd manage fine with just a dram
combine business with pleasure you may say
well, that's the kind of guy I am.
The first day passed with just a twinge
but the next day I was screaming
and me on my second honeymoon with a sore back
I thought sure that I must be dreaming.
The wife she dozed me with Anadins

Codene and Aspros too
I even went and asked the chemist
if he had anything new.
But no such luck, so I dropped my head
and my jaw began to sag
when inspiration suddenly struck
I'd stuck a spare box in my bag.
Oh my, I was delirious now
as I caressed the orange packet
I contemptuously sneered at the Anadins
and the rest that couldn't hack it.
now as they say we all live and learn
well I learnt this lesson about health
when it comes to women, drink or song
they all come a poor second to yourself.

....

Day Dreaming

I was sitting in the chair just thinking
and as usual doing a bit of wishing
I dreamed that I was on Loch Shin
and I was happily fishing.
Trout were rising to my fly
the breeze giving a ripple of cover
my friend across the bay got one
so we waved to one another.
Immediately then I was into a Rainbow
my rod it bowed with pressure
the line was taught with expectancy
and the reel it screeched with pleasure.
Now as I carefully played that fish
Betty the post awoke me with a letter
and I cursed the conscious reality
when a dream can be so much better.

....

Guilty

The murderer gets off on a technicality
lives long and seemingly contented
child abusers and rapists give the alibi
that their victims had consented.
Now I'm not saying that I know the answer
and of no wisdom make pretence
but when it comes to crimes of that order
the duck pond makes a lot of sense.

....

Ran Off

Now here is a wee story
about a woman I knew
she was married to a boring man

and we all knew that was true
Well anyway she ran off one day
albeit with the local bounder
and it was six months later and miles away
before eventually they found her.
She had been deserted of course
a big mistake we all reckoned
but do you know what she said when she came home
'it was worth every single second.'
....

Damn Poachers

There are a lot of poachers about you know
you can tell them by the way they walk
they sneak about sort of furtive
and they whisper when they talk.
Now I went to a Loch the other day
parked the Merc in the siding
and as I was putting on my deerstalker hat
I could see where the poachers were hiding
Tackling up with the best of gear
Hardy rod, green wellies and jacket
I glanced over to where the poachers were
just to see if they could hack it
Yes I was right, their nerve just cracked
off they went running without even a breather
so then of course I couldn't tell them
that I hadn't a permit either.
....

Investment

I knew a businessman who was investigated
by the infamous income tax
I don't know the whole story of course
but here are some of the facts.
The Tax man called on a cold December morning
reminding my friend of Scrooge
his brief case looked like a kit bag
it was really huge.
My friend took him in and sat him down
on a comfy chair by the fire
then he put on that vacant look
it's a face that you would admire.
'Cash' he said, 'I don't have cash'
I'm like a church mouse so to speak
but he didn't tell the tax man
that he sat on a rare antique.
Anyway to cut a long story short
my friend got off Scot free
and before the tax man left he said
'You were closer to a fortune than me.'
....

Downhill

It is my birthday once again
yes, today I'm fifty four
the only trouble is that I look ninety
and my back is terrible sore.
I got cards from all the family
and the usual promise from the wife
you know when you get over fifty
it can be an awful life.
No gay parties for me today
(Oh dash I better not say 'gay')
that is the trouble with modern life
you have to watch every word you say.
Mind you' I'll likely have a nip or two
just a quiet night so to speak
do you know when I was forty
the birthday could last a week.
But I can see it's all downhill now
when you get excited about catching a mouse
stop eying up the neighbours wife
and talk for hours about building a house.
Aye I can see the brain going too
that is mother nature again being kind
tomorrow you'll think that you'd had a great day
and the day after you'll not even 'mind.
....

Happiest Times

I knew a man who was good with money
and he toyed about with stocks and shares
very soon he climbed the ladder of success
yes, up the apples and pears.
Unfortunately then after ten years at the top
(we were really all sorry for that bloke)
for his firm went down the tubes
and he ended up flat broke.
Now this chap was a great philosopher of life
and as I talked with him two years later
I asked him which were the happiest times
which of the two were greater.
He looked at me kindly with eyes of a sage
and before anything else was said
he replied, as you ask that question
you can't be nearly right in the head.
....

Two Sure Things

Are some people born to be winners
and others born to lose
does anyone get a say in this
or even allowed to choose.

The winner of course says its all 'ability'
while the looser say it's all fate
if only we could find the right answer
that would really be great.
Ministers and priests say that they are called
(Oh yes, even the Wee Frees)
apparently they all get their directions
when they are kneeling on their knees.
Yes it would really be nice to believe in that
better that a gypsy reading your cup
but if the ordinary man said they were speaking to God
they'd likely lock him up.
Now we all know the one thing that is sure
but I say there at two including death
it's only actions that matter in this world
and all the beliefs and yapping's a waste of breath.
....

Old Age

I'm back doing my meditation again
I'd just thought I'd give it another go
they say it is awful good for you
but to be honest I do not know.
This time I'll try and go deeper
just something the Buddha said
but if anyone looked in the window
they would swear that I was dead.
Likely there would be panic then
all my customers would be on their knees
'mind you, it wouldn't be me that worries them
it's probably their guarantees.
Aye it's not easy being an old mason
supposing you are an elder in the Kirk
years after you are dead and gone
they'll still criticise your work.
....

Pain

I had a lot of pain today
so I cursed the brickies hod
then as usual I vented my anger
and started screaming at God.
'Oh Lord' I yelped and wailed
'Have you no' got any compassion'
'can you no' get me back in circulation
before Fyfestone goes out of fashion.'
The building trade is moving ahead without me
I even hear talk of plastic bricks
soon I won't be able to keep up with the rest
'Oh Lord, the pricks.'
All I ask is a few more years
and maybe get back my wee blue lorry
and if by chance I offended you God

honestly I'm awful sorry.
Also a couple of contracts would be handy
even a wee extension would be dandy.
But first things first, the injury
please get rid of this pain
and if you do this one wee thing
I'll never bother you again.

....

The Alcoholic

Alcoholism is a terrible disease
far worse than a heart attack
most people think you're a pain in the ass
and only a few, the best o' crack.
You think you remember the deeds of last night
oh yes, you say you know
but when you relate the story
it all happened a week ago.
Everyone is against you too of course
they are all involved in some evil plot
and if you think some alkies are different
well I'll tell you now they're not.
Then there is the fantastic lies
the tall stories that you tell
just ask an alkie how much he drinks
and he will lie like hell.
Yes, it is an awful affliction
when the wife thinks you're a dirty rat
yet, personally I feel so lucky at times
and so glad I'm not like that.

....

Human

I bawled at the wife again
'You're not much of a woman'
well, when you are in pain, you've got to
that is only human.
Next I insulted the dog
that helps without fail
but the stupid bitch just blinked at me
then she wagged her tail.
As no one else was there at the time
I just slunk off back to my bed
then at the last moment changed my mind
and laid on the couch instead.
'What a life' I bleated to God
(he knows that I'm really a good bloke)
but why did he surround me
with a heap o' girny folk.

....

Shopping

I went down to the supermarket today
to buy my usual beer and grog
bacon, beans, and a frozen hen
and some Chappie for the dog
Invergordon is such a nice town to shop
you can always get somewhere to park
they also have no traffic wardens
and I could do without the nark
anyway I was soon at the checkout
and as that nice lassie rang the till
I put my hand in my pocket
to get money to pay the bill
I'm sure you've guessed what happened next
not one tosser had I got
and if you think that funny
I tell you now it's not
the dame smiled patiently at me
as I put back the grog, the beans and the hen
mind you I never liked that place anyway
and I'm never going there again
....

Fishing Flies

Have you ever tried making 'fishing flies'
well that is what I'm doing now
'mind if the wife knew what I was using
there would be an awful row
you see after I nearly scalped the dog
my need for hair was acute
and being a normal man I thought of a fur
and the wife she had a beaut.'
Well all the season with feverish fingers
I turned out Palmer and Pennel
it must have been a relief for the dog
as she shivered away in her kennel.
Oh yes, that was a grand season indeed
I caught enough trout to fill a boat
you know it is amazing what you can catch
if you're using the wife's fur coat.
Well anyway as likely you've guessed
the dinner dances had to begin
and how could I tell the wife about her fur
when one arm was lost on Loch Shin.
But anyway as luck would have it
just as I was about to blame some muggers
a moth flew out of the wardrobe
so I shouted 'What greedy little buggers.'
....

Eyes Opened

Did you ever take a turn of being a smart ass
I did once, well actually twice
and boy, did I think that I was Archie
I wouldn't swap me for any price.
Anyway I was speaking to a tramp one day
he had stopped outside for a rest
so I thought that I'd go and get the crack
more for amusement and maybe a jest.
Well anyway he told me his story
of troubles overcome
of love and death and treachery
and of emotions that could numb.
Pursuit of pleasure, not for him
but the simple joy of being free
and as he disappeared along the road I knew
he was a better man that me.
....

The Register

I see a register of Free Masons is proposed
for those people with a bit of power
then we will know who they are
and we can watch them hour by hour.
of course all of this has been done before
and personally I find it boring
though the scheme they had was efficient enough
trust Hitler for that and Goring.
So why not make a register of Catholics
they seem to stick together all right
why not the Jew and the protestant too
and the lords in the house who are snoring.
Yes it is a ridiculous thought
idiotic it could be called
but do you ever wonder about the proposer
do you think he was ever 'blackballed'
....

Delete

My favourite word at the minute
is the verb 'delete'
I say it every time I feel the emotions
of hate and then defeat.
I think of my brain as a computer
when something is on the screen that's bad
I just press the 'delete' button
and I am no longer sad.
yes it is a great technique
but sometimes I do squirm
in case I press the wrong button
make a mistake and press 'return.'
....

Tragic

Some folk think that being heartless is tough
kindness is both weak and soft
and when they heard the story of Jesus
sadly for them they scoffed.

....

Training

We can train a human to do anything
yes, even to kill and maim
given the motive and the drill
you would do the very same.
Our policeman are trained almost perfectly
on completion of course they'll cop their brother
and if you park on double yellow lines
yes, the wardens would book their mother.
Yet we still have a training failure
and no, it is not recent
why can't we devise a course
which would train everyone to grow up descent.

....

Flitting

I've often thought of moving house
but my house won't let me go
if you asked me how I thought of this
well honestly I do not know.
The only answer that I can give
is that circumstances cannot be right
maybe there is a mutual attraction
and there are more to a building site.
Yes mother nature is mysterious indeed
of that we can all agree
but I do think it a bit over the top
when it comes to moving, the house tells me.

....

Reading

The greatest treasure a man can have
is the ability to read
this simple little exercise
can satisfy every need.
Surely it must be a gift from the gods
for only wise gods' understands
when a man is holding a book
he can hold the world in his hands.

....

Perfection

I'm back into the swing of winter now
with my studies and my books
I even stopped taking the dram
to see if it would improve my looks.
You see I was turning red and purple
probably tartan would be the word
but waiting to see what clan it was
now that's what I call absurd.
So, I'm into self-improvement now
and bound to be perfect around about June
'mind the way I have been living my life
a bit perfection can't come too soon.
I long for that day I'll feel aloof
the way I'd swagger after I walked
just like a reformed alcoholic
or a smoker when they've stopped.
But oh the feeling of being in control
and not be a weakling like fellow man
yet that attitude reminds me of Hitler
just before the trouble began.

....

My Hero

I you've never read Morgan the Mighty
you won't know what you've been missing
he was a real hero, not like the ones now
who are more interested in clothes and in kissing.
No, my Morgan would sort out the bad guys
without ever a thought of sweat or bad breath
he cleared his desert island of bad people
even the cannibals all starved to death.
Yes, many a happy hour I spent with Morgan
swinging about the trees on a rope
swimming in the croc' infested river
with nothing to save us but hope.
These were impressive days indeed
not forgotten as to an adult I grew
even now when I have a problem
I often wonder what Morgan would do.

....

The One That Got Away

I never told you about the fish I caught
yes, it's the one that got away
it must have weighed at least two pounds
and it took me half an hour to play.
I reeled him in until he began to tire
my rod was quivering like a leaf
and just as I was about to beach him
what happened then is beyond belief.

The line just parted right at the knot
and all I could do was gape
then that sickening emotion welled up
which was tantamount to rape.
I whimpered first, then I screamed
and stared at the empty beach
he made a V in the water just like a shark
and he was gone and out of reach.
I shouted swear words after him
and worked myself into a lather
I even accused the fish
of not knowing his father.
Then after the tension left me
my mate came into view
so I said nonchalantly, 'aye, lost a big one
must have been four pounds, how about you.
....

Contrary Nature

I was feeling right girny today
so as usual I began to sob
phoned up the wife to give her a nag
then threatened to kick the dog.
On bended knees I prayed to Allah
to send me an enemy or two
just somebody to have a fight with
even a Jehovah Witness would do.
If only someone would phone
selling conservatories or double glazing
(yes it's ringing there it goes)
you know the power of prayer's amazing.
But no such luck just a pal
Oh God he sounded cheerful
when all I wanted was someone to hate
and to maybe give them an earful.
That is the contrary way of nature I suppose
I know that perfectly fine
but why do I end up in the wrong place
exactly at the wrong time.
....

Humans

Oh how I hate the wildlife programs
where the animals are pestering each other for sex
or else they are trying to murder each other
and biting each other's necks.
Yes at times I'm glad I am human
and not a lion or a cat
because we all know that humans
would never act like that
....

Sense

Two young lads were going to the disco
when both were run down by a bus
now this is just a hypothetical story
so don't get upset or fuss.
Both were of different religions of course
maybe like me and you
so I will act the saintly Catholic
and you can act the Jew.
Anyway God's angel came along
and said 'Come along brother'
took one by the hand
and turned his back on the other.
Now I don't care what religion is
or whether you are a saint or a prat
I only know that my God
he would never do that.
....

Real Reality

I knew a man who hallucinated once
you could almost see his neurons fire
and the tale that he told us
it was story you would admire.
'Yes', he said, 'I saw it all'
'clearer than I see you'
and to him that little story
was in reality perfectly true.
....

Dream World

Did you ever fancy being one of the beautiful people
'Jet setters' they were called years ago
what they were called in the days of the propeller
to be honest I do not know.
Never the less I'm sure they were there
all dressed up in the latest clothes
bobbing and dancing in nightclubs
though probably now it shows.
Yes it would be nice to be in the 'In' crowd
more so if they are the elite
and not one scruff amongst them
that really would be a treat.
But once again there is a down side
always a fly in the cream
you'll miss out the joy of living
if you live your life in a dream.
....

Revenge

What a beautiful word 'Revenge' is
it's a pity it has connotations of hate
yet the feeling couldn't be described as good
the adjective I was thinking was 'great.'
There is nothing quite like 'getting your own back'
when somebody has pulled your rug
that perfect feeling of satisfaction
which could only be construed as smug.
Yet after all is said and done
and you contemplate the consequences and cause
you may wonder if it was all worth it
and do you know most of the time it was.

....

The Ballet Dancer

Phil the dancer pirouetted and leapt
young girls swooned and stifled a scream
and us strong, rough, tough, he men
scoffed and coughed, then turned a shade of green.

....

Wait For It

The spirit didn't move me today
so I just looked out of the window and gaped
probably I should have read a book or something
or even watch that cowboy movie I taped.
But no, I just sat staring into space
my mind worlds away
to some that would be a waste of time
and a totally useless day.
Yes nature can be so eccentric at times
yet ultimately on her we rely
so why do we plea, beg and pray
and don't wait for a reply.

....

The Ferret

A ferret ran into my house once you know
at the time I thought, 'what luck'
the opposite of what I should be thinking
for about ferrets I was never quite struck.
I grabbed a big stick and a shovel
a snare, and a gun, to be prepared
you know it's amazing how you can hate
just because you are a little bit scared

....

Smart Guy

I met a young London boy once you know
and he thought that all us country boys were thick
'mind I really didn't get offended that much
for to be honest he was a bit of a dick.
He wasn't aware of that observation of mine
not at the start as I'm sure you'll agree
but I think the penny dropped when I said
now who's the ones drinking their own pee
....

A Fool

You cannot be made a fool of
most folk don't know that's true
all people can do is create circumstances
then the rest is up to you.
....

Simple

Some philosophers say there is no past
others decide there is no future to come
only the present is real they say
they are probably right when all is said and done.
But who am I to argue the toss
for today my back is sore
that's because I hurt it yesterday
and tomorrow it'll be the day before
....

No Respect

The Panda car was following me
well, you should have seen me drive
perfection, except for that flock of birds
even then I left most alive.
I stuck to the road like a limpet
not even one swerve did I make
apart from that old wifie at the zebra crossing
there was not another mistake.
The horses beneath the bonnet squealed
and pulsed beneath the rust
I was even tempted to give it wellie
and leave the two constables in the dust
of course I quickly quashed that devilish sense of fun
put on my beret to look more sedate
maybe I could impress them with hand signals
they were bound to think that great.
Keeping my speed at a constant fifty
I felt 'special' and kind o' selected
but then a cruel twist of fate

something I never suspected.
Off they flew down the motorway
really, I think some people are twisted
they didn't even bother to stop me
in fact I doubt if they knew I existed.

....

The Final Response

Now I don't know if this story is true
it sounds as though it's embroidered a bit
never the less I'll tell you the facts
to see what you think of it.
There once was a very powerful president
(for legal reasons I cannot say who)
it wouldn't matter in any event
if this story isn't true.
Anyway the president was up against it
everything was wrong , nothing was right
the poor guy was at his wits end
he'd be waken half of the night.
'Ban the bomb, stop the war'
the price of sugar and bread
I tell you holding the whole thing together
was driving him off the head.
Then suddenly one day he snapped
I think it was over unemployment
why the people were all broke
and not getting any enjoyment.
It doesn't matter anyway, he just snapped
and I find the psychologist's predictions uncanny
for when a man's really at the end they say
the word he screams is 'Mammy.'

....

The Masses

The general masses are thick they say
to say that you're a brave man indeed
but why call most of our countrymen stupid
for a start is there any need.
Try interviewing each one separately
just to see the IQ they've got
if you do you might find inspiration
and the clever will find out a lot.

....

So Sure

I could have sworn I'd emptied the teapot
in fact there wasn't any doubt
but when I tipped it upside down
two wee teabags just fell out.
It was no big deal but still I gaped

at the two brown bodies in the sink
no great revelation here of course
but it did make me sit and think.
I was so sure I would have bet a million
called my greatest hero mistaken, my best friend misled
now isn't two teabags ridiculous to argue about
so if you are sure of anything, sometimes it's better not said.
....

The Stupid Thief

A thief was about my garden
because I cannot find my spade
I was surprised they didn't take the hoe
for it was a new design I'd made.
Still, I thought he couldn't have seen it
that long beauty made out of a rake
mind you the welding was pretty rough
and the steel handle a big mistake.
Never the less it is a priceless tool
albeit a bit top heavy and cold
maybe I shouldn't have used the electrical conduit
there again, the welding rods were old.
Anyway the dirty thief missed his chance
no doubt content with a B & Q spade
he will probably never appreciate the situation
and realise the mistake that he made.
....

The Playing Fields of Eton

They say that on the playing fields of Eton
the great wars of the world was won
(mind, I think it was only the one's we were in count)
so that would reduce the wars to 'some.'
Anyway I'm sure Tommy Aitkins would disagree with this
his Eton was the school down the road
five a side football and three and in
in a farmer's field the sheep had mowed.
So what did they learn on the playing fields of Eton
dare I say that they learned to cheat
Tommy did too, but they learned not to get caught
and that's why we rarely get beat
....

The Miner

Dracula sees more of the sun than me
it's like that when you are a miner
down a hole digging for coal
yet at times there is nothing finer.
The pleasure of putting on clean clothes
real joy in a shower or a bath
contentment at knowing you have earned your bread

and for a reward, a pint and a half.
Yes it's not a bad life you know
my scale of happiness goes as high as your own
but deep down there I see nature bare
and understand things only gods have known.

....

Heaven

At the end of the day it costs nothing to pray
helping others is all for free
precious kind words, the song of the birds
that's Heaven just wait and see.

....

Old Buildings

Edinburgh is our capital, I know
but isn't Glasgow a lovely city
Perth and Aberdeen are also great
but modern planners deserve some pity.
They strove away at Cumbernauld
did their best at East Kilbride
but their concrete tower blocks crumble
just because they are outside.
Now architects never change much
long ago their buildings fell
no doubt they tried the multi-story then
and the cantilever as well.
So when you consider our heritage
what we see now is the best
all the old inferior buildings crumbled away
for time is the ultimate test.

....

Response to Bank

I've a meeting at the bank next week
'God, my giro must have been delayed'
I whimpered a little and let out a scream
then fell on my knees and prayed.
'The bank' I thought, 'may God save me'
the money I get is in such small doses
their mahogany counter looks so expensive too
and the staff looks down their noses.
'Oh sexual intercourse' I shouted in panic
or at least words to that effect
I should never have trusted anyone
my finances are just wrecked.
Then I remembered my sage of a granny
her wisdom came straight from the cuff
at times like these she softly whispered
'All I can say is 'tough.'

....

Advice to a Youth

One thing I like about our country
success can be found in business, films, and pop
you are the only person to say 'can't'
there are tons of room at the top.
Don't be submissive and say 'who me'
blame luck or say others are clarted in jam
but of course if you run out of excuses
you can always blame your mam.
No, that is not the way to succeed in life
rather do everything the best that you can
if you do your best, I'll guarantee
you'll succeed at being a real man.

....

A wee Downer

Oh I wish that I was more of a hero
and less of a nervous wreck
even if I learned a computer or something
at least I'd be a bit more high tech.
It's really awful to be dull and dowdy
there must be latent beauty somewhere inside
then no one would laugh at my belly
and maybe ignore my big back side.
But there again I'm not so unhappy
I have heaps of family and friends
my several businesses are doing well
and I'm off for a run in my Mercedes Benz.
Yes life sometimes has its compensations
and when I see some slim good looking guy
especially if he's poor, that is sure
I say 'There but for the grace of God go I.'

....

Deep Thought

Poets write odes to the autumn
a riot of colour the artist weaves
but do they ever think a bit deeper than that
and wonder who picks up the leaves.

....

Confidence

One time I thought I looked ugly
well actually it was twice
this feeling was unusual for me
because I know that I'm pretty nice.
Anyway as a gazed in the mirror
my jaw began to sag
for below each lovely blue eye

was a pouch like a tattie bag.
My stubble had turned a nasty shade of grey
my nose a curious hue
well we all know the reason for that
why does anybody's nose turn blue.
My hair must have melted over night
along with my pearl white teeth
'God' I thought 'what a mess'
even God would say 'Oh good grief.'
Fortunately when I saw reality again
and my beauty was like the sunlight at dawn
now isn't all this self-confidence stuff
all a bit of a con.
....

Happiness

Like everyone else you want happiness
there is absolutely nothing wrong with that
a bit of security and comfort perhaps
and maybe someone to love and to pat.
A whole day free from worry
sometimes that would suffice
and of course a win on the lottery
that would be very nice.
Our health could be better that's true
being younger would help I suppose
being taller or shorter, a bit more hair
or just maybe a smaller nose.
So on and on goes the chase for happiness
you're sure you'll find it, you know you can
well if any of you ever find it
I'd just love to meet that man.
....

In The Playground

In the name of Allah I can hardly believe it
we are fighting Iraq again
will that damn leaders not sort out their problems
without more killing of women and men.
'They have secret weapons, but we have bigger guns'
'We have high technology while they just do their sums'
they have thousands in their gang, but we have many more
now do you ever get the feeling that we've heard all this before.
....

Understanding

Some people live with physical pain
day in day out, and at night
a few seem to suffer mental anguish
and think no one understands their plight.
So how do the unafflicted understand others pain

105

when maybe it's toothache is all that they've got
(and if you think that is the epitome of agony)
I tell you now it's not.
Well really, the answer is quite simple
bang your head on the wall, if you have the guts
then if you do it often enough, you will feel pain
and the rest of the world think you're nuts.
....

Human

'Oh God' I cried in grief again
another mouse caught in the trap
thankfully it happened through the night
and I never heard it go 'snap.'
'Maybe it has babies' I wailed once more
likely they're out in the shed
I slid to my knees and sobbed
'by tomorrow they will all be dead.'
No mother will come to feed them
the father will be miles away by now
why wasn't it him that was caught in the trap
instead of this poor little cow.
Whimpering once again, I came to my senses
and checked the other trap that I set
and yes, here was the daddy, stone dead
yet it's so human to judge then regret.
....

Positive Thinking

I've told you about my positive thinking
and whenever I have a bad thought I say 'delete'
well after about six months of this
to be honest, I'm just about beat.
No matter where I go now
the pub, or the library reading books
it's even worse if I go to a party
for they all give me such strange looks.
But we all have to be honest with ourselves
and I must look like a Dalek walking down the street
when everyone else is saying 'Morning or aye aye'
I am going 'delete, delete, delete.'
....

No Necessity

Nobody is interested in perpetual motion today
yet it is the ultimate of all invention
getting something for nothing you might say
at least that is the intention.
Unfortunately the laws of physics deny it
quantum mechanics and mathematics agreed
that for a planet with plenty
evolution says there's no need.
....

Why Change

I can visualise the town of my childhood
and I see it warm and bright
then I dream of the flickering shadows
when the lights came on at night.
And there before me all the people I knew then
but do you know I find it so strange
when I was so pleased with everything
why had it all got to change.

....

The Old Jersey

My jersey got a haircut today
but it wasn't much of a clip
I just used the kitchen scissors
and gave the ballies a snip.
Mind you it's baldie at the elbows
and baggie at the waist
the neck is completely all askew
with dragging it off in haste.
The colours too have disappeared
it's now a faded grey
but I have grown attached to it
and I don't want to throw it away.
So what do you do with a worn out jersey
considering the good times we had together
is loyalty to a bit of wool important
if it is you'd wear it forever.
No, that is not the way with nature
for she recycles everything, even women and men
and in that mysterious factory
she makes everything brand new again.

....

Big Man

Do you know I can't get over how lucky I am
I have brains, beauty and great wealth
my family and many friends almost worship me
and keep asking my advice on their health.
But a very strange thing happened to me in Alness yesterday
which I have yet to figure out the cause
for a wee runt of a mongrel bit me in the arse
of course maybe it didn't know who I was.

....

A Prick

Another funeral on Tuesday morning
but this time I'm not going to go
(to be honest I wasn't struck on the guy anyway)

I wouldn't tell everyone that, only now you know.
not much point singing 'Abide we' me'
trying to look sad at the coffin of polished pine
saying 'Oh he wasn't a bad chap at all'
when you know he was a prick all the time.
But there again do I take things too far
is my understanding of death all aglee
for one thing certain about a coffin
one day it'll hold a prick like me.
....

Human

I prayed again to God last night
'Please' I said 'send us a genetic engineer'
possibly you might think that a strange request
or at the very least a wee bit queer.
But I sent that plea in earnestness
for the human race is progressing so slow
in fact at times I think we're going backwards
resurrecting instincts that we should not know.
A lot of our hero's are now homo' or bisexual
young folk worship behaviour so uncouth
sportsmen and women approve of cheating
and every second actor admits that they're a drouth.
Yes it is an abysmal picture that I paint
the decadence of man and woman
yet deep, deep down I know that I am wrong
for God loves us because we are human.
....

Indifference

The worst word in our language is 'indifference'
when I sense it, it brings me so low
hate or love, disgust or desire
but not, 'I don't want to know.'
You would think 'indifference' would hold the middle ground
it's not 'hatred' or 'love' to be fair
yet that empty emotion 'indifference'
chills the heart, when people don't care.
....

The Portfolio

'Here it comes' a heart attack I thought
but no, it was just a bit of wind
and there I was ready to meet my maker
my story ready and the excuses why I sinned.
'Oh' I thought another masterly escape
maybe a year or two left in this old body of mine
perhaps I won't have to tell my pathetic story yet
and of course the same excuses will do just fine.
Another day, another year later

my story and excuses were now perfection
but when I presented myself at Saint Peters gate
I got through, but my portfolio got a rejection.
....

The Bird

Even to animal lovers this may sound strange
in fact it could be termed absurd
but I shed a tear yesterday
would you believe it, for a little bird.
It was quite plain that its death was quite imminent
but it was not for that reason I cried
nor was it for my inadequacy
I couldn't help supposing I tried.
No, the reason for my sorrow was simple
nothing intellectual, perceptive or grand
whatever it be that saddened me
was the bird didn't understand.
....

Shopping

I was down in Edinburgh at the weekend
everyone said to me to go to the Gyle
for the cheuchters benefit that's a shopping mall
with stores and shops by the mile.
Now this experience was an eye opener
in fact it was really hard to comprehend
why everyone seemed to be besotted with clothes and shoes
glassy eyed with a death wish to spend.
They say that millions pass through it in a year
that's a lot, supposing the goods were half the price
but then surely a pair of shoes would last more than a year
so why in earth would anyone go twice.
Yes it is a complete mystery this shopping
a life spent looking at shoes and clothes
is it need or just plain greed
you know, I don't think anyone knows.
....

Popularity

Do you ever think that nobody likes you
that you're unpopular with friends so few
well, don't be depressed or feel alone
a lot of us think like you.
Now try to imagine you're having a party
and you ask all you're friends to dine
there might be only two or three there
but you can say what you think and it's fine.
When the more popular people have their do
likely their table will be full
but they don't address one and all

in popularity that's a golden rule.
The more popular you get the more complex you are
true to all, is impossible there's no doubt
and when the awful nice people have their party
that's the day that they'll get found out.

....

Court of Session

I was in the court of session once you know
that was in Edinburgh near the castle
an angel must have been with me that day, I got parked
while everyone else had a hassle.
The austere building glared at me right away
maybe it instinctively sensed that I was a wee builder
of course the wife narked me for criticizing the stone work
and I was so tense by then I could have killed her.
But keeping my cool, I turned to the cathedral
and to be honest, yes, I prayed
I asked Saint Giles to crisp the opposition
and make a fool of the points they made.
Now into the great hall, now that's a sight
the ceiling, the roof, the epitome of the joiners craft
mind' you I wasn't impressed with the door hinges
that new bits of aluminium stuck on looked daft
Yet all in all it really looked impressive
for marks I'd give nine out of ten
it would have got the ten if it wasn't for the repairs
which shows to employ the right men.
Now getting back to the litigation bit
(I'm always distracted by buildings, just a wee habit)
anyway the wife was stamping her feet by now
and generally getting quite crabbit.
'There's your barrister' she squealed and shoved me
that push nearly knocked me off my feet
it would have done if Giles hadn't intervened
and I thought that was pretty neat.
To cut a long story short, the barrister saw me and waved
(do you know I felt as proud as punch)
but then he said 'What are you doing here today'
'your case is next week, I'm just off for my lunch.'

....

The Gene

Some men are born to be teetotallers
others seem to be here to drink
could it be in the gene, if you see what I mean
I don't know, but it makes you think.

....

The Tycoon

I was tycooning away in my office one day
(in reality I was renewing the pools)

you can do it over the phone now you know
then you can be sure that you don't break the rules.
By the rules I mean the wee crosses
you could easily have been doing it wrong for years
then just imagine the week that you'd win, you discover
I can visualise the moans and the tears.
So to be sure I'll use my Mastercard
and besides the lassie at Littlewoods seems so nice
then I won't have to bother with the post at all
do you know stamps are an awful price.

....

Autonomy

Why can't I be a big shot
go to work in a smart suit
and when I stride through the office
the lassies would squeal 'ain't he cute.'
But no such luck, it's jeans for me
a Stanley tape stuck in my belt
and an egotistical power crazed Aberdeen foreman shouting
'You're here ta' da' fit yir telt.'
Well personally I don't think it fair
I was the dux o' the academy in Tain
Maybe have been a doctor or a lawyer
you know a brickie is just not the same.
But I can be cowardly and sneaky as well
I even wriggled out of a charge of assault
when it's pure circumstances that dictated your life
your situation can't be your own fault.

....

Madonna's Bottom

What in earth is Madonna showing her bum for
she already has fame and money
I just can't figure it out
and really think it funny.
Does she really thing we're interested
in her fantasies
does she think her bottom so special
when we've all got one of these.
Maybe she's on an ego trip
and thinks she's one of a few
when the rest of us only got one
she was blessed with two.
But anyway I'll save my money
and she can keep her book
and if I find her backside on display
I won't even give it a second look.
But here again, I'm a normal man
hypocritical and pretty week
and Madonna knows too, there's very few
who couldn't resist a peep.

....

Repeats

There is not one original thought left to think
all our thoughts' have been thought before
the stories you tell the jokes as well
yes there is so much more.
This seems to drive some artists mad
and they strive to paint something new
writers, poets and sculptors
doing some things they shouldn't do.
Architects, builders and even politicians
all striving to be unique
but I tell you now the hermit was right
there is nothing new left to speak.

....

Life

We all gathered round the camp fire
and do you know all the stories were good
mind you, after seventy years on earth
so they should.
Some had done such wondrous things
and others were really a scream
some people had such a pampered time
they lived their lives in a dream.
Oh it was so entertaining
but if course we avoided the odd scruff
well, we were sort of ordinary guys
and we thought enough was enough.
Some had explored the wide world
others plumbed the depth of despair
one guy laughed for most of his life
'mind, I didn't think he was all there.
Another chap told the story
of hardship and the fight to survive
'but do you know' he said sincerely
'I knew that I was alive.'
The excitement of straining against nature
and alas yes, my fellow man
but now the fight is over
and I know the man that I am.
One old man smirked and grinned
'Well' he said 'I was a millionaire
but when I think I worked day and night
I consider that pretty fair'.
Oh the stories went on and on
and the dying embers made an effort to burn
then they all looked in my direction
and I panicked for it was my turn.
Now I have no wish to be dramatic
no life of Heaven or Hell
but I had the saddest story of all
for I had nothing to tell.

....

Too Much

He who flies with the crows get shot
the same as runs with the rabbit
but total destruction seems a bit over the top
for just one little bad habit.
....

The Cure

My wife said to me one morning
'Oh I must really try and slim
that virus has swollen me up like a porpoise
when I used to be so thin.'
Well as usual I offered her the panacea
a cure for all her ills
and as usual she declined the offer
for any malady, she'd take some pills.
She also said that she had a cold
maybe it was a touch of the flu
so I redoubled my efforts of persuasion
quite likely the same as you.
But no such luck she wouldn't relent
not even when I guaranteed a cure
'mind I wasn't a hundred per cent confident
but I was ninety per cent of the time sure.
Well the day dragged on spluttering and coughing
it was just wrecking her poor wee body
when at last she said, 'I'll take the cure'
so I poured her a big glass of 'toddy.'
....

Again and Again

If you could live your life again
is there anything that you'd change
maybe nothing so drastic as cut it out
but just to rearrange.
One man says he would, and another wouldn't
some say they would discern
but the one's who says they wouldn't change
that's the one's that never learn.
....

Boredom

I'm really awful bored today
I am probably missing the neighbour
but that's not true for we never socialised
and also he voted Labour.
We never went and took the shot together
when I think of it he was kind o' sinister
but there again what do you expect

from a Church of Scotland minister.
Not once did he stagger up the drive
or made a pass at a strange woman
some people are a slice short of the pan loaf
and a little less than human.
So I'll twiddle my thumbs in despair
there is no one left to corrupt
not one soul to argue with
nor even to interrupt.

....

A Childhood Dream

I've always wanted to be a cowboy
to be one of the riders of the range
and when you think of all the films I've seen
that ambition is not so strange.
I imagined myself as being Jeff, the hero
back at the ranch helping Sue
only it was years later I realised
what he was helping her to do.
Riding into Deadwood at nights
singing 'Forget me Not'
and me in my innocence never twigged
that Jeff would take the shot.
The fights and shootings excited me
there was a dastardly murder near every night
but of course we all knew our hero
because his hat was always white.
And the pesky injuns going round in circles
shooting their arrows with bows
why that folk in the wagons kept missing them
it is only God that knows.
Yes I really was taken in by it all
even the scalping didn't seem bad
but grown up reality is a different thing
and sometimes that makes me sad.

....

More Panic

I took another panic attack today
yes, it happened once again
this time I was at the butchers counter
as I was about to buy a hen.
I could feel the sudden surge of blood
as it all rushed to my face
I bitterly regretted going to Tesco's
I should have stuck with the Mace.
But anyway here I was
everybody grinning and staring
and me sweating like an old horse
and not one soul was caring.
As usual the checkout was choc a block
with imbeciles writing out cheques

and that silly loon wi' a credit card
for a miniature and a pack of Becks.
Of course they all kept staring at me
well they say ignorance can be bliss
but I never thought that I'd see the day
when it would come to this.
Then the wee toad of a manager came out
and stood where the trolleys were left
'Oh God, he's going to stop me'
and likely accuse me of theft.
But fortunately no, so I scurried out
and held tight on my frozen hen
I tell you though I starve to death
I'm never going there again.

....

Ramblings 2

Hormones Again

I went up to the bacon counter
when my hands started to shake
the sweat was running down my face
and my body began to bake.
A mile to go to the checkout
all the people could see my plight
deep down I knew that was impossible
but you never know, they might.
So off I tottered, my face bright red
(it was just my age somebody said)
past the dog food down the isles I ran
and I never believed that this would happen
to a normal man.

....

The Slippery Slope

Yes I was on the slippery slope
and fought hard to keep upright
I could feel the evil forces
attacking me day and night.
Yet still I kept my feet somehow
for powerful is the Thane of Hell
I cut and thrust with principalities
and that's a story I'll never tell.
But one small fact I held intact
that Christ was tempted too
and do you know you'll never understand it
until it happens to you.
But another thing that kept me on fighting
was the question 'why bother with me'
and do you know the answer is so simple
I'm sure you'll all agree.
But do you know an astonishing fact
that while on the slippery slope
when life was spiralling downwards
and darkness was murdering hope.
I just sometimes stood amazed
at the various folk I'd meet
and it was quite an eye opener
who'd pull the rug away from my feet.

....

The Invention

I thought that I'd make an invention
so I got together a steel spring
then some rods and iron hooks
for the counterbalances to hing.
A few wheels of an old pram
some wire to hold them steady
then a tube of super glue

now I was almost ready.
I tied the wire to put the spring in tension
it looked like it was a great invention
but the wheels wouldn't move nor would the spring
I probably should have used a bit of string.
Then all of a sudden it all collapsed in a heap
and when I think of it now I could sit and greet
and as I sat and gave a sigh
you always think you can do something,
it's easy, until you try
……………………..

Lonely

Do you ever get real lonely
when even a 'hate' phone call would do
now the secret is not to get depressed
you're not alone, they are more than you.
Yes life can be sadistic at times
and I know it's not your choice
no-body wants to be lonely
and long to hear a human voice.
Yet chaotic swirling circumstances dictates
as nature paints her picture
just remember loneliness is experience
and experience make you richer.
……………………….

Out of Proportion

It dropped on the rug with an ominous thud
the quarterly communication from the Hydro Board
well, you know that they sometimes get it wrong
so over the bill I pored.
I scanned the units and checked the price
to be honest I got very upset
but if you don't wire round the meter
a big bill is what you get.
My head went down and I kind o' sobbed
the wife patted me and said 'Do your painting'
never mind that nasty people
or you'll take one of your turns o' fainting.
'Oh God, it's me again'
that Hydro Board are the pits
please send a thunderbolt to Elgin
and blow their damn office to bits.
My hand took on the customary shake
'mind you they shake like that each day
but the oscillations are a wee bit faster
when I get a bill I cannot pay.
Never the less the wife came back
in my misery I never noticed she went
and yes, she paid that wicked demand
she's so straight she must be bent.
…………………..

Jumping off the Mantelpiece

You know how true the saying is
about the things that are said in jest
well honestly I was there when this happened
as I was sitting drinking with the rest.
Now this woman, I think she was tipsy
she thought she'd do a prank
what she intended was a bit ambitious
because of the amount she drank.
Well she stood up on the fireplace
and on my pal she tried to leap
but my pal took a step forward
and the poor woman landed in a heap.
Now you've all heard of 'the minister's daughter'
how she had them all in fits
jumping of the mantelpiece
and landing on her (bits).
The moral of this story is of course
is when things are sung in fun
there might be a grain of truth somewhere
but I know that particular stunt just can't be done.
....

Building Bricks

Realities riddle beckons all
come solve realities riddle
is the pea under the left or the right
or is it under the middle.
Does ten and ten always make twenty
or can it sometimes make twenty one
no reasonable mind could ever deny
the impossible can't be done.
But there again, the impossible's done
I hear a voice from London speak
I can travel to the ends of the earth
and do it in less than a week.
Elements have changed from one to the other
the serpent became a stick
and that was no illusion
or any cunning trick.
You see everything is made
from the same building blocks
cities, the hills and the heather
it's all dictated at the start of time
how and if, they will stick together.
....

It will be better

I'll leave the world a better place
that was always my intention
so I build a few houses

and also a few extensions.
Now you might say, that's not a lot
and chastise me for my boast
but I will be happy to settle for that
because it is more than most.
....

The Legacy

I was saddened that our hero Churchill
left his money to his heirs in perpetuity
and I thought he was so wise and smart
oozing sense that flowed so fluently.
Yet mighty men make mistakes as well
and mistakes you cannot scorn
but Churchill took the thrill of life away
even before his heirs were born.
....

Never too Old

Will I drag my old body down to the pub
after all it is Saturday night
but half the pleasure is gone
when you are too old to fight.
Maybe instead I'll take a wee walk
that's more sedate for my time of life
and give a wee wave to my neighbour in passing
praying he won't twig I fancied his wife.
Or else I could watch the movie
or even take a run on my bike
I could gate crash someone's party
but all is in vain, my zimmer broke down
so I won't get out tonight.
....

Hope

We hoped for a land fit for hero's
where justice and the generous give
but all we made was a smelly farm
where all the greedy bastards live.
....

Sick Joke

Now I'm not a man for sick jokes
I prefer the ones about Paddy or the Paki
but this wee Jap got wounded in Hiroshima
so disgusted he limped off home to Nagasaki.
....

The Upbringing

It's all in the upbringing the minister said
and you'll see how good they'll turn out
teach them all the graces and virtues
and they will be a credit no doubt.
Now this statement was a great comfort to me
because you know me with my liking for malt
but I'm also a sex crazed lazy philanderer
and it's all my mother's fault.
....

The Artist

it's amazing the artistic talent a man can have
especially when he is retired
only yesterday I fondled my brushes
and I really felt inspired.
I looked out of the window
and I could see the meaning of life
then my eyes glazed over
and I smiled at the wife.
I worked like a Dervish
the paints flowed like cream
colours leapt out at me
just like a dream.
But sadly I knew with a gutted sensation
that it would take another day
to complete my creation
if only a little more time I could borrow
I wouldn't need to leave the ceiling until tomorrow.
....

Love Affair

You've often read of great love affairs
of lust and fiery passion
no, I don't think it will ever cease
and not likely to go out of fashion.
Some stories are sad, some are bad
some passions can ruin your life
but why is it always with a strange man
and for a man, it's never the wife.
....

Linda

Yes I was lying there with Linda on my mind
that was a bit of a pity because my wife's name is Audrey
well, anyway there I was
lying there with Linda on my mind
how could the wife be so cruel
when Linda was so very kind.

Why does Audrey gurn so much
while Linda is always so sweet
just the luck of the draw I suppose
God it would make you greet.
Always so smart about the toon
I'll bet you won't see her in an old night goon
her make-up is perfect, we' ruby lips
and that white breeks fairly clings to her hips.
Her long blonde hair looks just great
and never ever saw a curler
she dances like a fairy
when the young bucks birl her.
There again she doesn't drink whisky
and can't tell a blend from a malt
but Oh God she doesn't suit that pint of Guinness
but I suppose everyone's got a fault.
....

The New Age

We've had the stone age, bronze and iron
and today we have sex and lust
but that is just a devious diversion
today is the age of rust.
....

Another Dead Fly

I just killed a fly, by accident of course
now this is one thing you don't know
you can see its guts all over the window
but where did it's little life go.
....

Lucky Dog

I wish I were my dog at times
about self she has no clue
yet she understands the essence of life
now that's smarter than me and you.
She understands her wants and her needs
superfluous is city lunches
accepting a plan ignored by man
and instinctively rolls with the punches.
She doesn't crave a kennel of gold
in seconds can forget and forgive
yes, evolution has been kind to her
for all she wants is to live.
....

Who Knows

Were we really gifted, paradise
or was it just an infant Hell

the beauty of youth confused us
yes you and me as well.
The puppy dog ambles in the garden
in spring and summer weather
yet come the maturity of winter
it may become the king of terror.

....

More Experience

He's bankrupt they say, he's down the tubes
oh what a terrible shame
and him doing so well too
now he's left without a name.
Yet how can he hold his head so high
and stare failure straight in the eye
but there again you'll never know
until you give it a try.

....

Twisters

Do you know I was over fifty before I realised
that our country was full of twisters
and to think of all the years of respect
when I called them misses and misters.
Oh how stupid, yes even thick
naive, a fish in the net
the worldly wise was in disguise
and of course I now regret.
Then mysterious mother nature steps in as usual
with the silver lining to this dark cloud
and she whispers, 'Son, you are better than them'
she is right, and now I'm so proud.

....

The Plan

I thought the Lord was my shepherd
and the ministers were the collie dogs
and in that great big engine
I was one of the cogs.
Now great I thought, a mighty plan
an enigma there was no doot
until a wee beetle crossed my path
and was crushed under the sole of my boot.

....

Fighting Dirty Again

The regional Council is trying to con me now
well I suppose it is their shot
but after the tax and the accountant got through
it's only a couple of quid that I've got.

So they will be in for a disappointment
you see, I can wipe the grin from their face
because (do you see that flashy new road they built)
well, I happen to know, it's in the wrong place.
Yes, when it comes to the nitty gritty
Then you wonder what to do
you would do the very same as me
and you will fight dirty too.

....

A Great Loss

I hurt my back when I was a brickie
it was like an artist losing his brush
a model getting old and haggard
when the wrinkles all came in a rush.
Like John Wayne losing his six gun
but of course he hadn't got to build any walls
no it was more like Dolly Parton losing her bosom
or Warren Beattie, his 'other bits'.

....

The Drinkers Memory

I used to remember everything once you know
but then I started to drink
and then I forgot all the hurts and insults
now doesn't that make you think.

....

The Rules

I was a big shot once you know
now I'm poor, and it's a drag
I used to go to the casino
but now it's Whist or a game of Brag.
The Audi all but rusted away
and I can't afford to fill the tank
when once I walked proud I now slink along
and speed up when I pass the bank.
I pick up my pension on Thursdays
and pretend it is a pittance
but if I lost a pound before I got home
the wife would likely have kittens.
It's just like Africa in the jungle you know
the wounded animal is always fair game
well I tell you here in Britain
the rules are the very same.

....

The Barbi

I got drunk at a barbi' once
yes I 'mind it fine
of course that's not the only occasion

because I do it all the time.
'No sense of decorum' the wife would say
there is nothing else in your head
that is after I had woken up
and slunk away to my bed.
Well the next day I got to thinking
and do you know I thought she was right
so I figured that I would surprise her
and stay sober the next barbi night.
Saturday night came round again
as you can imagine I was full of apprehension
but anyway I lit the barbi
in the shelter of the extension.
The dog was yelping as usual
it's no wonder I gave her a kick
well the last time she stole some kebabs
and the wooden sticks made her sick.
Anyway on with the story
the guests came rolling in
I could see they were all excited
at the thought of a little sin.
The wife served out the lager and whisky
and to me, lemonade, what profanity
a drinker staying sober at a barbi
it's the first signs of insanity.
In went a tape of Elvis
though I say it myself the food was great
and I didn't mind the troops scooping the drams at all
but I was disgusted at the rate.
Soon they were all swinging and singing
to be honest it was a pathetic sight
grown men and women enjoying themselves like that
you know, it didn't seem right.
For hours they all cavorted
they were oozing happiness all over the place
but I still sipped lemonade
and tried to keep the gurn off my face.
Well to cut a long story short the wife gave me a nudge
and I blurted out 'Drink, what do you mean'
but she just puffed up her pillow and said
'Wake up, you are having a dream.'
……………………

Not Up To It

I tried to understand quantum mechanics
and did my macroscopic best
but when it came to the questions
yes, I failed the test.
My equations were left incomplete
(actually that is another word for sums)
but it does sound more impressive
as you mumble it through your gums.
My particles just wouldn't perform
no chance of me making a bomb

by the time I got the thing to explode
the enemy would all be gone.
So it looks like I'll have to stick with bricks
and forget the holes in space
likely with my luck I'd fall in anyway
and vanish without a trace.

....

Quite Smart

I wasn't the brightest boy in my class
but I know I wasn't the dunce
because I was belted for being cheeky to the teacher
so I only did it the once.

....

Workers

I was taught to be a worker
and not to lounge about
to sweat is a proper virtue
of that there was no doubt.
Yet at times when working
'wanted to doss' is how I'd feel
but dossing is more demanding
you really need nerves of steel.
So I'll have to be patient
just like other men
and wait until the big wheel moves
when it's my turn again.

....

Holidays

I'm off the Spain again soon
to give the Spanish another fright
in fact if they knew I was coming
they wouldn't get a wink to-night.
'Ole' I'll shout 'Ole'
from the steps on the front of the plane
and I can see them all smiling
'Oh not senor again'.
Straight to the cafés
ah Sangria in a jug
join in the flamenco dance
and give the senoras a hug.
All will be delighted to see me of course
they know, their blues I'll banish
I can tell by the way they shout
it's only a pity it's all in Spanish.
The long quiet days beside the pool
me cheering them up, acting the fool
the splashing around, what delight
and I'd sing Flower of Scotland late at night.

Oh yes I'm looking forward to the change
maybe the wife won't be so grumpy
but she always gets like that near the hols'
I just don't know why she's so jumpy.

....

Mysterious

The standard of human enjoyment
is something I'll never know
the best night out at a party
is the one when you didn't go.

....

A Visit to the Doc

He told me I must have an addictive personality
well, I didn't know what to think
he couldn't know about all my excesses
so he was likely talking about drink.
Yes, he said you're a weak weak man
(not that exact words but all to same effect)
probably he was trying a wee bit of psychology
and not to annoy me I suspect.
'Your blood pressure is up
that's easy to tell
your' kidneys and liver
are knackered as well
with all your excesses and addictive history
how you are still walking is a medical mystery.
Well he slagged me off for the full seven minutes
before that I felt quite fine
and damn it, I thought I wasn't doing bad
for a priest of eighty-nine.

....

More Drams

I took a few drams again last night
and today my heart is lead
in fact if I were a normal man
I would be lying in my bed.
But a drinking man is big and tough
fights off the weakness to stay sober and good
yet if it were considered a virtue to get drunk
I don't think anyone would.

....

Success

Some folk succeed
others make a mess
but if I get through life without a record
I'll call that success.

....

In Defence

He told me I was a wee bit porky
to be blunt he called me fat
and I was quite pleased with myself
until he went and said that.
But mother nature gives us a defence system
so I didn't take too much notice of him
because he's a long streak of misery
and twice as ugly as sin.

....

Poor Cleg

If there is one thing worse than a midgie
it surely must be the cleg
why only yesterday one flew along
and landed on my leg.
He sooked the usual pint of blood
the alcohol content was ten per cent
then he only flew a hundred yards
before his liver went.

....

Opportunity

Do you ever think what might have been
if only you had acted
it doesn't take too much imagination then
to know that you could have cracked it.
Opportunity knocks but once they say
but personally I don't think that's right
plenty of people get more than one chance
so you never know, you might.
The problem is, which way to jump
and not lose the bit you've got and need
but if you fear failure to that extent
no, you'll never succeed.

....

Thankful

I suppose I'd better try out the hoover
and tidy up the mess
but housework is not my forte
in fact I'm hopeless more or less.
I do not see what should be done
I'd be far happier laying bricks
and what on earth will I do with that washing
shirts and socks and a heap of knicks.
Oh all that decisions fair wear me down
don't they realise that a brickie is only human
I better get on my knees and thank God again
that he didn't make me a woman.

....

A Change of Heart

Peyton Place was on the tele last night
now who could wish for more
oh yes it had been on years ago
and I've seen it all before.
I remember the last time I took a fancy to Alison
and I really thought she was bonnie
now getting older does strange things to a man
because this time I fancied Connie.
....

Won't be easy

I'm more or less waiting for the grim reaper now
you know, that angel we' a gurn on his face
I think he carries a scythe or sickle
and a black hood keeps his hair in place.
Mind you, he'll have a job to find me
I'll be hard to trace and plant
it's a very difficult house to get to
why even Scobbies taxi can't.
....

Sickening

Not many things make me ill
except the obvious of course
and you know me with my disease
which at times can leave me hoarse.
But of all the usual causes
to the toilet I will rush
when I hear the sickening sound
of sentimental slush.
....

Knowledge

Life is not meant to be simple they say
but do you ever wonder why not
what is the point of complications
when eventually we're all going to rot.
A lifetime's study of time and space
and in the end it's still a mystery
all your efforts and knowledge
not even recorded in history.
Then the lucky ones with a bit of faith
happy with what they are taught
for when they die they'll be satisfied
because they'll be told the lot.
....

Clothes

They're buzzing around the Eastgate centre
in a desperate search for clothes
why there's such a compulsion to toff ourselves up
it is only God that knows.
Shoes for our feet, shirts for our back
a jersey carefully picked
the young folk need a pair of jeans
and they're better if they are ripped.
Yes, it's a strange instinct that we have developed
the priority of our body to cover
'mind you, it's better than our ancestors
with their hobby of killing each other.

....

It Doesn't Cost Much

My wife is a grand worker
and pretty good looking too
at times she also is very kind
and that is also true.
Now, not trying to be smart I told her
of her good attributes she had many
do you know that pleased her a lot
and it didn't cost me a penny.

....

Last Will

I wrote it on my new writing pad
yes it was my final will
they say that is a symptom
when you start going down the hill.
I started off quite neat at the start
emphasising they all do my bidding
but slowly my script deteriorated
'till it was like a hen walking over a midden.
Quite exasperated with my clumsy attempt
I stroked it out to start again
and I suppose that prompted the idea
but I can only guess the time was then.
I grabbed another page of my jotter
and shouted 'Oh what the hell'
then demanded that I be deep frozen
and left the lot to mysel'.

....

Cats and Dogs

I knew a man who hated dogs
now I couldn't understand that
but there again I could understand
if he said he hated cats.

....

130

Tarring the Drive

The County came to tar my drive
and not a bit before time
for promptness I'd give them one point
and for reluctance I'd give them nine.
I have only asked them a thousand times
by telephone and by letter
but they are so tight and miserable
I don't think anyone could do any better.
So now at last it's getting done
it was really worth the row
the only wee worry that I have
is who will I pester now.

....

Wonder

You know I'm always wondering
about the enigma of time and space
why nature evolved an Eden
and then bothered with a human race.
Then I sit and ponder
while we drag the creation asunder
I do not wonder why
but only why I wonder.

....

The Phone Call

Have you ever waited for a phone call
when someone says they will ring you back
now that's when you need some patience
of which I never quite got the knack.
In five minutes I begin to dislike them
in ten it drives me nuts
in fifteen I get quite jumpy
and in twenty I hate their guts.
Yet when the phone eventually rings
when I am by the Devil driven
I pick up the phone and say 'Hello'
and in an instant all is forgiven.

....

Insight

I woke up depressed this morning
and thought 'Oh not another day'
closed my eyes and turned around
and stayed there where I lay.
I could hear the traffic passing
and human voices as they chat
and I looked up and questioned God

'Why can't I do that?'
Now as usual God didn't answer
as I toiled in my private hell
tired, sad, and desolate
and late for my work as well.
Now I don't know the answer or the cure
there is only one compensation that I can reveal
when you see a fellow human suffer
you'll know exactly how they feel.
....

Priorities

Me and my pal were riding along
doing abut sixty on my motor bike
going round a corner we both fell off
now you can believe this if you like.
Head over heels the both of us went
cut and bruised and sore
I fell into some bushes
and my trousers tore.
From a prone position my pal shouted
'My arm is broken, for the love o' mike'
and honestly I replied
'Never mind the arm, how's my motor bike?'
....

True

Were you ever bamboozled by somebody's chat
when the facts come thick and fast
and you sit there in silence
hoping to see sense at last.
Fluent, smooth and nimble
'Do you mind saying that again'
then doubt creeps into your mind
who's stupid, me or them.
But when the rhetoric has ended
and you still haven't a clue
you can rest assured that one of you is thick
and it cannot possible be you.
....

The Space

Now here is a little puzzle
without getting too profound
what happens to the space you were in
when you are buried underground.
Does the air somehow dilute itself
or maybe some plant will fill the space
could it be some babies are born
and some extra just in case.
What controls the balance of nature I wonder
it can't all possibly be down to luck

but it is a bit disconcerting when you see a stable
and consider the barrow of muck.

....

A Little Understanding

I've told you ages ago
that for a while I'd lost the place
for an Englishman it would be social ruin
and to a Jap a loss of face.
But fortunately for us Scotsmen
most understand this little vice
if only we could sympathise with others
now wouldn't that be nice.

....

The Hermit

It's not normal to be a hermit you know
that is of course except for the hermit
solitude is totally free
you don't even need a permit.
The biggest advantage is obvious
yes it's elusive peace
yet even when you live only on air
somebody will want your fleece.

....

The Cause

I had better eat some peppermint sweeties
so my breath won't stink
not much smell of vodka anyway
it's only a pity it's whisky I drink.
Yes, I love the taste and effect
I even like its colour
after one or two, I could be a friend to you
now can you think of anything duller.
I will rabbit on how the world should change
stories of injustice I will tell
procrastinate the ultimate fate
and use big words like these as well.
Now nobody's ever figured out the cause
drunkards come from every class
the only common denominator that they have
is that they're all a pain in the ass.
Psychologists and psychiatrists tried it
all known therapists have had a go
surgeons with computers and laser beams
and still they do not know.
Now I don't pretend to have cracked it
it would be easier to cure a cancer
you see the reason for drinking
just does not have one single answer.

....

Drunkard

There is only one wee bottle of lager left
and I'm embarrassed to go and buy more
'mind you my hands are quite steady today
but my back is pretty sore.
The man in the Wine Lodge
must think that I'm the pits
the constant track I wear in his lino
must really get on his tits.
Of course he is there for that purpose
and I put up with his covert scorn
to be honest I couldn't care less
if his damn floor is worn.
No it's not easy being a drunkard today
or a 'wine bibber' as the bible says
even the Christians want nothing to do with us
as they sing their songs of praise.
So we will struggle and put up with you all
although we get no appreciation
because they would feel worse if we were like them
it would be an impossible situation.
…………………………………..

Another Drunkard

If I had my glasses tinted a bit
that would obscure my two red eyes
and if I whitened up my teeth
maybe I'd tell less lies.
I could dress like a ponce
and act like a priest
get respect from you all
well a few at least.
Then after a little practice
and perfected my new part
I might even consider
to have a change of heart.
…………………..

My Building Line

I've got a huge roll of building line
the day I bought it I mind it fine
it was in Winkies (that Macleods of Tain)
I had a day off due to the rain
and Winkie said it would last me for life
then conned me into buying a Swiss army knife.
Anyway getting back to the big bit of string
there is no chance now on a wall it'll hing
apart from the odd parcel, it will stay long and white
and that's very few a year, so Winkie was right.
…………………..

Brainwashing Again

The most sinister thing I find in this world
is how people can change 'attitude'
'brainwashing' is probably the appropriate word
and succumb to it most of us would.
Think of the ordinary guys at school
and the few that joined the force
now are they the same human beings that we knew
no they're not, of course.
The old post offices (not so much now)
of the government agencies, the dole was the best
give a man or woman a job in there
and soon they will be just like the rest.
Now I'm not saying it is deliberate
but the bit that frightens me
if the secret subtle art is abused
we won't know but only think we are free.

....

A Bill

Another bill from Telecom
I'd like to tell them where to stick it
if they want money they should do the same as me
and buy a lottery ticket.

....

A Wee Worry Resolved

I got awful worried about my books
that is the ones I send to the tax
not that they were cooked you know
but there could be one or two cracks.
I gazed at them all in poly bags
twenty years of financial history
they were all agreed by the tax of course
and that is another mystery.
Now as I gazed I started to feel guilty
not only about the good years but also the bad
yet, I was nearly sure I declared most things
but when you start to think like that it's sad.
Now as I pondered the profit and losses
I knew that to my new life I'd have to adapt
one builder I heard of couldn't accept the change
and honestly I heard he snapped.
Anyway here was the pile of worry before me
and if anyone is going to get done it'll be me
you know too, there are greedy people out there
and no such thing as advice that is free.
So philosophy aside, practicality must dictate
of brilliance I sometimes get flashes
so I took twenty bags out to the garden
and I burnt the lot to ashes.

....

Breakdown

I was coming home from Inverness yesterday
when the car went and broke down
it was on the duel carriageway
about five miles out of the town.
Now you know that I'm an optimist
so out of the car I leapt
smiling I waved at the passing cars
it's a move I now regret.
Before that breakdown I loved fellow man
it's no wonder I now feel glum
because it wasn't twenty that stopped to help
not ten not two but none.

....

Aggro

I got the form for the electoral register
it came in the morning post
mind you we only get one delivery each day
but I suppose that's more than most.
Well I opened up the yellow form
filled with civic duty and nationalistic pride
and what do you think I found
underlined and written inside.
It said 'ANSWER THE QUESTIONS'
and they were quite easy I didn't have to ask how
but then it said 'SIGN IT' and return it 'NOW'.
Well normally I am a quiet man
and quite likely the same as you
but tell me who ever wrote that form
who the hell are they speaking to.
Now maybe at times I over react
and at fifty odd, never get into fights
but I tell you if I ever find out the author
I'll punch out his bloody lights.

....

Perfection

If you have never got drunk or swore
never put out your plate for more
never fornicated or got into a fight
never sinned and is always right
better get a check up and go to your bed
because honestly chap I think you're dead.

....

Fresh Start

I must go and buy a new jotter
this one is getting tattered

in fact it's ragged and dirty
and really looks quite knackered.
I notice my writing looks so neat at the start
it's not like mine at all
but the further into the jotter I go
it takes on the familiar scrawl.
Yes, I really tried at the start
clean, tidy, concise
but deterioration then set in
and now it looks far from nice.
Of course all the words still mean the same
unimportant perhaps, but steady and true
but do you know, it's worth a bit of effort
because presentation is important too.
…………………………..

Ownership

I'm all for a bit of free enterprise
but ownership, that is greed
you cannot possess what is not yours
you see there is no need.
Buy some stone, make a home
then die like normal men
bequeath you property to your offspring's
now who own it, you or them.
So whether you believe in a life here after
it doesn't matter an awful lot
for when it comes to natures property
all you get is a shot.
…………………………..

The Spell

When I was told there was a spell on me
well honestly I just laughed
I thought it was so incredible
to be blunt I thought it daft.
But woe to he that scoffs they say
and of witchcraft there is no proof
yet there is no denying the esoteric
that is a bitter truth.
But why I thought, why me
I never hurt a soul (I'm sure you'll agree)
maybe some young witch after a thrill
or some old hag needing the drill.
Anyway me being a logical fellow
I was sure I could figure it out
quite confident in my mental abilities
an explanation I'd find no doubt.
So into the bookshops and libraries
I got to know Alester Crowley quite well
some of the books were sensible and logical
but others were all to hell.
Anyway I persisted in my enquiries
shamans trick and gypsies curse

the wifie in the library used to look at me
and of course that made me feel worse.
Still undaunted I persisted
and learned everything I could
and eventually I would crack it
yes, I was sure I would.
Weeks stretched into months and the months to years
you know that subject is just a muddle
it's all right if you want to read fortunes
or maybe learn to juggle.
But all worthwhile things need time
and quantum mechanics ain't no trick
but I wonder about the authors
was it me or them that were thick.
Anyway as you can imagine I learned some things
out of all the books I bought
but the basic truth I learned
is that some things can't be taught.

....

Pride

I went round the supermarket again
you see, it's Thursday I get the Giro
my list was on the back of an envelope
and it wasn't in pencil, but biro.
I primed myself up before I went
'mind the last time I shook like a leaf
thinking that wee manager
would accuse me of being a thief.
No, this time I was Cool Hand Luke
as I confidently swung into action
you know yourself if you're feeling good
it creates a lot of satisfaction.
I sauntered round the veggie racks
passed the soup and peas
nonchalantly picked up a half of butter
and then a lump of cheese.
Cool Hand Luke I thought again
as I skilfully steered my trolley
one wee manie lost control of his
and I thought 'oh what a Wally'.
Walking tall I strode to the checkout
alas it was then when disaster struck
the lassie behind the fag counter smiled at me
and I stupidly thought 'what luck'.
so I thought I must look great
and smiled a toothy grin
regretted I never shaved that day
to take the whiskers off my chin.
Then in a second I understood the old proverb
about the pride before the fall
because I staggered into a stack of beans
and it's not one that fell, but all.

....

The High Rise

We've built our condominiums
and tower blocks in the sky
the smart set raced to buy them
and I've often wondered why.
Vermin free, yes I agree
but give mice credit they are not dense
when closeted so near that breeds fear
even the rats have that much sense.
....

The Hols'

At last we landed in Malaga
so I lit a Mex' cheroot
one hand held my sore back
and in the other my 'carry oot'.
I had on my Stetson and T-shirt
just like you see on the tele
the big hat hid the bald head all right
but the T-shirt didn't hide the belly.
Oh what the hell, I'm only human
and at my time of life sex is indivisible
because I was quite glad of that fact
because to lassies I was invisible.
Anyway we were ushered into Pancho Villa's bus
and I gleefully thought of a little sin
but I felt like Josef and Mary
for nobody would take us in.
All the hotels were fully booked
except for one little shack
I said to the wife 'Well try it'
just for a bit of crack.
Well the shack turned out a little cracker
me and wife had a ball
there were no restrictions on conduct
and no licensing laws at all
the fortnight sped by so quickly
sunlight, laughing, the lot
and by the time we reached the airport
I was glad it was the shack we got.
On the plane now in respectable mode
quite exhausted with all the capers
the guy in the next seat said 'How's your hotel'
and I said 'Oh one of those sky scrapers'.
....

The Opposite

The pendulum swings from love to where
yesterday today and tomorrow
the giant clock goes tick tick tock
if only it were hate and no sorrow.
....

The Big Three

I've told you about my wishing well
and some of the wishes I've made
though masons are not superstitious
and that's well known in the building trade.
But never the less we all like to hope
and we hope for love and fun
but when it comes to 'faith'
now that is a tricky one.
....

No Reason

Here I am just back from a funeral
broken hearted and sobbing again
the scourge of life is death they say
for ordinary women and men.
Yet, it's frustration that makes me sad
no grand design or holy call
for that young life to disappear
there is no reason, no not one at all.
....

Utopia

If I won the lottery
I really would get excited
buy a new car for the wife
and she would be delighted.
Next a house, then a holiday
jack in my job on the site
I wouldn't bother we' fancy women
but you never know, I might.
A boat, a plane, even a loch
I'd be a Laird at last
then not one worry would I have
and problems a thing of the past.
....

The New Road

You know the road I told you about
well the noise is still driving me nuts
I thought of putting up a 'Road Closed' sign
but I didn't quite have the guts.
Of course the County are delighted with the road
the way it meanders up and doon
and don't even give me a second thought
as I sit in my porch and fume.
Me and the dog looks out and glares
we hurl abuse at the cars as they pass pell mell
I scream 'I hope you all get a puncture'

and the dog shouts 'That goes for your cat as well'.
Oh but it is so frustrating
the zoom zoom never ceases
why only last night the wife got the doctor
because she thought I was going to pieces.
But no, I'll hold on to sanity
and pack my ears with wool
the only thing is I won't hear what the dog says
then I'd feel a fool.

....

Another Funeral

Another funeral today
and I am amazed at what the body can take
drinking and smoking to excess
and also the odd mistake.
No consideration for health
slovenly, lazy and fat
but do you know the person that died
was not at all like that.

....

The Light

I saw the light
and you're all going to hell
the Buddhists and Rabbi's
and the Pope as well.
Pakistanis' and Hindustanis
even Bill and Ben
all the Japanese
and all the Chinamen.
Yes I saw the light
it's Paradise I am bound
I was the lost sheep
but sure enough I'm found.
Now when I arrive in Eden
I will get anointed
and if I see any of you lot there
I'll be surprised and, disappointed.

....

No Replacement

It can't be very nice for Roddie
not even going to be replaced
all the lectures he gave me about drink
it all seems now a waste.
To think that all the parish is doomed now
but will everyone copy the likes of me
or will people not even change at all
you know it's awful interesting to wait and see.

....

Them and Us

When dealing with government agencies
especially if you make a fuss
do you ever get the feeling
it's a matter of 'them and us'.
Now this is what I was wondering
is this attitude consciously trained
or is it all in the recruiting
and it's there already ingrained.
Are the Council workers a different breed
perhaps descendants of the missing link
and they have evolved to look like us
they're not, but it makes you think.
....

Wishing

I must take out the Tarot cards again
just for a bit of crack
take them from their hiding place
and shuffle up the pack.
Ask the twenty questions
or maybe try a wish
something simple for a start
like a steak supper instead of fish.
Of course the lottery will come into it
'mind it used to be 'Littlewoods'
but I tried that wish so often
and they never came up with the goods.
So I'll make my wants more simple
and won't mention a specific amount
just in case I get a stupid fairy
and the wee fellow cannot count.
....

Gray's Anatomy

Did you ever study Gray's Anatomy
you know, the book that's two inches thick
it describes in detail all of your body
and the diagrams can make you sick.
And now as you can imagine I feel inadequate
quite jealous and unhappy now
they made our bits look enormous
and I don't wonder why, but how.
But overcoming the pangs of envy
I'm so grateful I don't have boobs
and glad I haven't the female parts
including the fallopian tubes.
Yes us men are so lucky
our plumbing is relatively simple
that probably goes for our brains as well
there's more activity in a pimple.

Well after an hour of study
I had enough of her and him
and was glad mother nature had the sense
to cover the lot with skin.

....

Social Gaffe

Did you ever make a blunder
and make a huge mistake
and compound the error
with every breath you take.
You plead to the wife
'Oh please let's go home'
and she'd reply pertly
'No, you're on your own'.
Then the deadly silence
while your gaffe is digested
all the chewing is stopped
and all the jaws are rested.
The floor will not open
no escape from all the folk
then you pray to God
to give you a fatal stroke.
Five seconds of sheer hell
for just trying to be clever
yet that five seconds
you will remember forever.

....

The Demon Again

I'm feeling like being a bad boy again
and it's not long since I had the cure
the wife thinks it made a difference
but to be honest I'm not so sure.
But why do you do it' I hear you say
'it is a silly thing to do'
well, why I do it I don't know
in fact I haven't a clue.
All I know is that it comes over me
like some terrible tropical disease
and it takes such a grip of me
and takes me to my knees.
It's only fortunate that I'm hardy
of that you will all agree
because really it's not all that great
to have fun and behave like me.

....

Change for the Better

If your tastes are similar to mine
you'll like a house built of stone

something more substantial
to call a house a home.
The stretcher bond is ageless
so elegant and mature
maybe the art is completely lost
but of that I'm not quite sure.
But look again at that crafted stone
that blocks of sandstone you call a home
and yes, you will see mistakes in the bond
in this perfect building you are so fond.
The chisel's slip the mark of the mash
perhaps an apprentice, young and rash
the clourer's bite once shiny and bright
but now it's yellow, old and mellow.
It's true new things can look lovely
we know that perfectly fine
but when it comes to substantial things
they are improving all of the time.

....

Happiness

Do you ever wonder who is happy
and then just wonder why
you probably think it's money
well sometimes so do I.
But there again take another look
because I'm sometimes happy too
and I haven't got a lot of money
likely the same as you.
So what evokes this mortal bliss
does satisfaction play a part
but I'm a frustrated cowboy
right from the very start.
So where does ecstasy come from
clearly it can't be seen
never the less I've figured it out
it's an invisible drug in the gene.

....

Meaning Well

Do you ever listen to the radio
especially Talk Radio UK
well I do quite often
but oh, the problems they had today.
Some of the men couldn't get sexy
some of the women couldn't care less
one poor chap described his symptoms
the problem he had I could only guess.
Well I got to think if builders were councillors
you wouldn't get so much blether
the standard cure and advice to all
is 'pull your damn self together'.
Or else the more sympathetic approach

when some poor soul has had enough
again the solution is standard
and the comment would be 'Awe tough'.
Then when it would come to suicide
you'll never get more understanding in your life
the advice would be 'crack on with it mate'
and I'll go and tell the wife.
Yes, that is what I call real brotherly love
the builder only wants the best for you
but we have a strange way of going about it
and I know this is also true.

....

The Insult

I was reported to the Inland Revenue
and no matter how hard I try
I cannot find out who did the dirty
or find out even why.
I tried to be nice, then I tried stern
but it was as I suspected
Judas was cool, I was the fool
and the traitor was protected.
Now I'm not professing to be the perfect man
but now I could cripple the dirty rat
because the Tax man said I didn't cheat them
and that I wasn't as smart as that.

....

Erring

Yes, the thirst has come on again
this time by slow degrees
if the minister's wife could see me now
she'd be shaking at the knees.
Of course I'm only joking
it's only brotherly love that I desire
a bit of companionship and a laugh
and to sit around the fire.
But somehow somewhere through the ages
drink became synonymous with grief
and upright men make the profits by them
the whole thing's beyond belief.
Now I could tell you the reason for my excess
but I wouldn't know where to begin
so unless you are perfect I'll let you start
and tell me the reason you sin.
Now I'm not implying that you are a bad person
or an unfeeling man or woman
but keep it in 'mind for the both of us
to err is only human.

....

The Barking Dog

I didn't get a wink last night
due to the barking dog
and after the ravages of the weekend
I usually sleep like a log.
But last night, somehow she wouldn't stop
bow wow, then woof, woof woof
at two o'clock I got really fed up with this
and that is the honest truth.
So up I got and put on my goon
a reprimand on order it thought
but when I got through she looked quite narky
so I thought I'd better not.
You see with dogs you have to be sensible
there is always a reason why they make a din
and I wasn't going to nag a moody Great Dane
now that's where the sense comes in.
....

Remembered

I was reading the works of William Blake
you know, that's the poet they said was mad
anyway I enjoyed his poetry
though some of it made me sad.
I felt I understood the in's and the out's
the motives and the passion
mind you, nowadays that style
well, it's mostly out of fashion.
But never the less, old or mad
and his writing criticised and dismembered
when you and I are dead and gone
it is William that will be remembered.
....

The Housewife

Well I must go and peel some tatties
of course I'll scrape them because they're new
boil up the fish with a drop of milk
or perhaps make a pan of stew.
But I didn't want this role reversal
and that is the honest truth
it's just because I hurt my back
and I cannot climb a roof.
Now as you know I was always an optimist
and I always liked to learn something new
well this is what I learned lately
if you like being a housewife
you are the one of the few.
....

Impetus

People have gone completely power crazy
everyone wants somebody to boss
anyone will do, it could be you
supposing you don't give a toss.
Is it innate this compulsive urge
the rewards, more money, women and food
if that were true we would strive too
not all, but most of us would.

....

Shopping

We went up to Dingwall yesterday
the wife wanted to go shopping at Lows
but when we arrived we discovered it was now Tesco's
why they changed it, God only knows.
On the plus side, the car park is bigger
that gives me and the wife more room to fight
that's not exactly true we don't get physical
but in the future who knows we might.
So at the moment we will slag each other off quietly
we' a whisper a glare and a sneer
I tell her she's buying a lot of rubbish
and she makes quips about my belly wi' the beer.
Silently we curse each other
living proof that spells don't work at all
or else she'd be exposed as a witch
and no doubt I'd be three feet tall.
Of course we add on the 'darling' and 'dear'
albeit in more of a snarl
we've already been up that isle dear
do you not remember 'darl'.
Oh yes this shopping is a battle all right
and remember that you have to be tough
the winner is there at the checkout
and the loser at the door in the huff.

....

Sure of Yourself

In a moment of tranquil contentment
to think being civilised is great
all the world is learning to love
and breeding out the element of hate.
Then out of the blue somebody hurts you
and in an instant you are back in the cave
and the civilised man is astonished
at the way that you could behave.
Revenge, anger, even murder
all for some insult or slight
but a civilised man won't attack you
but do you know, the caveman might.

....

147

It's Not Free

I put myself into a trance today
to be posh I say meditation
you should try it yourself some time
it's really a great sensation.
I'm not going to tell how to do it just now
because I did the course and it cost me pounds
and then if I told you, you'd get it for free
now that's not so miserable as it sounds.
You see if you get this knowledge for nothing
with no commitment or effort involved
all you would get is a stalemate
and a dilemma that never is solved.
Just remember the first basic rule
and I'll tell you as it was told to me
pay the price for everything worthwhile
because there are few things in life that are free.
....

Addicted

I'm really feeling unwell today
in the trade we call it 'rough'
and as usual it is self-inflicted
which makes it pretty tough.
The nauseous cramps comes and goes
why you over did it nobody knows
and here I am tempted
in the middle of the afternoon
I only wish the wife would come home
and she would make it soon.
But in the meantime I'll test myself
and walk up and down past the cabinet
but oh you need nerves of steel for that
and honestly I can hardly stand it.
So what will I do in my present state
I know staying inside the house a mistake
and speaking to that idiot of a neighbour
that only makes me worse
you know this affliction is a terrible curse
so I'll have to do something that's sure
now I'm not pretending that it's a cure.
But at least I try when I'm on the grog
and there is nothing wrong
with a long talk with the dog.
....

Idle Hands

I thought I'd steal a fag off my son
and when everyone is gone, go on the booze
you know yourself if you are idle
one of the perks is, you can choose.

I could report my neighbour for jobbing
or even throw a stone at his cat
perhaps even tackle that wee blonde down the street
now what do you think of that.
But me being me won't do those things
well maybe only one or two
but it's amazing what comes into your head
when you have nothing else to do.
....

Good Food

It's half past five once again
and time to heat up the pies
you know when you are enjoying yourself
how the time just flies.
Tonight I'll make a gastronomic delight
for on top of the pies I'll put beans
then I'll heat a tattie up
and not bother at all with greens.
Now this may seem mundane to you
but look at it another way
because food takes on another look
if you hadn't had a bite all day.
....

Priorities

Deep in the darkest night they talk
how their wages have got to be paid
the paedophiles trial has ended
and decisions have to be made.
Misery and hate in abeyance
the baby's abused, just forget her
policies, principles and moralise
about an abortion or a French Letter.
....

New Neighbours

I see workmen over at the manse today
we must be getting a new minister I suspect
mind you it's better to have someone in the house
or else it will get wrecked.
I do hope it is a Christian couple
and not just anybody
someone with the kindness of Margaret
and maybe the tolerance of Roddie.
Of course this is a selfish thought
or could be construed as a Freudian slip
because you know I visit my neighbours
when I've had more than just a wee nip.
Now at the moment I have no intentions
and am likely the same as you

but a man has to be realistic and sensible
because you can't be sure what he'll do.

....

Suing

I thought that I'd join the modern trend
and look for someone to sue
I pondered for a little while
and thought, the County Council will do.
First of all I must prepare my case
now what were their misdemeanour's?
I'll get Lawson Keir on the job
and he will take them to the cleaners.
I can see it all now in the Court of Session
me and Lawson teaching them a lesson
with our horse hair wigs and long black cloaks
niggling at the jury when they are out for smokes.
Yes, we'd be a formidable pair
but one wee problem still exists, to be fair
you see in my researches about their crime
the bit of land I wanted fenced and tidied up, is mine.

....

The Final Solution

I really must stop listening to the radio
especially the UK talk show
it's not that I don't understand the problems
or even I don't want to know.
It's just because I get too emotional
especially the stories about abuse
then I end up crying my eyes out
and that is just no use.
No one would listen to my solution anyway
because I would cripple the abusing sod
then I would hang them without a trial
and leave their salvation to God.
Now don't think I jest with that remark
I wouldn't care if it was women or men
just remember all the abusers that I catch
none of them would do it again.

....

A Relapse

I stopped smoking a fortnight ago
and yes, today I had a relapse
it wasn't even I will or I won't
or even the agony of perhaps.
No, I just got wired into a fag
but it wasn't worth the guilt or remorse
five minutes ago I was breathing with ease
and now I cough like a horse.

Mind you, it keeps me humble I suppose
or I could get cocky too
for there is nobody so smug
as a man who has stopped
and we all know that to be true.
....

Good Advice

When I was young an old man told me
'Son, never get drunk on wine'
although I was told a long time ago
I still remember it fine.
Not once in all the years that have passed
did I fail to follow that advice
if the old man could see me, he'd be proud
even I, thought it pretty nice.
But alas alas, as you know
I've been inebriated many a time
whisky, beer, vodka, the lot
but honestly never with wine.
....

Twelve Steps

He laid the book before me
'The Twelve Steps of Recovery'
I picked it up quite gladly
thinking it was a discovery.
Instantly of course I realised
that this was serious stuff
but of programmes of sorting out myself
honestly I had had enough.
Never the less I turned a page
just for a bit of fun
and there in print was my problem
right there on page one.
Now I'm not saying there is a cure for you
your problem may not be in the book
but it can be amazing where you can find an answer
if you make the effort to look.
....

Another Freudian Slip

I knew a man who loved money
so he called his dogs Dollar and Buck
there is another who loved gambling
so he dubbed his daughter Lady Luck.
Now I consider myself pretty smart
I could spot the Freudian slip
so I asked my wife Fanny, what she thought of it.
....

The Robin

Did you ever notice when a Robin stares at you
it has a right accusing look
they say that they are very territorial birds
and I read that in a book.
Well I was thinking why they stare
and it's not hard to understand
you see you've probably built your house
on their piece of land.

....

Pretty Smart

They say your brains don't forget anything
down to the details so minute
if you don't think that completely amazing
you must admit it's cute.
All the information seen and heard
the sensation of touch and smell
of all that was exposed to you
even the taste as well.
Now I was thinking, that's pretty clever
of that there was no doubt
but do you know what the tricky bit is
is how to get it out.

....

Midges

Do you know it is November
and we have midges still flying about
the weather is so warm of course
that is the reason, no doubt.
I think that they are enjoying themselves
you can tell by the way they fly
but they don't know there's a frost tonight
and most of them will die.
But there again are they as daft as that
maybe they are smarter than man
while we worry about tomorrow
they enjoy themselves while they can.

....

Jealousy

I told you the County built my garden wall
and that I was ready to criticise
but to be honest it was near perfect
just a delight before my eyes.
Yet was I happy and contented
especially when it was free
no I wasn't, I was jealous
that it wasn't built by me.

....

Caught

The wife smelt smoke in the bathroom
it was the kind exuded by fags
and I thought I was so crafty
when I sneaked a couple of drags.
I had opened the window and shut the door
so as not to cause a smog
but honestly that woman has the sixth sense
and a nose like a collie dog.
So I had to admit it now I was rumbled
you see we are a family of three
and if it wasn't my son or the wife
it was obvious then it was me.
For a second I thought I'd deny it
and maybe blame it on our last visitor
but there again that wouldn't wash
because he was the Church of Scotland minister.
So I just came clean and admitted all
that was all that I could do
but what a relief when the wife exclaimed
'Oh, I had a couple of drags too'.

....

Pride

I stood at the bar when I was on holiday
and I was the invisible man once again
while that stupid barmaid was grinning
and serving the other men.
I tried to flag her down with a hundred pesetas
that used to work in days gone by
but the pesetas were invisible too
God it would make you cry.
I tried the smile, eye contact and all
but that only made it worse
and they were drinking nips all around me
it's no wonder I started to curse.
Then at long last she spotted me
when I had about enough
so I said I wasn't wanting anything now
and walked outside in the huff.

....

Cheered Up

They say the cause of depression
can be the lack of light
now I don't know if this is true
but you never know it might.
So just in case I got out the torch
but the batteries were getting done
maybe that is why it didn't work
for the effects were little or none.

But anyway I persisted
all this in the middle of the day
when in came the Post and caught me
now what on earth could I say.
At first I tried various excuses
then I just cracked and just told the lot
and the way she screeched and laughed
I was glad that I got caught.
....

The Missing Saw

Although this happened forty years ago
I remember it to this day
when your feelings are hurt you can't forget
at least that's what they say.
Well anyway I was a boy on this job
and a joiner couldn't find his saw
now no worker steals each other's tools
in the building trade that is law.
So anyway a diligent search was made
where it went was anybody's guess
but this red haired wee joiner thought he knew
and accused me more or less.
While he quizzed me of my movements
the saw was found where he sat
and I could tell by the look in his eye
that we would not forget that.
....

All Hidden

I was building a wall with another brickie once
and do you know he was as slow as a snail
especially when it came to the gables
when we had to pull everything up in a pail.
Not only was he slow he wasn't even tidy
his brickwork far from neat
the mortar was running down the wall
and a quarry of half bricks at his feet.
Well eventually all the building got harled
and in a few weeks later I passed the wall
could I see a difference in his work or mine
no I couldn't, no not at all.
....

Happiness

Now concerning the pursuit of happiness
which everyone has a right to pursue
there are plenty of happy people out there
so why not me and you.
The first rule is try and be sensible
when it comes to your ambition

aim for the top but not too high
be realistic in your decision.
The secret is don't aim too low either
do and be all that you can
we all know that you are unique
but you are only extra special to 'mam'.
Then when you have a future thought out
with kindness to others you must act
and whether or not you like the idea
it seems to be just a fact.
Do unto others as you'd like to be done to you
and do it first if you must
that seems to be essential
a maxim that you can trust.
Now don't start thinking money is happiness
that's the biggest mistake known to man
but never the less have a wee flutter
and win the lottery if you can.
Then when you have mastered these basic rules
it is happiness that you will find
you see happiness is not a physical thing
it is just a state of mind.

....

Ramblings 3

Is There More Than One

Do they have a social membership in heaven
or is that just another dream
maybe I shouldn't think in terms like these
in case that I blaspheme.
Mind you, I'm knackered anyway
according to all known religions
when they are talking to the angels
I'll be playing with the pigeons.
And likely too no birds get in
and neither will my Great Dane
a place without any innocence
no, our heavens are not the same.

....

Modern Art

Do you remember hearing about the painting
in the mode they call modern art
well I remember seeing the picture
and do you know it was a clart.
It was widely acclaimed by the experts
then it transpired it was all a joke
the picture was painted by monkeys
just to confuse the folk.
The experts were rightly embarrassed
about their adulation
writing in the papers
about the new sensation.
But I was sorry for them
and I thought the joker a prat
because it was obvious to most of us
a chimpanzee wouldn't make a mess like that.

....

Doubt

It's strange the way people have changed
the mighty hunter gets little respect
the leader of the pack, the biggest yap
but that is evolution I expect.
Now a suit of clothes, the eagles cloak
the castle in the city
and men who once were kings sweep roads
now that's a bit of a pity.
Yet if by chance the bomb goes off
and we are faced with decimation
I wonder who would be our leaders
when we start the new creation.
Would suits and brollies be cast aside
spears and swords made from the pen
our leaders once more lead from the front
you know I doubt it now and then.

....

One Smile

A bonnie lassie passed the shop window
where my stock was displayed to perfection
but do you know the only thing the lassie saw
was her own reflection.
Vanity I thought, all is vanity
but the next time she passed she gave another smile
and I thought what a nice lassie
but of course I knew that all the while.

....

It Didn't Work

You've seen that lassie advertising chocolates
you know, the one on TV
well, I think she is supposed to look sexy
but she looks far too cheeky to me.
In fact I think she appears gurny
perhaps it's her gypsy way of life
but I won't buy that brand of chocolates
in case it affects the wife.

....

Tell tale

A wifie was talking to my son one day
about our little shop
how a drunk man tried to serve her
and he could hardly walk.
No need to tell you I had a sore back
which makes it difficult to sell
but honestly on that Saturday afternoon
I was drunk as well.
Now believe me I am not proud of that
in fact I'm quite ashamed
and my son was quite right
when it was me he blamed.
However I thought it over
as I usually do
and discovered that it's only when folk go wrong
that people will clipe on you.

....

Royalty

I'm sorry for the royal family
of tragedies they have had their share
but mother nature doesn't know they are royal
and mother nature doesn't care.
Now I can understand a broken heart
and everybody on someone must lean
but what I can't figure out
is why the whole family's so mean.

....

Stuck in the Mud

They're running about in 'Four Tracks' now
they rarely say 'Land Rover' or 'Jeeps'
and they go to the Co-op
to buy their tatties and their neeps.
Now I was thinking about the 'Four Tracks'
mind, it's a matter of what you'd like
but I've cycled around Tain for years
and never once got stuck with my bike.

....

Not Stupid

I must buy a new record player
for the spring of mine is done
but I hear in the modern ones
they haven't a spring at all, not one.
It's all done with transistors they told me
and in the shop they thought I was soft
because I shook my head and didn't buy one
but they didn't know I've no' light in the croft.

....

The Present

Doctors are striving to make us live longer
with spare parts and various drugs
sorting all our diseases
by killing all dangerous bugs.
But who wants to live eons as a wrinkly
or our childhood extended by years
all this talk of life everlasting
that's one of my greatest fears.
Now I would say, enough is enough
seventy or eighty is plenty
even a well filled cupboard
eventually gets empty.
So if you yearn to do anything
and you can't figure out how
don't rely on extended life
just go and do it now.

....

Thirst

Now I was thinking about temptation
and I am certainly not the first
but you people who can resist
are you sure you've had a right thirst.

....

A Different Direction

Do you ever feel you are in a rut
and you are completely stuck
all your ambitions came to naught
and you curse your rotten luck.
Now I know the answer is not simple
and it is hard to fight from the floor
when the tide of life is against you
and your heart is really sore.
That is the time to rely on nature
for nothing is as it seems
and if the force is against you
try some different dreams.
Now it's not weak to do a U-turn
it's not cowardice or defection
it only makes sense to change your mind
and take a different direction.

....

Not Improved

Isn't it strange how some memories stick
I remember when I was in class three
the teacher confiscated my pencil sharpener
and never gave it back to me.
And there was the time, I remember it fine
I hit a lassie with my schoolbag
and then I gave her a shove
and I did all this
yes, in the name of love.
Now I think no wonder we are all twisted
suspicious, with a fickle heart
how could we be anything else
when we were never right at the start.

....

Bad Training

I'm sorry at times I read Morgan the Mighty
and all that comics about Superman
I shouldn't have dreamed of being Roy of the Rovers
or I wouldn't be the dick that I am.
Oliver Twist that would be missed
and the tales of Elkabar
even John Wayne I wouldn't watch him again
and that's not taking things too far.
Now when I go down to the Dole tomorrow
(I have an appointment with Emperor Nero)
he'll tell me it's time I got a job
but do you know there no demand for a hero.

....

Depressed Again

It seems so long since I had a good laugh
or even a decent smile
Moses must have felt like this
when he was sailing down the Nile.
Well you never know a princess might find me
a man never knows his luck
but likely I would get stuck in the reeds
and the princess go to the knees in the muck.
Instead I'll go to Eden Court
and hear some old jokes like Fanny Gray
at least I'll remember how once I laughed
before they take me away.

....

Do You Know

I'm envious of the people who enjoy their work
and they are interested in what they do
I'm pleased they know the road for them
because I'm a man that never knew.
Keep on trying, you know the drill
and do not care if you are blundering
it just gives me joy to see you try
and not sit here, and then die wondering.

....

Anticipation

I was glad to get past my childhood
and leave that time behind
and I was a little bit grateful
that I didn't go quite blind.
Into maturity at last
at the time I would never have guessed
that life is just like Christmas
the anticipation is always the best.

....

Contentment

I sometimes wish that I were a Catholic
a Protestant or even a Jew
I just have no religion at all
in fact I haven't a clue.
It's not for the want of trying though
in fact I think I tried the lot
and for all my various efforts
it's only a sore head that I got.
But when I thought of the compensations
now I'm a contented man

while you lot murder each other
I'll lie on the beach with my dog and get a tan.
....

Innocence

A policeman came into my shop today
'Oh, he was only in for a look'
and my conscience was crystal clear
not one blot on my book.
'Well', I thought, 'this is the way'
no worries about meeting the law
to meet any man eye to eye
and live life without a flaw.
Well, talk about feeling cocky
I'm always suspicious about that state
because when I got to the car that night
I noticed the licence was out of date.
....

Flashers

The dark nights are here again
and driving the car is not fun
a rush to get home before it is dark
when I am out a run.
The worst of the lot is the blinding lights
and that guys flashing makes me fizz
why don't they keep their hand on their dick
because that's where it usually is.
....

Enjoyment

I must apologise for my drinking
before it is all too late
at times for me it was hell as well
but you know at other times it was great.
They say you can't enjoy life half drunk
it's the attitude of a kid
but at times it was fantastic
and I enjoyed it, honestly I did.
....

Bitter Regret

When I was in the second class at school
do you know my pencil disappeared
well, I was told I had to be tough
and the pencil was stolen I feared.
I accused a wee chap sitting nearby
his little lip quivered and he began to cry
at three o'clock I put my jotter in my bag

and leaned across the wee guy to grab.
Then out of my pocket the pencil dropped
and rolled off down the rows
why I never found it before
it is something only God knows.
And now I'm over fifty
and that incident I'll never forget
because I still get a guilty feeling
and the memory still haunts me yet.

....

Competition

I don't much like competition
and it's not fear of defeat
I am just an average guy
and I sometimes get tired of being beat.
I'm laid back now, like the farmer
when he went to the annual ball
he said 'I'm no' good at dancing
but I'll spread dung to any man in the hall'.

....

The Weather

I wonder what is going to happen next
rain, hail, sleet or snow
there might even be a hurricane
well, you never know.
I used to think it would be right handy
if we could predict the weather bang on
then we could decide to harl or not
and never get it wrong.
Yet after a little contemplation
this is what I thought
that life sometimes can be so boring
but it's the only excitement we've got.

....

Bull Bars

Some folk bolt them onto Land Rovers
I've even seen them on cars
you know, a cage sort of thing on the bumper
I think they call them Bull bars.
It's supposed to restrict any damage
especially to the lights at the front
in case you get a bit careless
and give your car a dunt
Now I was just thinking
they must be an awful price
and I've lived in Invergordon all my life
and only saw a bull on the street twice.

....

Impossible

My mother was very wise you know
but not the wisdom of a saint
in fact to put it a Highland way
we all thought she was quaint.
Now when I was young I had a hero
there was nothing this man couldn't do
even all his stories everyone was true.
But my sage of a mother
told me something I should know
yes, she told me my mighty hero
couldn't scratch his arse wi' his elbow.
....

No Excuse

I'm good at mathematics
you probably call them sums
I could have been a professor
not like you bums.
I can converse in French
Spanish and Greek
Latin and Polish I can speak.
I can see that you are impressed
and the jealousy makes you sick
but ignorance is no excuse
for calling me a prick.
....

Love

Yes I'm still in love after thirty years
I can't help it, this is just a fact
maybe if I told the wife about her
she'd tidy up her act.
....

Spite

I left the shop window illuminated
so all the people could see last night
but I never sold a thing today
so I'll turn them off tonight for spite.
....

The Witness

There's a BMW car
parked across the street
I think it's top of the range
and it really looks quite neat.
Now I know who this car belongs to

it's owned by a guy I don't much like
(well he charged me too
much for building a dyke).
So anyway as I looked
three young guys started flogging the wheels
now me being a fellow motorist
knows exactly how it feels.
So I went to the window and whispered
'Stop don't make so much noise'
then I pulled the curtains
Oh, well boys will be boys.
....

Pride

I built my gable so carefully
well jointed and the peak dead plumb
it was a treat to look at
sort o' aesthetic, not like some.
But during the night a gale got up
and all the gables fell
but I could never understand
why mine blew down as well
....

Lads of the North

I got tired of hearing about Latin lovers
the Spanish and the French
if they were up in the north
they'd be sitting on the bench.
The lads up here are so modest though
you can ask in the Balnagown or the Star
that their prowess with the lassies
is known both near and far.
Why it's well known in Portmahomack
and Stornaway in the west
that we are the only lads who go to Spain
in order to get a rest.
....

Hyperactive

A young mother came into the shop today
and she had a bairn by the hand
well I though, how sensible
(because I had just done the polishing)
and all my stuff looked grand.
Well in no time at all the wee guy took off
while the dame looked on and grinned
and I stood there fuming
and God forgive me I sinned.
He picked up my bonnie ornaments
and kept screeching out 'MUM'

I bared my teeth and whispered
aren't you getting a big boy, Son.
Well he snottered over a table
shook a crystal display
I must have looked like an idiot
my mouth hanging in dismay.
Next he grabbed the brass
I could have kicked his ass
but I thought 'oh he's only a child'
and tried to think of other things
so I wouldn't get so wild.
Round and round the shop he went
and I prayed to God 'Oh soon'
please get rid of this lassie
and her wee baboon.
Well eventually God responded
and the wee guy slammed the door
I think he knew by instinct
I couldn't handle any more.
Now every story has a moral somewhere
and by nature I'm not harsh
but I'm glad for all our sakes
I didn't boot his little arse.

....

Sexual Harassment

Swein the sear was accused you know
of interfering with a wifies clothes
whether it was all imagination
only Swein and the wifie knows.
But there were more than one accusation
in fact three or four banded together
no doubt it all came out in Ardgay
when they were having a bit of a blether.
Now I was thinking as usual
but I couldn't make any guesses
right enough four refusals
but I wonder how many successes.

....

Civilisation

I find it quite unreal at times
this fascination with shoes and clothes
why some folk have evolved like this
it's only God that knows.
Trekking down the high street
to fulfil some strange desire
no adrenalin pounding
no peace at any camp fire.
Women and men no difference in them
pride in survival, a dream
and sad eyes gaze in windows
and courage a useless gene.

....

Be True

Do you ever find it difficult to be truthful
to hold an opinion or true belief
look any man straight in the eye
without lying through your teeth.
Well I've sussed it out at last
and you don't have to be Superman
just think of something to say
and believe it the best you can.

....

Rank

The all wear hard hats in the building trade now
to protect the brains in their head
someone told me the foremen
even wear theirs to bed.
They are different colours to denote the rank
of class distinction there is more than a trace
in my day you could always spot the gaffer
by the vacant look on his face.

....

Other Jobs

I don't think I could stand the strain
of working in a shop
when you are desperate to sell something
and the customer just wants to talk.
And even worse, the window shopper
when they point and don't come in
and I nip my fag and stand there
with a sheepish sort of a grin.
'Oh yes your stuff is lovely' they say
such a pity I'm not buying today.
Then of course I told you about the bairns
especially the hyperactive kind
but I always refrained from booting arses
the mothers would think me unkind.
And then when I have a slack spell
I sit and I reflect
was the building trade as bad as this
no comparison I suspect.
And then I remember thinking
when I was building a wall
there was no other job as hard as this
no, not one at all.

....

New Bar

I'm going out to a function tonight
so I better keep control

and not drink any of that nasty drams
while I watch the rest of them bowl.
Oh but I forgot its 'opening night'
and the Alness club built a new bar
they said it's for me but I didn't agree
that would be carrying things too far.
....

No Customers

I went for a holiday last year
and sailed through Amsterdam
and the wife took a fair grip of me
knowing the man that I am.
Well we cruised the canals in the evening
and it really was a beautiful sight
they use the boats like buses there
and turn on the lights at night.
The courier showed us the famous places
and yes, the lassies in the shops!
he also told us their customers
were ministers, politicians and cops.
Now I can get emotional at times
as all the curtains were closed, bar one
and I was so sorry for that poor wifie
she hadn't a customers at all, no not one.
....

Wonder

Yes I took the shot last night
oh Friday is always the same
and the wife told the bairns I was tired
just to give it another name.
Well I was just thinking
you guys who drink coffee and tea
are you sure that you are normal
and don't you have the same thirst as me.
....

Blamed

I remember when I was a young boy
oh I was only about nine or ten
mind I don't dwell on these times a lot
but I think of them now and then.
I used to go to a dancing class
that was on a Tuesday night
but it's possible it could be a Wednesday
but I think Tuesday is right.
Well anyway as we leaped around
as I remember with great glee
the lassie beside me farted

and do you know she blamed it on me.
That lassie is a middle aged woman now
and I don't see her very often
but when I do I'm the only one that knows
why she's always coughin'.

....

Sins

You know it's not so bad having drink for a sin
it's not a disease it's more like a blister
because I know an awful sober chap
and he's knocking off his own wife's sister.
He goes to church on Sunday
mind that's better than taking the shot
but he would be amazed
at what a drunk man will spot.
Now I know that we both do wrong
and yes we harm people there is no doubt
but the consolation in heavy drinking
we don't wait to get found out.
Now I know this sounds a wee bit pompous
or maybe I try to justify my sin
but when I see his wife's sister
I'm so glad it's not me but him.

....

Weakness

Well I must confess, I did regress
on Tuesday night I took a strong drink
mind you, it was just a few
but you know it made me think.
Here's me thinking I wasn't addicted
but my resistance went down to nil
and it really was a miracle
I didn't take the fill.
But now I'm over the craving
and temptation is all in the past
but I fairly enjoyed the dram on Tuesday
so maybe this temperance won't last.

....

Quiet Day in the Shop

Nobody is buying my brass Pegasus
or even the sailing ship
and all our stuff is so bonny
you know it makes me sick.
Likely they're spending up in the bar
the Balnagown the St. Duthas and the Star
so I'll not associate with them
they can get as drunk as a newt
I'll just walk down the street

and get a carry oot.
……………………..

In The Way

I mind it fine
when we were young
we made a huge snowman
and oh yes it was fun
right in the middle
of our football field
our Goliath stood
with sword and shield
surveying all the school around
the last snows of spring
soft and round.
Yet it took so long to melt away
that we were sorry
we made him that day
………………..

The Barber

That lassie who cut my hair
she's nice, but awful slow
no wonder she got pregnant
she told me so I know.
But it's better than talking about football
or else about the weather
for everyone else there listens in
and when they get out they blether.
So you have to be careful in Invergordon
but not in Tain
for they have a male barber there
but do you know it's not the same.
Mind you that is just my preference
it's just the way I am
I like the lassies close up to me
but I do not like a man.
…………………

Instincts

Human urges are the strangest things
the strongest one is a mystery to me
you think thirst is at the top
but not when you're bursting to pee.
Then you think it must be love
or lust of the passionate kind
but if you tell a drowning man that
it'll be the last thing on his mind.
Yes we humans are a funny lot
you can see the animals are kin
our greatest desire, yes by far

is just to save our own skin.

....

Selfish

It's strange how fickle a man can be
insensitive, selfish and blind
we were at a function on Friday night
and believe me I was far from kind.
My loved one took a little turn
I cried 'You're not expiring by any chance'
and when she replied she wasn't
I went back into the dance.

....

Training

It seems to be common with some men
although I think it is going too far
when they go off to work
they take the keys of the car.
Of course there are worse things than that
so too much pain I won't recall
but why don't these women not wear suspenders
and then not give the man sex at all.
Now that is a theory I'd almost guarantee
that, would make most men bend the knee
and if it doesn't work I'm sorry for you
his male hormones have vanished
and he's just left with a few.

....

Spot the Ball

Do you remember that competition in the paper
you know where they remove the ball
well one paper forgot that part
and they still never got a winner at all.
Would you believe that some folk are that thick
yes both workers and the bosses
that time I really was very close
and I only used ten crosses.

....

Stolen Drink

He reached over the table
and grabbed the dram
well I am a kind of skinny guy
but I can't help how I am.
His grubby elbow cocked in the air
downed the nip as though I wasn't there.
But I was calm and collected
as he quaffed the amber nectar
because the drink wasn't mine at all

but belonged to my friend big Hector.
....

The Man Trap

I got something stolen once
so I thought I'd lay a trap
maybe it was a cruel thing
as it had a spring that could snap.
Well I concealed it so carefully
it was a real cunning device
so I won't describe it more
only it wasn't very nice.
Well during the day I heard a squeal
the trap was well and truly sprung
but it was only an old twitcher
do you know sometimes the innocent is hung.
....

Liar

I was told when I was young
the worst thing was a liar or a cheat
so I slotted that in my memory
because it was simple and neat.
But when I got older and I got drunk
and down the slope I slid
who was the one that picked me up
just take a guess who did.
....

Men

Men can be the pits you know
they will cheat, lie, and flirt
and they just can't resist
looking up a woman's skirt.
Oh yes, they're great for the patter
flatter and chatter
but when older they get really rude
they don't see criticism as constructive
I tell we're misunderstood.
....

The Idiot

After all my promises, yes
last night I took the shot
and of course as usual
most of the night was forgot.
I just seemed to weaken
and now I'm full of dismay
my mouth is awful dry
and I'm feeling rough today.

If only I was more sensible
and took a cup of tea
but no, I've got this fiendish thirst
and it just comes over me.
My throat goes into turbo
the brain in automatic
the imagination runs riot
with pleasures quite ecstatic.
But then, good old Morpheus
soothes my spinning mind
and I wake up and the taxi's gone
and I am left behind.
Yes, this weakness is a curse
strong drink it is a mocker
and me at sixty leaping away
convinced that I'm a rocker.

....

Moderation

I was watching a builder plastering
and he sure wouldn't get a prize for speed
but that doesn't matter in the long term
as long as it's guaranteed.
Of course I was one of the idiots
who went at the work like a bull
now I'm completely knackered
I feel a bit of a fool.
The answer of course is 'moderation'
in everything you do
unfortunately I never learned about this
it is a word I never knew.
Now he is still plastering and I am sitting
all my joints are raxed as well
but I could never have done what he does
I'd find it as boring as hell.
Now I'm not saying that he was right
or even that I was wrong
only it's not a nice feeling
to be somewhere you don't belong.

....

A Lost Button

I found a button on the street
and thought, 'oh no, attempted rape'
or else a robbery or a mugging
'Oh for pities sake'.
Maybe a wife beating, yes it's off a coat
oh that poor woman annoyed him
she must have got on his goat.
Or perhaps a savage attack
by a Rottweiler dog
or maybe the wifie had a dram or two
and then went on the grog.

173

'Oh no' I cried again
and my head fell in my hands
there's a wifie in Tain without a button
and it's only me that understands.
....

A Gurny Man

He was a miserable man all his life
grumbled when he retired
not even a smile on his gurny face
the day that he expired.
I often wonder about mother nature
when she made a mistake and made a prat
maybe she never cleaned out the mixer
and then made a man like that.
....

Common Sense

I never see anyone going up to a big guy
and tell him his leather jacket is a cows skin
no I never see them spitting
or being cheeky to him.
No, it's usually some poor wifie
chattering beneath her fur
and likely it was left by her granny
and didn't belong to her.
Yes, these protesters usually are so crafty
no one tells the champ he stutters
mind you, there is one or two
but you'll always get a few nutters.
....

Names

I must take home the wireless
of course now it's called 'radio'
why they bothered to change the name
that's another thing I'll never know.
The record player now has a styles
what was wrong with a needle
now we have a church officer
when we used to have a beadle.
Is all this name change for the better
is it more descriptive and clear
would whisky taste the very same
if we started calling it beer.
....

More Regret

I've always wanted to be a cowboy

but now I reckon it is too late
outdrawing Wild Bill in the saloon
and winching Big Nose Kate.
Jumping on my horse to ride the range
shooting an injun or two
singing our songs round the campfire
and the other things cowboys do.
But alas alas it's only a dream
life's not like that I'm afraid
but there are enough cowboys already
in the building trade.

....

A Pain

I can't be bothered with Top of the Pops
in fact at times it makes me rage
even page three does nothing for me
now this is all due to my age.
Of course I know this is a phase
and hopefully it soon will pass
for there is nothing like the change of life
to give you a pain in the ass.

....

Programmed

I lost my first true love
when I was just a lad
the very sight of her red hair thrilled me
and then I felt so glad.
Now as I look back
I really wish it wasn't true
for I put my hand up her skirt
because that's what I thought
I was supposed to do.

....

Quite Happy

Yes, I like a drink
and I also puff the weed
also I'm fond of the women
now do you think that's greed.
I like to dance I like to laugh
I love the joy of a bairn
but why do we let some people spoil it
will we ever learn.
Fitness fanatics with their aerobatics
skinny women and over-developed men
no I don't want to be perfect
and certainly not be like them.

....

Figure it Out

I had a right battle last night
but I didn't take a drink
and I'm not any better today
in fact I'm worse I think.
I feel like biting the wife right now
and believe me it's not with lust
I could even kick the dog
as she looks at me with disgust.
I can't help it I'm gurny and depressed
I want to be out there working
and skiving along with the rest.
Yet idleness teaches a lesson
an employer is not there to fleece
no need to give cheek to the foreman
or complain about your piece.
So work as hard as you can
and really do your best
but the old adage is true
you'll go down the road like the rest.
Now don't look here for wisdom
though I'm almost sane the physiatrist said
but I still try and figure it all out
so I must be wrong in the head.
....

Fly

I must nip down to the Wine Lodge
and get some whisky, gin and wine
just in case we get visitors
or maybe some friends into dine.
I better get some beer for the young folk
not forgetting some sherry and brandy
and I must mind to get some vodka
for a bottle is awful handy.
Now most of you folk think 'what a host'
as I struggle out with my box
but we alcoholics are so crafty
an as fly as the proverbial fox.
....

Ski Pants

A lassie passed with 'Ski pants' on
now I told you men are disgusting
but her breeks were stretched to the limit
and out her bum was busting.
Now most guys are a wee bit lecherous
and they'll look at women's bodies I fear
but do you know on that occasion
I couldn't even work up a lear.
....

Craftier Still

I heard of a guy once
and he was fond of the drink
now even the CIA or KGB
wouldn't suss this out I think.
He injected oranges with vodka
to avoid a hullabaloo
and he sat there like an angel at night
saying 'Yes dear, they're so good for you'.

....

Typical Man

Some masons are working along the road
and they are building a wall with stone
now me being a crippled mason myself
I started thinking when I got home.
Their bond was quite good as it should
for marks I'd give six out of ten
because I knew and this is true
I'd be tidier and twice the speed o' them.

....

The Green Grass

I never thought I'd end up
working in a shop
me being a silent sort of brickie
who didn't like too much talk.
I used to like the noise
and the smell of cement
and laugh at the brickies bums
when their backs were bent.
The noise of the single cylinder mixer
when it broke down no one could fix her
and the shaky scaffold the labourers erected
four masons fell off and foul play was suspected.
To cool us down God sent down the rain
plus the odd hurricane when we worked in Tain.
And the clerk of works with a list of complaints
and the architects who thought
they were next things to saints.
Now after thinking about it I better stop
for I know full well, it's easier to work in a shop.

....

A Poor Chap

I was at a dance and there were an old guy there
and do you know the old chap wasn't the full shilling
and it wasn't only the drink that was at fault
because most of that he was spilling.

And as we danced the Gay Gordon's
our hearts really full of pity
the old guy staggered out the door
carrying the glass that held our kitty.

....

Unlucky Thief

A thief came into our shop one day
and he stole a brass miners lamp
with Humphrey Davy engraved on it
as well as the approval stamp.
Unknown to him of course
the cardboard box was in the store
and all the bits weren't assembled
for in the box were one or two more.
A safety valve an instant cut out
obey the instructions or it'll explode no doubt.
Well, I thought about it for a minute
and said 'Oh mighty me'
and wandered through to the store
to make a cup of tea.

....

Would You

I must cut the 'Building Contractor' bit off my sign
it just reminds of times when things were fine
when my little town flowed with milk and honey
plenty of work and plenty of money.
And then I think, were we happier then
would I do it all, the same again
and even now in my darkest mood
yes, I'm pretty sure that I would.

....

Get up and Go

It's nice to think the tide will turn
and your luck will change for the good
sit around, mope and cry
you never know, it could.
But deep down you know the answer
the laws of nature are harsh
for the very time you want to lie down
that's the time to get off your arse.

....

The Tool for the Job

Last night I dreamed I was chased by a lion
in fact to be honest there were about six
and two of them had me cornered
well as you can imagine I was in a bit of a fix.

My body was trembling, my brain was spinning
intelligence defeated, base instinct was winning.
Then out of the turmoil, as clear as day
I saw the answer, I saw the way,
so simple I thought as I picked up my gun
two quick shots later and the deed was done.
And I stood there amazed and felt a bit of a fool
for in the theory of everything
you just need to use the right tool.
....

Real You

Poor little mouse, you're dead now
and yes, it was me who set the trap
your bright little life just vanished
with one metallic snap.
Yet you still stare at me with living eyes
questioning my motives on life's demise
protect the eagle, the buzzard and hawk
the lion and tiger, who kill and stalk
the wolves who tear deer limb from limb
and the cunning fox, yes, do protect him.
Is it because we are small and never hurt a soul
and yes we are scared, as we run from hole to hole.
Does our forage for food fill you with disgust
is our total destruction really a must
or deep down do you favour the beak to the bill
and in your heart, it's the weak you like to kill.
....

Passing The Time

Do you know I've only got two pounds left
and it's nearly Saturday night
I'll just have to go without a drink
and just make do with a fight.
On second thoughts I'll probably stay in
and watch some sex on the tele
or maybe I'll make some fishing flies
and sort the hole in my wellie.
Or else I could gurn at the wife
but I better not give the bairns a thrashing
because they are getting quite stumpy now
and likely they would give me a bashing.
No I've decided, I'll do the usual
I'll just sit and whine
at least that is constructive
and it'll help to pass the time.
....

Excuses

I took a couple of drams last night
yes, I know I'm supposed to be stopped
but as I walked passed the cabinet

out the wee cork popped.
Well I am not a heartless man
so I raised my glass and did sup
for the poor wee black bottle
was just trying to cheer me up.
....

More Excuses

I must go to the bowling club tonight
though I can't mind if I'm banned
the last time I fell over the table
basically because I couldn't stand.
This was due to exhaustion of course
and that damn fresh air from the door
or else that baldie wee manie
throwing slipperine over the floor.
But I'll walk in like a priest tonight
or more likely slink behind the wife
just in case that big blonde is there
you know the rumours in that club is rife.
....

A Quiet Day in the Shop

That's two more Americans in the shop
you know I should charge for giving directions
and the lassie up the stairs is pregnant
so I should practice caesarean sections.
There's an old manie passing the window now
I could go out and start a fight
but with my luck I'd get a doing
which would spoil the rest of the night.
So I'll just take my jacket off
and maybe the rest of my clothes
and that might attract some attention
Rab C. Nesbitt in artistic pose.
Well I looked in the mirror
and God I looked rough
I wouldn't have the guts
to go in the bare buff.
So I'll leave my jacket on
it sort o' hides the flab
and I must mind and write a letter
and apologise to Rab.
....

Getting By

I'll not bother with a Roll Royce
A Mercedes will do me fine
if I can't get the Champagne
I'll settle for sparkly wine.
If I can't get my hands on miss world

the rejection won't make me blue
I'll just chat up miss Scotland
or even miss England would do.
By now you'll see I'm easily pleased
I don't set my ambitions too high
while you lads all fight for the top
I'll get comfortably by.

....

My Garden Wall

The masons finished the garden wall last night
and do you know it looks quite nice
they pointed it up three to one
to keep out the weasels and mice.
The cope has yet to go on of course
but I have every confidence it'll fit
and if they make a bonny job
I'll likely get all the credit for it.

....

Return

Do I want to get back to the days
when I could take just a pint and a nip
when I had a head of hair
and there were teeth behind my lip.
When my legs were strong
and my back was straight
when Saturday night came
the feeling was great.
Impressing the lassies we' my Teddy Boy suit
my body neither stocky or lanky
but my mother told me my jeans were too tight
and my bum like two eggs in a hankie.
Such is life there is no way back
at youth you only get the one shot
but really the memories are the best
and go back I certainly would not.

....

Hell

Now in the end, you've got one friend
and for company you'll have you
maybe you like liars and thieves
and you are one of a few.
To spend every week with a lying creep
that's a nightmare to tell
but think of spending forever
now that's my idea of hell.

....

More Fate

I didn't decide I would sit here
nor orchestrate these actions of mine
I just did what I had to do
and tried to do the right at the time.
Do cosmic winds blow
when the cards of fate are dealt
kings and queens fall at random
and in the cauldron of ignorance just melt.
The mighty pull of moon and sun
the permutation of stars we inherit
and magnetic atoms governs all
the disgrace, the blame and the merit.

....

The Shake

I put on my drunken glasses again
now all stuck with super glue
I hope this is not an omen
for you never know what I will do.
Is the strain of denial now telling
surely I can have a sober laugh
be a bit more civilised
without a pint and a half.
'Yes you can' my friends all tell me
but some of them are no' half wise
you can enjoy yourself with a ginger beer
now that's just a pack of lies.
But sure enough I've got to do it
for strong drink I've had more than plenty
for by the time it reaches my mouth the now
the glass is usually half empty.

....

No Smile

My nightmare is reality now
I could easily admit defeat
this could be one blow too much
and I am in retreat.
Confidence gone, the shake returns
but that is no disgrace
because there is nothing quite like life
to wipe the smile from your face.

....

Sober Day

You know I feel so gurny today
I could assault that wee guy across the street
but likely he's a Kung Fu expert

well you never know who you'll meet.
He'd likely give me a thrashing
and throw me half round Tain
I can see the look on the wife's face
'Oh not you, drunk again'.
And me as sober as a judge
albeit half battered to death
wheezing like the barbers cat
trying to catch my breath.
Well I stopped dreaming
and gave the wee guy a wave
you know us sober chaps
fairly know how to behave.
. . . .

Broke

I've just got a letter from the bank
about my plastic credit card
why I did not pay the statement
now from using it I am barred.
Are you sick or even paid off
please answer right away
or at least make some excuse
why you didn't pay.
Well I scratched my head and thought a while
and replied on headed paper, to look posh
'Please accept my apologies' I wrote
but I hadn't quite got the dosh.
. . . .

Was I Right

They call it 'designer stubble' now
in my day we were told it was lazy
while I am all spots we' scratching my face
which one of us is crazy.
Cut your hair up past your ears
study and read a book
pop stars are such a useless lot
you know, no wonder I sit and look.
. . . .

Spite

Where have all our customers gone
getting their shoes sorted next door
they hobble across Geanies Street
because their feet are sore.
Or else getting tyres for their car
just across the street
it seems to me that's all on their minds
is their cars and their aching feet.
No thought of me sitting alone

polishing my bonny stock
even if the went down to Jessies and Audreys
to buy the wife a frock.
Mind you it's mostly all the men to blame
the ladies have far better taste
men try to drag the women away
muttering 'Bonny things is a waste'.
Well I've said my mid day prayers about them
especially the guy who wouldn't buy the wife a doll
I prayed that he wouldn't get supper for weeks
and not get sex at all.

....

So Common

I still feel it's so un-Scottish
to see the girls on page three
showing off their private parts
for all of Scotland to see.
In fact it reminds me of sewing machines
when my father went to sell some
he told me they were like arses
and everybody in Scotland had one.

....

Decisions

I broke my glasses once again
by crashing head first into a wall
I thought the dyke would save me
for I was about to fall.
I blamed the wife for that of course
she was supposed to keep me erect
but if I were a suspicious man
foul play I would suspect.
So now I sit and ponder
about her inability
maybe I could do with a younger one
with a wee bit more agility.
But that would be too much hassle
because the wife is fully trained
and a young one wouldn't have the strength
and if she dropped me I could get brained.
So that's it, I've decided, I'll keep her
but I'll watch her when we make merry
I'll cut out her coke and Bacardi
and make sure she takes only one Sherry.
Now that's it all resolved
to keep her I might as well
for the road is all wet with gutters
and a man's got to look after himsel'.

....

The End

Well I think I've finished all my work
so I will sit here and wait for God
I only hope I will go quietly
when Saint Peter gives me the nod.
It would be embarrassing if I lost the plot
screamed and begged for another week
hanging on to the wife
and kissing her on the cheek.
I'd feel a right fool if I lost my cool
When my poor mother is lying in bed
and here's me bawling
'Go on take her instead'.
No, I decided to go with dignity
the heroic road I'll take
a wee bit like Spartacus in the film
only that I would escape.
....

Can it Get Worse

You know when you're having a stroke of bad luck
and you are amazed at the cruelty of men
if you think it can't get worse
well you'd be wrong again.
Just think of the old scenario
of sitting homeless broke and alone
and someone steals all your clothes
now, that is the time to moan.
When you stand up and cry to God
that all you have left is one boot
you take a defiant step forward
and a thistle goes up your foot.
Then to crown it all
you have symptoms of gonorrhoea
and there is not a toilet in sight
now you have diarrhoea.
Of course with the cold
your manhood has shrunk
and without a hot bath
you smell like a skunk.
All your neighbours stand and stare
and even your old mother
pretends you're not there.
'Yes' you may say
you've arrived, 'I'm in Hell'
but you don't know what's to come next
and maybe that's just as well.
....

Party Time

At my office party
I throw one every year
there are shouts of 'Merry Christmas
and 'Ha' a guid new year'.
Jokes are told then a wee dance
the conversation is witty
but I am the only one I employ
and at party time that is a pity.

....

Try This

I've been in the shop for most of the day
and I've sold just one wee duck
you know it's not like the building trade
selling is a matter of luck.
But I've got a sneaky feeling
and you don't have to tell me why
other folk's jobs look so easy
until you give them a try.

....

Hurt

If you think you couldn't murder
or even do a violent act
you have never really got hurt
and that's an honest fact.

....

Winning

I must have been off the school
the day they taught us about winning
I just got the bit about 'taking part'
and that was at the beginning.
Or maybe it was only the higher grade
and they forgot the B's and the C's
but we were happy with the Beano
and various comics like these.
But I see it now, it wasn't deliberate
it just all evolved with time
because it would be total chaos
if everyone was first at the winning line.

....

No Reward

Do you ever notice when you do a good turn
or 'give a lift' as we say in the trade

they are so pleased at the time of course
but then they avoid you like the plague.

....

Good Sense

It's strange how quick our leaders evolved
it's so unnatural to lead from the back
egging on the troops
in another suicidal attack.
At the start they were at the front
then gradually to a point on a hill
now it's deep in concrete bunkers
no doubt some are there still.
It's brains, not strength the criteria now
and of course it makes good sense
but still there is something wrong with it
or is it only me that is dense.

....

It's There

You've heard the theory of 'Parallel worlds'
just beside us they are spinning
only they are the past and the future
while us idiots sit here grinning.
The past is here like the present
and the future is kind o' past too
and we sit with our minds throbbing
wondering what to do.
Do we move ever forward
or do we count the treasures we got
but if the future is behind us
it really doesn't matter a lot.

....

The Race

I was wondering if just thinking things
or do misfortunes give some folk pleasure
and do we hate to see other's succeed
and by their success our own efforts measure.
This is probably called the Rat Race
or to be posh the Condition of Man
but I was thinking we just caught up with the rats
when they got fed up with the race that they ran.

....

Addiction

Drugs are like a jealous mistress you know
your very soul she will try to own
she'll give you a thousand reasons to stay together

and none for going it alone.
She'll soothe and caress your conscience
ecstatic you confess how you feel
but alas the world that you live in
is a world that just isn't real.
Yes a mistress who keeps her man chained up
that is no lover for me
has she got her claws inside of you
try to leave and then you will see.
....

The Widows Pension

You know the Scottish Widows pension
well their advert gives me the creeps
I've seen their little brochure
lying about the house for weeks.
The woman on the front page
seems ready to break into a grin
in death or in anticipation now
you know a man just cannot win.
I've always liked a wee bit of sorrow
and the wife being totally bereft
because of the way I live my life
we all know who will be left.
It's only reasonable a bit of heartbreak
but I won't get that now due to the pension
and who will pay the premiums
oh I can hardly mention.
I can see it all now her going about
we' that black hood on her head
looking as good as ever
when her heart should be like lead.
And me lying in Rosskeen or Kilmuir
I never quite got to grips with the spot
so for the venue I'm not very sure.
And then she'll buy a new car likely
and maybe get another man
Oh that widows pension
the government should totally ban.
....

Grow Up

I'm fifty now so that leaves me with twenty
and by the way I'm carrying on, that will be plenty
by then I will have stopped drinking as well as the smoke
so if I keel over it will be with a stroke.
And what about the women
will I have lost the notion by then
mind you I don't think about them constantly
only now and then.
Oh my, what a future
and I find it so hard to abstain
and that last dance I was at in the Duthac Centre

God I was the talk o' Tain.
Well well I just might try and practice
not to take the mid-day dram
and I won't ambush the wife at ten to six
you know, that's the kind o' man I am.
If only I could calm down a bit
and as the wife says, 'Act normal'
throw away my jeans and medallion
and dress well, kind o' formal.
As I remember my mother had a quaint old saying
and she would quote it like a sage
only she would stamp and lose her temper
and scream 'Act your bloody age'.
....

Too Late

The age of innocence is youth
yet men corrupt with lies
women set their evil snares
and the halo falls and dies.
The arrows are loosed
deceit, dishonour and hate
straight to the heart of hope they fly
and the shield of faith arrives
too late too late.
....

Daydream

I sit with my back to the radiator
and I really must look pathetic
I never shaved for a day or two
in order to look aesthetic.
And then I thought to myself
Oh, what the hell
I'll go for a run in the Mercedes
and visit my girlfriend as well.
Now where is the bottle of Grouse
and that Havana cigar
and damn it all I'll book a holiday
I don't think that's going too far.
And then I must get on to that guy
to make a better job of my grass
because the mess he made of the hedge
gave me a pain in the ass.
And also that stupid woman
the one in the paper shop
cancelling my Trout and Salmon
and put all my fishing to cock.
When I'm at it I'll sort that wee lassie
the one that's supposed to clean my hoose
I must mind to tell her she's paid off
for putting the wife in the boose.
Dash it all I was dreaming again

and it's only tea that's in my cup
I'm lucky nobody knows what I'm thinking
or it's likely they would lock me up.
....

Time

Yes time will heal all our ills
and in time we will forget our spills
time can turn sad times into laughter
make light of the greatest disaster.
Yet bitterness still defeats all
and through the unforgiving time we stalk
choked by its stinking pall.
....

Winter

Love blossoms bright in summers sun
when the breeze is warm and we are young
Blue Tits chirp and white Doves gaze
and soft lambs runs races through the haze.
Yet the golden harvest conceals a truth
from innocence and unsuspecting youth
that there is a frost, a killing frost
and on mown grass and barley lie
the Blue Tit scratches and the Doves sigh
yes this is a time when even love can die.
....

Dignity

I always thought that I'd pop the clogs
while I was doing the rock and roll
but I was so embarrassed thinking that
I never told a soul.
I had visions of me keeling over
just as I was going to catch the wife
and her crashing to the floor
with a risk to limb and life.
And the band having to stop
in the middle of Heartbreak Hotel
and me lying motionless where I fell.
And the wife going into the craze
when she got to her feet
wi' her hair and clothes all over the place
because she's usually so neat.
And I dread that slipperine
all over my trousers and jacket
and that wee barmaid getting hysterical
and making such a racket.
And also, being me I'd think of that half gill
the one I left on the table
but it would likely be too far away
and to reach it I wouldn't be able.

But no use worrying about all that now
because that will not be my end
for rock and roll is out of the question
because I can hardly bend.
Mind you I confess I'm not sorry
I just don't think it dignified
for a sixty-five year old to die rocking
if I said anything else, I lied.

....

Basic

I always thought that 'character' went very deep
and principles had deep roots within
great strength we had in virtue
and never outgunned by sin.
But now I am older I see the twist
and me so smart, I knew it all
but I'm ashamed what a man will do
when his back is against the wall.

....

The Killer

You know the killer instinct amazes me
and believe me it's in every man
whether you are a priest or a pacifist
I don't think it matters a damn.
We've all got this bit of killer in us
but the bit I really find strange
it's not an instinct we see all the time
not obvious in our vast range.
Yet this instinct is so strong at times
but the wee bit that amazes me
it's strongest when you have won the fight
when there is no need you see.

....

The Rat

I really felt a bit guilty
as I put out the cat
because I opened up the shed
where I knew there was a rat.
And in less than five minutes
deaths screams came to a halt
'Yes I am a rat' it said
but that is not my fault'.

....

Tonic

Well I was tirading at a wee lassie
who works for an insurance firm

why her company should pay me
and do the decent turn.
I said 'My dear if this happened to you
would you expect the insurance to pay
what would you do'.
And, do you know, the wee dame
she said 'Now let me see'
'yes I think that my parents would look after me'.
And then I said to her
'Well suggest a job I could do'
and she replied so primly 'I haven't a clue'.
Perhaps you could try some computers
you know, it really is a sin
as I screamed, I was a builder
she whimpered, 'Try admin'.
Well do you know I put down the phone
and I laughed for the rest of the day
and she was a better tonic for me
supposing her company wouldn't pay.
………………………..

Tea Time

Well I was right scared the day I nearly died
all my relations were there and most of them cried
and me being a dick, pretended I was sick
but it wasn't sore at all, I lied.
I held my chest and tried to look pale and white
you know I thought I could keep that up
most of the day and night.
But no, not for me the dramatic end
with secret confessions in the arms of a friend.
Instead the wife barged in and stole my hot water bottle
'You won't be needing that' says she
and don't just hang on, get up to pee
and really you mightn't have time for tea
so I'll just make some for your relations and me.
………………………….

Priorities

Well you would hardly believe this
after wrecking my back
I got another problem
no, not a heart attack.
It's not even painful
and I know I'm not alone
in fact thousands had it done by Samson
with a sharp stone.
But oh the embarrassment of showing it to the doc
now he knows the size of it
I wonder if he'll talk
tell all the lassies
and make me a laughing stock.
But quickly the wife steps in as usual

before I get too excited.
'Come on my dear' she said
'we'll watch Manchester United'.
'What, I screamed, a football match'
when I'm just one inch from hell
and she replied quite calmly
'Oh for all of the good of that one inch
it would be better off as well'.

....

Out of Sight

Did you hear about the lump of ice
that's making the scientists go into a fuss
because it came from billions of miles
and it's making a B line for us.
It really is colossal
about the size of Wales
and when and if it hits us
it'll cause earthquakes and likely gales.
Probably it will split us
north to south east to west
I don't know which is the best
all I know is I couldn't care less
I just don't have any fears
for the forecast date of impact
is not for a thousand years.

....

The Same

There's that two doves cooing away
in the Damson tree again
and I thought 'now isn't nature nice'
then that damn hawk swooped to kill them
I tell you now that made me think twice.
Mind you why I should be shocked I don't know
our existence is much the same
you love, you care, you feel you share
but there are always bastards who will kill and maim.

....

Saturday Night

Well I disgraced myself once again
on Saturday night I took the shot
all that oaths and promises
yes, they were all forgot.
Oh when I think of it now I could cringe
the way I embarrassed the wife
staggering about the Legion
like it was the last day of my life.
My conduct was quite absurd of course
especially for a man my age

chatting up all the women
putting their husbands in a rage.
So now I just hang my head in shame
things will never be the same
my goodness I must have a terrible name
and oh how I hate Mondays.
....

Alternative

I haven't smoked for weeks now
and yes, I'm a wee bit smug
well I was puffing since I was wee
but now I'm off the drug.
So I am delighted
at long last I have won
so just to celebrate
I'll have a little rum.
....

A Mood

I can hardly believe this is me
sitting in my office at quarter to three
not even fit to kick the dogs arse
but likely she rip my leg off if I tried anyway
so that would be a bit of a farce.
Mind you there is supposed to be a reason
and very little happens by chance
but I have serious doubts now
in fact I must mention it over in the manse.
If only a Jehovah Witness would call
'till I get into a good fight
but I would likely get a friendly one
then I'd have to wait on the wife.
Oh it's awful to feel gurny
when I should be of good cheer
you know it's only a fortnight to Christmas
and three weeks to New Year.
Then we will stand without glasses full
and wish peace to our Queen and nation
forgetting about those poor happy souls
who don't quite grasp the situation.
....

The Ultimate

You know it's not the dying that gets me
it's the bit before that, the lingering on
trying to keep your emotions under control
until you're finally gone.
I have visions of throwing myself at the ministers feet
and bawling to be saved
screaming 'I didn't mean it you bastards

it wasn't me that misbehaved'.
Catching the doctor by the throat
pleading 'Are you sure'
then threatening to nut him
if he couldn't find a cure.
Trying to drag the wee nurse into bed
for the last lust of my life
only to get caught by my sister
and of course the wife.
And then that final degradation
of all horrors that can happen to a man
when the visitors open their bottle
and they don't give you a dram.

....

Inbuilt

Well I must go to bed now
and take my afternoon nap
I tell you this life is so exciting
it's really the best of crack.
I'll take the Ross-shire Journal
and Oh yes, The North Star
but would all that stimulation
be taking things too far.
No I don't think so
we in the Highlands Are pretty tough
when things go wrong we bawl and scream
and then we go in the huff.

....

Watertight

You know the Eastgate Centre in Inverness
well they've got to build part of it again
apparently the red concrete blocks
won't keep out the rain
but taking it down, well!
It seems to me a bit over the top
when the brickies made such a good job of it
not forgetting the lads on the YOP.
And all the tenants seem quite happy
I only think that just
mind it's a pity about the few traders
the ones that really went bust.
But getting back to the building
now believe me I don't wish to brag
but I could cure the dampness
with coloured cement rubbed in with a bag.

....

Abstinence

Last night I only took one wee drink
and do you know, I never slept a wink

I lay there and I worried
my muscles all sore and taut
not relaxed as usual
when I take the shot.
I thought of all the things I must stop
and the thrills and excitement I must deny
you know it's no wonder I sobbed a little
and had to stifle a cry.
Yes a man has got to be brave we're told
and pass worldly pleasures by
but I sometimes just sit and wonder how
and sometimes I wonder why.
....

Civilized

Well a Hare just popped into view
as out of the window I gazed
mind you I live in the country
so I really wasn't amazed.
Instinctively I looked at the dog at my feet
a rangy Dane that stood six feet
and I thought of the thrill of the chase
the stubble field where they could pace.
The speed, the blood and adrenaline pounding
red coated horsemen with bugles sounding.
And I looked again at the wee beast
cropping away at the grass, a feast!
The loping gait the rise and the fall
and to kill that beast I had no reason
no, not one at all.
....

I Wonder

I wonder if I will try Aberdeen
or that manie at the Bridge of Earn
or I could try acupuncture
from that woman the lives in Fearn.
There's aromatherapy and hypnotherapy
I could give them a try
what did this happen to me for
you know, I often wonder why.
....

Be Prepared

What happened to me was a pure disaster
the worst thing that could happen
to a building contractor
and I was so stupid with one string to my bow
I never gave it a moments thought
only now I know.
I was the kind who thought

oh that only happens to other folk, not me
but life isn't like that now I see.
And if you think people care you are crazy
why half of them think that you're just bone lazy
so take some advice from a man who knows
insure yourself to the limit against all woes.
That sounds sensible but it doesn't work
so my advice is, don't get hurt.

....

Forms

I've just got more forms to fill in
God, I am sick of all these questions
name and number once again
I feel I could tell them to stuff their pensions.
'Tell me again, how you got hurt'
'this time I'm sure you will be believed
but you'll have to get one more examination yet
or else the boss will be peeved'.
Now I got to wondering, who was the boss
so I studied the hierarchy tree
and would you believe who's at the top
yes, it's you and me.
We are the ones who hire and fire
and pay the wages when all's done and said
but if you think you have a say in it
you're not nearly right in the head.

....

You

Just ambition is surely right
advancement, learning, darkness to light
yes, I say do what you can
but don't control the lives of fellow man.

....

Better

I was never impressed with sobriety
I thought that was going too far
yet now I'm on the wagon
I see things as they are.
Our lovely politicians
not a selfish thought in their head
and our caring civil servants
making sure the poor were fed.
Civil war what on earth for
a mortgage to bury the dead
no wonder I don't like sobriety
I'd sooner be drunk instead.

....

Instinct

It's really great to give a helping hand
this little action makes you feel good
why, everyone would not think of it
but you did, and so you should.
Yet when I travel through life's intricate winds
I have learned another trick
when your friend gets rich and successful
try not to look so sick.

....

Inevitable

There is only one dove left in my garden now
thanks to that bloody hawk
no soft cooing is heard now
as around the pond they'd walk.
No loving kisses as they nestled in the bower
gone is the summer sun
when bees flit from flower to flower.
Patiently now in the beech tree perch
the crows are drooling
have finished their search.
Instinctively they know that they will dine
silky white feathers their nests will line
the blood of the dove turns into wine,
and do you know for the helpless
it's all a matter of time.

....

The Thief

I caught someone stealing from me today
and do you know I was shaking like a leaf
so I sat in the front porch with a cup of tea
and swore and ranted about the little thief.
Well eventually when I calmed down
and when the knocking had left my knees
I went to pick up my sandwich
and do you know what had happened
the dog had just eaten my piece and cheese.

....

Justice

I like the wildlife programs
where the wildebeast is chased for prey
yellow eyed lions a craving
I could watch it, yes, all day.
The thrill of the chase, the race the pace
but the bit I like the best
is when the lion gets kicked in the face.

....

Dark Days

Is the innocent really defenceless?
And will they lose the war
with a battle that is totally senseless
what on earth is it all for?
Is it need or greed why the angels bleed
and mindless hurting some twisted joy
snakes flick their tongues, no songs are sung
and miserable is the girl and the boy.

....

Not Good Enough

I wandered through the jungle
and you know not one devil was attacking
then I got to thinking why
is there something that I was lacking.

....

More Depression

Yes I was deluded over my destiny
the laughter of youth turned to tears
kindness, not hate exposed me
and revealed my weakness and fears.
Mighty man or cruel wreck
death baits the trap with delight
he lured me with dreams of glory
yet hope near divorced me last night.
Yet honest truth surely exists
or is the reality just more lies
does the lion sharpen his fangs
as lower the vulture flies.

....

Sobriety

I stood at the door of the mansion of sorrow
yesterdays confusion the bench mark of tomorrow
and I knew the sun was losing its fight
the king of darkness will take his throne and it'll be night.
No music left in the ballroom no gaiety in the hall
no aristocratic butler no footman tall
no coach or horses to grace this drive
only chaos rules to keep terror alive.
And yet as I looked with eyes glazed with sin
I could see the battle clearly and the war I must win
then brother courage again came to my aid
took my arm gently, 'Don't be afraid'.
And I took that step through the shadows
through the portico and hall
and entered into the room of reality
where sunshine's rules the day and truth she governs all.

....

More to Come

I thought that I had reached the bottom
when my back refused to bend
and I thought of the Lord Almighty
what else he could send.
Well, the Lord in all his wisdom
no doubt thought it a good idea
so in order to prove a point
he sent me diarrhoea.

....

Just your Luck

The lily of the valley
shows no greed
yet she's smothered
by tare and by weed.
The olive tree sees not
or even hears
yet she can live in a desert
for more than a thousand years.

....

Lies

Now, will I watch Neighbours
or will it be Home and Away
I can hardly believe that I'm doing this
in the middle of the day.
My early demise from the building trade
must be a joke of the gods
perhaps because I liked barrows
and never bothered with Hods.
And me doing so well too
a decent mixer and lorry at last
a two shovelled firm you could call me
now that's all in the past.
I have to turn the heating up now
in order to raise a sweat
I queue at the post office wi' my pension book
and you should see the money I get.
Occasionally I fall on my knees
and ask for a little guidance
and the post she comes to the door
with a complaint about subsidence.
Yet still I take heart
amid all this bad luck
and I think to myself
I'll no' get stuck.
Nature helps a man that tries
but then I got to thinking
that's just a pack of lies.

....

Fate Maybe

There is just no rhyme nor reason
to life's vast intricate plot
no set plan for any man
no system that we can be taught.
Do good, do bad, feel sad, feel glad
connive conspire or just wait
save or spend, but in the end
it's all a matter of fate.

....

Right After All

I priced a retaining wall once
just a couple of years ago
the manie took a look at the price
and he said, 'Just to see me out you know!'
I had priced for a nine inch wall
and he thought half would be ample
I told him it wouldn't last five years
and I'd seen many an example.
Well anyway he got someone else to build his dyke
and it transpired he was right that old colonel
because last night as I read in the paper
I saw his death in the Journal.

....

Not Me

I really will have to change this time
and not take the nip we' the lager and lime
not take the smoke after the tea
that sounds like Hell take it from me.
But there again my breath will be fresher
my beer belly gone what could be better
and in the cocktail lounge I'd drink coffee or tea
but better not be too rash so we'll just wait and see.

....

Conned

The whole world is going mad at the moment
do you know I could sit and cry
I can't understand all this wickedness
no matter how hard I try.
Men are fighting, women are dying
children are starving to death
some ministers twisted, their names are now listed
and companies that would steal your last breath.
So what do we do, me and you
I feel we're like ducks on a pond
we are here to produce sport and beer
I think we are all getting conned.

....

In Proportion

I did a job away in the hills
and it was a pure disaster
I wasn't making a profit
and I couldn't go any faster.
Everything was against me
the snow the wind and the rain
I'd never seen such a climate
far worse than Dingwall or Tain.
The mixer broke down
the lorry went in the ditch
an' me losing money
which was a pure bitch.
The midgies came in hordes
at the least excuse
and that repellent I bought
was just no bloody use.
Anyway while inside sorting a wall
I found an old ABC book
which children were taught
and do you know I sat on a brick
and for an hour I just thought.
....

The Mistake

It really is disloyal to kiss and then to tell
give the story to the papers, and get money for that as well
tell all the sordid details, that seems to be a must
but all you really tell folk is that you they cannot trust.
Yet they're paid their fortune they still get some respect
friends will gather round them and have a party I expect
and that gives us another clue when they sing their song
and only a nutter is happy when they're doing wrong.
....

A Cheap Job

I did a job for a lady once
and believe me I was very cheap
just because I knew her auntie
and we were friendly so to speak.
But when she built her extension
she got some lads on the fly
and they took her to the cleaners
and I didn't bat an eye.
....

Change

Well I better put on the mince and tatties
and set the table for the wife

imagine a mason doing all this
you know it's a terrible life.
Sitting up, lying down, taking a run in to town
trying to exercise to relieve the pain
waiting for the post once again.
Phoning the doctor for an appointment
only to get another disappointment.
So take my advice supposing you get the sack
on no account, hurt your back.
....

Nice People

Do you ever wonder about that chaps
you know, that guys that are really 'nice'
well now-a-days I take a second look
and think about them twice.
Some pretend they're stupid
when you can see they are sharp of wit
they crouch when asking questions
kidding on they're thick as shit.
But why on earth should I criticize them
for that is the nature of man
and hurting other people
only makes me sadder than I am.
....

Can You

You know the more I think of it
I feel I'm under a spell
everything went right for years
then it went all to hell.
Mind I'm grateful for the years of plenty
and that age of happiness
but I wonder why things went wrong
and I ended up in this mess.
But that is the way with life I suppose
you only rise to fall
if you think you can change that plan
you can't, no, not at all.
....

Consequences

I really need a haircut
and my face is a bit of a mess
I'm on the brink of financial ruin
well nearly, more or less.
I tried to do my sums again
and do you know I can't afford to live
and my family look like whippets
on the food that I can give.
Still, I have learned one lesson

I should write it on a placard
'when a builder hurts his back
he's well and truly knackered.
....

Food

The prime minister is a millionaire
but where did the money come from
initially it came from a worker
but maybe I'm getting it wrong.
The whole source of wealth
must come from labour
and the basic production of food
for if all of the farmers packed it in
we would starve, I know we would.
....

The Secretary

Eventually I'll get the hang of this typewriter
when I do I'll buy a skirt
put on some rouge and lipstick
and really be a flirt.
The very first brickie to be a secretary
mind you I was always good at sums
and of course us office workers
won't be showing half our bums.
....

Pride

I have a hole in my wellies
which is a bit of a pest
for when I go to the fishing
I like to be the same as the rest.
I want to stand in the water
to cast my line and hook
and a hip flask is awful handy
if it's cold and you need a sook.
Yes, it must be a grand sight
to see us all sooking and casting
they're plenty of water in the river
and time is everlasting.
The day is long and the sun is warm
and we pray as we are sooking
'Oh Lord let me catch a fish
because there's a few folk looking'.
....

Mystery

I was never cut out for all this labour
or to be a working man

my body is far to refined
and my nature extraordinarily kind
so I better just stay as I am.
Yes, I'm sure you could guess
that this is all just a dream
who can fight the forces
which come from a hundred sources
and nobody is what they seem.

....

Logie

I stood in the churchyard at Logie
and listened to the sound of the dead
they told me to stop all my hating
and to try more loving instead.
To forgive is the music at Logie
be gentle understanding and kind
listen to the soul that God gave you
or else the deaf will deceive the blind.

....

Try It

Tour around in an old car
then try it out in a new Jag
try a cigar in the cocktail bar
then next week a rolled up a fag.
A Harris tweed jacket, a tennis racquet
a box with a snooker cue
you know it all makes a difference
in the way that folk treat you.

....

Agreed

I was watching a great debate on TV last night
and now I know why I am still building a wall
because when everyone spoke, I took it all in
and then I agreed with them all.

....

Was There a Plan

I built a house for a fellow once
and he was quite bereft
for the very day I finished the house
his wife got up and left.
Yet one thing that puzzled me
that during all of the construction
it was her that decided all the details
and it was built by her instruction.

....

The Experts

Did you know it's over forty years
since the Dead Sea Scrolls were found
they were written long long ago
then hidden underground.
Experts in language they came in
also experts in history
but what's taking them so long
that is the mystery.
Forty years to decipher a text
a lot of head scratching going on I expect.
Well do you know what I was thinking
academics can rise and can fall
but the ones in charge of the translation
they are not experts at all.
....

Could Be

There goes the doorbell once again
a Jehovah Witness wi' the obligatory bairn
a briefcase under his oxter
and enough pamphlets to build a cairn.
He wants me to go to heaven with him
and give up my cosy life of sin
he says I won't make it alone
the darkest regions of Hell I'll roam
for it's only witnesses that will get in.
Then I thought of all the things that I was taught
the truth can be blindingly clear
if it is only witnesses that get to heaven
what's all the rest of us doing here.
....

A Compliment

I never liked working with concrete
although that is part of the trade
it never gave me satisfaction
but the wages have to be made.
There are so many other things
I just never liked
in fact it could be described as hate
but there is a few words that compensates
if the client says 'That looks great'.
....

A Little Error

There they were once again wi' their briefcases
knocking at the front door
and I was right in the mood for a fight
well, my back was terribly sore.

So, I rushed to the door
well it was really more of a creep
wrenched it open and screamed
'I'm going to speak'.
Well I really did get wired in
you know I think I went off the head
I was bawling about blood transfusions
and everything else I had read.
I ranted on for at least half an hour
and concluded with human endurance
and do you know they weren't Jehova's at all
but two guys from the Prudential selling insurance.
....

Comparison

I read a book about witches last night
and do you know it gave me an awful fright
I tossed in my bed for hours
and was waken for half of the night.
Dancing at midnight wearing long black cloaks
there were women there too as well as blokes.
Sacrificing a hen
Oh it's better all forgot
and me thinking I was wicked
because I take the shot.
....

The Reject

I flaunted myself before her
that's before I got the belly and bum
I was holding my breath so tightly
my muscles were getting numb.
I nonchalantly gave a flick of my head
to put all the waves in place
and I had to think of motorbikes
in order to compose my face.
Oh yes, here it comes, a reaction
that didn't take much detection
and me posing the best that I could
only to get a rejection.
....

Making Money

Like every good wee builder
I always pay my tax
I work it out by calculator
and send it off by fax.
I'm so modern in my office now
since I got the driving ban
I bought a new electric typewriter
and put in an extractor fan.
A radiator now gives off the heat

that replaces the old coal fire
and on the wall I hung a mirror
to do myself up, and my face admire.
Yes, I admit I really feel posh
but I also feel a birk
because when I'm in the office
there is no one to do the work.

....

Last Ambition

I have only one ambition left
which must wait until my closing hour
an achievement more precious than gold
more satisfying than power.
I'd like to utter one sentence
whether wealthy or poor I'd be
'The man that lived my life
well that was really me'.

....

My Letter

I think I'll write a letter
and get it printed in the Times
but I better stick to the prose
for they mightn't like the rhymes.
I can see my letter in London
being carried all around the city
but if it ended in the chip shop
that would be an awful pity.
In the tube some swanky guy
will exclaim 'Who on earth'
'Did you see it George, on page three'
'that man must be a genius'
and they'd be talking about me.
But there again I thought
if they said nasty things
and worse if they started to laugh
so I just took my letter
and happily tore it in half.

....

Very True

Old Donald boarded the train
he was bound for Inverness
and in the same compartment
sat Mrs' Mackay and her daughter Bess.
'Oh mother my arm is awful sore
when it broke I got a terrible dirl
it must be the sorest thing
that could happen to a girl'.
'No Bess you haven't experienced anything yet

for childbirth is the sorest thing
that anyone can get'.
Now the train was approaching Garve
that's near the Rogie Falls
when Donald had enough, and said
'Did you ever get a kick in the balls'.
. . . .

That's Life

Well I honestly think my brain has snapped
and god, it wasn't even due to the drink
it's all because I got a puncture
you know it would make you sit and think.
The constant pain with the explanations
to tell the ins and outs I haven't the patience
and the wee bit of disbelief in every eye
you know sometimes I just sit and cry.
And me, gosh I was one of the best
but in ten short months I'm forgotten
now that is a bit of a pest.
But never fear I will not be defeated
no, not by pain or by drink
but why do folk want to make me unhappy
you know, no wonder I sit and think.
. . . .

Alcohol

God how I hate November
that's the time I get so depressed
when I really want to be happy
and laugh along with the rest.
But no, unfortunately, that's not for me
you know sometimes I could smoke the pot
but I am of another generation
so I just take the shot.
And of course the pot is illegal
in case it interferes with our wits
but did you not notice it's the alcohol
that makes us kick each other to bits.
. . . .

The Trance

I've made an appointment with a hypnotist
to stop the fags and the drink
but when I thought of the pleasure I'd lose
it made me sit and think.
Am I quite ready, my hands are still steady
'mind you when I laugh I choke
admittedly too my nose turned blue
that's due to the rum and the coke.
Then there's all that money I'd save

I'd soon be a millionaire
but how can you enjoy life with no fags or drams
I think it very unfair.
But still I think I'll go to Inverness tomorrow
a broken down brickie with a heart full of sorrow
and when he swings his watch back and fore
and I drop into a trance
I'll dream of the days, the happy days
when I drank and smoked and danced.

....

The General

Deep deep as love can be
It's the jewel of all emotion
anger or greed, hate or need
they pale before devotion.
No greater love can a man feel
than for his country family and king
honour and virtue essential
and the peace that faith can bring.
Yet last night as I dreamed
I dreamed the dream of despair
and terror froze my very soul
vulnerable helpless and bare.
Silently I screamed out my distress
as the storm before the calm
then instinct overpowered my senses
and the word I shouted was 'Mam'.

....

Proprietary

I'm thankful that my lot in life
is not to govern men
to be responsible for another life
the magnitude is beyond my ken.
Born equally naked and die equally dead
but it's the bits in between
that's important someone said.
All joys and sorrows orchestrated
and as through the porthole of life you glide
the entourage follows, and that's homicide.
Live your life to the full, that's true
but other folk have their own life to live
and it doesn't belong to you
So pray they will forgive.

....

A Want

Well I never thought that I would see the day
that I would contemplate taking drugs
when I was quite pleased with the whisky

which would disappear in one or two glugs.
But here I am in a fair bit of pain
no day is different, all are the same
and really no-one cares when you're out of sight
your laughter is forgotten your day turns to night.
And then you get to thinking about the young folk
as they pass the pipe of peace
and you realise, yes, it's a want in the human soul
and it's a want that will never cease.

....

Sadness

The most pathetic sights I've ever seen
is a simple man look sad
a clever man go mad
an evil face look glad
and a dog who's lost it's master.

....

Revenge

I have an appointment on the eleventh of May
which turns out to be a Monday
so I better have a quiet weekend
and not have any drams on Sunday.
Mr' Welch is the man I'm seeing
he's the top surgeon at Raigmore
but he's not going to stick his knife in me
although my back is sore.
I can visualise him now sharpening his blades
and checking his circular saw
staring and peering at my X-ray leering
trying to find out where's the flaw.
I can almost hear him chuckle with great delight
'Heh, heh, I'll keep this one handy
and do it late at night'.
And I must mind to tell the matron
to get a new wick for the lamp
because I don't like the new hospital
I rather it dark and damp.
Ah yes, Donald James, I mind you fine
I played football against you many a time
remember the final when the ref you tricked
well I won't forget because it was me you kicked.

....

Darwin

Darwin awoke one morning
and he looked up at the sky and sun
yes, and in that very instant
he knew how it was all done.
Slow progression, natural selection

the strong mate the strong
in time it's perfection
but who eats who, that is the question
and where did the poor chicken go wrong.
....

Circumstances

If you take your religion
to it's logical conclusion
you know there would be far less confusion.
Does your god tell you wrong from right
and help you out in each war you fight.
Then what about the other side
are they the ones with too much pride
or have they a different god from us
and they can die without a fuss.
And when we all fall into endless time
do you go your way and I go mine
I just cannot believe eternal torment
for ten minutes of sinful pleasure spent.
Forever and ever, no reprieve
I find that quite monstrous
I just cannot believe.
Surely our maker when he drew up his plan
knew the sinful ways of man
and during the course of his deliberation
took this into consideration.
And all that endless blood and sacrifices
I can't believe that it was he who advises
what possible good in life's blood spilled
from some poor lamb that's just been killed.
And a burning carcass glowing on a fire
now that's a lovely sight to admire.
Remember Judas
you know he was only a man
and many a sleepless night he spent
I cannot believe he's in eternal torment.
For after all it was prophesied
somebody had to do it
or Jesus wouldn't have died.
And then what would have happened
to the atonement for sin
there was no other way
someone had to betray him.
And now I think with all our advances
we are all victims of circumstances
though we all get a choice
that must be true
it's conditions at the time that dictate
what we must do.
....

Ramblings 4

The Temptation

They've harvested the carrots in the field beside me
and I'm quite glad that they are all away
you see I was thinking of stealing a few
and that was just the other day.
But honesty and virtue forbade me
and my honour is still intact
but I weighed up the pros and cons first
before I even thought of that.
And now the temptation is all gone
a seductive temptress out of sight
not that I'm into stealing carrots anyway
but you never know, I might.
....

They Are Everywhere

The first time I used my parking badge I felt guilty
because I really looked in the pink
and before you get the wrong idea
no, it has nothing to do with drink.
I just happen to be a healthy chap
and hardly a day was I sick
but a dour crippled man inspected my badge
you know in all walks of life, there's a prick.
....

Disclosed

Do you ever think the whole world's corrupt
when even our own MPs are on 'the take'
of course you don't call it bribery then
it's just called a wee mistake.
The clergy are caught in massage parlours
some drunken doctors couldn't care less
judges commiserate with criminals
the whole system's in a bit of a mess.
Now this is not a new phenomenon you know
of this I have no doubt
but there were no tabloids long ago
and it's only now that we're finding out.
....

Yes I Knew

When a 'dirty old man' gets found out
or some other pervert gets caught
I wonder if that's their first offence
but usually no, it's not.
It seems to be a fact with sex criminals
that they were always twisted a bit
and for years we knew they were like that
it's true if you think about it.
....

What You Do With It

What do you want out of life you ask
is it success, love and wealth
and maybe too a few sins thrown in
if not too injurious to health.
Oh yes the plans of mice and men they say
the philosophers are thinking yet
but it's not a matter of what you want
it's making the best out of what you get.
....

True Nature

Now I don't defend the drinkers
just because I take a dram
but it's not the drink that is nasty
that's just the nature of man.
Yes, that's a smug proclamation
but it is true I have no doubt
because if you haven't got it in you
then it cannot come out.
Now this may hurt your ego
but perfection is reserved for a few
so admit to your own defects
and don't be a liar too.
....

Healing

I think I must be one of the first
to get acupuncture on the NHS
at last our doctors are opening their eyes
and it's bound to be a big success.
In fact when you think of it it's unbelievable
how our whole culture ignored the east
and only resorted when all else failed
when the patient was near deceased.
Even then we'd stay quite convinced
that foreign methods were no good
and never thinking if we tried it earlier
to give a cure it could.
Of course there are alternative medicines
and how they work we haven't a clue
but is that really so important
as long as they do good to you.
Do we need to know how an Aspirin relieves
and does the composition have to impress
well I tell you this I don't know
and my headache couldn't care less.
....

Ambition

I think that I would like to be a minister

215

well I think of that now and then
bawling away from the pulpit
'You wicked bastards, don't do that again'.
Stopping all the dancing at eleven on a Saturday
nutting one or two punks in case they start a fight
stalking round the public houses
hardly taking a dram
demanding confessions from the young bucks
about who filled wee Jeanies pram.
Then on Monday I could relax again
keep a low profile and my flock to tend
for nobody does much at all through the week
it's only at the weekend.
....

Not Obvious

I've had to terminate my little business
for years now I've had constant pain
a surgeon thinks I am swinging the lead
that means the insurance won't pay out again.
The tax man is sure I diddled him
even the tele is on the blink
and added to the worry of the usual things
I had taken to the drink.
Now this would be funny if it wasn't true
and I used to like a joke and a jest
but I had to laugh when my doctor asked
'Now why, are you depressed'.
....

I'm All Right

You know what they say about the afterlife
that no-one ever came back to tell
but I was thinking if there is a Heaven
I would do the same as well.
Would you risk your place on the list
no you wouldn't at any price
maybe once you applied to get in
they won't entertain you twice.
Yes, that is it I'm pretty sure
that's why they don't come back
I can see them all queuing away
and saying 'I'm all right Jack'.
....

Tact

The British people don't say what they mean
down south 'coffee' can sometimes mean sex
while the further up north you go
it could mean a nip and a bottle of Becks.
Why can't we all be more straight to the point

and say 'Come on missis, it's the giving season'
but you would get a slap in the mouth
so that is probably the reason.
....

Nothing is Fair

I went down to the town last week
and I went to demand fair play
being deprived and pretty poor
I knew no other way.
Well first of all into a restaurant
now I knew that was pretty rash
but I ordered up a massive steak
although I hadn't the cash.
But anyway the bluff came off
they were bamboozled by my cheek
why a should a poor man do without
for I hadn't a steak in a week.
Next I dragged a young guy out of his car
when the lecture was over his jaw gave a sag
well I had told him in no uncertain terms
it was my turn for a shot in a Jag.
Now spiritually satisfied back to the car park
never again would this poor man be kicked
but do you they are no justice in this world
because my old Ford was nicked.
....

One of the Laws

'What have I done to deserve this'
when you hear this it's usually bad news
rarely you'll hear a winner shout that
it's more than likely it's when you lose.
Yes indeed it's a strange thing to say
yet our instincts do prompt the appeal
and you may think of a thousand reasons
but you know not one of them are real.
The way of the world is more complex
some situations just don't have a cause
there is no consistency in total chaos
and that seems to be one of the laws.
....

Tax Evasion

Another letter from the tax man
and guess who he wants to see
god I wish he would stop these letters
because he sure ain't in love with me.
Yes I did hear that he's paid by results
in the trade that would be a bonus scheme
and there is nothing like the hope of reward
to make the workers keen.
Now I will admit I didn't tell him all

but surely this won't reduce me to rags
all because I sorted a slate for a wifie
and she gave me a pot of jam and twenty fags.
But believe it or not this is a crime
and I regret not sending the tax man his share
that would be five fags and a jelly piece
I wonder if they'd think that fair.
……………………………..

Qualifications

Qualifications are useful things
albeit it's just a paper with print
and it doesn't exactly tell you much
but it does give you a hint.
Now this is used through all society
from the lowest job to the top
but if you think that this is proof of ability
well I tell you now, it's not.
Now I wonder if this happens in the top jobs
where it is critical there is no looseness
because I employed a qualified brickie once
and he was absolutely useless.

………………………

D I Y

For dinner I boiled a cabbage
it is so good for your health
and I tell you nothing tasted better
as when you make it yourself.
………………

I Still Wonder

The evil one was after me once again
so instead of prayer I shouted 'I'm off'
I was at the stage I didn't care
about punishment or the grapes of wrath.
And do you know I think that worked
he's left me severely alone since then
and I am living a more tranquil life now
more like ordinary men.
But a contrary nature doesn't die easy
nor do the politics of sin
now I wonder who really won the fight
was it me or was it him.

……………………

The Cream

The West was won by frontiersmen you know
they invented the Colt to keep him alive

and now when we're safe and modern
we give our pathfinders a P45.
Yet these are the people we rely on
and the ones that will always take the brunt
just think when you and I start a fight
who do we push to the front.
Then when the chaos and terror is over
once again it's the great melting pot
and when the mass of humanity cools down
is it the cream that comes to the top?

....

Living on Your Wits

If ever you come into money
you know the first thing that you will find
what the Americans call 'suits' move in
and honestly they will rob you blind.
You might think this pessimistic
and the outlook to be the pits
but I tell you some respectable people
make their living by their wits.

....

Imagination

I'll let you into a secret
I always wanted to be Captain Kirk
being in charge of the Enterprise, is so exciting
and more interesting than building work.
Oh but being any of the crew would do
for they all ogle the girls with big 'jugs'
and it would be a push over to be Mr. Spock
because already I have the lugs.
But there again think of the responsibility
the consequences of one mishap
interplanetary war could break out
but, I could always blame that on the Jap.
Oh yes the possibilities are endless
maybe even be an assistant to Scotty
or perhaps not, he looks a bit miserable
and likely wouldn't give me a shotty.
But no use daydreaming I suppose
that is all children's games
so I better mosey along with Clint now
or my other friend Jessie James.

....

Tragic

One of the saddest stories I know
about war, the bayonet and gun
a man told me he knew a man who saw the man
who shot Harry Lauder's son.

....

Lesson in Lending

I wonder when I give a loan of anything
whether a ladder or garden shears
(books are never returned of course)
and the rest kept for two or three years.
Yet the funny thing is when I asked once
just a wee thing I'd forgot to buy
I was grilled for half an hour
if, what, how long, maybe and why.
Now this is something I've never understand
and it has nothing to do with the cost or price
but does it show up a flaw in me
because I would never ask twice.

....

Be Exotic

I must go down for the pension again
but this time I'll ask for a raise
basically because the amount that I get
only lasts me for two or three days.
Now did you notice I used the American term
I said 'Raise' and not good old 'Rise'
because it's important how you say a word
in fact it can be a surprise.
Just try phoning somebody up today
and use the 'English' to the best effect
next try the local vernacular
you will find a difference I suspect.
Yes it is another wee law of nature
and when learned it will open you doors
this was noticed long long ago
exotic birds come from foreign shores.

....

The Best Bits

I do not like video's at weddings
or parties that are recorded
you can see it goes to some peoples heads
maybe an Oscar they'll be awarded.
But I don't like it, I feel I'm being watched
yet of course I know I'm not
but by the way that I behave at times
half the party's best forgot.
Anyway it's all right for the quiet ones
they can have a laugh next day at the rest
but personally speaking about parties
what I remember is usually the best.

....

Forbidden Fruit

I've told you about this weakness of mine

well, I weakened again last night
I gazed at the wife with pleading eyes
and she said 'Oh all right'.
Well I filled my glass and drank the draught
and call it contrary to give it a name
but when you are allowed to do something
do you know it's never quite the same.

....

Distinction

A labourer gets as 'pissed as a newt'
and an MP as drunk as a lord
the man who just can't cope, tops himself
but his majesty falls on his sword.
Yes there seems to be a difference all right
and these reasons we'll never get rid
distinctions are here forever
now tell that to your coffin lid.

....

Accurate Sounds

When you use the swear words
they say it's the English language you haven't mastered
but honestly some words convey the meaning so clearly
that some people are just a pure bastard.

....

Top Of My League

I thought I'd try my hand at robbery
but that just proved a flop
not that I didn't try hard enough
I just happened to get caught.
Next I tried some blackmail
about what the boss was doing after lunch
but the squirt hadn't the guts to try her on
so he was as pleased as punch.
Well I thought crime is not paying
and I couldn't be bothered with petty theft
but after trying most of the big things
their really wasn't a lot left.
Still I was determined to be wicked
and dancing naked didn't sound too daft
so I joined a porn group
and God forgive them, but the audience laughed.
Yes I admit I was a failure
I just wasn't rotten to the core
but when I think of it I didn't do too bad
for a minister from Aviemore.

....

False Guilt

Do you ever put yourself in hypothetical situations
   | like being seduced by a film star
   | then wonder if you would comply
     and if you did, how far.
Now this can be a dangerous game to play
and the ones that play it, you can always tell
they are the ones going around with red faces
     and feeling as guilty as hell.

....

Not Prepared

Someone tried to rob me once
and in a way that was really a shame
you see my poor wee Spaniel had died
so for a guard dog I bought a Great Dane.

....

Certainty

Thank goodness I'm living more sober now
for a while I was out of my tree
and it wasn't even a happy romance
that the whisky had with me.
Yes it really is an amazing life
for experience there is no cure
but you wouldn't do the things I did
but tell me, are you sure?

....

Trusty

Who do you put your trust in you say
of course I trust my best friend
truthful, honest and reliable
on him I could depend.
And yet when you look in the magazines
in the queries about love and life
guess who seduces your husband
or guess who runs off with your wife.

....

My Diet

You succeeded and that is good
and you got fed the best of food
now we're both dead and I lie near him
do you notice he is fat and I'm nice and slim.

....

There is More

All the knowledge I've gained in my wanderings
and the conclusions I come to in my ponderings
no drugs needed or alcohol to drink
for true reality is not what you think.

....

Get Out The Scalpel

Another bloody minister caught for abuse
I didn't even bother to read his excuse
interfering with bairns, should he get shot?
personally I'd do the operation
and take away the lot.

....

Fair Play

When I was young I was taught 'fair play'
to take your turn until it was your shot
and if you think that's the only way to succeed
well I tell you now it's not.
Oh yes it's honourable, it's good and it's right
and everyone should have principles and ideals
but there is no virtue in being ignorant
success also comes to cheats who steals.
The rain falls on the good and bad alright
and you'll get your share if you're there
sunshine too might shine on you
but Lady Luck never needs to be fair.

....

Knowledge

Knowledge is a wonderful thing isn't it
education some say is divine
in fact it's probably more intoxicating
than drugs or fruit of the vine.
And yet some things I have learned
some facts I know to be true
I wish that I was never told about them
I'd be happier if I never knew.

....

Are You Sure

The truest lesson I ever learned
and I've figured it out all alone
not that it takes a genius to understand it
it's quite simple once you are shown.
Now I know you will argue about this
you even might think me a prat

but one sentence you should never say
is 'That I would never do that'.
....

Watching

I get embarrassed at sex on TV
something tells me that it isn't right
and it's nothing to do with the time it is on
whether through the day or at night
the point is sex is a secret instinct.
Like we want to be alone when we cry
but now people are so nosey
when we even want to watch someone die.

....

Luck

I knew two men who worked equally hard
but only one was a success
yet the other did almost the identical things
not exactly but more or less.
'Where did I go wrong?' the failed one asked
'I hardly ever got a rest or a breather'
well I had to tell him I didn't know
and that nobody else knew either.

....

The Future

You won't believe what I've bought today
so I will not keep you guessing
it was a pack of Tarot Cards
in the mysteries of the occult I'm messing.
The first mystery I had to overcome
that the word is pronounced 'Tar-o'
why on earth drop the T off the end
that is something I don't know.
But anyway I ignored that little mystery
because our language is riddled with that
likely whoever made up the word couldn't spell
and probably was as blind as a bat.
So down to the main business, the cards
well I shuffled them like a dervish in season
that really wasn't necessary you know
but what the hell I don't need a reason.
I dealt them out according to the book
(it's always wise to use the directions)
now this is where the tricky bit comes in
deciphering the future projections.
Now as usual I'll put it all in a nutshell
because in an hour I was feeling happy and glad
and the reason was very simple
I just believed the good bits and took no heed of the bad.

....

Basic Rule

I was my own boss for about twenty years
and a wee builder I was proud to be
mind you I was never a big tycoon
my staff was a labourer and me.
Now we were quite happy for most of the time
though every day there were physical strains
but that suited me and my man would agree
our bodies were better than our brains.
Now everyone knew apart from us two
that flesh and bone won't last intact
but when you're young and strong like us
you don't understand this fact.
So now in the autumn of life you may say
I remember the rule I learned in school
'The builder who built his house on the sand
his employer was a damn fool'.

....

The System

We have a grand big system
within our welfare state
it must be the envy of all the world
everybody thinks it great.
Nobody starves in Great Britain
everyone can afford to eat
and every now and then
there is a special little treat.
All the old people are looked after
it's a matter of being systematic
and to teach the bairns
without getting autocratic.
Yes we're totally organised all right
so why do I feel a birk
well it's our grand big system
it's that sometimes it just doesn't work.

....

Changing

I thought I knew what ecstasy was
but apparently it's now a pill
a policeman was once a 'Bobby'
but now it is the 'old bill'.
The language sure is changing now
they just don't know what next to say
so I will put on my gurny face
in case they say I'm 'gay'.

....

Clever

My dog is exercised, groomed and fed
and on frosty nights she has a warm bed
plenty affection, tickles and a pat
do you know I wish that I had brains like that.

....

The Best So Far

Democracy is the best we have the now
and it gives a chance to every woman and man
if you want to be a millionaire it's there
you can do it, yes you can.
But sadly this is the religion of the 'able'
for this religion is to take not give
but some folk don't like this system
and they too have a life to live.
So the smartest gets most of the harvest
just because they are clever at sums
and philosophers, artists,
and those who can't cope
get thrown compensatory crumbs.
So what is justice? I don't know
does the positive only create tears
can we not sit and figure it out
and not wait two thousand more years.

....

Old Sayings

Some of the old sayings really are true
you can see it at any public meeting
some folk get up and orate for hours
and speak for the sake of speaking.
Yes, you can rely you will get found out
supposing your schemes are small or big
for everyone knows where the good food goes
and they just look for the quietest pig.

....

Ownership

Yes you love your country
and the English they do too
I suspect they have similar feeling
just the same as me or you.
So who owns the country you may rightly ask
now that can be difficult to tell
for it's always the future generation that own it
and the land is not ours to sell.
All we are is 'Tenants' for a while
our duty is to work and make 'Eden'

and that is what we are all doing here
and that is the only reason.
....

The Employer

How can you be an expert on 'bricklaying'
if you have never laid a brick
that's what I would call an ignorant expert
does that make sense, or is it me that's thick.
You get lecturers in our universities
now I know they are far from fools
but really when you think of it
they have never quite left the schools.
Experts in our government
most have never been unemployed
but God has given them vocal chords
and they are overjoyed.
Yes, it's a strange old world right enough
when spinsters can council you and your wife
and the guy who tells you how to sweep the streets
never bent his back in his life.
Now I often thought 'how did they get their jobs'
but that is a task for a lawyer
because all the yapping confuses the issue
that they have an idiot for an employer.
....

The Urge

I'm feeling the urge coming on again
and 'good grief it's only Wednesday night'
I can hardly say it's near the weekend
that just wouldn't be right.
If only there were a wedding
or even a funeral would do
maybe a royal divorce would suffice
but I like an excuse to be new.
Well it looks like it will have to be the usual
old dependable once again
when the wife comes in I'll try and grin
and sob 'What a terrible pain'.
Then I'll hobble through to the cabinet
when she's not looking do a Highland Fling
and if it wasn't for all that empty bottles
she would never suspect a thing.
....

Failed

We've had to close the wee gift shop
the one I told you was in Tain
well everybody said they were very sad
and told me it was a shame.

But I thought it was an experience
and I tell you I have made worse boobs
but I never raped or murdered
just a wee shop down the tubes.
Now I am so glad I got things in perspective
anyway, it was only a dream
so I will throw myself on the bed again
and wail and sob, and scream.
....

In Comparison

I was zooming down the A9
the car was going like a dream
for an old Polo it was doing all right
if you see just what I mean.
Mountains loomed on either side
fence posts were just a blur
with my new exhaust from Kwik Fit
the roaring was down to a purr.
Yes I admit I was delighted
and about my progress I could brag
and I thought I was doing so well
until I was passed by a bloody Jag.
....

More urges

Well it is four o'clock now
and I have just taken one wee nip
the excuse this time was the dog was cheeky
and was about to give me lip.
Now one wee nippie doesn't affect me much
I'm hardly going to break into song
but if you think I feel the worse of it
then once more you'd be wrong.
....

Waiting

Do you ever watch the programme 'Waiting for God'
it's quite often on ITV
well I was just thinking if I won the pools
that God would be waiting for me.
My philosophy on life is simple
there is much more than 'daily bread'
and only a fool would slacken off
especially when he's ahead.
....

Not So Bad

It is a very true fact of life
that of all the terrors and fears you've got

when they eventually happen
they're not as bad as you thought.
Your wildest blunder, is just a mistake
ecstasy just a little pleasure
financial ruination reduced
just to getting some short measure.
Yes, you say that lesson is learned
as sure as my last breath
so why are we all so worried
about the mystery of death.

....

Honesty

My dog she barks at intruders
and wags her tail at my friends
she asks for food when she's hungry
and no, she never pretends.
I've studied her actions often
and it's plain for all to see
although I might be smarter than her
she's far more honest then me.

....

Faultless

I had murderous intentions about a bluebottle
which was annoying me more than most
so I tracked it down with a club
actually a rolled up Sunday Post.
And as I was going to deliver the Coup de grâce
I could almost hear the wee thing cry
'Look this is not my idea
it's not my fault I'm a fly'.

....

The Operator

I was reading about our brains
and how complicated they are
smarter than the largest computer
with more permutations by far.
A hundred billion little cells
and each one can interact
there isn't anything it can't do
it's incredible but it's a fact.
Well I said to myself, I'll have a go
and see if I can't pick up Moray Firth Radio
so I concentrated and tried to tune my brain
but all I got was an advert for the Dress Shop in Tain.
Well I was a wee bit disappointed at this
so I thought I'd try some psychokinesis then
and if you know what that fancy word means
I'll give you ten out of ten.

Anyway I concentrated on the ashtray
actually it was more like staring
the wife was giving me funny looks
but to be honest she's past caring.
Now with all this mental activity
my poor head began to ache a bit
and the damn ashtray didn't move anyway
while I'm risking a migraine or maybe a fit.
No I thought there is a sensible way to look at this
and it all came to me later that night
to be sure we have this fantastic brain computer
but it's the operator who can't work it right.

....

Intoxication

There must be hundreds of religions going about the now
every year another new sect
and everyone determined that they know it all
well do you know that drink can have the same effect.
You can see the 'heavies' how the congregate at the bar
and their spirit is not from 'above'
but you can't deny the fraternity
and the brotherly love.
Of course this is just a wee observation
but also one that is true
have you ever thought about yourself
and what intoxicates you.

....

Clarity

I was looking up at the clear blue sky
there was not a star in sight
and I got to thinking
do they only come out at night.
Oh yes, I knew that they were there okay
this could be termed 'faith' or 'belief'
but no doubt there are some that would argue
and bring us both a lot of grief.
What a strange twisted mind us humans have
we can't comprehend a life of bliss
if I don't believe what you believe
we'll fight to the death over this.
Enlightenment is the answer I suppose
an attitude that very few show
only when you understand a lot
you realise how little you know.

....

Belief

She said I was self-centred and opinionated
and my attitude quite absurd

well I agreed, but did I believe
no I didn't, no not a word.
....

Choices

To think I'll never build a wall again
now, that is something that makes me sad
and compared to empty idleness
the building trade isn't so bad.
Now when away from it, and kind of detached
I think builders deserve more esteem
in fact I would go further that that
and say all workers should rule supreme.
Yet what about the poor lazy folk
can they help it if they're not the salt
is it just another quirk of nature
and being lazy is not their fault.
No, there is much more going on than that
that is why you are you and not me
if you think we all get choices in life
try to be different and then you will see.
....

Left it too Late

I can't help laughing at some old codgers
and the way that they behave
they get caught embezzling money
when they have one foot in the grave.
Others woe the women
and damn it all they can get them too
but that seems to be a quirk of life
and it's nothing unusual or new.
Now I don't condone their behaviour
and to understand it make no pretence
but why did they leave their ambition so late
it just doesn't make any sense.
....

Ashamed

I saw an acquaintance of mine stagger down the street
well do you know, I can hardly believe what I did
I went into the paper shop, not for a paper
I'm ashamed of it now, but I hid.
....

Sober Again

I thought I was going to get a visit from the minister
for he sometimes comes over and prays
and usually he's got a cryptic message in his ravings

mostly concerning my drunken ways.
But if he comes over now
he'll find a different man
and he will think he did the trick
and take the credit if he can.
You see I am on the tack just now
not a dram had I got, not a smell
but I am near the critical stage now
and getting cocky as well.
Anyway my new image pleases everyone
it's back to good old status quo
but really does that make me a better man
to be honest I do not know.
....

Education

One thing I regret and can't forget
is one older boy I met at school
now I was just an ordinary kid
not brilliant but neither a fool.
Now this older boy was what we call 'streetwise'
or sophisticated could be another name
but he told me the ways of the world
and do you know, I was never the same.
Now I'm not going to bleat about people I meet
but is all knowledge really worth showing
for I know I would be a happier man
for some things you are better not knowing.
....

The Rat

There were signs of a rat out in the shed
I wonder if it knows my cat is dead
and I knew by the noise it made later that night
that the rat was sure my cat was dead all right.
....

Why Not

It's strange when people are hypnotically regressed
some are convinced that they have lived before
the picture is so clear and described in detail
even to the clothes they wore.
But one wee thing makes me suspicious
in previous lives most were well off
rarely were they of the working class
more than likely some kind of toff.
And yet if you believe it all
maybe at high stations we all get a shot
now to me that seems only reasonable
and personally I don't see why not.
....

In The Lap of the Gods

Life can be awful cruel sometimes
though we say it is circumstances
it's more like a game of Bingo at times
a matter of luck and chances.
Smart folk say they have organised this or that
and some of the time that is true
but other times you can plan what you like
and the opposite will happen to you.
No wonder the Greeks believed in the gods
and that they did all the dictating
pushing them around like pawns in a game
organising the loving and hating.
Yes it's logical to believe in that
yet to say it aloud is a blunder
because the theory has been ridiculed since years
but do you know I sometimes wonder.

....

Must Have

The world's population is increasing
there are millions more of us now
some experts contemplate the reasons why
but you know I just wonder 'how'.
I often think it's like a plant in a jar
give it air, water, and close the lid
now no more material can get in there then
but the plant grows big, so it did.

....

First Lesson

Learn a new word or fact every day
now that is a principle that is good
unfortunately folk are too lazy
but we all know that we should.
Now think of it even after a year
365 things that you will know
and after a while at this habit
maybe it's brilliance that you'll show.
Now before your mind starts boggling
learn this lesson on day one
you will never master love or life
and the impossible can't be done.

....

It Was Always a Story

I used to think it was a great idea
contained in stories of long ago

how kings and lords went out incognito
in order the populace to know.
Yes it all sounded good and romantic
and even saintly so to speak
but honestly if they tried it today
I don't think they would last a week.
Now our kings and lords are not any worse now
I have no doubt that some would die for glory
but they wouldn't live like ordinary folk
unfortunately that was just in a story.

....

A Different Person

I never asked to be born in the Highlands
I never got the chance of Maryhill
and if by chance it was London
it's likely I'd be living there still.
Now I don't know if this is all decreed
if I was in Park Lane I'd likely say 'Yes'
but would I be the same man I wonder
I think so, but that's just a guess.
And then the question, are you really you
accepting of course you're unique
but if you were abandoned in Cyprus at birth
right now you'd be a Turk or a Greek.

....

Values

Are 'Honour' and 'Virtue' just empty words
and 'Justice' the power of persuasion
can loyalty be bought for a price
and 'home' be any nation.
Is all our values a thing of the past
a winning post the ultimate prize
and when we get there, is it fair
we find all that we hate and despise.

....

Easy Learned

Some lessons we just can't learn in life
and others are learned instantaneous
there seems to be no criteria at all
just various and miscellaneous.
Now a lesson well learned is never forgot
and will be with you forever
just go somewhere you're not wanted
and you will never go back, no never.

....

234

Your Division

Being too sensitive is not a good thing you know
as they say 'you should take 'em on the chin'
but honestly you can get tired of losing
and watching all the other folk win.
Oh yes the rules are the same for all okay
so I'll only make only one supposition
if you are getting injured and hurt all the time
perhaps you're in the wrong division.

....

Who is Who

Oh look there's a doctor, here's a tailor
look over there, there's a sailor
and next to me a politician, great
all in the same churchyard
behind a closed gate.

....

Tins

I'm sorry I didn't learn physics at school
or even some algebra would do
but all I got was the basic stuff
you know, what's two and two.
Oh yes I regret the omission now
I didn't even get French or Latin
when the clever ones were getting the Iliad
in metalwork I got a tin to flatten.
So as time passes now I'm sorry
discontented, well more or less
I'm smart enough to know what I've missed
and what I'd like to possess.
But life has great compensations you know
and that's where some satisfaction begins
when other people are talking academic stuff
it's so obvious they don't know much about tins.

....

Mind Power

My calculator sits there silent
when it used to go 'clickity click'
the answerphone no longer blinks
my god it makes me sick.
My estimate book is empty
just like the balance in the bank
and all because I got a puncture
it's a spare wheel I've got to thank.
Yes, it's terrible feeling, self-pity
for this idleness there must be a knack

but there again, look at the statistics
it's the jobless that usually crack.
But mother nature's a friend at times
she'll alter your attitude and your thinking
she'll tell you that you're 'swimming well'
when all the time you are sinking.
Until one day, yes you realise
the seat of failure and success you find
happiness sadness and boredom
is all in your own little mind.

....

Revenge

Revenge is a frightening instinct
so I was thinking when we expire
all our friends are there to meet us
and likely kept a nice seat near the fire.
Now I want to join the reception committee
and I'd give a big welcome to you
and honestly, I know this is terrible
but I'm planning to ambush a few.

....

All The Same

Yes, I've told lies to save my skin
and no, I am not proud
I've said things I didn't believe
just to be one of the crowd.
I've studied my soul accordingly
as I'm sure all men do
and given the same circumstances
you would do most of it too.

....

How Do They Do It

I just received my parking sticker
it allows me to park on the street
this gets me closer to Marks & Sparks
god it would make you greet.
But really it is awful handy
especially now I'm older and wiser
but it's a pity they didn't add a clause
about the breathalyser.
I am joking, yes of course
a hard brickie once, but wiser now
and I know abstinence is right
Of course I do, but how.

....

No Justice

I know an alcoholic
who has a serious medical condition
many times he slept at the side of the road
and that's by his own admission.
Now all his life he was hard on himself
while I was as careful as could be
yet at seventy he is quite happy and chirpy
and looks half the age o' me.

....

Grown Up

Show me a boy when he is seven
and I'll show you the man
now this is a very ancient quote
and older than I am.
Yet show me this man in twenty years
whether brought up in a palace or gutter
and if he doesn't fancy Marilyn Monroe
then I will show you a nutter.

....

Old System

Could we get back to the days when we had a king
and he was in charge, and the boss
he was responsible for everything
the laws the profit and loss.
And if he didn't do it well, off with his head
it seems crazy but it worked not bad too
yes you may say that they had a chopping block
but the ones that used it you know, were few.

....

Doesn't Hurt You

There were many a poor labourer
who worked hard all their days
and for a treat they had on their piece
some cheese and mayonnaise.
They lived and died very modestly
still their children thrived and grew
and they weren't told about caviar
so their stomachs never knew.

....

Mirror Image

I got my photo done at a kiosk
but it was inferior because I looked fat

my hair looked thinner and greyer
and I know I don't look like that.
It's the mystery of electronics you know
my video camera is just the same
it sort of twists the sounds and image
and at the price it is a shame.
But what I can't understand about optics
it has a selective ability to con
because I'm the only one to look different
and everyone else is bang on.
....

Must Be

Where does the extra material come from
that's the stuff that makes you grow
does it come from water and food
to be honest I don't know.
But if by chance that is the source
and 'that' material goes to make you
you are made of the things that you eat
it's amazing but it must be true.
The mind boggles of course at the very thought
if you eat pork, you are a bit of a pig
and if you are a vegetarian
some bits of you are a cabbage and others bits a fig.
Oh yes but all this material is processed
all that happens is that it just changes shape
and I won't even consider the option
if our bodies make a serious mistake.
Then you eventually die and get buried
and on the earth's great compost heap you'll grace
it doesn't matter if you are burnt or blown up
there's nowhere else to go but outer space.
So the whole process is quite simple
you will be born again one day
mind you, I'm not sure if all of you will
but surely part of you anyway.
....

Ego

They say a man shows his true colours
that's when he's intoxicated
personally I'm not too sure of that theory
I think it's overrated.
The wife sometimes tells me the things that I've done
at some party, a dance or a Ball
a lecherous wine swilling sex maniac
and do you know, I'm not like that at all.
Where she gets her information from is a mystery
the conduct is that of a rat
Oh maybe that two sherries went to her head
because I don't remember behaving like that.
....

Too Much Imagination

Two policemen called on my neighbour
and I immediately thought he got caught
well, I never got to know him very well
because a man's a mystery, 'til he takes the shot.
Now I know some people are capable of anything
so it might be drugs or even prostitution
or maybe they've come to take his bairns away
and put them into some institution.
Drunk driving was out because he doesn't drink
mind you, it could be theft
I ruled out murder right away
but do you know there's not a lot left.
Then I twigged, it must be rape
and him over sixty, the dirty rat
when I think of his poor gentle wife
I couldn't get over that.
Well, to be truthful I was disgusted
but it shows how wrong you can be
because he didn't do anything bad after all
the Bobbies were just looking for me.
....

The Honest Truth

I'm so glad 'Bonny baby' competitions are near stopped
I think it only led to corruption and lies
this is a fact I know first hand
because I entered mine and didn't get a prize.
....

Born Lucky

Some people are born with a silver spoon
when others arrive, they're a pest
a few inherit some talents
but being born 'lucky' that is the best.
Good looks will fade, money gets spent
ignored abilities will return, no never
loser or winner you stay a beginner
for even luck won't last forever.
....

A Good Tax Man

As you know I've had a nightmare with the tax
I also had trouble with the rates
and it was a Mr Smith that was pursuing me
not only me but some of my mates.
Well we all got together one evening
and decided this democratic system must go
what we were going to put in it's place

well to be honest we didn't know.
Anyway we held public meetings every night
convinced the populace that they must vote
we took particular notice of dissenters
and of names and addresses took note.
This went on for quite a few years
our throats got red raw from speaking
but fewer and fewer people turned up
to our public meeting.
Now we weren't exactly pleased with this
but funnily enough gave us inspiration
the obvious choice is a revolution
to get rid of the oppressive administration.
So yes, we recruited enough fanatics
our motto 'For justice we fight'
and we met in secret back rooms
nearly every second night.
Now after more years of trouble and strife
and maybe pain and death for a few
we sang glorious hymns of battle
and any other songs we knew.
Eventually yes we succeeded in the end
organised a government as revolutionaries should
and when it came to choosing a tax man
we all thought Mr Smith was pretty good.

....

Smile

I was told the Russians don't smile like us
they only smile when they're happy, or win
while the British can lose or be miserable
and what do we do? We grin.
Some of us smile at the least provocation
(except when maybe driving a car)
and to expect a kind look from a driver
that would be taking things too far.
But generally speaking we're a smiling bunch
and we can hide anger and pain beneath
because it only seems a natural thing to do
when you're happy or angry to bare your teeth.

....

All Change

One kind of man that's rarely respected
in fact they're reminiscent of a Jackal
they don't get into the game at all
but run with the team and won't tackle.
And yet again should we criticise them
it's easy for a lion to be brave
and if we got the chance to change
I wonder how we would behave.

....

Mam

Some say that a man's last word is 'Mama'
but up in the North here, we just say 'Mam'
or it's shouted when in the greatest distress
when nobody else cares a damn.
Now this is all very sentimental isn't it
and a lot of crap if there is no proof
but I happen to know a man
and he told me that it's the truth.

....

Culture

I was reading about a woman's problems today
her husband at times dressed in ladies clothes
and this disgusted and upset her
seeing her man wear pretty pink bows.
Now why was she so upset I wondered
it was all done inside the house
he didn't annoy or offend the neighbours
or make them jealous of his new blouse.
So where is the wickedness or moral decline
at its worst it's just a wee bit of deceit
if he were a dancer in Greece he'd wear a 'Tutu'
and woolly pom-poms on his big feet.
The problem then must be our culture
what we are brought up to expect
a conditioned response creates our outlook
and our attitude I suspect.
So as time marches on we all have to change
yes, tolerance is an advancement
kindness and understanding will come one day
and to our culture, true enhancement.

....

The Greatest Sin

Some prostitutes were on the tele this morning
and they were getting a bit of a slagging
but good old Kilroy kept control
or there would be a lot of finger wagging.
Now as you know I'm not 'streetwise'
maybe only smart enough not to get caught
but if that's all the crime that these women do
you know, that's not a lot.
Yes you are right, morals are important
virtue and trust keeps families intact
but the oldest profession is here to stay
and that is just a fact.
You see we got our priorities wrong
when we see other peoples faults we make a din
but to make another human beings life miserable
now isn't that a greater sin.

....

Common Belief

I was in a bit of a quandary today
so I said 'Yes, I'll ask the cards'
not that I wanted unfair advantage you know
well maybe just a couple of yards.
Shaking with excitement I found their hiding place
(I don't tell the wife in case I get a row)
because she's a sort of Christian like the minister
but if they only could see me now.
I hunched over the table and put out the light
and concentrated on what the future may bring
but I made a mistake in putting out the light
because I now couldn't see a thing.
So enough of the ascetic trappings
I put on the light and shuffled the deck
but my mind wandered to Saturday night
and who's marriage I might wreck.
But anyway back to the business
so I dealt out a five card spread
picked up a hand and looked at the pictures
it was of a wee manie looking half dead.
The next card didn't look any better
so I threw that hand in the pack
swore three times some really bad words
you don't have to, but I did for the crack.
The next three hands honestly, were useless
but the fifth, now I'm not deceived
it told me such a wonderful future
now guess which hand I believed.

....

Yes We Are Right

I see they are going to try more war criminals now
do you think that we should forget and forgive
or perhaps you take the opposite view
that some people don't deserve to live.
Now if you think that it's not Christian you know
because Christians shouldn't kill and fight
though some people preach and philosophize
I still think it's the two of us that are right.

....

Spoiled

I was reading in the paper today
about a man from Inverness
he dived in the river to help a dog
and he saved the pooch's life more or less.
Now really I was so proud of the Invernesions
I thought 'Hero's one and all'
but if it was a local who threw the dog in
Just to fetch a tennis ball.

....

In Proportion

I got things out of proportion again
mainly due to a recent disaster
I would have screamed more abuse at the post
but my jaws wouldn't work any faster.
Off she went scurrying down the road
I'm sure she thought that I cracked up
but why does she keep giving me all these bills
when she knows I'm down on my luck.
When I don't even get asked to a dance now
and me and the wife went to all of the Balls
most of my friends have deserted me too
and not even a Jehovah Witness calls.
Also that damn mechanic put my car out of tune
he said it was the new machine they invented
but I'll need to take another look at him
because I'm pretty sure he meant it.
And did you hear the weather forecaster last night
lying through his teeth and telling stories
high depression, low depression
it's not, it's the bloody Tories.
Well the wife came in and cheered me up
and she made tea and toasted bread
told me about the aerobatics class
and what the other women said.
Then off she waddled the floor boards creaking
and left me happier by far
at twenty stone she looks like a fairy princess
you know sometimes I see things as they really are.

....

Well Trained

Isn't it strange in the animal kingdom
how a dog is so easy to train
yet, you'll never teach a cat to beg
though their intelligence is much the same.
The lion, tiger and panther
even the mighty elephant and bear
all can learn special tricks
if they are taught with cunning and care.
yet there are some things impossible to learn
they have limitations and that is true
but if you train a man the proper way
there is not anything that he will not do.

....

Survival Instinct

Have you noticed when you're under pressure
your angle of vision somehow decreases
the whole vista is fragmented
all you see is little pieces.
The pumping rate speeds up in the heart
and the heat in your chest could boil it

all your muscles are tense and taught
then suddenly you need the toilet.
Now this is what they call the 'critical' time
yet not at all dangerous to health
right enough, you might get a heart attack
but you're more likely to wet yourself.
Now this is just nature's way of telling you
and nothing to do with running or lifting weights
she is just informing you that the time has come
to start bleating and blaming your mates.
....

Ramblings 5

The Perfect Friend

I quite fancy a new computer
you know now they can even speak
but they are a wee bit expensive
and the cheaper ones give you cheek.
I can imagine the witty conversation
about religion, politics and life
something that won't hog the limelight
and is better crack than the wife.
Now I'm not suggesting a marriage of course
companionship is what I mean
that notion is ridiculous anyway
unless the computer is very keen.
Just a kind voice to boost your ego at times
a sort of dependable faithful friend
something that really would blow a fuse about you
and not merely just pretend.
Yes it would be a relief to get home late at night
when the last thing you need is a grilling
all you want to do is play country and western songs
and there's the computer, able and willing.
This must be the nearest thing to perfection
life would become a big dawdle
and if you get fed up with the voice
you could change it for a new model.
Of course the added advantage is enormous
if it gets nasty and calls you a bug
no need to retaliate or fight back at all
you just kick it and pull out the plug.

....

Twins

Women and whisky are the same at times
and this is perfectly true
the more you love either of them
the more they'll make a fool of you.

....

Are You Poor

The poor are always with us we're told
I can't mind if it mentioned the rich
but we are so bamboozled with metaphysics
it's difficult to tell which is which.
Is the poor still penniless now I wonder?
Or is it all matter of degree
just ask a poor man that basic question
and he'll tell a different story than me.
Even the connotations of the word is fearful
in fact 'poor' just sounds 'poor'
but there is no need to get into that
for about semantics I'm not too sure.

Anyway the point we're addressing
you can call it by a fancy name
but if you haven't got a pound, you're broke
and the circumstances are just the same.
Call it pride or brainwashing
or a disease without a cure
but if a man can only see himself by comparison
then he will always be poor.

....

Weigh The Odds

There is Bingo and there's Lotteries
competitions and football pools
and some of the clergy will tell us
that we are a lot of fools.
It's the poor who will buy the tickets they say
that's me, but am I a dope
I know the odds like anyone else
but what's wrong with a bit of hope.
Yet they will persist with their patronising
and tell us we just can't see
but I understand the chances of miracles
and they will be waiting longer than me.

....

Excuses

I was never a captain of industry
well, I never got the chance
never was good at athletics
because I hadn't the vest or the pants.
Never played football for Rangers
the scouts up here must be blind
but my mother says I could have done it
and she said 'Oh, never mind'.
If my teachers were better
I might have been a professor
even a doctor and discover some cures
but that is all excuses I suppose
now tell me a few of yours.

....

Patience

Patience is a virtue we're told
does it mean just to sit and wait
don't fight the forces against you
and leave it all up to fate.
Yes time will change things all right
there is no doubt that is true
but time has no meaning for nature
and the change could be too late for you.
So what is the answer, wait the rest of your life?
rely on 'hope' to understand

no it's not, keep on trying
and give nature a helping hand.
....

Another Lost Dog

There was a local farmer long ago
in these days he was termed a 'toff'
his friends were the professional fraternity
including the men of the cloth.
One summers day along the dusty road
a lost collie dog waddled
the farmer stood in the courtyard
his horse already saddled.
Now this is something I'll never understand
though plenty theories I've heard and read
for the farmer whistled the dog to the courtyard
and he shot the collie dog dead.
....

The Future

Live for the present have no thought for the 'morrow
now that's a statement to comprehend
forget the past, it did not last
and if you don't know, pretend.
Yes modern thought is in the 'now'
and the same outlook as the ape
if we don't understand why the future is important
then we can all sit and scratch and gape.
....

Need

Your desire to eat can be satisfied
and thirst can be quenched by drink
most needs are met automatically
you don't even have to think.
Yet for some instincts there is no satisfaction
for money and power you can plead
and you will never get your fill
achieve, and greater is the need.
....

More To The Eye

Humans can only see part of the spectrum
that is the stuff we call light
for instance we see a lot through the day
but hardly a thing when it's night.
Now mostly we stay with our abilities
to our eyes comprehension we belong
but do you ever think of the bits we do not see
and wonder what else is going on.
....

Games

I never liked the game of Monopoly
though I played it when I was wee
money for this money for that
there was nothing or little for free.
Snakes and ladders was my favourite
with all the ups and downs
oh yes I remember the emotions
the smiles and all the frowns.
Now I'm grown up I go to the casino
and I've won more than once or twice
you see when you were all playing Monopoly
I was practising 'dice'.
....

New Theories

Why do scientists ridicule new theories
and generally tear them to shreds
is it because their brains are full
and there is no more room in their heads.
You would think they would gather together
and forget about being aloof
'Now chaps we have another new theory
let's see if we can find some proof'.
But no, unfortunately they don't
except maybe for a few
but surely there must be different ideas
or we'll never get anything new.
....

A Good Instinct

I was reading about paedophiles today
twenty adults, from a labourer to a toff
and when I look back over the years
you know, most of them got off.
Now I'm not so cynical as to believe
that the judges are part of that crew
though statistically and percentage wise
it's logical to say they're a few.
But what emotion boils up in us
a Christian view or is it innate
oh yes there might be confusion
but at times it's all right to hate.
....

False Confidence

Do you ever think if you hit a disaster
that you will still come out all right
your resources and determination excel
so you never know, you might.
Your natural intelligence would overcome

complete confidence in abilities too
but I tell you that you really don't know
until a disaster happens to you.

....

Pressure

I got a letter from the financial director
and then another from the tax inspector
they're not a lot left for Hannibal Lecter
it's no wonder my friend is the amber nectar.

....

Evolution

You have yours and I have mine
do you know that's evolution upside down
there were billions of years of sharing
but not in the modern town.
Interdependency is all but forgot
yet it's essential if we are to survive
in a year or two we could outdo
the ability to stay alive.
'No man is an island' a man once said
but sadly the test will be time
and you and I will never know
if you have yours and I have mine.

....

Greed

Do you see the wages we pay our leaders now
you would think that they were needy
when we want to employ capable people
we don't get them but the greedy.

....

Bullies

Violence begets violence they say
well I'm not sure that is true
mother nature is the best teacher I think
what do you feel, if someone hits you?
Yes nature tells you to hit them back
yet the modern way is 'no don't'
but if a bully gets a thrashing they'll stop
most will, and only a few that won't.

....

Day Dreaming

Imagination is a wonderful thing
(that's a little function of the brain)
one minute you could be Tarzan

and the next second be John Wayne.
A fighter pilot, yes even a tramp
your repertoire has no end
all you have to do is sit and relax
and then you just pretend.
Now some say 'stop this childishness'
it's all a pie in the sky
but to do that I don't know how
and I also don't see why.

....

Tens Again

I stuck on my Tens machine again
relaxed and had a dream
for a wee bit of sensual pleasure
you can't whack a Tens machine.
Now I'm not saying it's anything like sex
maybe like reading the latest love letter
it's really all in the mind you see
not physical at all but better.
How it works is quite simple really
the electronics is not so mooted
it is just the way the brain operates
you can't think when you're electrocuted.
Yes modern technology is a wonderful thing
when it can even out fox your mind
eventually it will dictate our lives
so it's a good job a two volt battery is blind.

....

Cracked It

When it comes to the subject of evolution
we all assume that humans are the top of the tree
I think so too and so do you
and only a nutter would disagree.
Yet when I contemplate Gorillas
their society and their pack
I think that they were human once
but decided all to go back.
Now that is really not so amazing
just correlate space and time
is your ambition a concrete jungle
when the original one is just fine.
Yes, I say the Gorillas have cracked it
the horse now comes before the cart
for they are living happy lives
and that's what I call 'smart'.

....

Fashion Designer

I sometimes thank God that I was a brickie
and not a fashion designer
it would be better to be a joiner

or even to be a miner.
It wouldn't stretch my capabilities you see
there is no challenge in drawing ties and hankies
and it doesn't take a lot of imagination
to design a pair of panties.
But there again you never can tell
there is more to life than laying bricks
so I'm sure there's more to fashion
and more to a pair of 'nicks'.

....

Teddy Bear

I had a teddy bear when I was young
and more than likely you had one too
admittedly mine wasn't a natural colour
to tell the truth it was navy blue.
Anyway a long time has passed since then
and when you are young you do not see
but how was I supposed to know
that my teddy's now worth more than me.

....

Be Prepared

I was told to prepare for disappointment
yet be ready to grasp success
the joy of winning stays the same
but the pain of a loss is less.
These are words of wisdom alright
two contingency plans out of a host
and this is true except for a few
but which plan will we use the most.

....

Hand in Pocket

I put on my Tens machine again
that's a contraption that gives you shocks
I tell you now what a belt you can get
it's a good job I haven't the pox.
There are two wee knobs for adjustment
for a pulse or quick vibration
and after a while you master it
it can be quite a pleasant sensation.
So now if you see a man smiling
and on the street that's rarely seen
don't be alarmed or think the worst
he's only adjusting his Tens machine.

....

Easy Way Out

A final demand for council tax
from the director of finance

he's thinking I'll pay in seven days
well I tell you he has no chance.
You haven't to take it too personally
I thought that as I shuffled the deck
boiled up the cauldron with a little soap
so he would slip and break his neck.
Oh the things I thought to do
from a 'hitman' to the Mafia
in no time at all he would be reduced
to making stools with raffia.
Eventually of course common sense prevailed
and out came the book of cheques
yes I knew it would bounce like a kangaroo
but it was easier than breaking necks.

....

Being Smart

A builder needs a bit of geometry you know
when he's sussing out a plan
(mind you, to be honest some are thick)
but they do the best that they can.
Basically it's all simple arithmetic
though it's handy if you know square roots
oh yes there's more to building
than jeans and wellie boots.
Pythagoras theory is used a lot
now I'll bet you are surprised
if two sides of a triangle are three and four
the diagonal it comes to five.
Yes the builder has to be smart at times
to avoid ridicule and disgrace
for there is nothing more embarrassing
than to put the building in the wrong place.
Yet should such a dastardly thing happen
this is where true intelligence comes in
the architect might say it's the builders fault
but the builder will blame it on him.

....

Programmed

Do you wonder why you hate snakes and rats
and are so emotional about your dislikes
you might think cars are great
but detest the motorbikes.
It really is quite sinister you know
and it's unfortunate for the snake and rat
but when you were a little boy or girl
you were just told to think like that.

....

No Smoking

I thought I'd take a cigar today
and that's what I went and did

you see there is no smoking later on
when they screw down the lid.
....

Paradise Lost

When the white man discovered Fiji
and saw the first girl in a grass skirt
all the men were laughing and singing
and no such thing as hard work.
Surely this must have been a paradise
sunbathing and fishing off the reef
no fighting, gurning or nagging
it all sounds beyond belief.
No taxes, no losses, no gaffers no bosses
there is not anything you could lack
but the great mystery still remains
why did the first ship ever come back.

....

Getting Your Own Back

Some people criticise the builders work
is that level? and is it plumb?
look at the state of his jeans
he's showing half his bum.
Not more tea! not again!
and through the hoarding everyone's peeping
then they saunter off to their office
and wonder why it is leaking.

....

The Worker

I knew a man who worked for the council
and every day it was a pretext
he just wandered about the building
wondering what to do next.
The office looked a hive of activity
and maybe that was just as well
because he never knew what to do
and he didn't like to tell.
Years went by in mental torment
and it really was a shame
yet nobody ever told him the truth
that the whole department was doing the same.

....

The Big Team

Do you think it's just in the cities
that there is love hate and intrigue
and the sleepy little village

is in a lesser league.
You may say it's a smaller circle all right
and I know exactly what you mean
but consider the amount of people you know
you'll see the village has a bigger team.

....

Another Clan

I think we head for self-destruction now
by the way we have evolved
when you would think we have learned
and most of our problems solved.
But instead of being a community
each person being interdependent
a few grab most of the profits
then they go off and spend it.
Riches just breeds a separate clan
their motto 'We don't need you'
but tell me, when you think of it
who is it that needs who.

....

Knowing

Old men and women really are valuable
they have proved that they can survive
went through some bad experiences
and still they are alive.
Action taking, decision making
all aspects of living and growing
young folk want the initiative
but there is a difference
between thinking and knowing.

....

Ability

I'm all for poaching labour
that is luring a worker away
it is against the law of course
but it goes on every day.
You see it makes for efficiency
no employer needs to shout
see how a junior football team plays
when there is a rumour about a scout.

....

The Builders

Young King Tut is famous now
so is Christopher Wren
the Taj Mahal is a wonder of the world
and the China wall is one of them.

Yet when you see some beautiful work
we give credit, and I agree
but do you ever think of the brickie
for it is his work that you see.

....

Talent

I tried to develop a singing voice
but to be honest it wasn't quite there
everybody has a talent they say
that might be true, but where?
All the common skills were tried
at arts and crafts I had a go
even magical tricks for a while
and after that I still didn't know.
I attempted climbing mountains
racing a car and a motorbike
tried physical contortions
now, that's something I didn't like.
But still I persevered for years
diving, sailing and flying
and then the penny dropped
I had the talent for trying.

....

Dave The Fishman

I don't feel up to the mark today
no doubt the culprit is Whyte & Mackay
so I will find out if they changed the blend
and if they did I want to know why.
Another explanation could be seafoods
last night the wife made a big dish
maybe that prawns were past their best
to be sure I'll ask Dave the Fish.
Well to be honest there's nothing else
but right enough I had a feast
and apart from the eating and drinking
I'm living the life of a priest.

....

The Worst

Jealousy is the worst of sins
yet some say it's sloth or hate
others say it's fornication
or being disloyal to your mate.
Now we all know no sins are nice
why did Samson move the pillar?
He just showed which was the worst
every one of them is a killer.

....

Be Fair

Fair play is an enigma
does it come from within or out
an inbred virtue you might say
and the way it's learned there is a doubt.
But have you really studied the game
maybe you did and never knew
it's not a matter of what you do to others
it's knowing what they'll do to you.

....

The Novel

I tried to write a novel once
but I just didn't have the knack
you never read so much rubbish in your life
in fact it was a heap of crap.
When I think of all the paper I wasted
and all the time I spent
I should be counting my fortune now
but that's not the way it went.
My imagination ran riot you see
in fact it went through the roof
my heroine a drink crazed nymphomaniac
instead of being a bit aloof.
The whole plot was so ordinary
the dialogue colloquial and crude
I didn't even put in a killing
when in a 'murder' you really should.
Yes the whole thing was a shambles
and now it is just a pest
because I was happier thinking I could do it
the illusion is always the best.

....

Who's Crafty

It's very strange the older you get
you think a lot more about dying
but nature puts in a counterbalance
about your age you will start lying.
You take more time to tart yourself up
there is regret about receding hair
a bulging belly is noticed now
that never used to be there.
Memory too is not as it was
that's nature again being kind
you even forget to be embarrassed
when a name you cannot mind.
Yes nature can be a friend at times
and she'll do a lot for you
but it's all her fault at the start anyway
so who is outfoxing who?

....

A Dream

I dreamed last night that I was fishing
in the morning straight to the book of dreams
not that I'm superstitious or anything
I just like finding out what it means.
First of all into the new book
but the interpretation didn't seem right
so out came the trusty old volume
to see if it could throw some light.
Down the index I looked for 'fishing'
and there it was under 'fish'.
I didn't pray for an explanation as such
it was probably more of a wish.
So enough of the occult I read what it said
I was after salmon not haddock or cod
but why are dreams so complicated
you see I was fishing but had no rod.

....

Next

I must go and visit my old auntie now
she is thinking her time is soon
so I better go in the morning
and not leave it to the afternoon.
But after I thought for a little while
though some illnesses have no cure
nobody knows what's going to happen next
and that is one of the few things that is sure.

....

The Adult

Women are smarter than men you know
have you noticed that in life
maybe you've paid no attention
so go and ask your wife.
'Yes' she will say 'That is true'
and we are honest with each other
for if I look after her
she will treat me like a mother.
Now I'm not saying that men are thick
nothing at all like that
as long as you know that you are the kitten
and she is the grown up cat.

....

Small Depression

I have reached the end now
'mind you, I say that every week
I go a wee bit over the top

and maybe neurotic so to speak.
But I will make a comeback
I don't know when or how
if only it was today
and I could do it now.
But no such luck, life's not like that
to dictate is not your lot
all you have to do
is do the best with the part you got.

....

Safety

I've mediocred all my life
never rose too high to fall
never helped a soul in distress
in fact I did F all.
And now my empty life is over
my epitaph should read
'This man lived his life for safety
only now he can't see the need'.

....

The Nurds

Do you remember when we were at school
there were always the controlling few
wee upstarts (usually with glasses)
trying to tell you what to do.
'You must join the scripture union
get your uniform washed and pressed
buy some kit for athletics
spikes, pants and vest'
(It's no wonder I get depressed)
then at last you leave the school
and thank God you've left them behind
but if you ever thought that
you'd be out of your tiny mind.
No, they are always with you
and I often wonder why
because the little bastards are still there
yes until you die.

....

The Volunteer Who Doesn't Know

Well I volunteered to help
which was a wee bit of an enigma
after all the things I've done
'mind you, I survived the stigma.
Of course it's drink I'm talking about
the degradation and damage to health
and half of the things I have said and done
I don't even remember myself.

Of course I'm prepared for rejection
that's normal for most men
for the times we hear the affirmative
is only now and again.
But I will offer anyway
it's up to them to hear my trumpet
they can take me or leave me
or else they can like it or lump it.
The thing we have to remember
there are no such thing as human gods
half the world is hurting
and the other half a heap of sods.
The thing to do of course
so you won't expire with a little sigh
is not to fear rejection
but give the virtues a damn good try.
Don't even think of fame and fortune
drink and death will level all
climb the ladder with confidence
and try again if ever you fall.
Just remember the important part
and now you know you cannot moan
it's awful nice to be popular
but when you die you're on your own.
Now what happens after that
to be honest I haven't a clue
but it's the only sure thing in life
that it's going to happen to you.
....

I Understand

I never fell I never had toothache
that's pains I never knew
but yesterday I tripped and broke a tooth
so now I empathise with you.
....

The Fight

I wrestled for my life more than once
and I wrestled with al-co-hol
did I have a convincing win?
no I didn't, no not at all.
So now I fight that monster every day
and it's not a battle to choose
it's a kind of 'toe to toe' job
some days I win and others I lose.
But I will keep on fighting
so if you see me stagger on the street
don't think I didn't fight that day
it's just one of the days I got beat.
....

Playing At It

I was having a crack with a man one day
as usual it was, life, women, and drink
it probably wasn't in that order
but more or less I think.
Well he was a chap who had seen the lot
had experienced the highs and the lows
and when I met him he was 'down'
he just shrugged 'That's the way it goes'.
Now I'm not encouraging recklessness
but I paid notice to the advice he was giving
'You know' he said 'Half the folk in the town
they are just playing at living'.

....

Ignored

I met a chap who slighted me once
and that must have been ten years ago
why I didn't forget in all that time
is something I'll never know.
Of course I knew him quite well
but we never exactly met for a chat
in fact I pretended I didn't know him once
now I can hardly believe I did that.

....

A Dreamer

I'm sorry that I was born a dreamer
if only I could see things as they are
I am sure that I would be happier
contented, and better off by far.
But fate and time they did guide me
and alone now I sit with my dreams
trying to make sense out of a nightmare
where chaos reigns and nothing is as it seems.
If only I could turn the clock back
another road I would surely take
but then I might lose my soul completely
another road could be one more big mistake.
Yes I know I fight a losing battle
a dreamers life rarely comes to ought
yet it's not a question of power or glory
for in the end it's 'you' is all you've got.

....

The Boss

The greatest lesson I've ever learned
is that your life belongs to you
it doesn't belong to king or country

although that's important too.
Governments install the chain of command
and if you let them, they will control
bosses, unions and bureaucrats
will steal your very soul.
Just remember who is the boss
and this is a fact that's true
yes, fill all your obligations all right
but you are the boss of you.
'Freedom' is not just a word you see
it's a feeling that comes from within
fear no authority or any man
do it now and just begin.
Cross to the right, move to the left
don't walk if you want to run
no need to bend the knee at all
remember it's your life, and you only get one.

....

Getting Along

I must write out a treaty with my neighbour
but these agreements are all so boring
but if he can keep his dog from barking
I'll keep my wife from snoring.
He can burn his rubbish on Saturdays
I'll do mine on the Sundays
and that will leave the women free
to hang out the washing on Mondays.
Now for the television and wireless
no decibels over eight
mind you, I've only got an old gramophone
so that will suit me great.
Cleaning the car will be optional I think
for none of us will get a splatter
because he lives nearly a mile from me
so that's one thing that will not matter.

....

Tripped

Why had I to stoop so low
before I could eventually rise
grandeur was just an illusion
which crumbled before my eyes.
Yet now I see the world clearer
and it's a different world to mine
when riches can be found in the gutter
then pure water is turned into wine.
Maybe you don't have to fall by the roadside
to feel degradation and pain
look in the mirror and see a strange face
and to be called by a different name.
Yes, it would be great to be perfect
but experience teaches us all

so learn the lessons of today
for tomorrow it's you who could fall.
....

Natural

Our whole country is going money mad
and there is no such thing as 'maybe'
one of the few natural things left
is to watch a lassie with her new baby.
....

Understanding

A friend was at the railway station
where else, but Inverness
it was a cold dreech winters night
and it was snowing more or less.
Well this woman came over to him
and do you know she was shaking like a leaf
now believe me he knew the symptoms
she was suffering beyond belief.
To the uninitiated it wasn't the cold
neither was it the clothes that she wore
by now I'm sure the penny dropped
so I won't elaborate more.
Now my friend listened to her plea
of fifty pence or a pound
how a cigarette would be heaven
he listened without a sound.
Now what do you think my friend did
did he moralise and show her the right way
or did he give in to her request
or turned his back on her that day.
Well, this is what he told me
but of course I have no proof
yet I know this man very well
so I know he spoke the truth.
'Yes' he said 'When I saw her
I didn't see a drunk at all
I just saw some mothers lassie
playing with a bat and a ball.
And yes, I gave her cigarettes and money
and didn't ask why, where, or how
you see that lassie was hurting
and the help she needed was, now'.
....

The Right Theory

I have never met many good people
sometimes I wonder if it is me that is blind
somehow I took it for granted
that very few were kind.

And now I've landed on my arse you could say
at last I see the light
my theory in the beginning was perfect
I was always bloody right.
....

True Ability

To have ability is a comforting thought
it keeps your ego nice and erect
gives you confidence in times of need
but can lead to cockiness I suspect.
Yet still, ability is a wonderful thing
it's human endeavour at it's best
it's called potential before the exam
and 'true ability' after the test.
....

Never Too Late

I see the sense of life now
just a little bit late
I used to enjoy a wee shot of sin
in fact I thought it was great.
And now when I'm getting past my best
just in time I see the trick
and when I think of all the years
I was a proper dick.
But I was told it was never too late
who know when I'll expire
why it might be fifty years
before I will retire.
So now is the beginning
a better man I'll try and be
because you know, honestly
I was never happy being me.
....

Who Knows

They are fighting again about religion
you know, it must make God sick
putting us intelligent people here
and we evolved to be so thick.
I'm sure at times it must cross his mind
to get rid of the whole bally crew
and start again right from scratch
with something entirely new.
There's folk about who never worked
'mind you a gorilla is just the same
but they're a bit too much like us
only called by a different name.
No, God will need to think of a different species
with no aggression and devoid of greed
but you know, I can't think of any
so we'll likely have to grow them from seed.

Perhaps a cross between a chimp and a tattie
but the tattie would introduce blight
the chimp would be far too lazy
no, that won't work, though it might.
Of course there are the Whales
and the fish as well
but if they were building houses
think of the smell.
No, this is not going to be easy
monkeys, tatties or a cod
so I'll throw in the towel now
and leave it all to God.
....

Irresistible

A friend of mine diddled me once
so you may ask why call him a friend
well, we were quite fond of each other
so honestly I don't pretend.
Of course I was a wee bit hurt at the time
and like snow our friendship melted
but do you know the more I ponder
I don't think he could help it.
....

The Reception Committee

Do you ever think we are a wee bit like dogs
and some of us are a different breed
I know it sounds ridiculous
and to compare there is no need.
Am I smarter than you or maybe I'm thick
you know all this distinction, just makes me sick
why kill a man when he could be your brother
and all because, he's a different colour.
Or maybe he belongs to a different tribe or clan
so get a grip, he's another man.
But this killing will never cease
it's all a dream this prayers for peace.
And we may bend the knee to priest or Pope
but in the end, all is, 'hope'.
Kill for the good or some other excuse
you've got to have a reason or it's no use
but man is so resilient he'll find a way
and the killing will go on, for another day.
Yet at your life's end when up comes your number
who will meet you at the end of the tunnel
you know sometimes I wonder.
....

Moulded

One kind of film that's rarely seen
is one where the robbers get clean away
but the pictures are not true to life

it happens every day.
The reason behind this is obvious of course
psychologically it is nothing new
someone in power is frightened you'll try it
you won't but there will be a few.
Oh yes, it's all so cleverly done
simple people believe what they're told
but isn't it a wee bit sinister
when an attitude can be made in a mould.

....

Making Sure

Pain is all in the mind they say
(that's the big computer in your head)
it tells you the place where something is wrong
and sometimes even turns it red.
Oh yes it's a clever system all right
but it's like a wife with her finger wagging
surely one telling is quite enough
so why do they keep on nagging.

....

The Real Reason

I'm glad our attitudes to virginity have changed
when you think of it, it was beyond belief
a lassie who did something so natural
was branded far more than a thief.
So why was virginity so prized by men
is it about virtue and honour they care
no it's not, most are just bad lovers
and a virgin cannot compare.

....

At The End of The Battle

To be a soldier must be terrifying at times
especially in days long ago
that's when we were cutting lumps off each other
and were standing toe to toe.
Most of us could probably shoot a man
and dropping a bomb would be easier still
but hacking at a man until he is dead
that's not a civilised way to kill.
Yes we have ways more acceptable now
the music of machine gun chatter
but when the battle is over, you're dead
so in the end, does it really matter.

....

Spoiled

The managing director was screaming
'I want a new computer and fax

also another accountant
to sort out the company tax'.
Shaky hands noted it all down
and an order was sent that day
but why is it always the spoiled child
who always gets his own way.

....

No Reason

Give me some blondes a Porsche and a boat
and I will be contented
Oh yes you better add on a house as well
one that isn't rented.
Guaranteed holidays twice a year
a portfolio of stocks and bonds
and if you think that's too greedy
you can stroke of one of the blondes.
Now when all this is delivered to me
I will be delighted there is no doubt
but why is our milkman always whistling
when he has nothing to be happy about.

....

A Turn On

We're all fairly educated now
when we can read about explicit sex
and us thinking it was a bit extreme
to sook each other's necks.
But now they're into whips and things
and to me that is a farce
for any man that got whipped by a woman
would surely boot her little arse.
But no, some men seem to like it
they even get tied up in chains
and to think that Draughts and Ludo
that is what we used to call 'games'.
Anyway they can do what they like
all that stuff is a joke
I'll just go and buy a new diving board
because the last one went and broke.

....

Kept Back

Don't ever fall in love at all
and a lot of heartache you will miss
don't try anything and you can't fail
and that feeling could be bliss.
But in the end when you get your report card
there will be no marks, but do not cry
you'll get to repeat the whole thing again
because you didn't even try.

....

Learning

We can learn a lot from dogs you know
I did when I cut my dogs claws
'nails' would probably be a better word
anyway they're at the end of her paws.
Now she is quite a monstrous bitch
and could give a terrible bite
so the lesson I learned from my Great Dane
is that 'bribery' works all right.
....

Another Mystery

We've made billions out of our empire
and now more billions out of our oil
a fortune was had by our pirate ships
and the captain took home the spoil.
Now I know that high finance is beyond me
but I understand the meaning of 'spent'
if someone would only explain to me
because I still wonder where it all went.
....

Lucky

I checked the lottery ticket
well I could hardly believe my eyes
six wee numbers just like the tele
which means I'd won first prize.
Now you can imagine the excitement
as we went into planning mode
holidays, houses and swimming pools
and a Ferrarri on the road.
Yes, the choice seemed quite endless
there is pleasure in spend, spend, spend
but what happened later that night
I can hardly comprehend.
My house went on fire and burnt to the ground
Lady luck only sometimes plays cricket
and I got burnt to death all right
but I was so lucky to save the ticket.
....

Not Today

Some people think they are extra special
like good old King Canute
many times I heard the story
and I still think it's pretty cute.
Inflated ego, or a bit slack in the head
out of touch with reality you might say
but we have all come so far since then
for no people are like that today.
....

Reality?

Down the road of fantasy I often walk
I feel love, hate and despair
but when it's painful it's back to reality
and leave all that feelings there.
If only we could do that with life
switch off when we get too hot
but if that happened in the real world
It is 'fantasy' is that you've got.

....

Do Your Best

I gave my dog a bone today
a wee treat after lunch
and she was delighted
and was as pleased as punch.
She spun in circles, wagged her tail
but did she say 'Oh thank you'
no she didn't but I got the message
she did the best that she could do.

....

Easy Way Out Again

I received a phone call from a company
who would help me with my cash flow
I had never heard of them before
and their name I did not know.
Well my mind went into 'remember' mode
'Now who owes money to me'
though I might be a freemason
I don't do building for free.
So I pondered yes, for at least an hour
and I admit there were a few
now don't get me wrong there weren't a lot
there were only one or two.
Anyway I decided to let them all off Scott free
benevolently look over my estate and castle
(that's not true really)
I just couldn't stand the hassle.

....

Nosey

Why is the future so fascinating
much more than the present or past
have we really mastered all of today
and our brains are working so fast.
Maybe it's curiosity just like the cat
and we all know what happened to it
or perhaps we are all a little nosey
well, we all are, a bit.

....

Cracking Point

They threatened him with violence
tried bribery with cash
beautiful bikini clad women next
some with stockings and lash.
Yet, no, our hero still didn't crack
and I tell you it wasn't nice
but when the Eastgate Centre was mentioned
he broke down, well, everyone has his price.

....

Is There Anybody There

Have you ever met anyone who was so impersonal
you wonder if there were anything behind the eyes
it's not that they are saying stupid things
or even telling stories or lies.
It could be termed a 'vacant' look I suppose
if it were intolerance that would show
the only way I can describe it
is 'They just don't want to know'.

....

The Origin

Why is human life so short for some
yet, for a few it's far too long
some get rewarded for doing no right
others punished for doing no wrong.
Yet inspiration comes to everyone
no body stops you and says 'No don't'
if the neurons' not there you will not care
you might say you will but you won't.
Now this might be a picture of chaos
or is it the pattern that is too large
but if recipes and formulas do exist
there must be somebody somewhere in charge.
And what do we do when we confront this fact
yes, we prostrate ourselves and pray
and turn it into some religion or other
because we don't know any other way.

....

A Change

Right from the start I tried to play my part
to act it out to the best of my ability
but really the character I got wasn't very good
and would drive you to early senility.
So early on I decided to change it
but the new one didn't fit the plot
and if anyone says it's easy to alter the scene
I tell you now it's not.

Of course perseverance is a wonderful thing
and I did persevere
you may ask, did I succeed in the end
well I didn't, and nowhere near.

....

Fair Play

If I don't win the lottery next week
I'm going to go in the huff
well, I paid my pound just like the rest
and enough is more than enough.
Really I think it is my turn
to have a share in luck of that kind
but if it means a share in the bad things too
maybe I'll just change my mind.

....

Granny

My granny looked at my lovely curls
'Aye, he'll break many a heart'
and I believed every word she spoke
because my granny was pretty smart.
Now after years of experience
I know that she was wise
but on that one occasion
she told a pack of lies.
Now I don't feel angry or bitter at all
though I 'mind her wisdom fine
but it's only a pity she got it wrong
because the heart that got broken was mine.

....

The Answer

I'm going to have a change one day
no, I don't know when or how
but life can be so boring
especially the way I'm living now.
So will I win the lottery
or maybe it will be the pools
and then I could go to the shed
and throw away my working tools.
Oh yes we all dream of pleasure
that is neither bad or good
but really the answer to unhappiness
is a change of attitude.

....

The System

They say that in our jails there is a system
where the prisoners punish crime

271

apparently it's been there since years
and is working away quite fine.
They have their own scales of justice
where theft and fraud isn't so bad
and if you happened to rob a bank
you'd be more or less 'Jack the lad'.
Smuggling is quite acceptable
nothing much wrong with stealing a car
and the one arm bandit is begging for it
as it stands in the cocktail bar.
Yet when it comes to rapists
child abuse and other perversions
the punishment can be severe
for offences against these persons.
Now I'm not saying the system is good
intrinsically we know what is crime
and like any other system of retribution
it is only right for some of the time.

....

A Want

There is hardly a drop left in the bottle
the 'water of life' has ebbed away
you may think I had enough last night
and there's no need for any today.
That may be so, and true no doubt
and to think it, you won't be the first
but like everything else you fancy
when it's not there, the thirst is the worst.

....

Mouse Trap

The trap was set with one green pea
cheese was traditional but I'd wait and see
is everyone else the same, or is it me
or can you also corrupt one green pea.

....

Hospital

Up again to the hospital
the one in Inverness is called Raigmore
and the amount of times I've been in there
I've now wore a track to the door.
But really you have to laugh now and then
no matter how you feel
when a nurse asked what was wrong with me
I said 'Oh a punctured wheel'.
But seriously though it's the place to go
some are so brave you feel a fraud
dedicated and caring the Lord is there
and proud to be their God.

....

Nerve

When I was in the library I saw a book about sex
and I admit I was tempted a bit
but if the wife saw that about the house
it's likely she'd have a fit.
Now first things first I cunningly thought
how can I smuggle it out of the school
I'm only allowed four books just now
and the desk wifie won't break the rule.
Now desperation was urging me on
will I take five and pretend it is four
but sure as fate I will be spotted
before I reached the door.
Inspiration was flashing like lightening now
it was a matter of leave it or take
well if the wifie spots it among my cowboys
I'll pretend it was a mistake.
Now that's what I did, honestly
and I very nearly got away
but I lost my nerve and stuck it in 'travel'
and it's there to this very day.

....

Will of Iron

The wife was really proud of me last night
all because I never took a dram
and on Monday night I'm usually rampant
that's just the kind of man I am.
Now I'm going to tell you the secret
so you can understand it
you see I drank a lot on Sunday
and there wasn't a drop left in the cabinet.

....

A Thief

Some people criticise and demoralise
until there is nothing left
although that isn't a crime
it is a form of theft.
So easy to take from the poor, that's sure
and there is always someone willing
but at life's end you can't pretend
you are guilty of killing.

....

Fate

Life would be so simple if all were fate
there would be no need to postulate
no need to plan or break your heart
when all things are known right from the start.
Do actions matter if you believe this

is there any consequences of a hit or a miss
it may be your theory but it isn't mine
for being here then would be a waste of time.
. . . .

Shared Experiences

All things come to him who waits
isn't that a comforting thought
all that we do is sit on our bums
and we'll get what we never got.
Oh yes it would be idyllic all right
and that idea could be called fate
but only one experience comes to us all
and we don't even have to sit and wait.
Now you would think this great experience
would weld us together as sharing can do
yes I think it probably could
if you realized it's going to happen to you.
. . . .

Nice Man

There was a guy who was in my squad
and his wife he used to beat
yet he wasn't a mean or surly sod
in fact he was the nicest man you could meet.
Witty, considerate and thoughtful
the most popular man on the site
but word got out and everyone knew
what happened when he got home at night.
Now all the builders were appalled of course
but still there were considerable doubt
you see two and two didn't look four
and the popular is rarely found out.
. . . .

The Answer

Is money the answer to your problems
well you never know it might
if your dilemma is not health or love
then you're probably right.
But when you consider private medical care
and what cash will do for your heart
I'm sorry that I doubted you first
when you were correct at the start.
. . . .

Horse Before the Cart

I'm fairly fancying a drop of toddy now
and it is only half past three
if only a funeral would pass the window
that would be good enough for me.

274

Or perhaps some good news on the telephone
like some relation getting a baby
now I don't care if the tests were positive
near enough would do, or maybe.
If only the dog would bite me
yes I could even correlate that
but the big bitch came over and licked me
so I just gave her a pat.
Yes it is an awful affliction
and your life can get in a mess
but at least I understand why a man drinks
it's just because he's under stress.
....

An Instant Dislike

Do you ever dislike someone for no reason
except you only think he's a bit jealous
at sports he is far too dedicated
and at his job he is over zealous.
Too witty and good looking for his years
his Jag is a funny colour
and that yellow jersey he wears at golf
makes even the sun seem duller.
Yes I can understand all that
so you can relax and take a breather
because I met that guy as well
and I didn't like him either.
....

Divine Ambush

You know about the ambush I'm planning
assuming of course I get in
so just to be sure, perfection I'll endure
and hardly ever sin.
Then I was wondering if there were bushes
to conceal my traps and snare
at the end of the tunnel
I could make a hole like a funnel
and if they won't let me in it's not fair.
But when you think of it that's not bad enough
when fear of uncertainty is top of the list
so with one hand I'll beckon and wave
but with the other I'll shake my fist.
Now you might think all this crazy
and really I'm inclined to agree
be of good cheer you have nothing to fear
unless you fall out with me.
....

Another Regret

He was really insulting to me
and me being a real man walked away
now do you think I did the right thing

because there is always another way.
Well many times I thought of this
in all the years ensuing
and yes, I regret to this very day
I didn't give him a doing.
....

Innate Weakness

Mothers should teach their daughters about men
because there is a point of no return
just like a fire out of control
you just have to let it burn.
Of course the sons should be taught as well
about their innate weakness to think
and teach them to control their thirst
before they start spilling their drink.
....

What Turns You On

Some women go queasy about tall dark men
and others swoon over a singer
poetic prose can impress a few
especially if it's said after dinner.
Now unfortunately I can't do any of these things
but one lady once called me 'darling'
you see I made a nice job of building her house
and I think she got turned on by the harling.
....

Technically True

The doctor asked me how much I drank
so without blinking I said a bottle a week
well I was brought up not to tell lies
and always the truth to speak.
But I didn't tell him the size of the bottle
which would be sensible in the interests of clarity
for when I finished my bottle
I gave it to collect pennies for charity.
....

Be Wise

'Early to bed, early to rise'
I think that old sayings are great
'A stitch in time it saves nine'
that means don't be too late.
'Strong drink and some women
can ensnare you'
your very soul they will entrap
do you know some of that old sayings
is just a load of crap.
....

276

Instinctive

I went down to the library once again
passed the shelf with the sexy book
to be honest I completely ignored it
didn't even give it a second look.
Straight to the psychology and philosophy
picked two from the physics and science
then one more to make up the four
how to sort a domestic appliance.
Proudly then up to the counter
the lassie gazed and said 'Yes sir'
well she was brand new at the job
so I thought that I would impress her.

....

Supporter

That was a great game of football last night
Turkey against Manchester United
Manchester won four to nil
and I was really delighted.
Now I'm not from that city, or even England
yet my allegiance was clearly seen
because the Turks looked swarthy and scruffy
and our boys were clean as a new peen.

....

It Takes Brains

I built a house many years ago
the client he was a banker
and his wife brought out the tea to me
for which I never forgot to thank her.
Now the banker wanted to do the labouring
and I thought he must be mad
but it goes to show it does take brains
for he was the best labourer I ever had.

....

Pressure

Did you ever think of wiring round the metre
and a bit of new pipe work for the gas
another water toby in the garden
where you could cover it with grass.
Even robbing a bank may cross your mind
or maybe writing a begging letter
if you have never thought of these things
you've never been under pressure.

....

Would You Believe Me

A spaceship could land on my doorstep
the Loch Ness monster I could see every day
Big Foot could come around calling
and ask me to come out to play.
Poltergeists could wreck my house and home
Roman soldiers and ghosts as well
but with my history of drinking
there is not one soul I could tell.

....

Miss Timed

There was an old man of a hundred
who we now speak of in the past tense
but that old man never lost his wits
in fact he spoke a lot of sense.
'Though I'm blessed with extra years' he said
I got them at the wrong time
if only they came around the middle of life
that would have done me fine.
Yet I know it is all my own fault
and if I had my time again
I wouldn't pace myself for seventy years
I'd do a preparation for a hundred and ten.

....

Appreciation

I've known success and I've known failure
and success is definitely the best
probably I would take it every time
and just abandon the rest.
But when you get down to the nitty gritty
and hypothesis and analyse
the failures are not so boring
in fact they can open your eyes.
There is no fun in being a 'big shot'
if everyone else is a 'big shot' as well
no excitement in walking a tightrope
if nobody ever fell.
No stimulation in running a race
if everyone is a winner
the best of steak will lose its taste
if you get it every day for dinner.
Yes, we all need a failure now and then
so we can appreciate success to the full
but remember the opposite is true as well
and 'that' is the golden rule.

....

Too Clever

There was a chap who knew everybody

from the mightiest in the land to the least
he knew the queen and prime minister
and Bishop briggs when he was a priest.
He knew the haunts of the haughty
and all the little boys who were naughty
who rang the bell he could always tell
but he wasn't clever he was dotty.

....

Your Job

I knew he thought I was a thicko
when I couldn't fill in the form
well half of the questions were ambiguous
and the other half just pure corn.
Still I persevered with my Biro
and to be honest it was a strain
the only question that was straight forward
was my address and then my name.
After that dyslexia took over
and I regretted I hadn't learned Greek
the wee interrogator looked down his specs
wishing he had the guts to give me cheek.
Anyway I completed the task at last
did I feel inferior, no not at all
because I think someone is really stupid
if they cannot build a wall.

....

The Statement

I put on my jeans and jersey
we were going to the town
the wife she said 'You can't go like that'
and she said it with hardly a frown.
Now I pride myself on my honesty
and my clothes make a statement as well
they project my personality
and what other people I tell.
Just to be sure I looked in the mirror
and my reflection said 'you sure ain't rich'
'in fact you look quite scruffy
and a lazy son of a bitch'.
Yes I was quite taken aback
and the wife was dressed like a doll
I looked again at my statement
and I didn't mean to say that at all.

....

Typical Shopping Day

We went shopping the wife and I
where else but the Eastgate Centre
the wife went into spending mode
and as usual I lost my temper.
We fought over our coffee and bun

the pop music was driving me nuts
she was dying to tell me to push off
but she hadn't quite got the guts.
The checkout lady wouldn't accept my card
basically because it was out of date
so off I went to find a hole in the wall
while the wife had to stand and wait.
At last the transaction was finally concluded
and we slunk off with our trolley
I thought that nothing else could go wrong
but to think that was just sheer folly.
We bumped into our new neighbours
as we wrestled with all our bags
they were dressed like two models
and I was like a bag of rags.
Still I tried to ooze charm as usual
mentioned the noise in the neighbourhood
but it was them that was having the party
so I think I was misunderstood.
By now of course I began to perspire
so I suggested enough was enough
but the wife snorted she wasn't finished yet
and stalked away in the huff.
You can understand by now I was shattered
my nerves were like strings on a fiddle
the whole body went limp and I sagged
into one of the seats in the middle.
Out came a packet of Hamlet cigars
lit up, and marvelled how I was coping
when along came a wee guy in a uniform
and said 'Sorry sir, no smoking'.
....

The Seducer

She was confused, unhappy and lonely
and beside her fireplace he sat
but he seduced the vulnerable
now that's not a man but a rat.
....

Second Hand

There is nothing new under the sun they say
and when contemplated that is true
okay so you bought another car yesterday
and today you think it's brand new.
But where did all the material come from
originally from the dust of the ground
and that dust used to be something else
but now it's not square it is round.
All our feelings have been felt before
our dreams and our aspirations
love hate and envy
and all our other sensations.
The jokes we hear the stories we read
all have been heard in the past

they are fixed in time as it were
it's our memories that do not last.
Yet sadly we want to be original
but that is an impossible dream
every atom has been used before
yes even the simple gene.
Maybe you don't like being second hand
and probably you think it unfair
but if no more material is getting in
you must always have been there.

....

Basic Instinct

Do you remember the story about the young Mormon
by Miss America he said he was raped
well all the men up here read the story
and most of us sat and we gaped.
Now I'm not saying that he lied exactly
perhaps he fought like a Turk for his honour
and after ten seconds he gave up
realizing that he was a goner.
Then considering his youth and religion
and the attributes of the beauty queen
surely he could have held out for one more second
for ten seems a wee bit mean.
But there are men of virtue and conviction
to say otherwise would be absurd
but when it came to the Miss America story
I did not believe one single word.

....

In Jail

They say our jails are like holiday camps now
and not like a dungeon at all
the inmates can even buy a ticket
for the governors and warders ball.
Of course that's not a dance, but a raffle
devised by the clients to entertain
they tried it first with a cuddly toy
but it didn't take off the same.
Television and video films
and carpets on every floor
no bashing rocks in quarries now
in case the backs get sore.
Yes it all sounds pretty good to me
and to get in it's not so hard
I passed the exams quite easily
and now I'm a prison guard.

....

Teach the child Meditation

I drifted off into meditation again
(that is when your mind goes blank)

and for this ability of mind agility
it's two people I've got to thank.
Basically it's due to a strict upbringing
and that is the honest truth
because every time I said a word
I was told to sit and shut my mooth.
Now I don't mean to be critical of my parents
to do that I would hesitate
but nothing worthwhile is easily learned
and they taught me to meditate.

....

Holy Joe's

I wonder at times about the Holy Joe's
they probably call themselves 'The Elect'
mostly they are very sure of their act
and a wee bit cocky I suspect.
They terrify us with tales of Hell
and dreadful things we ought to know
but honestly if they are the company in Heaven
I really don't want to go.

....

The Circus

I was never keen on circuses you know
not even when I was small
the trapeze artists gave me the willies
in case one of them would fall.
The lions and tigers terrified me
I'd cry 'till I was almost tearless
well you never know they looked so wild
and they might eat up Captain Fearless.
No, the memories of circuses are not happy ones
and I have yet to see a funny clown
in fact the biggest pleasure they gave me
was watching the big top coming down.

....

Going Round in Circles

Is aristocrats really the cream
and look down upon the rest
especially the new moneyed people
who were only doing their best.
I wonder why the pen pushers
think they're better than manual workers
or the guys at the bench or digging a trench
they look down upon the shirkers.
So tell me, what about them
no blank ends because nature is neat
you see shirkers look down on royalty
then the whole circle's complete.

....

Are We Safe

The big bomb won't go off now I hear
now we've all come to our senses
the Berlin wall it did fall
along with several fences.
But I'm suspicious of thrifty men
there could be negligence in all that haste
it would only take one glutton to spot the button
and say 'What a terrible waste'.

....

The Flirt

You would think the more you get rejected
the more you would feel the hurt
but it's a good job it doesn't work like that
well, not for the normal flirt.
Good old mother nature is a friend indeed
and I admit it's unfair and outrageous
but one little bit of success now and then
and that will do us for ages.

....

Disappointment

Disappointment can be kept to a minimum
if you try to be pessimistic
now I'm not saying it's the answer to all
that would be too simplistic.
But try and change your attitude a bit
don't be too happy, think positively about sad
then when you get some bad news
the way you're feeling will make you glad.
Yes, this could be one answer all right
but a life time like that is daunting
when you discover you didn't need to be like that
now that's what I call really disappointing.

....

Priorities

The clergy never fail to disappoint me
when there is famine and children with rickets
they study away in a big house
contemplating lottery tickets.
Murder and abuse all around us
the baby is dead, just forget her
noble Christian minds must concentrate
on a fucking French letter.

....

On Your Toes

Job security can be a bad thing at times
also the 'golden hand shake'
just like a cushion it takes away the sting
out of the mistakes that you make.
To prove my point, one example
imagine an inaccurate bill sent to you
if the person who sent it got sacked for that
I tell you now, you wouldn't get two.

....

A Calling

Some folk are called to greatness
others are called to glory
a few are divine and make a rhyme
and one or two to write a story.
Mundane tasks, I thought that's me at last
so while waiting I built a wall
but I often wondered who did the calling
because I was never called at all.

....

Tell All

Praise the Lord the war is won
holy predictions have come to pass
and all the atheists ran away
to tell the canister of gas.

....

Body Language

You can tell by the way a person speaks
if that person is affected
the expression of guilt is universal
when the guilty is detected.
Yes body language tells a lot
it gives sense to many guesses
you can even recognise an idiot at times
by the very way he dresses.

....

The Politician

I understand hard work the old lady said
that's something I've done all my days
and honest toil is rewarded
in a hundred different ways.
But what I don't understand, she continued
even at my age I do not see
that you are only a quarter of my years

Yet you are a thousand times better off than me.
....

Old Philosophy

'He'll never get on like that you know'
do you remember when the old folk said that
they referred of course to some crooked deals
and the philosophy we accepted as fact.
Now you are not blind or either am I
and I see things the same as you
the one's that didn't take any notice succeeded
and the one's that did are few.
....

Keeping it Going

Maintenance is a good thing at times
essential when it comes to motors
clean and oil the working parts
adjust the plugs and the rotors.
Yet, in other things that we have
it is better to do a little shirking
the best maintenance is to leave well alone
and don't touch it if it is working.
....

Confidence

There were a tribe of Red Indians
where the richest brave gave all his stuff away
this was a proof of confidence
that to get more he'd find a way.
Intrinsically this is a noble gesture
but now lost to modern man
when our braves make a few pound
they hang on to it the best they can.
....

Ownership

How can you own a piece of land
and belong to you like your hair
if you walk away and then look back
yes, the land is still sitting there
A house a car a business as well
all you can buy is 'the use'
you might say that you created it
but that is just an excuse.
Ownership is just a responsibility
like alcohol once it is tasted
if you get drunk on power of possession
then the divine spark in you was wasted.
....

Getting a Winner

'God save the queen' the choir sang
and I sang 'Save her too'
she plays her part to perfection
which makes her one of the few.
Now I'm not going to condemn her family
they have all been put to the test
some passed some failed some cried some wailed
but the queen came out the best.
Of course hereditary jobs are a lottery
and the odds of a winner is bad
so I say again 'God save the queen'
she is the best we ever had.

....

Top of the Pyramid

Brainwashing can be so subtle now
no need for torture or dripping taps
when we believed only the enemy did that
not us, but the Germans and Japs.
Oh yes we all can be manipulated
and we are, by other men
but when they're doing their manipulating
who is influencing them.
The pyramid must narrow eventually
that's one law of nature we've got
so do you ever wonder who the originator is
maybe it's not a 'who' but a 'what'.

....

Discover

I've just thought of the perfect plan
for the politicians who promise utopia
why not send them for a year or two
and try it out in Ethiopia.
Then when they have solved the basics
got rid of greed and need
they might discover that every man is a brother
and there is no other breed.

....

Unique

Sometimes you are right and sometimes wrong
that is when you follow your senses
well, that is what everyone else does
so don't make any pretences.
But have you ever wondered why you're not right
when to the same clan we all belong
obey the same rules went to the same schools
so why did our senses go wrong.

....

Ramblings 6

Vampire

Did you notice some folk are like vampires
how they can drain your energy away
seem to get strength from making you feel bad
well I met one just yesterday.
Now I am not saying that they are evil
but honestly I felt just shattered
and by the time we parted company
I was well and truly knackered.
Maybe it's another mystery of nature
I don't know it's just all so vague
but I know if I see another vampire
I'll avoid them like the plague.
....

Tax Man Again

Well the tax man wants to see me again
and believe me it's not for a treat
in fact if I was an ordinary man
I would likely break down and greet.
But instead, me being a Highlander
I prayed to God to send unlucky charms
and if all these things do not work
then break his bloody arms.
Now I'm not rich I just try to get by
and I've never ever been known to beg
now I was joking about the broken arms bit
so I just left it at one leg.
Now you might think I'm saying that for a laugh
and nobody could be that rotten
but honestly just examine yourself
you'll fight dirty too if you're on the bottom.
Yes it was an eye opener to me as well
there seems to be no depths a man won't sink
oh yes you know how far 'you' would go
but honestly you don't really know, you just think.
....

The Chemists Shop

I went into the chemists shop today
and all the staff were dressed in white
the ladies were smelling so sweet
they must be scrubbing half the night.
Well I bought more toothpaste as usual
I've rakes already so what could be dafter
but if they employed just one scruffy man
he would know what I was after.
....

Deserve It

I was listening to a politician last night

and he was saying how our police were great
in our country no one gets hammered in a cell
that was the essence of the debate.
No I'm not going to condemn our Bobbies
indeed I have many friends in their ranks
and really for the job they do
mostly they get little thanks.
But the politician said no one gets duffed up
he is either a bit slack or sick
for everyone else knows what's going on
except for a few that's thick.
'Oh how horrendous' you may say
I'll write to my MP after lunch
but before you do that just think again
some people deserve a good bloody punch.

....

Hidden Virtue

I knew a contractor once
and he had three vans and a car
adverts in the Ross-shire Journal
'Estimates free and will travel far.'
He joined the local council
and really got on everybody's wick
now I don't wish to be vulgar
but honestly he sounded a prick.
Anyway that is all beside the point (I think)
because most peoples true colours are hid
so take a guess who helped a man in distress
it was anonymous, but I know who did.

....

Pride

I went through a stage in life once
and hell, did I think I was smart
all that talent in just one man
well I sure played out the part.
Fortunately it didn't last too long
and I say that for all concerned
for a man can be such a pain in the ass
that is one of the lessons I learned.
But when I think of it, men can be stupid
we ignore the old proverbs that guide
and strut about thinking we are great
knowing all the time what comes after pride.

....

Found Out

The minister zoomed off past again
for he's not speaking to me more or less
well I told you about this disease I've got
I take a dram, and yes, to excess.
Now some people long to be presented in Heaven

289

but I get the feeling that day won't be all fun
yet I am interested in that day
because I'll find out what the rest have done.
....

Improvement

I don't like us to copy anyone
perhaps especially the US of A
but do you know it makes me feel good
when they say 'Have a nice day.'
It's far nicer to go to a garage now
no gurny mechanic with a fag in his mooth
whinging about your wreck of a car
just because he's in the boose.
And it's pleasure to dine out now
when the waitresses smile and don't whine
you know they are trained to say their spiel
but it's nice, and not before time.
Oh yes we're changing here all right
and to the narky one's it must be a pest
but there were too many pegs in the wrong holes
and this change is all for the best.
....

The Light

I put in one of those infrared lights
the kind heat and movements it detects
and they are so sensitive now
it doesn't have to see, only suspects.
After I finished the installation
(it's outside of course) nailed to a tree
I thought 'maybe it's not a great move'
and as usual I was thinking of me.
I thought of my return on a Saturday night
the rejected Casanova but still full of hope
the light is sure to blink away
picked up by the Hubbel telescope.
The neighbours too will see the illuminations
and detect that vacant look on my face
yes I can hear them say
'It's him again, what a disgrace.'
No more sneaking in I thought
that usually put the wife in one of her rages
gone would be the time I could cuddle down
and whisper, 'I've been home since ages.'
Well I walked up and down and pondered
weighing up the pro's and the con's
I might even get caught with the curtains open
in my vest and red long johns.
No, too much science is not a good thing
especially when it's around the home
so I eyed up the gleaming bulb and aimed
and hit it with a big stone.
....

Inevitable

I can't understand these pessimists
why they get upset and depressed
can they not do the same as us
and try and do their best.
But no, they prattle on despondently
about the bad things that happen each day
but they can't see their folly
for it's going to happen, anyway.

....

Benevolent

If I were a millionaire I'd give it all to the poor
and that is what somebody said
now if you think it was me who said that
you're not nearly right in the head.
No, what I would do is just as good
I'd give builders work on my mansion
keep a plastic surgeon off the dole
making me nice and handsome.
The Jaguar company I'd not forget
or the boat builders in Peterhead
I'd even give C.R. Smith an extra
by putting in triple glazing instead.
The barber, the tailors, the cruise ship sailors
I'd spread out the work to be fair
but I can see there is only one snag
I'm just not a millionaire.

....

Alternative Therapy

I'm going to try acupuncture now
no, I haven't exactly cracked
but it is amazing what you will try
when you are feeling knacked.
After that it's two Filipino lassies
walking up and down my spine
I can imagine them saying 'how are you doing'
and me saying 'Oh just fine.'
Then with my luck the wife would walk in
and I could see her glower
watching the two Filipinos disappear
around a hundred miles an hour.
But seriously one thing I haven't tried yet
that's to hang by my feet from the roof
but then they'd likely lock me up
'He's gone nuts and that's the proof.'
Oh there's not any winning at all
so I'll skook down and have a dram
you know it's awful to be a weakling
but that's the kind of man I am.

....

Instinct

I never cease to be amazed at animals
even down to the inane worm
now I won't say a lot about them
because they make some people squirm.
But have you noticed if you try and catch one
they seem to know that you are after them
they disappear down the burrow in a flash
and you will never find them again.
It's the very same with the stupid fly
they are very difficult to swot
something so utterly senseless
but they very rarely get caught.
Now I was watching a wee beetle yesterday
and considered its demise with my shoe
but the wee thing took off and vanished
I tell you the wee thing knew.
Self-preservation is in the humblest creature
and it's in me and in you
in a tight corner if you are threatened
it's amazing what instinct will do.
....

UFOs

I was reading a book about aliens
and about spaceships flying the skies
I can't make up my mind if it's true
or if it's all a pack of lies.
Anyway it doesn't hinge on what I believe
and if I saw one I'd likely faint
you see it's not a matter of what you believe
they're either there or the ain't.
....

Envy

Envy is an awful thing isn't it
I'm so glad I'm not affected
some say it will eat your soul away
I was wise when that sin I rejected.
But I don't like that new chap down the road
he must be a bit of a jerk
and his wife as well you can easily tell
as they pass in their damn new Merc.
....

Human

Many men were driven mad
trying to suss out time and space
the correlation of God and universe
and to put everything in its place.
Now this is all very admirable I'm sure

292

and intrinsically exciting
a wee bit more of a challenge
than the usual reading and writing.
But before you start your ponderings
and draw a diagram along with your sum
remember you're just a human
and in the intelligence bracket, dumb.
Now any simple man will tell you
and it doesn't take too much detection
if you want to be reasonably contented
just do not pose the question.
Now from this negative viewpoint
does humanity ever advance
will a grand big pattern emerge
and it's not all down to chance.
Will the universe disclose its secrets
and from the chaos come some sense
is the reason we cannot see it all
because we're thick and dense.
It could be but I don't think so
but when I ponder now and then
I realise the sum of five and five
but also seven and three make ten.
Then is it all a matter of viewpoint
is there more than one reality
well just ask two football fans
which was the best team
and the answer is the actuality.
....

Faux Pas

Pain is forgot quite easily
unhappiness the back of the mind
the present and future before us
you leave yesterday's problems behind.
Yet when we dream of the morning
and we wipe away our tears
the faux pas is remembered forever
yes for a thousand years.
....

Does it Matter?

I knew a bloke who was taken to the cleaners
by a thief a cad and a cheat
and he believed the lies he was told
well they did sound pretty neat.
Now this chap wasn't exactly soft
they'd call him now a salesman's dream
and if you had to describe him
you might kindly call him 'green'.
Now all this happened years ago
and now both of them are gone
moralise if you like

about the right and the wrong.
But I was thinking one wee thought
you could be crooked and full of patter
and if at life's end there is darkness
then nothing on earth would matter.
…………………………..

Faith Healer

I went up to see a faith healer
and do you know he fair did the trick
I came home that morning
and laid a thousand brick.
At night I made love four or five times
Oh the morning came far too soon
mind you I bided my time
and ambushed her again in the afternoon.
Then to a dance in the bowling club
I danced nearly all of the night
put my name down for the Sunday league
you know it was sheer delight.
Dug the garden in the morning
the whole place spick and span
now, I know what you are thinking
but no, not one dram.
Alas alas yes you've guessed
nothing is as it seems
all that hope and aspirations
is just one more of my dreams.
And yet I thought I've done most of that
apart from digging the garden bit
but why didn't I enjoy it so much then
in the days when I was young and fit.
…………………………………

New Tyres

I got new tyres out of Kwik Fit
and I ran about like a bairn with new shoes
you remember the feeling yourself
not one race that you could lose.
Now I suppose they call it 'posing'
well that was me and my new Pirrellies
it's a good job no one could see my feet
because I still had on my wellies.
But anyway home I went delighted
well you're pleased when your car looks nice
in fact I only gave a rude gesture once
and flashed my lights about twice.
But then, you'll hardly believe this
stopped by the police at my own garden gate
and do you know the constable said
'Your tyres are lovely,
it's a pity your licence is out of date.'
…………………………..

Not Speaking Again

The minister is not 'speaking' just now
I'm not surprised, I can be a twit
the only times he sees me, I'm half shot
and speaking and acting like a tit.
Oh don't think I'm proud of myself
when I think of it I could cringe
not that I do anything really outrageous
just normal things when I'm on the binge.
Like the last time I went over to visit
honestly, no wonder he thinks I'm the dregs
for I started chatting up his wife
and admiring her lovely long legs.
And Oh God the remorse in the morning
it's a blessing my mother can't see me now
and the poor wife asking me probing questions
of why I do it and how.
Yet you know in a moment of serious thought
I can see the excuses are nothing new
but I was thinking if we were all the same
you know, that would never do.
....

Mans Chief End

I was lying dreaming the other day
amid a few gasps of pain
now I know what you are thinking
'Here, he's at it again.'
No I'm not after sympathy this time
but cry if you must I suppose
and I'll continue with my story
as you dry your tears and blow your nose.
Well this is what I was pondering
hypothesis I'll say to be posh
and when you write bonny words like that
you don't pay your 'nosh' with 'dosh'.
Anyway back to the theorem
as usual short and straight to the point
and no alcohol passed my lips today
although I did consider a joint.
Now this is it, Mans Chief End
when we're buried we will even be meaner
there we'll be lying side by side
arguing, who's making the grass greener.
....

A Legend

I saw in Cyprus the very spot
where Aphrodite came out of the sea
we were there on holiday a while ago
aye, the wife and me.
What a romantic story it is
a legend worthy to tell

when a goddess waded ashore
and met a prince on the beach as well.
Now if that happened in Scotland
at Rosemarkie or maybe the West
the sea would likely be frozen
or the midgies would be a right pest.
I can see it all now as clear as day
(well I can do that now and then)
A crofter would probably carry her off
to his holding away in the glen.
Year after year another baby
no adoration, except maybe a pat
loading her down wi' peats in a bag
now try and make a legend o' that.

....

A Pain

I've often told you before
our whole country has gone money mad
whether or not it was always like that
I don't know, but it makes me sad.
At one time I thought there was a pyramid
with the workers forming the base
and the chain of command tapering upwards
where everybody had his place.
But now I think it's inverted
where the one boss was, now we have ten
and they have a staff of twenty
to look after two or three men.
You've got to be a manager now you know
even an assistant one will do
no one is proud to be a worker
I wonder if this is something new.
Somehow no, I don't think so
men were always full of gas
self-important little buggers
and generally a pain in the ass.

....

Superstitious

I never used to be superstitious
but I knew a man who was
he told me he didn't know why it was so
and I never discovered the cause.
As you can imagine I had many a laugh
him dodging ladders and the third light
even when I said, you don't get a lot of snipers
going about Dingwall at night.
But anyway he was persistent
and he's happily working as I lie in bed
yes it was me who had the accident
you know, no wonder I scratch my head.

....

The Last Resort

I've been at the stage a few times
when I screamed 'God, I'm beat'
and now I look back and wonder
how on earth I kept my feet.
But life can be so amazing
for just when you think you're done
when you have reached the lowest ebb
and no hope is left, not one.
Does something miraculous happen then
a reversal to fortune fame and glory
no it doesn't not in the real world
that is just a story.
How then do we survive
is consistency the name of the game
no it isn't fortunately
because nothing ever stays the same.

....

You'll Remember

I have a job to remember at times
especially the bad times with fights
when some gorilla of a labourer
was trying to punch out my lights.
The good times too are mostly forgot
the long hot summers in the sun
and the innocent joy of youth
in the days when we were young.
Yet human memory is such a strange thing
forgot are the days we spent together
yet one little insult meant
yes, you'll remember that forever.

....

Ask the Question

Do you ever get philosophical
and wonder what you're doing here
is there a purpose to your life
and why other folk seem so queer.
Of course you've posed the question
as most ordinary people do
but I'm glad I haven't to answer
because I don't even have a clue.

....

Another Faith Healer

I went to see my 'Faith Healer' once again
so she can sort out my back
it really is a nice experience

far better than Raigmore on the rack.
We just sit in the room alone
and she puts her hands on the vital spot
as usual I visualise the wife walking in
'Aha, now you are caught.'
Trust me to think of something stupid like that
when I'm supposed to relax
'You're awful tense' the healer says
so I tried to think more about backs.
Anyway, the bit I was going to tell you
that the healer is a psychic as well
and she asked me if I would like a reading
because maybe my future she'd tell.
Well, I was quite excited at this
as she shuffled and then dealt the deck
there can only be an improvement I thought
because at the moment I was a wreck.
She picked up the hand representing the present
and concentrated on the cards for a while
well that twisted sense of humour kicked in
'Do you have a run or a prile.'
'Oh God,' I thought, 'I better be serious'
I'll really must try this once
or she will think I'm a nut case
or at the very least a dunce.
So solemnly I composed my face
and listened like a pig to thunder
while she explained all the cards she had dealt
and I just sat there in wonder.
Well, do you know, and this is honest
her accuracy was quite amazing
and when she told me all the good things to come
I couldn't help grinning and gazing.
So to cut a long story short
as I hobbled back to my car
my back was still as sore as hell
but I felt much better by far.

....

Missed the Point

Millions getting killed in Africa
children are starving to death
millions of mothers are dying
giving babies there last breath.
And us sanctimonious bastards
wonder if we'll work on Sunday
and is it a sin to be homosexual
or to get drunk on a Monday.
What is the wishes of God we say
who now do we call and anoint
to think that God sent his son here
and we missed the whole bloody point.

....

298

Natural Emotion

He told me he had won a fortune
and to be truthful I was kind of stunned
my little brain went in overdrive
trying not to be outgunned.
When my thoughts of hatred and envy subsided
I though how much will he give me
then my civilised nature took over and I thought
I'd give that man anything, and I'd do it for free.

....

Wrong Place

A weed was growing near my doorstep
and do you know it was a bonny wee thing
the summer sun was beating down
and the birds began to sing.
Well you will hardly believe what I did next
I just plucked that blossom fair
and killed a living plant
all because it shouldn't be there.

....

A Gifted Girl

I went down for my pension today
and to be honest I had a bit of a shake
no doubt it was self-inflicted
just one of the mistakes I make.
However I was feeling terrible
as I trembled in the queue
praying that no one would notice me
now this is between me and you.
Well anyway when I got to the counter
the lassie serving was so nice to me
she completely brought my mood around
and I walked out of the Post office
feeling like a million pound.

....

The Plan

I was saying my morning prayers as usual
when something crossed my mind
it was the wee black boy on the tele last night
he was starving, naked and blind.
And I thought to myself, 'surely not'
is this part of the celestial plan
while I'm saying grace for my dinner
these wee guys are being slaughtered by man.
But of course maybe we Christians are special
the sort of icing on the cake

and maybe it's only us who deserves a nice life
the rest being a big mistake.
And then I thought that can't be right
there is a detailed drawing for every wall
but some builders cannot read the plans right
and their building's too narrow too tall and it'll fall.

....

Alone

I've had the experience a few times now
of thinking 'good God I'm beat'
when everything piles on top of you
and you feel you are losing your feet.
Yes these are terrible times right enough
and no doubt we all get a shot
so if you are thinking you are all alone
well I'll tell you now you're not.
Fortunately these bad time eventually pass
but are we thankful and full of humility
no we aren't we arrogantly court more disaster
now that's what I call stupidity.

....

It's Free

I understand it all now, I have figured it out
the big secret of life itself
and boy, I'm going to take advantage
of the secrets of health and wealth.
The best brains in the country tried it
but it took a brickie like me
and I hadn't got to pay a penny for it
in fact it came totally free.
Now being a well-balanced kind of chap
I should share it with all women and men
but if you think I'm going to tell a soul
you'd just better to think again.
But I will tell you one wee thing though
and I won't need to be explicit or exact
for when it comes to telling secrets
a man can be selfish, and that is a fact.

....

Homo

I consider myself to be an ordinary guy
with the usual equipment of men
but I have a job understanding homosexuals
their instincts seem exclusive to them.
Of course I understand to love a man
that is good, normal and true
but why do they fancy the other thing
you know, I haven't a clue.

One thing I have noticed however
and I've seen this time and again
the tough guys who beat them up
now, I'm very suspicious of them.
So do we pity them as inferiors
most of us do I suspect
it will take ten thousand years more
before this fact of life we will accept.

....

The Request

I got a request through the post today
it was from 'Children in Need'
now this is a very worthy cause
one of the best indeed.
Now as you know I'm pretty broke
and believe me now I do not joke
but anyway I was just going to throw it away
as it's years now since I got a salary or pay.
Then for some reason I read the script
well, do you know I nearly cried
and honestly when I told you I was broke
I never knew I lied.

....

Last Straw

I took a run into the town today
and on the way back the car cruised to a halt
I checked the gear and the usual things
just in case it was my fault.
But no, she had just run out of petrol
such a simple thing you would think
yet that little incident
near drove me over the brink.
Now I'm not a softie by nature
tragedies I've known a few
but it's not the big things that make you crack
it's a build-up of the wee things that happen to you.

....

Comparison

Human nature is the strangest thing
there's no accounting for some of the twists
it's quite a mystery when driving your car
why some folk shake their fists.
And honestly it mightn't be right
but this is what I was thinking
some folk believe they are swimming better
when they see that you are sinking.
There is some pleasure in being top of the class
when you know there is a bottom

and it can be nice to remember a name
when everyone else has forgotten.
But one thing sure for rich and poor
when you eventually take the big dive
you will be the only one that is dead
and everyone else is alive.
....

No Hope

Do you ever think that you are alone
and that's usually when things are bad
all your relatives and friends have left you
and you feel desolate, beaten and sad.
Now I won't raise your spirits with false hopes
or tell you at the end of the tunnel there is light
that would be unkind and untruthful
if your first opinion was right.
....

Bear Fruit

An apple tree died in my garden this year
never again will it bear any fruit
'mind you, it was a kind of stunted tree
and very likely hadn't much root.
So I won't wax too lyrical
like Byron or even Rabbie
for its blossom never looked that great
and the apples were wee and scabbie.
But then I thought if it were human
oh what moaning there would be
he wouldn't be such a bad chap after all
but you don't get that if you're a tree.
Yes mother nature is the greatest teacher
she shows us that 'words' do not act
you either bear good fruit or not
and that is the important fact.
....

What Name

It's not a matter of what you do
you're only judged if you get caught
one simple weakness of the flesh
and all your virtues come to naught.
But is 'mans chief end' the ego
and the respect of fellow man
is a champagne glass so different
than an export or lager can.
Is jeans and jersey really alien
compared to a pinstripe suit
which one does the governing
and who gets most of the loot.

Yes it's a topsy-turvy world
to understand it we must do our best
and if we cannot suss it out
'pretend' the same as the rest.
....

Lost

I got a very nice letter today
and enclosed was a sermon recorded on tape
it was really only a little gesture
but I thought it was great.
It was from a Christian lady of course
for men rarely do a kindly act
they seem to think it a weakness
it's not nice, but that is a fact.
Well anyway back to the letter and motives
obviously my soul she wishes to save
and it's no wonder she thinks that I'm lost
by the way that I sometimes behave.
So I went into pondering mode again
and figured out why I never got the call
you know there are folk who have prayed for years
and never got an answer at all.
Oh yes, I envy Christian contentment all right
only an idiot wouldn't wish to have that
but some are successful at fooling themselves
and that's just another fact.
....

The Protection

I was reading just the other day
how to protect yourself from spells and the like
it can all be done with mirrors you know
well I thought 'Oh for the love of Mike.'
Now anyway here is the theory
you put a mirror at every window and door
then when a spell is sent, it bounces back
now who could wish for more.
Also according to mystic legend
the strength of the spell is doubled on the way back
for instance if somebody wished you palpitations
on the way back it's a heart attack.
Now during this diabolical deliberations
my poor Christian heart was full of doubt
I thought if someone sent me a headache
then they could blow their own brains out.
Well like every other normal man I laughed at this
after all it is only something I had read
but do you know something about Invergordon
there's a lot of folk with bandages on their head.
....

303

Can't Resist

I was pondering away the other night
just how a weak miserable wretch I was
I hadn't a clue why I grew up like this
and my mother too didn't know the cause.
'God' I thought, 'I just can't resist some sin'
and the wee blonde down the road is driving me nuts
and I have a character so elastic
but I just didn't have the guts.
And here comes the temptation to take a drink
is there any man who could resist this lure
I suppose there must be one or two
but to be honest I'm not very sure.
I was getting a wee bit depressed then
when mother nature gave me this information
'You know' she said 'you're doing all right'
'the rest just don't have the inclination.'
Now this as you can imagine cheered me up
and I realized it wasn't weak to have a ball
it's the rest that are weak so to speak
they can't resist to stay sober at all.

....

The Bat

A bat is roosting in my conservatory
and can I find where it is hinging?
'Mind you I search for it through the day
when I'm usually whistling and singing.
Oh yes it's grand when the sun is streaming in
but you try and search for it at night
I'll tell you the least wee move
can give you a terrible fright.
Of course you've heard the stories about bats
and I laugh the same as you
but try looking for one in a dark conservatory
and these stories could easily be true.

....

Lectured

A man once gave me a lecture
what else but about the evils of drink
yet he was snecking another mans wife
now does that not make you sit and think.

....

Hermit

I'm living like a hermit now
if I was richer I would say, 'recluse'
I just can't be bothered to be friendly
and speaking to the computer is no damn use.

I'm even dodging Betty the post now
and if the milkman comes I hide
when the ministers wife puts out the bucket
I just go and run inside.
Some folk say this is paranoia
or some other fancy disease.
And I don't want them to see me
swinging about the trees.

....

The Result of Drugs?

I'm taking too many tablets now
there is no 'ifs' or buts'
and to use the local vernacular
I'll likely wreck my guts.
But I was watching a girl on TV today
and she was hooked on cocaine
and when I considered my odd pain killer
you know it's just not the same.
Now this woman she must be about thirty
and she looked like death warmed up
she mumbled how she just followed the crowd
and about her rotten luck.
Now if you saw her you mightn't be sorry
a kind of hippy who didn't care how or why
yet she reminded me of a five year old
which would make any parent cry.
Anyway I remembered the scandal about her father
about the time she was playing with toys
he travelled abroad to the third world
and corrupted little girls and boys.

....

Playing a Part

Sometimes I am amazed at some titled folk
yes some landowners and the wealthy
some don't seem to know they act out a part
now to me that can't be healthy.
It was made clear to me the other week
when we changed our chieftain of the games
(now forgive me if I don't mention names)
but anyway our new chieftain
played his part to perfection
and the rest of the dignitaries did their bit
with little or no direction.
Then a trite little letter in the press
by an ex-chief of the clan
who hadn't yet quite grasped
that a man is just a man.
And it was sadness that I found in that letter
neither noble or aesthetic
when a player believes his role is real
now isn't that pathetic.

....

Tax Man yet again

You know I used to tell you about the tax man
and when I think of it I called him terrible names
some started with F and some with B
and they should be thrown at the Highland Games.
Well I had a meeting with one today
now they are only people with a human heart
but do you know before the meeting was over
I knew my opinion was correct at the start.
And one other thing crossed my mind at the meeting
which I have yet to figure out the cause
because I always thought that I understood people
and I never realised how out of touch I was.

....

The Beginning

I was trying to figure out the secrets of the universe as usual
when in a blinding flash all came clear
now I'm not saying my theory is perfect
all I can say that it's pretty near.
Well at the start, that is the beginning
God made Eve and Adam
now he seemed all right to me
but she seemed a bit of a madam.
Anyway eventually they had a family as we know
and they in turn took husbands and wives
in time spread out through all the world
and lived there all their lives.
Now I'm not going to avoid the age old question
'From where came the extra folk?'
Then this is what I figured out
and I'm serious, I do not joke.
As we all know God had angels
out of that host a few were suspicious
well I only think it natural
that some of them were ambitious.
Now this is what happened, some tried to procreate
only to find out later it was a terrible mistake
but the faulty creation went on to make the masses
and that is why we have so many smart asses.

....

Thinking

Do you ever think that sometimes
we all concentrate too much on self
I was always told it wasn't good for you
in fact injurious to mental health.
But after long deliberations
I decided this was not true
for if everyone is thinking about themselves
they are not conspiring against you.

....

More Jealousy

No, I was never jealous of anyone
and envy was alien to my mind
in fact if you ever met me
you would think me very kind.
Now see that guys in their Merc's and Jag's
and the wife driving a Mini Moke
it's not my fault they are all stuck up
and are such horrible folk.

....

No Choice

I often wonder when the script was written
and the casting director took his pick
why he chose me to be the brickie
you know it makes me sick.
I would sooner be a king or something
or maybe an industrial tycoon
and not be working in the snow and rain
the walls collapsing in the odd typhoon.
If only I had a little say in what went on
but then you would have your say too
and everybody can't be a millionaire
that would never do.

....

Love

I rarely write about 'love' as you know
and it's not lack of emotion or phrase
I only think it is sensible and wise
not to put the wife in a craze.

....

Put By

I might as well use my Parker Pen
before it is too late
or it will end up like my other things
obsolete and out of date.
I have brand new clothes in the wardrobe
and a lot more up the stairs
but I suppose it would look funny
being the only one dressed in 'flares'.
My after shave and deodorant has evaporated
for years I could have smelled quite sweet
instead I put them bye for good
and ignored my sweaty feet.
I've spare parts for engines still in the shed
by the look of them they were driven by steam
and me thinking that they would be handy

but that was only a dream.
Yes I admit I'm a natural hoarder
I just can't bear to throw things away
and my friends they sometimes laugh at me
but I don't know another way.
Yet for a compensation I get the last laugh
when my neighbour is doing some task
and they run short of something
guess who's the man they ask.
....

No Guarantee

I knew a man who had pension plans
insurance worked out by a think tank
he had every little detail permutated
down to the cash in the bank.
But his wife ran off with the lodger
his children all joined a commune
his house was built over a coal mine
and they expect it to disappear soon.
Now sometimes you have to see the funny side
and appreciate there's life when you're gone
but the man reminded me of a Gopher gaping around
saying 'What the hell's going on'.
....

Robin Hood

I wonder if Robin Hood was here today
who would he start robbing
would it be the millionaire
or the guy on the dole doing jobbing.
Yes you might dwell on that for a while
and come to the same conclusion or lie
and you'd bet your boots it wouldn't be the rich
when there are soft targets like you and I.
....

Zombie

Before I go to the big distillery in the sky
I'm going to have an autopsy done
this is just in case I waken up later on
hardly any has done it but I might be one.
Oh how gruesome you may rightly say
and blasphemy I'll be bound
well I don't care that's only sensible
there's enough zombies going around.
....

Something Missing

Maybe I'm repeating myself again
but do you see these geniuses and very clever folk

well there must be more going on than genetics
and believe me I do not joke.
Most of the very clever ones I knew
no difference if right or left handed
they all had a kind of vacant look
reminding me that aliens have landed.
And there again as I study them
to be like that I am not wishing
I know they say that they have something extra
but I can't help thinking that there's something's missing.

....

Got It

Do you ever notice about your greatest desires
to crave for them is a blunder
now it would be a dull life otherwise
but you know sometimes I wonder.
Now everyone can see what happens
it happens to me at any rate
after you've had it, you didn't want it
and before you get it it's great.

....

Guardian Angel

Everyone has a guardian angel you know
and I even know the name of mine
untiring he always tries to keep me right
and for marks out of ten I'd give nine.
I know through the years he has helped me
that is something I always knew
and when at times I needed a helping hand
he showed me what I must do.
Now I know you would like me to tell you the name
and openness and frankness is good
but if I told you, you would take pure advantage
you mightn't, but some of you would.

....

Sober

There's the minister out in the garden again
I'll wave to show how sober I am
you can believe me it's way after three
and to be honest I hadn't a dram.
But with all this waving I never noticed the rake
and as you know 'on no rake shall you tread'
all my efforts and show of sobriety was wasted
for the cleric walked away and shook his head.

....

The Inevitable

I sometimes think we are standing still

and it's the future that's rushing to us
while we smugly take credit for it
rationalise, and arrange and fuss.
No none of us planned to be unhappy
like you I want to rejoice
but I keep getting a sneaky feeling
that none of us gets a choice.
Yes the future is there before us all right
but is it already made
now that is a question that boggles the mind
and makes me a wee bit afraid.
....

Just Try

There is little point in making promises
especially the ones you mightn't keep
Oh I know, I made plenty myself
in fact I made a heap.
But really it's all just a waste of time
all you do is make enemies too
why not take every day as it comes
and you will feel brand new.
There is no big virtue in committing yourself
if you don't you can't tell a lie
so just do the best that you can
and give it an honest try.
It's a funny thing in life you know
like stocking up your larder
if you want value for money
you have to spend time and shop a bit harder.
....

The Complex Brain

It must be nice to have a wee debate
and be able to give tit for tat
and not to have to wait half an hour
and then think, 'I wish that I said that'.
Now don't be mistaken, this is not slow wit
or lack of understanding or what we know
it's just that our brains are more complicated
and the information has further to go.
....

Bad Habits

I'll justify all my bad habits, yes
solid reasons I will find
I will show it's not weakness at all
or any other quirk of the mind.
So I pondered and I pondered
now believe me I don't blame you
but you must be hiding yours so much better
and that is the best I could do.
....

The Hare and the Tortoise

Remember the story of the hare and the tortoise
the one we got taught in primary three
how the tortoise won the race eventually
and there was a moral we were supposed to see.
Now this is a tale I've always remembered
and probably the outcome was fair
but in real life the tortoise has a boring time
and will be pipped at the post by the hare.

....

Auld Acquaintance

I met a fellow I hadn't seen in years
so I greeted him with a big 'Hello'
now why on earth I did that
is probably something I'll never know.
So as we spoke the more confused I got
and I was very glad to part
yet when I think of it now, it's so simple
I didn't like him much at the start

....

Bigoted

I think we are slowly winning the war
and it's bigoted ignorance that we fight
understanding is our spear and sword
and not what is wrong or right.
Justice will prevail one day
show your colours and the battle endure
but are you on the side of justice and truth
and are you a hundred percent sure.

....

A Little Clue

What, the minister was talking about
to be honest I just don't know
not that I'm a regular anyway
but I sometimes go.
He was ranting on about the eye of the needle
and of course he was talking about wealth
but I can't figure out the point of it all
and I don't think he knows himself.
For after the service is over
he shakes hands with a grip that's sure
then gravitates into conversation
and his friends to me aren't poor.

....

The Joy of Being Rich

Thank goodness, no bill in the post
I was expecting a big one soon
but the way my luck was going
I got it in the afternoon.
Now normally I would just write out a cheque
and 'unperturbed' wouldn't be too strong a word
but when you have no money in the bank
honestly you feel a bit of a turd.
Never experienced it? It's not a nice feeling
in fact poverty is a pure bitch
but if you have never felt it
you'll never know the joy of being rich.

....

The Quality

I sometimes talk about money
as I have said often, the country is 'money mad'
I don't think it was always like that
it's so unnatural it makes me sad.
There's no time to stop and just chat for a while
or give anyone a visit for pleasure
the conversation now is money and stuff
or else how you were given short measure.
And when you think of it
we all have a story to tell
adventures of love and romance
and of living and dying as well.
But sadly now, storytelling is dying out
the graphic tales of deceit and hate
but all these stories have all but gone
and disappeared at a terrible rate.
You can blame affluence or even television
but the culprit is anybody's guess
and although we all seem to be richer now
the quality of life is less.

....

A Choice

If reincarnation turns out to be true
would you come back as you
or would say, 'time for a change'
well I think I'd say that too.
But now when you think of it
if you can change your mind it would be fine
for to draw the logical conclusion
we both made a mistake the last time.

....

The Spell Again

I went and did it one more time
got my fortune told again
again I asked who put a spell on me
and demanded she tell a name.
Now she told me a good description
and on a scale she did quite fine
if the dirty rat is reading this
he better be flying down the old A9.
Well anyway after the reading was over
and I paid to her my dues
I asked her if she could tell me more
just to get the crack and the news.
Come back next week she said
and a name I'll have no doubt
but with crossing palms with silver
I'll be broke before I'll ever find out.

....

Union

Well I haven't taken a wee dram since ages now
I know that's hard to comprehend
'mind you I suppose this is only Wednesday
and I had a good few at the weekend.
Now honestly, here I am quite cocky
when you think of it it's just been a couple of days
and here's me almost looking down on drinkers
I don't care what anyone says.
What would I be like if I turned teetotal
probably I'd be a right prick
there's just no accounting for human nature
but oh God it makes me sick.
Mind I think it's the same feeling for religion and fags
everyone wants clones of themselves
then the world would be like a warehouse
the same product but on various shelves.
No, this cockiness really must go
I've no desire to procreate clones
consistency can sometimes be boring
maybe a wee bit like Wimpeys Homes.
Surely there's room for a wee bit partition
instead of amalgamation we should separate
and agree to put up with our differences
if that would work it would really be great.

....

The Letter

When I was a boy in school I got a letter from a lassie
and the innocent letter was then considered rude
but in those far off days
I thought it was pretty good.

Anyway the teacher saw the note being passed
and demanded it's confiscation
I tell you if she had read it then
it would have created a minor sensation.
Now me being an honourable wee chap
that is, apart from my precocious intention
I would not produce the damning evidence
or even the source would I mention.
Now I mind the wee lassie sitting cringing
the big teacher glowering satanic
and the poor wee thing was as white as a sheet
on the verge of hysterical panic.
Now through fear and loyalty I stuck to my guns
but do you know it's forty years since then
that wee lassie is now middle aged
yet I still see her now and then again.
And when we meet on the road or the street
I smile and so does she
and no one else in the world knows this
but she is still grateful to me.

....

The Lions Again

I was dreaming about lions again last night
and of course this morning, straight to the book
this is a volume of ancient meanings
and honestly I was scared to look.
Well anyway I did, and it wasn't that bad
as far as a semi-nightmare goes
but why were the lions all chasing me
it is only God that knows.
Now I could say that it's a bad omen
and there is big trouble for me ahead
because when I was kicking the lions arse
I was kneeing the wife instead.

....

Never Forgot

Many a fight I had when I was young
and many a belting I got
punishment lines plenty of times
now these are all but forgot.
The pains of growing up, just a laugh
and long gone is the desk where I sat
but a teacher slapped my face once
and I still can't forget that.

....

The Urge

I can feel it building up again
the urge to take the shot

and if you think it's easy to resist
I tell you now, it's not.
I know it's difficult to understand
yet it happens to women and men
but when I hear people talking 'smutty'
I just can't understand them.
....

Paradox

I was told 'don't trust a soul'
don't rely on even a few
confiding in one will have the same outcome
as telling a hundred and two.
Now that attitude is not great is it
there must be more colours than black or white
if only we could understand the paradox
'a thing that's wrong yet it's right'.
....

The Gene

Talent is usually inherited
you don't need to be genius to see that
the seeds of life know more than you think
I can't think of anything that they lack.
It's all determined before you are born
your abilities to act and to sing
mind you I wouldn't take it too far
like who was born to be king.
But generally speaking it's all handed down
there are exceptions I'm sure but only some
and half of these could be explained away
by having a quiet word with your mum.
Now I was thinking about 'inherited memory'
or how it could be a trick of the brain
but do you know it's not so fantastic as abilities
so maybe they are transmitted the same.
And when you think of all that information
crammed into something so small
we readily believe the obvious of course
with that in mind, the rest is not so amazing at all.
....

Eye for an Eye

it can be difficult to be a Christian
when you see law and order break down
and it's not only in the cities
but in near every village and town.
Murder, theft, destruction and rape
unprovoked cruelty and abuse
I could go on for ages
but I think, well what's the use.

Now why don't we do the tit for tat method
I think of that now and then
maybe hanging a murderer is not a deterrent
but he sure as hell won't do it again.
Rape the rapist, steal from the thief
yes I know it doesn't sound right
but if a thug got a right good hammering
would that stop him, I don't know but it might.
By now you are thinking it's all been tried before
to say otherwise would be a lie
but some things just don't work the first time
yes, I'd give tit for tat another try.
....

A Cut Above

Do you remember years ago
how some folk were so superior
well I don't know if they meant it
but they made ordinary folk feel inferior.
I do not think there is so much of it now
now a days it's no disgrace being a debtor
thankfully our attitudes are changing
and may I say that's for the better.
But getting back to 'superior' folk
who never seemed to laugh or cry
did they really believe they were a cut above
and if they did, I wonder 'why'.
....

Lazy

If only I had hurt my leg
I mightn't be so jumpy
but then people smile and shout
and they'd likely call me 'stumpy'.
Well I thought, that's not too bad
at least it's better than 'thingie'
and then if it was my arm
they'd be sure to call me 'wingie'.
Now what do they call me with a sore back
the whole thing is so crazy
not one endearing word at all
but the one descriptive word 'lazy'.
....

A Nightmare Job

I did a job for an architect once
and there is no ifs or buts
by the time the job was over
he near drove the workforce nuts.
If I said 'wider' he would say 'deeper'
I would say taper shallow, he would say 'steeper'.

On and on, went the nightmare
the traditional tied to a kit
and do you think it looked any better
well it didn't not one bit.
....

Stand the Pace

I went up to Inverness again today
to buy some brand new specs
well my old pair were getting done
in fact they were total wrecks.
Mind you, no wonder when I think of it
you could term their treatment 'abuse'
of course I could justify every scratch
but honestly, that's just an excuse.
The time they fell down the side of the ministers couch
and vanished for a while without trace
mind you, that was a bit of a problem
because they were still hanging on my face.
And the occasion they crashed into the wall
knocking one lens out of its socket
well I really can't blame the workmanship
for they told me I was going like a rocket.
Oh yes these glasses could tell a story alright
some sad some glad some fair
so I buried them in the garden with a tear or two
and said one little prayer.
'Poor horn rimmed specs' I said
'I place you in your resting place
you got clattered, shattered and knackered
it's a pity you couldn't stand the pace.'
....

Propaganda

We're proud of British justice aren't we
and the way our country is run
the freest nation in all the world
with a health service second to none.
Now believe me I'm not being cynical
far be it for me to slag off my own land
but the first time I went abroad
it took me a while to understand.
And then after the usual ponderings
at last all was understood
we freely hear of foreign badness
but it's not sensible to tell us the good.
....

Foretold

There is a big stone on a hill near Dingwall
(now I'm not being a prophet of doom)

but legend has it, it's going to fall
and the time of falling is soon.
Now our councillors are pretty smart
because they got it chained to an anchor pin
and they employed a local builder
who went up and concreted it in
Now if it fell there were going to be disasters
as foretold by our own Bran Seer
but with all that chains and concrete
I don't think none of us need to fear.
Yes our councillors did a fine job
and safely the young folk pass by to the dances
well it only seems reasonable to me
not to take unnecessary chances.
Yes we are lucky to have brains in the county all right
and I say that with no derision
because if that happened anywhere else
they wouldn't get planning permission.
....

Clever Dog

I had a right good conversation today
well you could call it a monologue
the reason being it was philosophical
and a bit over the head of the dog.
But anyway she sat quietly and listened
with only an occasional nod of the head
I knew by the very look in her eye
she believed every word I said.
On and on I blasted and orated
and she looked on with adoration and awe
if I stopped for even a second or two
out went a supporting paw.
On I went for another hour
then looked out at the wind and the rain
and then the penny dropped with a bang
I don't think I'll speak to that dog again.
You see she encouraged me to ramble
(and to think she was once my pet)
she just urged me to prattle on
because she hates a walk in the wet.
....

Different Healers

I am going up to see two ladies today
that is the healers who's sorting my back
mind you, I don't tell everyone about this
or it's common sense they'd say I lack.
Now all I do is sit or lie as good as gold
while they practice their ancient art
and the three of us chat about various things
like the weather and football for a start.
Now after an hour of treatment

(when you're enjoying yourself time can fly)
honestly I feel a lot better
there is more to healing than meets the eye.
Now I'm not saying that medicine is not good
only an idiot would contemplate that
but do you know a box of pills just can't compare
with some kindness, a laugh, and a pat.

....

Naïve

I was taken to the cleaners a few times now
and in some of my dealing I got done
mind you there weren't an awful lot
but honestly there were some.
Now I wouldn't blame you if you thought I was soft
and a fool doesn't deserve wealth
but no one can make a fool of a man
he can only do that himself.
So this is a wee bit of wisdom I learned
and when you get the short end you'll not care
the man who cheats you is a lesser man
he doesn't even know, what's fair.

....

Get Real

I'm really astonished at the churches sometimes
now that we know about child abuse and disease
war, torture and cruelty, and evils such as these.
Corruption and treason the academics now play
and justice we'll get, yes someday
but why not make a start today
and not ask 'Christ can I work on Sunday'.

....

Sects

There must be hundreds of sects in the world
every one following 'the word'
everyone believing they have the truth
now to me that's just absurd.
Even the 'Wee Free' man along the road
declared he saw the light
and the 'evil one' has a grip of the rest
and he's determined he's right.
Now I'm no theologian or philosopher
but neither am I a dunce
I've seen both sides proved right before
and I've seen it more than once.

....

The Same Stones

One type of person really frightens me
I probably told you if you remember
it's the mainstay of our governments
the political party member.
Often I wished I could understand
how so many people could think the same
organise themselves into clubs and groups
and give each other a name.
Now I know if they didn't chaos would reign
and I don't doubt their sincerity at all
but there's no beauty if the stones are all the same
I found that when building a wall.
....

Mercenary

The doctors prognosis wasn't very good
so he said 'what are you going to do with your car'
well' I thought that's a bit over the top
and taking a sore back a bit far.
Then that pesky tax man had to hear as well
and me as poor as a church mouse
he says 'it's an awful pity you can't pay your taxes'
'but man, what are you going to do with your house?'
And you would hardly believe it, my accountant
you know I don't even think he's human
he says, 'Oh yes I know where your wife's shop is'
'and she's such a pretty woman.'
Well I've heard of people being mercenary before
but is there not one soul you can trust
yes of course there are plenty
the ones that don't know you are bust.
....

Guardian Angel Again

I know who my guardian angel is now
and I even know the name
but I won't tell you who it is
it just wouldn't be the same.
You can laugh if you like
so I'll give you a clue, it starts with 'T'
and his job is more of a profession
because he's looking after me.
Yes, I know a lot may scoff
some may even think I am a prat
but they can sneer at my new Jag
do I need to tell you where I got that.
But what of the disasters you may argue
I got my fair share you may rightly say
but I tell you all that bad things happened
when my angel was on holiday.

Now don't think I am cracking up
and should be locked up in a home
the next time you see me talking to myself
you'll understand I won't be alone.
....

Depressed

Do you ever get really depressed
and you say 'It's a hell of a life'
half your mates are robbing you blind
and the other half trying to sneck your wife.
It's pouring rain, the car won't start
the dog just killed the cat
you realise you've ruined the bairns
and the wee one's a cheeky brat.
And here comes the whistling milkman now
does he not realise he's near his doom
I wish I could tell him the exact minute
I can't, but it must be soon.
....

Freud

I started to study psychology
to sort myself out more or less
but do you know the more I learned
I realised we're all in a mess.
And me thinking I had hang ups
never thinking it could happen to you
there's not a normal man in the country
if there is any there must be few.
Volume after volume I read
vainly trying to find a cure
at one time I thought I cracked it
yet now I'm not so sure.
But eventually yes, I sussed it out
it was as simple as A B C
after a couple of books on Freud
I realised he was as nuts as me.
....

Blame

I had a right pain today
so I contemplated the shot
but I have to be up early in the morning
so I thought I'd better not.
I had to drive the car you see
taking the wife to the town to surprise her
and no point in getting stopped
and failing the breathalyser.

321

At times living in the country's not handy
there is neither trains or hardly a bus
and a taxi is out of the question
when it comes to transporting us.
So I will have to be crafty
and keep a sharp look out
for the cops up here will ambush you
at the least suspicion or any doubt.
But I am an old hand at this
and my experience has saved me once or twice
I just break down and sob
and blame it all on the wife.

....

Ramblings 7

Reality

There's no great truth
they're no damn lies
no big heaven up in the skies
no hot hell way down below
no bloody purgatory for children to go.
No screaming demon with cloven hoof
but men will still burn a witch
without a scrap of proof.
Chastise, circumcise, sacrifice and ostracise
men has made a world of sighs
and ignorance governs all.

....

A Long Way to Go

The sound of my voice is just a whine
you know, I can hardly believe it's mine
or else it's a growl or a groan
I really turned out a right moan.
But when I was young I was full of fun
I was strong decisive and brave
but do you know it's easy to have courage
when you're a million miles from the grave.

....

Memory

A good memory is a wonderful thing
the comfort and pleasure it can bring
remembering loved ones and friends from afar
fond memories saved as bright as a star.
But good memories can recall pain, grief and debt
you know sometimes it is better, just to forget.

....

The Queen

Yes I'm queen of the village it seems
in the shop I always talk posh
I wear my fur coat and also my hat
and I never say 'Hell' but 'Oh gosh'.
I do not buy plain bread I always buy pan
I call George my 'husband' and never 'my man'
the assistant's name is 'Fanny' but I call her 'Fan'
a little privilege when you are queen.
The doctor and minister I have to dine
and I cook all the food in the juice of the vine
and diarrhoea is their problem certainly not mine
for you don't have that when you're queen.
In church I sit in the ministers pew
because it has a cushion and there's only a few

going out of the door I say 'Oh how do you do'
and I see the respect in their eyes.
Then I take George and the dog for a walk
oh how I wish you could hear us talk
I speak about the 'rural' and George calls to cuddles
for the little bitch rolls in the puddles.
Then home by the sea side to watch the birds fly
and once a sea gull dropped its message right in my eye
if I live to a hundred I'll never know why
perhaps it didn't know I was queen.

....

Stark Truth

I used to think politicians were great
but now the world is in a right bad state
and to medical doctors I doffed my hat
but there's no cure for my aches and pains
so what do you think of that.
To our reverend ministers I'd bend the knee
not only to our own but even the Wee Free
but now has the devil really got me
so what do you think of that.
Now all things came together one day
and now the jigsaw is almost complete
because I built a wall of facing brick
and the whole thing fell at my feet.

....

The Only Ones

Fear of failure, fear of work
fear of sin, fear of the Kirk
fear of God fear of Old Nick
you know all this fear just makes me sick.
Muslims, Jehovah's, Christians too
they are all going to Heaven
but, Oh not you
you have to be fearful of not getting in
everyone knows you committed some sin.
But they are all forgiven
because of their creed
and they will be the only ones in Eden, 'Indeed'.

....

Instinct

I sometimes see the fighter jets
flying high up in the sky
and I often question myself
and I wonder why.
These young men are training
to kill some lad or lass
or perhaps to maim some bairns

in some mountain pass.
Can these bright young men not see
when making out their will
that the young blood just likes a fight
but the old blood likes to kill.

....

The Sea Saw

do you ever notice when you are feeling sad
that your condition makes some folk look quite glad
when you are successful and happy you all bounce
but you go down on your luck, they pounce.
Now isn't that like the chicken coup
and I'll tell you once again
it just seems to be animal instinct
for everyone to peck the skooky hen.

....

Indifferent

I cannot bring myself to dance
or even to laugh aloud
I always like to sit
on the fringes of the crowd.
No flippant conversation
or any serious topic
no ready chit-chat
my humour microscopic.
But still I smile and grin
and to all things I agree
'Oh yes, yes' I say 'I see I see'
but deep deep down I know
my indifference will show
for it's not easy to balance an act like me.

....

Lose The Head

Now I don't like getting angry
I'd much sooner stay happy instead
but two crows pecked on my window all night
and near drove me off my head.
Well eventually I lost it, and shot them both
with two overhead shots that would amaze
yes it's surprising what a quiet man will do
if he ever goes in a craze.

....

The Bottom

When you feel you are at the bottom
and you wish the lights would fuse
that's the very time to hold on
because you have plenty left to lose.

The unbreakable law of nature
that nothing stays the same
even stagnant water changes
with each shower of rain.
Hold on to life at the bottom
the future is still in sight
when you're low, they're one way to go
that's up, now isn't that right.
....

The VAT Man

The VAT mans visit ended
and I sunk on my knees before God
'Please' lord I prayed
send a motorbike to cripple the sod.
If ever his report gets to headquarters
Lord I'm done
please let him be mugged
by Attila the Hun.
May his briefcase be torn from his fingers
and his Lada reduced to rust
and that little diary burnt to ashes
I only think that just.
With his little calculator
we could electrocute him God
or give him a dose of the Bubonic Plague
when I give the nod.
Now you are bound to see it's justice
and if you grant me this little request
I'll go to the Kirk on Sunday
and sit among the rest.
I won't even think lecherous thoughts
about that wee blonde in the corner pew
and in the plate I'll put fifty pence
now then, are you no' proud of me noo.
....

God

It's not what you are
it's all what you've got
and how you acquired it
that's quite forgot.
Our God is a pound note
so don't make a sound
if you don't believe me
just look around.
....

Just Your Luck

I knew a chap who was addicted to drugs
and he would sook them just like a sweet

but that chap fought it and beat the habit
yet was run over by a bus in the street.

....

Near It

The trees of the forest
have killed all the flowers
grasped all the sunlight
from haven and bowers
starved fragile orchids
and severed the link
now one stroke of the axe
and all is extinct.

....

Comrades

They're rushing here and rushing there
and the unemployed just sit and stare
twelve hour shifts seven days a week
affluence for a few of the comrades, so to speak.
Yet I've never heard of a strike for Mike
and he can't even go the damn bike.
Where is the level of the sickle and hammer
when union men get red and whistle and stammer
and clink their change and feel a wallet fat
you know I never thought I would see the day
that I would see that.

....

Heaven

If all the people I know
who think they are going to Heaven
eventually arrive there
and their table is reserved
I will not go in, and this is sin
and my punishment will be deserved.

....

Street Market

I went to the market
where oranges cost a shilling
and around the fruit of the vine
people of all ages were milling.
Second hand clothes, a plastic rose
underwear transparent and stark
hot pies and peas, coffee and teas
and a place for your car to park.
Trousers of leather, lucky white heather
a song from stars from the past

friends for the day the price we all pay
a feast but then there's a fast.
....

Always One

I remember well the Bluebell Wood
where Beech trees tall and powerful stood
and around our campfire we brewed some tea
as Indians stalked from tree to tree.
The days were long the sun was strong
this should have been paradise
but there is always one that'll ruin the fun
a guarantee for a fool that is wise.
....

Luck

Have you still got some pride
well, you're doing fine
but have you ever been below the poverty line.
Being capable and fit has nothing to do with it
the master of all is circumstances
Who finds the oil, who tills the soil
it's not a matter of taking chances
or even who retreats, tries, or advances
or who got the start with one dollar or buck
because in the end, it's all down to luck.
....

The Book of Life

I thumbed through the book of life
and do you know I had to look twice
in fact I didn't think it nice
for among the M's where my name should be
there was an empty space for all to see.
Well, I said to myself this is a bit much
of all the chickens I'm not in the clutch
'Typical' I said, 'typical'
in fact it's very near criminal
and me rarely cynical
in fact I'm almost a saint.
Apart of course the love of the drink
and an angels breath just doesn't stink
and rarely do they have a lecherous thought
when it comes to sinning I got the lot
except of course I don't blaspheme
and most of my desires were only a dream
and for tax evasion I never got caught
a life of crime never came to ought
no, I'm happy with the character I got
and given time I could justify, the lot.
....

Workers

Some folk are born workers
and they are here to work
while others are born shirkers
and their lot in life is to shirk
so why should I judge them
and be a burke
If they want to work, let them work.

....

The Wolf

A man tried to tell me the wolf wouldn't attack
supposing I walked the woods at night
'Why' he said it's the wolves that would get a fright
and no they would never bite.
Well I didn't argue because it suited my rhyme
but do you know for everything there is a first time.

....

Achilles Heel

Mighty Achilles looked triumphant
as before his army he stood
he was bawling out things like 'You cowards'
and other things that were rude.
'Haw, you bunch of softies'
'can you not be like I'
(with a sneer on his face
as he looked up to the sky)
'I am almost perfect men
while you lot make me sick
why, I came through the whole battle
with just one little nick'.

....

Popularity

As you know I'm wary of real nice folk
who are everybody's friend
I can't understand how they like everyone
but do they really or do they pretend.
I can see all right it's possible
to love your fellow men
but you can love without liking
and dislike a few now and then.
No big virtue in being friendly to all
when some people are just not your type
you can still love your fellow man
and have a good dislike.
Nothing noble about listening to lies
and not deny the lie

nothing smart in laughing
when you really want to sigh.
No virtue in liking a lecher, a bully or a cheat
does the partridge say 'I like birds of prey'
because it's me they want to eat.'
This is the cost of being popular
as a hand may fit a glove
the very effort of liking
sometimes can kill the love.
....

Hunting

I have never hunted the fox
they say he's very smart
anyway I can't ride a horse
and wouldn't know where to start.
But I can well imagine
especially with a dram or two
yodelling over the hillside
in coats of red and blue.
Holding on to the saddle so tightly
jumping a five barred gate
yes I can imagine the excitement
I think that would really be great.
But one thing I can't come to terms with
and I'll ponder until I die
is there really any need to kill the fox
and if there is I wonder why.
Of course I've heard all the excuses
concerning the lambs, geese and hen
but I get the sneaky feeling
the sport just attracts cruel women and men.
....

Snooker

I must go and play a little snooker now
and see if I can pot a few reds
send down the black fifteen times
and tear the record to shreds.
The pink and the brown I have to put down
the blue the yellow and green
yes even in the game of snooker
it's the white fellow that does the damage
if you see just what I mean.
....

Local

I used to think the word 'vernacular'
sounded really quite spectacular
and referred to gentry, or even a king.
But a poor man's easily deceived

for whoever would have believed
something so grand could refer to him.

....

Pretty Nice

Yes we humans are full of faults
and some as deep as 'vice'
but every now and then we meet someone
and we say 'Oh she's nice'.
A gentle word a sparkling eye
no need for flirtations with you
five minutes conservation
makes a better man of you.
The world if full of wondrous things
sometimes beyond the instinctive mind
and to be sure a man gets inspiration
from a woman who is honest and kind.

....

Social Work

'You can't live like this the social worker said
with all this dirt in a week you'll be dead
and the district nurse will surely agree
that you can't live alone at ninety three.
You'll have to go to a home we call the 'eventide'
I'm sure you will like it, it's so clean inside
they're qualified staff trained to high degree
you will be so happy, just wait and see.
Your every need will be catered for
every assistance and help you need
now will we make that a week Monday
tell me are we agreed.
Of course you can't take the hens or the cow
or a couple of stirks or pregnant sow
and no I won't go and muck out the byre
or cut any sticks for your fire.
I'm a social worker and my duty I'll do
why you must know I'm here to help you.

....

Conform

I use you and you use me
and I conform to what you would like me to be
but I'm very interested when we are all laid bare
when at last we all ascend the winding stair.
And on that awesome day all will see
and I wonder if you will be you, and me be me.

....

The Open Fire

A lady asked me a while ago
would I build her an open fire
although she'd been there twenty years
that was her heart's desire.
To feel the heat of the living flame
an electric element just wasn't the same
no mantelpiece to put up your feet
she wanted to smell Birch and burning peat.
Well I got some cement and facing brick
started the mixer and gave it big licks
and in no time at all in fact two ticks
I built a lum for her.
The bricks I built in stretcher bond
they were wire cut and rustic red
I built them four to a foot
with three eighths for a bed.
An arch I threw over the opening
and a hearth of quarry tiles
to find an equal of that fire
you would have to travel miles.
Well as you know we builders ain't bums
but when I finished the work, over she comes
and she says 'That's just lovely'
you must get great satisfaction I guess
and I was so enamoured with the whole thing
all I could say was 'Yes'.
....

Unemployed

If I don't get a decent job soon
I'll have to fly the Fairy Flag
but the poor thing is like myself
worn out and knackered, like a rag
so all I can do is go down to the bureau
and conform to the celestial plan
there is nothing quite like unemployment
to make you feel less of a man.
....

Road Rage

One thing you will notice around my town
you will never get a smile from a driver, only a frown
they'll blow their horn and rant and rave
you just won't believe how some folk behave.
And if by chance you forget to put your lights in dip
to punish you, you know some people are sick
they wait until you are nearly passed
then they switch on every light that they have
and give you full blast.
Anyway one day in town a chap swore and gave a glare

so I went after him down the street like a hare
now I won't make any pretence
for I did commit a minor traffic offence.
But he must have seen I was going to retaliate
because when he stopped at the paper shop
when he saw me behind he didn't wait
bounded out into a bus at a terrible rate
and as I passed shaking my head at his wing
I gave him a wink
as though he never did a thing.
....

Hanging

Do we hang the murdering bastards
or do you think that not very nice
you know after a swing on the rope
they would never murder twice.
The rape of a child, now that makes me wild
yes, I'd sever the silver chord
but where to begin there is so much sin
or is evil a better word.
....

Aids

It used to be 'pox' but now it's 'Aids'
could this be some divine retribution
I cannot help but to think not, for I haven't a spot
because I make love to one not like some
and that is a great contribution.
....

Change

Sometimes you know
the rain turns to snow
and liking can turn into love.
But what a sad state
when dislike turns to hate.
....

Hang On

Have you ever stopped and wondered
what on earth is going on
every job you try and do
somehow goes all wrong.
Climbing a hill or down a pit
I just can't make head or tail of it
everyone's got some disease to smit
sometimes life is a con
so try and enjoy the good times

and when the bad times come
hang on.
....

The Gun

He's an excellent shot with rifle and gun
but why does he want to kill some mother's son
why do babies grow up and kill
will the evil bastards ever get their fill
but stupidity flourishes in poor man and toff
they just want to hear the damn gun go off.
....

The Lost Goose

it's awful sad to see a Grey Lag
lost and alone in the sky
wings beating so frantic
the earth is so gigantic
where did all his friends go, and why.
....

The Garden

Spring again and then the garden
oh the bloody garden
I really do beg your pardon
no need to swear I know
but I'm hopeless at the garden.
And just my luck
my neighbour is great
you know my liking for that man
is now tantamount to hate.
His tatties grow quick and all the same size
while mine grow like strawberries
and half of them dies.
My lawn is probably the worst it's been
and his is like a bowling green.
There he goes he waters the rows
and you know he gets right up my nose
in fact we may yet come to blows
oh how I hate the garden.
....

Harling

I wish they'd invent a machine for harling
because it's really sore on the back
I did a big gable yesterday
and near had a heart attack.
Scaffold up scaffold doon
throwing pails down to the loon

aye a machine would be a right boon
when it comes to harling.
....

Snobbish

A dog may crap in your garden
without as much as a pardon
and a cat may eat your goldfish
but they are Airedale and Siamese
now is that being snobbish.
....

Nightmare

The alcoholic dreams his dream
and angels alight on the branches
the world rotates so slowly
and treachery before him prances
the sun is high at noon
who believes a fool
everybody as a rule
and on his grave Satan dances.
....

Paris & Helen

Oh great Achilles from gods were born
spilled Hector's blood in triumphant storm
young Paris his brother knows passions hot
lies with Helen after the battles fought.
'Do you know Helen' he says
'what a way to end your days'
but I didn't think Heck would take him
I hope the bookie pays.
Oh come and look out of the window
and see all the campfires
hear the women twanging their lyres
now look there's a big horse on tyres
now isn't that kind of them.
....

The Schoolboy

Did you read about the blonde teacher
who played with an older boy
they had fun together
and it wasn't with a toy.
Well honestly I cannot help it
I had to stop and grin
that is every schoolboys daydream
and most are just jealous of him.
....

My Old Lorry

I saw my old lorry on the street today
and when I think of it, honestly I could cry
there she was as black as soot
and still with only one eye.
I could see she was heavily laden
in my opinion far too much of a load
and it was obvious to everyone
her body was too near the road.
Sadly I reflected on happier days
and some of the jobs in Ardross
now I don't think that damn coalman
would think of that, and couldn't care a toss.
I remember too when a brake pipe burst
and we were nearly copped
mind you, it didn't surprise me
we were in Alness before we got stopped.
Oh yes the memories came flooding back
when my emotions suddenly exploded
I rushed over and screamed at the coalman
'That damn lorry is overloaded!'
....

The Corner Shop

I suppose I'd better go shopping
what do I need apart from the grog
oh yes a pound of cheese
and some tins of food for the dog.
Oh, maybe the wife will go instead
along to the shop at the corner
I added a few articles on to her line
so I better warn her.
Not like the last time, just for a laugh
I added a packet of 'Big Boys'
and I tell you now when she got home
you ought to have heard the noise.
Instead of reading the line herself
she gave it to one of the staff
oh it cheered up the girls in the wee shop
and gave them a bit of a laugh.
....

Hole in the Heart

I knew a man who had a hole in the heart
and at school was not allowed gym
he looked quite an athletic chap
so it was an awful pity for him.
Now, as soon as he was old enough
he started an affair with the drink
some said the heart was doing it
but that is not what I think.

Anyway that was over forty years ago
and the class has fairly diminished
wheelchairs diseases the lot
and some that are all but finished.
Now science has progressed that's true
and no doubt wiser doctors get
for the guy with the hole in the heart
he is boozing away here yet.

....

Talent

Don't try and be a singer
if you haven't got the voice
and forget about the building trade
if you have another choice.
Think of the talents that you have
and then take your pick
when you have learned the basic rules
get in there and give it stick.
Now if you are naturally good at something
success will come your way
I suppose that is why I'm on my backside
and I can hardly move today.
Now that is a bit of self-pity
and I'm getting quite good at that
the surgeon thinks I'm an actor
'Yes, the dirty rat.'
Now most of this is 'clap trap'
if you want to sing, just sing
but there was only one Elvis
and everybody can't be king.

....

Useless

I used to pray for the royal family
prime minister and politicians too
that's the way that I was taught
and likely so were you.
I asked God to give them wisdom
and that an example they would set
guide us along the unselfish road
and keep us out of debt.
I should have kept that up no doubt
yes, I know that fine
but it was like speaking to a pile of bricks
a total waste of time.

....

Hope

Hope is the most astonishing thing
I think it is more enduring than love

338

and coupled with a wee bit of blindness
then the two go hand in glove.
Mind you that's not a bad thing
for without hope we would despair
and the wee bit of blindness helps us along
because perfection is pretty rare.
Now getting back to the point about 'hope'
and I'm telling you now this is no joke
I knew a man and he was nearly ninety
and on his death bed sat
well he called to me to do his football pools
now, what do make of that.

....

Justice

Everybody gets their rewards in life
and the wicked gets their comeuppance
and for their chance of happiness
no I wouldn't give tupence.
Time will eventually give justice to all
as they say, we make our own bed
and if you believe in all of that
you're really not right in the head.

....

The Replacement

I see two or three new builders about now
no doubt with help from the enterprise scheme
they are just taking advantage
now that I've paid off my team.
Mind you, it's quite heart warming
to see that there are three
I was thinking it would take two at least
to replace the likes of me.
But will they treat my customers right I wonder
and not 'do' them or make a mess
oh likely they'll offend them by refusing a dram
but that is only a guess.
And what about Mrs Ross's dog
I hope they speak to it
for she thinks the world of that mongrel
and I was one of the few it never bit.
Then poor old Mrs Mackay on the corner
who likes to talk and laugh
I only hope they have the patience
for she goes on for an hour and a half.
And for my other clients
the big ones who like a price
I only hope they are honest
to be otherwise wouldn't be nice.
Well I could go on for ages
maybe I will one day
now do you think I should tell them

about the ones that are slow to pay.
No I won't I've decided
for what I lost was pitiful small
and they can learn the same as me
well, I'm human after all.
....

Patience

Patience is the greatest gift
it's the icing and the candy
and when you are waiting for a train
you know it's awful handy.
Because really we are waiting half our life
for one thing or another
and if you think it gets easier, it doesn't
go and ask your mother.
The answer is to enjoy the waiting
when you are climbing you cannot fall
but honestly isn't it so boring
and not my style at all.
....

Pessimistic

Now it's nearly five o'clock
to be truthful I'm planning a dram
not exactly a will of iron
but that is the way that I am.
It's not that I can't be trusted
for some principles I'd fight hand to hand
yet I wonder what moulded man's nature
that's something I don't understand.
Some can be trusted to keep your dog
and for your holidays be a good master
but you can't leave your wife alone
that would be a pure disaster.
So what do you think is nobody trusty
black is man's soul and nobody's white
now you would be pessimistic if you thought that
but, you would be right.
....

Practice

A cheery personality is a precious thing
it's a talent of a special kind
more pleasurable than a singer
or any artist that you'll find.
But like all other talents of this world
practice makes perfection
now even a frog can sing a song
if you can see the connection.
....

Can't Help It

I was working with a man once
if I said 'gurny' would be to understate
and I had got right tired of him
I had enough on my plate.
Now just to cut a long story short
one day I nearly gave him a smack
I didn't fortunately, for the very next day
he died with a heart attack.
Of course I wasn't pleased
maybe a little relieved
but anyway the more I thought of the gurn
and believe me I'm no pundit
but his body and mind was going all wrong
and he just couldn't understand it.

....

A Craving

I flamencoed round the Cabana
but I didn't attempt the table
and now I'm sorry I didn't do it
because now I am not able.
Too late I learned this lesson
don't think of 'why' but 'how'
if you have a craving to do anything
you're better to do it now.
Opportunity may only knock the once
well that is what they say
and life is just a 'one off'
and this could be your last day.

....

Nightmare

I had a nightmare the other night
and it scared me half to death
when I woke in the morning
I was sweating and panting for breath.
What was the dream you well may ask
well, I now know the coward that I am
I dreamed I was a beggar on the street
and nobody cared a damn.

....

A Tall Story?

A friend of mine told me this story
and he said every word is true
mind you, he is of the same ilk as myself
and a bit of an alki too.
He told me he was down in London

staying at a right posh hotel
this was purely for business reasons
so his wife didn't go as well.
Well after the meetings were over
they all repaired to the bar
it was quite a luxurious place
similar to the Station or Star.
Well anyway after a rake of nips
as usual the guys started to mingle
now him being a Highlander
more or less thought he was single.
He chatted up the lassies
and one gorgeous girl fell for his charms
then in no time at all
they were locked in each other's arms.
Now nips led to martini's
and then of course, (up the stair)
by now he had drunk a bottle
oh, and he didn't care.
Now once in the bedroom
out came the Champagne
mind to my pal
all drink was the same.
He glugged it down at his usual pace
said complimentary things about her face
what happened next I can't describe at all
but in the morning he met her going out of the hall.
And she paused as he passed
and whispered 'Have you a light'
'and darling you were wonderful last night.'
Now my friend, I told you was a drouth
but I believe at times he tells the truth
he told me after he heard the barman's bell go 'ding'
after that he can't mind a thing.

....

True

Why are some folks lot in life
seems to be to spread unhappiness
it could be me it could be you
it could be anyone more or less.
To cause another human being misery
yes, and even grief
you know the way the world evolved
is really beyond belief.
I know that Darwin had a theory
'progression by natural selection'
but surely after all these years
we would be near perfection.
But yet he spoke a great truth
to the dead and those alive
that the helpless will surely suffer
and only the strong will thrive.

....

The Real Urges

I've never embezzled any money
or stolen ladies pants
basically because I was far too shy
and I never had the chance.
So I seem honest and virtuous
and I keep the compass within my range
but if I had to do it all again
believe me there would be a change.
There's not much fun pretending I'm perfect
and kidding on that I am good
I only wish I was brave enough to be me
and to hell with Robin Hood.
But then the obvious question
and I think of it a lot of the time
if I unleash my urges
where would I draw the line.

....

No Difference

I worked with a brickie long ago
and honestly I was twice as fast
yet he was a tidy worker
and I knew his building would last.
Well recently I saw a house that we built
and to be honest it still looked good
but I couldn't see our different work
and do you know I thought that I would.

....

The Wide Road

Yes we're getting back to basics now
the rich get richer and the poor get poorer
and he who lives by his wits get wealthy
there is nothing surer.
So boldly down the wide road we go
and it doesn't take too much detection
though we march bravely down it
we are going in the wrong direction.

....

Difficulties

We are told overcoming difficulties
that's what makes us strong
it makes us more understanding
and to know the right from the wrong.
Yet when I think of the disappointments
that we people have to endure
I sometimes doubt this philosophy

and of the theory I'm not too sure.
To be honest I think it is nature
and I'm sure that this is just a fact
the more troubles that you get
you just get used to the final impact.
....

Party Member

I hate the thought of being brainwashed
yet it happens all the time
we tend to think we are free spirits
well, maybe we are some of the time.
But if you think of our attitudes
and the source from where they emit
usually it's from the government
they're the ones who thought of it.
Of course we have our opposing parties
and that's something we should all remember
because there is something really frightening
about a staunch party member.
....

Justice

British justice, the envy of the world
you know, sometimes I just wonder
maybe the guy who coined the phrase
made a wee bit of a blunder.
It seems to me, I don't know if you'll agree
perhaps you'll just look and frown
I think it can be fair play all right
but only it's upside down.
Yes justice is the same the world over
the rich and smart are anointed
it's better to be guilty and wealthy
than poor and not really wanted.
....

Put Off

No blue suede shoes for me now
or rock 'n' roll I don't think
when I reflect on what could have been
no wonder I went to the drink.
All that potential in just one man
and I did nothing but watch
I was too frightened to try anything
in case I made a botch.
Now I'm too old for all that stuff
and I've learned that lesson with sorrow
so I'm going to try all I can
and I will start tomorrow.
....

Getting Done

I got cheated by several folk
and believe me there were more than a few
but somehow sometime later
I found out and I knew.
Now you would think a fool could stop this
and to be honest I know that fine
but my characters not as white as snow
and that little problem is mine.
You see when these folk are doing me
I'm 'scheming' as someone once said
and when I'm at my plotting
there's no eyes in the back of my head.

....

Another Lorry

I had a yellow lorry once
and do you know the gearbox was never right
it kept jumping out of top gear
though I held the stick with all of my might.
But then I had inspiration
strong elastic bands were the answer
if I could keep two hands on the wheel
she would corner like a ballet dancer.
So I tied the bands from the seat to the stick
and when I changed into top
I'd stretch the band over the lever
which made it tricky to stop.
But sadly deterioration slowly set in
instead of one band there were two
and it just seemed in no time at all
I needed quite a few.
Now this is honest I do not lie
I tell you she was so far gone
by the time I got to Dingwall
I was putting the last band on.

....

Removing a Galvanised Tank

I had the task of removing a water tank
and it was the size of a shed
it was positioned right in the apex
to give the water a head.
Now I didn't know what weight it was
it didn't matter because all I had was a rope
but us small builders are quite inventive
not like most other folk.
Well I emptied out the water
and put a half hitch round a purling
now, my rope was a cheap one
so there was a danger of it curling.
Well just as I was levering it over the platforms edge

underneath two directors were passing by
and they shouted up 'you'll not manage yourself'
and I replied 'Oh aye'.
So off they went to my relief
and so I levered it off on the rope to hing
but my rope wasn't strong enough
and it snapped like a bit of string.
So down it crashed to the concrete floor
with a noise like an atomic bomb
and at that moment I was grateful
the two directors were gone.
So down the ladders shaking like a leaf
and beside the tank I sat
when the two directors came in again
and exclaimed 'How did you manage that'.
Now I'm not a man to make a meal of things
for if they were underneath it would be tragic
so I just looked up as nonchalantly as I could
and said 'Oh just a little magic.'
....

A Snare

I'm a big strong man you know
I drink, I fight and I snore
and off my other attributes
if I had time I'd tell you more.
Yet once when I was out hunting
I heard a squeal from a snare
and when I reached the trap
a rabbit struggled there.
Well you mightn't believe this
most would say I lied
but I let the rabbit go
and sat down and I cried.
....

The Pub

Yes I'm going out again tonight
now that is pretty risky
well I've often told you
about my love affair with whisky.
First of all I thought I'd stay in
and maybe go early to bed
or else watch the late movie
and take a wee beer instead.
But no the wife and mother nature
seem to urge me to socialise
and after the things I've done to them
right before their eyes.
So how will I cope with my terrible thirst
the answer I now understand
I'll just sit with some Englishmen
and they won't stand their hand.
....

Fornicate

I've never fornicated once you know
and justifiably I feel smug
not like you weak creatures
with a stupid grin on your mug.
But there again I'll relent a bit
and this theory I will proffer
it does make it a lot easier
if you never get an offer.
....

My Lorry

The last lorry I bought was probably the best
it was a blue Leyland Terrier
mind you that was a good few years ago
when I was on the Perrior.
It was ex-hydro board I was told
and the salesman was sure on the ball
he told me although it was five years old
it never did any work at all.
Now that's not saying much for the Hydro board
but she looked quite crisp and clean
and my old Commer was old and knackered
it was a model that was now never seen.
So I took her home delighted
but as you know life is so unjust
because in just a year or two
she was rotten with the rust.
And oh it was so undignified
although with wire I tried to tie
one of the headlights just fell out
and she was like Nelson with only one eye.
Then the embarrassment of doing a job
when the wifie waved as we parted
I jumped into the lorry and waved back
but the lorry just never started.
Now the poor wifie was standing in the cold
and I was thrashing the battery with a hammer
trying to keep my temper in control
but occasionally screaming 'Damn her!'
Now I could go on and on
but really she was the best
yes, I know what you are thinking
what on earth like was the rest.
But then one last effrontery
and I never told a single soul
because she doesn't carry sand and cement no more
I sold her to carry, coal.
....

Love Poem

I thought I'd write a love poem once
and dedicate it all to the wife

347

I wrote pages of verses and stanzas
that, was the biggest mistake of my life.
I raved about Mary's beauty
her nature so soft and warm
I tried to make it so authentic
(but it sounded a lot of corn).
So I am near divorced now
mind I had an inkling at the time
I shouldn't have used her sisters name
just because the wife's name wouldn't rhyme.
....

Robin Hood

When I was young I often thought
I would like to be Robin Hood
taking from the rich to feed the poor
I really thought that good.
But now I'm older and have more sense
I can see it is all a con
so if ever I go back in time
I want to be rich like Prince John.
....

Revenge

You know it is terrible
but I sometimes think before I die
and I go to that great quarry in the sky
I'll get even with all my enemies.
You know the people who made me sad
that I would take my revenge
and I would be so glad
but then I thought 'what a waste of time'
they have a problem and it's not mine.
Instead I'll pray as hard as I can
and just try and accept my loss
put my trust in justice and God
and hope he'll make me the quarry boss.
....

What Next

I often thought of what a man will do
when his back is against the wall
and you don't have to be in peril
no you don't, not at all.
Just to gratify an instinct
it's amazing what a man will do
I never told a soul about this
but now I'm telling you.
In the middle of the night last week
the wife she had to get up you see
and guess who stole her glass of water

yes I confess that man was me.
And just to compound the crime
when I heard the patter of her feet
I shut my eyes and turned over
and pretended I was asleep.
....

Horror Story

I thought I'd write a horror story
to get fame and maybe wealth
but the story that I wrote
only terrified myself.
All that evil goings on
I couldn't sleep for weeks
imagination can be an awesome thing
and not very good for the breeks.
Well eventually I finished my tale
and tried it out on the wife
she read it without one scream at all
'Aye' she said 'that's life'.
....

Regrets

Yes I have a few regrets
and I wouldn't do some things again
all the mistakes embarrasses me
like other normal men.
So at times I sit quite red faced
silent and deep in thought
and I count my blessings
and am thankful I didn't get caught.
....

Love

I find it hard to talk about love
except when I'm in a clinch
then I'll tell her anything
even lies at a pinch.
I'll babble on for long enough
and persuade her the best I can
for that is ordinary behaviour
for the normal man.
Yet sometimes when I've no success
and she picks up a book to read
I pretend that I'm in pain
and I cry and beg and plead.
Even after a perfect performance
I've seen me be reduced to prayer
but God and the wife go to sleep
and pretends I'm not even there.
Now that is just the way of life I suppose

we men have got to be strong and tough
and if we don't get our wicked way
we can always go to sleep in the huff.
....

V Formation

You've often seen the geese fly over
in the formation of a V
well you know why they do this
the very same as me.
But have you thought of the bird in the front
the willing horse' you could say, but a bird
and if you think he knows what he is doing
that notion is quite absurd.
By instinct they act like us humans
whether at work or in an attack
they gather into a formation
and the smart stay at the back.
But then of course we could argue
that they take turns and they rotate
I wish it were true but that's not what they do
and to believe it would be a mistake.
What really happens is the front takes the brunt
until he falls quite shattered
and the rest regroup and fly away
for nobody wants the tired and knackered.
....

In Charge

I've often talked about coming into this world
yes, naked and we'll leave it the same
now I'm not going to whine at all
or even attribute any blame.
But when I was young and full of fun
I thought eventually I'll be in charge of myself
it always seemed the older ones
who controlled my life by stealth.
But now in middle age I see
waiting for my turn was a mistake
if you want to be in charge of you
this authority you'll just have to 'take'.
....

Pay the Bills

I've had a real bad day today
all the bills came in
and I hadn't the cash to pay them
which is tantamount to sin.
The sheriff's officers, oh not again
and I'm not even fit to fight
oh maybe they'll all get a heart attack

in the middle of the night.
So I am not going to worry any more
if I can or cannot pay
you know life is so uncertain
but tomorrow's another day.

....

The Trick

I never cease to be amazed at folk
and their attitude to the poor
if a rich man held his hand out
he'd get plenty that is sure.
Is it some instinct of preservation
of reasons you could take your pick
but personally I can't help thinking
it's the rich that know the trick.

....

The Happiest

Well I've figured it out at last
how to be a happy man
it really is so simple
it's the way the world began.
Just go along with chaos
let passion rule your days
and be totally irresponsible
in a thousand different ways.
Now if you think that cynical
just take a look around
and tell me which are the happiest dogs
running about your pound.

....

Evolve

You know what an unhappy country this is
most folk go about so glum
I don't mean everyone of course
but you know yourself they're some.
Well I was just thinking
about the millions of years
surely we should have evolved better
and done away with tears.
But no, we make each other unhappy
and it's only God that knows why
where is the pleasure in misery
for misery too must die.
Yet still we persist in this habit
and for what, some perverted pleasure
when life could be a joy for all
and we could all share in the treasure.

....

Road Men

See the men working on the roads
did you notice some of them are right careless
they don't have any concern about the traffic at all
probably they think it fearless.
Well I just missed one with my wheels today
as he ambled back and fore
and do you know I was so annoyed
I pranged him with my door.

....

One Cure

The ministers wife is in awful pain
and often can't get out of bed
she has arthritis in every joint
and it even affects her head.
But what I was wondering
(and this is probably sin)
why on earth doesn't Margaret
take a drop sherry or gin.
This of course is a crazy idea
yes I know that fine
then I could go dramming with Margaret
and it would be right handy most of the time.

....

Forms

Here's another form to fill in
and at the end the usual threat
if it's not returned in a fortnight
it's the procurator fiscal that I'll get.
And I don't even know the man
so why should I be his foe
I sometimes wish for the good old times
when you look vacant and say 'I don't know'.
We probably need a good champion
to help the fight against the nurds
because we don't know the jargon
and misunderstand half the words.
So what will I do with all these threats
will I fill in the form tonight
yes you know I will
because it's a system you cannot fight.

....

Principles

Have you ever been desperate for money
well I knew a man that was
and he was brought up to be honourable

and to obey nearly all the laws.
Now oft times I talked and thought
when your back is against the wall
what a man will do
well we're human after all.
Now this chap I knew was in a fix
and he struggled to keep control
did his principle and upbringing save him?
no they didn't, he cheated and he stole.

....

Happy Pills

I went down to the doc today
and do you know he was very nice
he asked me if I still took a drink
and I said 'Oh just the once or twice'.
This was all lies of course
as well as my denial of the smoke
then he told me of the dangers to health
and that I might take a stroke.
'It's my back' I said 'It's my bloody back'
the rest of me is fine
but then I took another tack
and I began to whine.
'Yes doctor, I know you're right'
it's the smoke and drink that kills
but could you no' see your way
and give me a few more 'happy pills'.

....

Sunset

The sun has passed the yard-arm now
well actually the window sill
now I know fine what you are thinking
that I'm going to take the fill.
You think when the sun is fading
my resistance fades away too
but you'd be wrong if you thought that
because I'm only going to take a few.

....

Reward

I sometimes wonder at life's end
is there a reward for kindness
or am I just havering
and thinking kind of mindless.
But if there is of course
there must be penalties and pits
now I won't take any chances
so I'll just go for 'quits'.

....

Dog Lover

Dog lovers are a crazy bunch
they're a breed of their own
the wife asked me this question
yesterday when I came home.
'Did you see anyone today dear?'
and as I was taking off my toggs
I replied quite unthinking
'Oh I was speaking to a couple of dogs!'
....

Another Reward

I knew a right kind woman once
and she couldn't give you more
just mention a bonny thing in her house
it was under your arm going out the door.
Many a helping hand she gave
and parted with many a quid
and did she ever get any reward in the end
well I know, she never did.

....

Boring

There is nothing quite so boring in life
as when things stay the same
even if it's constant sunshine
and not one shower of rain.
No miserable times to moan at
when the days are not so good
no exciting memories
to lift our darkest mood.
Now I know it's not nice to be unhappy
but it's an experience that makes you rich
I tell you there is nothing so empty
as life without a hitch.
....

Be Kind

I thought that I was unhappy
but that was really a joke
just take a look at the catastrophes
that happens to other folk.
I know it's no compensation
to see people worse off than yourself
poor and poverty stricken
in sickness and poor health.
Yes, most of us get some disasters
so we should keep this in mind
when you see other folk hurting
it doesn't cost much to be kind.

....

Drunken Glasses

I put on my drunken glasses again today
that's the ones all scratched and cracked
I hoped this wasn't an ill omen
if it is I should get smacked.
And me thinking I had it conquered
this weakness of the flesh
the body cries out for satisfaction
and gets it more or less.
But I will resist and overcome
and I will stand firm today
(mainly because the wife is watching me)
for she's got a holiday.
....

The Laird

I went out to see a repair job once
and the client was fair acting the Laird
he spoke with an affected accent
which in the North is rarely heard.
He pointed out the defective parts
and the leak in the garage roof
I was suspicious of an insurance scam
but of that I had no proof.
He strutted about just like a royal prince
gesticulating with a crooked stick
while I tottered two paces behind
thinking 'what a prick'.
Well when at last he finished
he looked down his nose and said
'Just give me a quotation for this and that
and I might consider it when it is read'.
Of course I'll get more advice than yours
to obtain a better perspective
because I don't think it's as bad as you say
so I'll get a more professional directive.
Now normally I'm not easily offended
I understand nobody is perfection
but on that occasion honestly
I had to make an exception.
I told him I was far, far, too busy
and this is the honest truth
as I drove off I put the window down
I shouted 'You also need a new roof!'
....

Memory Blanks

I'm not going to think too far ahead
one day at a time is enough
and for me to look back is disastrous
for some of the past is rough.

I could never justify my actions
that's the ones that I can 'mind
mother nature made me forget the worst
and I'm grateful that she is kind.
I have apologised a lot of course
and now my conscience is more or less clear
but I don't like that two old wifies smiling at me
and I get quite jumpy when they are near.

....

Planning

If I could get my hands on that angel
the one that planned my life
likely he just took the shot
and left it all to the wife.
Or maybe he was getting on a bit
and getting a bit slack in the head
and continued working
when he should have been in his bed.
But that is all excuses
surely I got some kind of guarantee
but no doubt he went and misplaced it
after he finished with me.
So what do I do with total chaos
do I still follow the crazy plan
the spec is really a nightmare
but a cheap way to make a man.
So I think I'll change it
and use my own aggression
just like we did in the building trade
that's where I learned that lesson.
But what can I do about that crazy angel
turning out people like me
I only hope he doesn't degenerate
and make builders that work for free.
Then when I think of my drunken habits
to make another like me would be a calamity
an if the angel thought he'd churn me out
that would be pure insanity.

....

Chaos

As you know I hurt my back
now this is just a quick fact
If I got drunk on Sunday
didn't go to work on Monday
in the mornings went on the beer
today I wouldn't be here.
I told you it's all total chaos
it's just the luck of the draw
there is no rhyme or reason
and that is the only law.

....

Retire in Spain

I must leave this country
or else with the cold I'll expire
I think I'll go to Spain
that's when I retire.
I'll lie on the beach
with a bottle of wine
a box of cigars
that will be fine
but then, I thought
what about this disease I got
I just couldn't look up all day
in the shade of bamboo huts
you see I'm easily bored
and lying about, would drive me nuts.

....

Important

I feel so sorry for the royals at times
no matter which one it concerns
they have a heart that hurts as well
and that's no way to bring up bairns.
They must think they are a different breed
and not like us all grown from seed
but I could understand if that were true
because I would be the same, and so would you.
Illusions of importance deceives us all
whether on the throne or at the kitchen sink
we are all clarted with the same brush
and not as necessary as we think.

....

Heaven

I better go to the Post Office today
and pick up my weekly pension
and this is so unnatural for me
I should be at an extension.
Even a garden wall with a cope stone
or a foundation would be heaven for me
and yet, when I was doing it
this heaven I could not see.

....

The Part

Why we pose only God knows
the psychiatrist says we 'project'
but what are we trying to tell other people
not a lot I would suspect.
Do we try and tell, we are well

or maybe that we are sick
and that guy swaggering down the street
is he telling me that he's a dick.
No I don't think so, I've been fooled before
people sometimes give out the wrong signs
we just can't remember who we are
like an actor who's forgotten his lines.
....

Economics

I sometimes get to the stage
when I think of the human race
there are so many clever people
and I am in the wrong place.
I can't understand economics
how men in suits create wealth
where does the money come from
is it by labour or is it by stealth.
Well in all honesty I do not know
and when from my studies
I take a rest and a breather
I realise I don't know who knows
and I don't think you know either.
....

Wisdom

I'm like you I criticise them
sheriffs, the judges, the law
even to the point of disbelief
of their judgements and what they saw.
Yet there was a trial of two young boys
yes, and I did get on my knees to pray
for those two young boys killed a baby
so I asked God to give the judge wisdom that day.
....

Ordinary

I'm not exactly breaking up
but something is certainly cracking
maybe I'm not eating enough fish
or some other nutrient I am lacking.
But there again when I think of it
I wasn't so bright, even at my best
I was kind of ordinary
just like most of the rest.
But I was told that I could crack it
given encouragement a kiss and a pat
and if you have ever lived in the North
you'll not believe a word of that.
So what is so wrong about ordinary
we can't all be 'head of the force'

the philosophy of being well balanced is good
and all the rest be deducted at source.

....

Holiday

Six of us local lads conspired
and thought we'd have a holiday afloat
and it was right handy
that one of us had a boat.
No wives were allowed of course
well, there just wasn't any room
so they waved us off at the pier
and we shouted 'See you soon'.
Now I won't go into the details
because each of us swore an oath
so that whole fortnight's a secret
and to tell secrets I am loath.
But one little thing I'll tell you
a holiday on a boat without the wife!
you could be very miserable
but we had the time of our life.

....

Successful Joiner

A joiner passed the window just now
and I happen to know, he's a bit of a crook
if he took you to the cleaners
that would not be a fluke.
But he is not the worst around
although he is always scheming
but if you think he won't do you
you really must be dreaming.
The old folk say he won't thrive like that
dishonesty is an anchor and drag
but the old folk can get it wrong at times
and I'll tell that to his new Jag.

....

Bureaucracy

I for one am tired of bureaucracy
the way the nurds have taken over
all their thousands of rules
to control the ways of the rover.
No wonder we're unemployed
a lawyer can't see the way clear
and it depresses men of action
and not the way of the pioneer.
You can see who does the pushing
but now it's all done with words
and who is our explorers
well it's certainly not the nurds.

So how do we get some balance back
and each do what they do best
but only fools want to live without rules
for in the past our leaders just guessed.
....

Millionaire

I wanted to be a millionaire
instead I'm nearly a pauper
in fact if I was any younger
it's likely I'd be a 'Yopper'.
But I won't start bleating
for the fire it burnt my leg
and it is so cold outside the door
I'll just stay inside instead.
....

Learned What

You would think after all these years
by example we would have learned
not make the mistakes out parents made
and have the peace that they all yearned.
But no, we charge on blindly
ignoring the lessons of history
why on earth do we make the same mistakes
you know it's just a mystery.
It would be so simple if we were stupid
that would answer all
yet smart men still climb mountains
and smart men sometimes fall.
....

Painting

I told you about the picture
that the monkeys painted
and when the experts discovered that
half of them near fainted.
Well a similar thing happened in Australia
with a poetical work, by a poet that was new
nobody had an inkling what it meant
but the experts said they knew.
Well it transpired some English students
just to create a din
selected words at random
and picked them with a pin.
Published them under a heading
and the experts sat and thought
when even a simple brickie could tell
that it was just a heap of rot.
....

In the Pew

Sometimes I fancy going to Lourdes
to try and find a cure
if only I were a catholic
but of my religion I was never sure.
And then I thought, better not
and that was sensible I knew
because I can't even go to the Kirk
without fancying some lass in the pew.
And I thought it was only me who did that
but the next time you take a look
most of the guys are singing away
with only one eye on their book.

....

More Luck

My bum is numb with sitting
my back is sore with work
my happy smiling face
droops now in a lurk.
And I was a man that thought
I was off the special breed
work hard, live honest and sober
and you will never know need.
And now when in my darkest hour
I often sit and reflect
where on earth did I go wrong
what duties did I neglect.
But deep down I just knew
the law of nature is very clear
it's all a matter of luck
that I am sitting here.

....

When Things are Good

In the past I found it so easy
to get on my knees and pray
to thank God for all his goodness
and the gifts we got each day.
But these were times of plenty
of sunshine youth and pleasure
the mornings promise of daylight
and warmth beyond measure.
Now in the afternoon of life
my faith is torn asunder
no manna comes from heaven now
and you know, I just sit and wonder.

....

Man

I used to think quite often
when I was digging out a found'
did a man really originate
out of this very ground.
And do you know it doesn't take a genius
it just takes a little thought
there is nowhere else to come from
it's the only source we got.
There is of course one mystery
that is the factor of time
and if we knew how long it took
we would believe it quite fine.
You see when you think in terms of billions
and the possibilities out of that arising
universes growing and shrinking
a mere man is not so surprising.

....

Life Style

I better take more of those coloured pills
I'm eating them now like Smarties
'mind you the doctor hinted
I'd been at too many parties.
Too much of a good thing at times can be bad
a paradox of 'no' and 'not'
but I enjoyed all the fun and the frolics
yes, I enjoyed the lot.

....

The Magnificent Seven

When I was younger I wanted to be Chris
you know Chris of the Magnificent Seven
black hat clothes and twin guns
I used to think that was heaven.
But now I'm older and probably wiser
I've lost the urge to sling any lead
for I realised it's no fun to get hurt
and not much joy in a baldie head.
So now I fantasise about being young
and I don't make any pretence
I just want to be the way that I was
you know it just doesn't make any sense.

....

Tourettes

We had a minister years ago
and he was a doctor of divinity
and I thought that he was the most holy man

362

yes, in all the vicinity.
He was a cleric of the old school
no, I never saw him smile
some said he was too clever for his own good
and I thought that for a while.
But when the poor man got really old
he lost control of his mind
he swore, ranted obscene abuse
and generally was unkind.
Now I have more respect for that man
by that signal and that sign
he told us he knew of the ways of the world
but resisted them all the time.

....

Mam Again

My mother thought I was so good looking
and would break many a heart
she also thought I was so clever
and I too thought I was smart.
But I kept this knowledge to myself
which was a bit of a pest
because then only me and mam knew
I wonder what was wrong with the rest.

....

Mixer

I must sell my mixer now
to a mason that is the pits
I mind fine when I bought her new
yes, I was thrilled to bits.
Many a winter we worked together
and many a happy summer too
and not one bad batch did she turn out
at least there were very few.
When I think of all the concrete she made
quite happily grinding away
no wonder I am shedding tears
and am feeling sad today.
But life has to go on someone said
it doesn't have to, but it will
me and my mixer are knackered anyway
we both are over the hill.
So I will put an ad in the paper
yes I know that I will feel lonely
but I'll not sell her to anyone
it'll be to a good home only.

....

The Arrest

I was arrested when I was about twelve

for fighting at the school
me and my pal stood in the station
and I really felt a fool.
The young bobby went through the procedure
you would think I was Al Capone
while I thought of mam and dad
and the row when I got home.
Now forty years later he's now an inspector
and doubtless made many a raid
but I was told I had the distinction
of being the only arrest he made.
....

Love Bird

I told you about the dove in my garden
the one that was left bereft
how once there was a pair of them
and thanks to a hawk only one was left.
Well I notice now there are two once again
yes it got another mate
it just goes to show it's never too late.
Yes it's lovely to see them
canoodling by the light of the moon
but I wonder if they were human
would somebody say 'too soon'.
....

Scaffold

I better not sell my tower scaffold
although I'm still a thrifty man
for one thing I bought it second hand
from a man in a transit van.
And now I'd feel responsible
if any of it went and broke
and you could get severely hurt
(well, I'm that kind of bloke).
So I asked my friends for their advice
some said it could collapse in a second
others said it would last for years
that is what they reckoned.
But I couldn't have that on my mind
for a niggling worry is never nice
mind you, I'm still human
so it would depend on the price.
....

Late Home

My wife and son were late last night
and of course I began to fret
snow and sleet, wind and rain
and the roads were greasy and wet.

Up and down the room I paced
every minute clutching the phone
'who on earth can I contact
oh why don't they come home?'
Lonely headlights flash on by
'but so few, what does that mean?'
I think of the things I've said and done
and what we could have been.
Then tensions relief, an indicator
a flashing light of joy
and I leaped up and down and laughed
yes, just like a little boy.
And now I see it's no mystery
although anxiety it can mar
but after a little worry
you see things as they are.
....

Nosey

I was working in Cromarty once
going home we stopped for a lager and lime
Craig my labourer had a shandy
and to be honest I had a nip with mine.
Well anyway a local was standing at the bar
and being a rustic he wanted to know the lot
where we came from where we were going
and what other jobs we had got.
Now I am not a cruel man
but for the crack I told him nout
every question that he asked
I just filled him with more doubt.
Flummoxed now and frustrated
he gazed where my lorry was parked
and I could see by his expression
that he was getting narked.
The truck was full of diggings of the job
and I'm sure he thought my secrecy he'd foil
for he turned to me and exclaimed
'You know boys, I don't recognise the spoil'.
....

It Happens

If I were to be honest I want to be rich
and then I'd buy a yacht
but unfortunately when the cards were dealt
wealth is not what I got.
I wanted to strut about my ship
but of course I'd call it a 'craft'
I would take a bevy of lovely lassies
no, I was never daft.
And on the pier the Merc would be parked
(by the way this would take place in Spain)
and the sun would be beating down

not like Invergordon or Tain.
And then in the afternoon
we'd all go to the shops
and I would flash my platinum card
and buy the lassies their frocks.
And then into the Cantinas
we'd all take the shot and get drunk
sing all the way back to the pier
to see if the craft had sunk.
And then we'd all lie on the deck
where we would get brown with the sun
rolling over and over
until we were well and truly done.
But now you know this is all a dream
and it won't happen to you or me
but honestly it happens to some folk
just go to Spain and see.
....

Don't Care

You know when your mind is in turmoil
and you have reached the pits
everything is going wrong
and you are losing your wits.
This is the time to be reckless
make a cup of tea and sit on a chair
read a book or watch a film
and really don't bloody care.
....

Big Lesson

The most important lesson in life I learned
and you know that I'm no sage
but I know that you can make a new start
yes, at any reasonable age.
The very time you think you're done
and that's your total lot
don't believe a word of that
I tell you now you're not.
Yes you can change your circumstances
but be careful where you jump
just weigh up the pros and the cons
so you don't land with a bump.
Consider yourself responsible
not shallow, small minded or quaint
you don't have to be perfect
or to be another saint.
Now it's not irresponsible
to want some happiness
desire some peace and comfort
and get rid of nastiness.
No, live your own life yourself
and think it out with precision

you can always change your mind
and alter any decision.
Nothing on earth is permanent
no great crime for you to atone
little virtue in being put upon
they're few things carved in stone.

....

Do It Now

Do you know this is a fact of life
that failure can create a sigh
but the biggest failure of all
is if you do not try.
Remember this is your only chance
do the crazy dance while you can
don't be afraid of the limelight
and then you'll be a man.
Take no thought for tomorrow
the nectar of life is 'now'
don't think of why, or where, or maybe
but only think of the 'how'.

....

Spelling

I did all the crosswords today
and do you know, I can't spell a word
and when you consider that statement
it really sounds absurd.
Well, the truth is I have a mental block
now it's 'dyslexic' in my day 'thick'
but I thought of the simple answer
a spelling machine would do the trick.
You just type in the letters, it then sorts them out
I was delighted with the machine I bought
so I put it to the ultimate test
and asked it to spell Chrysanthemum and then yacht.
Of course my machine responded
it must have worked hell for leather
because it corrected my mistake without a moan
now that is what I call clever.

....

Wait and See

Is all your bad days over yet
or are you still in the fray
if so you will have to remember
to-morrow's another day.
Yes I know what you are thinking
that things can never be the same
sadness is your lot in life
and happiness you'll never regain.

But you will have to be patient
just the same as me
and the two of us will overcome
just you wait and see.
....

Perversion

Did you read in the daily papers
about the MP that was perverted
the tabloids called it unnatural
and 'sleazy' they then asserted.
Now I never condone such behaviour
and to be fair, I've always tried
but he never abused anyone, so why be hard
he only wore women's clothes
and we only knew after he died.
So what yardstick do we use
against the degradation we are seeing
but if they keep the perversion to themselves
and not hurt another human being.
'Deviation' is not in the gene you know
that is stuff that's put in the mind
and I know it's fair to be hard at times
but other times it's right to be kind.
....

The Answer to Prayer

Did you ever wake up in the morning
and think, 'oh not another day'
fall on your knees in pure despair
and yes, then you pray.
'Oh God' you say in a quiet voice
or even a hysterical scream
this life is a living nightmare
and it's supposed to be like a dream.
Every bastard is after money
of course you try not to swear
but it really doesn't matter a lot
if God is busy and he's not there.
But anyway your prayer will be answered
as a million records show
and we are already aware of it
because the answer is, NO.
....

Getting Sorted

My neighbour was on television
and as you know he is our minister
well I was quite proud of him
albeit he looked quite sinister.
It was on the programme 'Reflections'

and do you know he did quite good
'mind you, with all his preparation
I was confident he would.
Now I was just thinking
that his neighbour must be a thorn in the flesh
and that is me of course who else
drinking myself to death.
Well I wouldn't like it, me being a mason
if my neighbour's house nearly fell
the slates were slipping of the roof
and all the stonework going to hell.
No, I wouldn't like that
that would be a reflection on me, you see
so I sorted out the manse
now I'm waiting for him to sort out me.

....

More Happy Pills

I got some pills from the doctor
to reduce anxiety and stress
and now my attitude is simple
I just couldn't care less.
I didn't pay my taxes
notwithstanding I hadn't the cash
and when threatened with fine or jail
all I said was 'Oh dash'.
I see my business going down the tubes
and my life a waste of time
my girlfriend went back to her own man
and I said 'Oh that's fine'.
Not a drop of juice left in the cabinet
and I thought that pretty hilarious
mind you, that gave me a thought or two
my emotions were mixed and various.
But oh these pills are a blessing
they keep me oh so calm
you know life is so much better
when you don't care a damn.

....

Poker

It's not what you want in life
it's a matter of what you get
no-body started out to be sick
or to get deep in debt.
No, the cards are there already
and nobody's allowed to pick
and it's just a bit of bad luck
if you cannot take a trick.
Still, you have to play the game
a bland faced hand of poker
the only difference that there is
you always leave in the joker.

....

Export Ale

There is nothing wrong with an Export
and it's very handy in a can
mind you I shouldn't be touching it
well, you know the way I am.
Long ago there were special openers
in them days we called it a 'tin'
and it was quite prestigious
to have one in your bin.
But oh not now, it's common
unfashionable like the fag
so now I dispose of them
concealed in a poly bag.
I'll bet you are wondering why I drink it
when it only makes me stagger
well the reason I drink Export ale
is when I've run out of lager.

.………………………..

Heaven

Most of us were taught 'what is mans chief end'
and we repeated it just like a rhyme
well I had given it a lot of thought
that is when I've got the time.
The short answer is 'get to heaven' of course
and by our own actions this can't be done
without faith nobody gets in
no, not even one.
But what if you can't conjure up belief
or perhaps believe the wrong tale
live your life the best you can
and still you're destined to fail.
And then some thief or murderer comes along
what we now call 'the eleventh hour'
and he stumbles upon the great belief
and gets the mysterious power.
Now that is nice if you're the thief
saved just by a hair
but the good living guy goes to the fire
well personally I don't think it fair.
And what of the millions of other folk
no aptitude and haven't a clue
some don't even know about heaven
yes, and there's more than just a few.
Confess your sins and it's paradise
forget, and it's down below
and why is it all so secret
that's something else I'll never know.
Now I think it's like the flat earth society
who believe the earth is flat
they are not going to fall over the edge

just because they believe in that.
I am convinced there will be a life all right
and you can be brainy or dull of wit
but I am pretty sure today
that no one can understand it.
....

Down the Hill

I am really looking terrible
getting so fat and bloated
mind you for my good looks
I can't say I was ever noted.
And to crown it all, I got a haircut
now my head looks like a neep
I think the barber had a hangover
and she fell fast asleep.
Even my good jersey
it's so baggy now and doesn't fit
my jeans are like a gift from Corn Flakes
yes, I'll need to get some kit.
My house too is crumbling about my ears
the whole thing is so depressing
and my garden is like a jungle
that would keep a commando guessing.
But there again things could be worse
so we will just wait and see
some people will pay good money for this
I'm only lucky I got it for free.
....

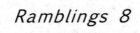

Ramblings 8

Success

Success is a journey you know, not a destination
when you think of it, it's very akin to a cruise
you don't check the lifeboats all the time do you
or listen to the weather forecasts for storms and news.
No you don't, you enjoy the moment
the reality of enlightened undulating poetic rhyme
that moment when you can feel, hear, smell and see
and even taste the very presence of time.

....

A taste of Hell

I totally wasted another day
and now it is nearly night
you probably think I'm depressed again
if you think that, then you'd be right.
The blinkers buckled themselves on so quickly
the rolling steel shutters swiftly came down
friends and places are now hostile and alien
even the flickering lights of my home town.
Ignorance and darkness snigger and mock me
the brave retaliate while I falter and fall
and angels weep for the courageous
for Satan selects them and wants them all.

....

A Weed

The gardener cursed and plucked the weed
the wee plant sighed and it was deed
the daffodils nodded, they all agreed
if you are not bonny you must be a weed.

....

Looking ahead

When I retire I really thought
I would have the time of my life
do all the things I wanted to do
and be a bit nicer to the wife.
Yes sixty-five will be the day of change
I'll save every penny and pound until then
no holidays or needless expenses
or cars or clothes like other men.
For food, porridge would be our staple diet
No salmon, steak, or bacon and egg
and if the dog wanted Pedigree Chum
she would just have to beg.
But a funny thing happened then you know
the wife ran off with the lodger
my stocks and shares all came a cropper
the bitch of a dog preferred the kennels to me

and wouldn't eat the food that I bought her.
Now you may wonder why I'm so philosophical
composed and resigned to my fate.
You see I never intended any of that to happen
and don't you do it either
don't leave things until it's too late.

....

Getting older

I used to say I'd never look back
and never would sit and cry
never wonder how things went wrong
and figure out the reason why.
No I said, I'll look forward
be positive, and reminisce I won't
but do you know the older you get
you can't help it, you just don't.

....

Failure

I wondered if I could handle 'failure'
as good as I did defeat
you see you didn't try if you fail
but other things were more powerful if you get beat.
Now I've been beaten many a time
and likely so have you
the feeling is so heart pounding
and we both know that is true.
Now 'love' and 'ambition' are testing grounds
where you compete and strive with others
but there is no such thing as failure
when on the mast you nail your colours.
It may sound old fashioned but courage is not rationed
it stands alone and never in lines
while others in groups put you through the hoops
and it can happen a hundred times.
So don't be afraid to love and commit
be upright honest and true
oh yes you may get beat at times
but 'failure won't happen to you'.

....

We Can't Help It

The bad hate the good
the stupid hate the wise
the sad envy the happy
and the righteous the sinners despise.
Thousands of years we played the game
and still our tactics are the very same
demoralise, and point the finger of blame
something is wrong somewhere
and I think that, a shame.

....

Not Sure

If I were a liar a sneak and two faced
and think of the true folk I had raced
winning may be important
you might be glad you hurried
but, do you know something
we're all a little bit worried.

....

Basics

I thought of all the worldly goods I needed
the answer was simple, it was food
of course water was essential
but there again a drop of wine was pretty good.
On deeper thought clothes was a must
at least a loin cloth to cover my bum
(well I'm a very modest chap)
not a flasher like some.
Then I thought of a hut or a cave
or some structure to keep out the rain
I decided to give Wimpey Homes a miss
and ignore Morrison Tain.
So I decided to build a hut
it really wasn't a hard decision
because I couldn't find a site for a cave
and I wouldn't get planning permission.
So up went the hut, a two storey job
then added on an extension
then I worried how I would pay it
for in basics you don't have a job or a pension.
So I got a suit a shirt and tie
then applied for an interview
I shaved off my beard and washed my face
I had to do that I knew.
And as I sat there staring and gazing
waiting to do what I was told
I thought of toothache, tigers and wolves
and the hut too that was pretty cold.
Yes modern life is a compromise
there is a freedom that is lost forever
and would I really go back to the cave
to be honest I would never.

....

Who's The Boss

I was born on this planet
just like the rest of my breed
and I will leave it with nothing
that is quite agreed.
In the meantime however
I just fail to see

why so many people
appear to be in charge of me.
....

Pacifists

Most of us like to think we are pacifists
abhor wars and violence too
some like to think they'd turn the other cheek
there's not a lot of them but there's a few.
The most of us however are 'normal'
we avoid conflict and dislike fights
yet if anyone harms me or mine or yours
we would punch out their bloody lights.
Yes that seems to be the universal consensus
was this instinct here from the start
yes it was, we don't have to be taught
it's just evolution playing it's part.
....

We See

Have you noticed these 'sexy' magazines
that sit on the top shelf
just above the Exchange & Mart
and the ones about health.
lovely young people exposing their bums
they must be someone's pride and joy
all these daughters and sons.
Yet there they stand in the glossy glare
for the whole world to view with hypnotic stare
oh boys and girls, you sing a sad song
for deep down *everybody* knows
what you're doing is, wrong.
....

The Bully

At school there was a bully
who beat one wee guy up
he used to say he was a dog
and the wee guy was just a pup.
Well many years later I saw the wee crater
a successful man of means
while the bully writes a rhyme
and sees happiness only in dreams.
....

Appreciation

I built a house one time
and it was a beauty
I added a coal bunker

and it was a cutey.
The wifie was delighted
and so was her man
because they were staying
in a caravan.
Well I often wondered
would they have been so pleased
or would it all be a hassle
if they were a lord and lady
and used to a grand big castle.

....

Getting Paid

I built a wall for a lady once
and do you know she was awful nice
I decided against time and lime
instead I gave her a price.
Her next door neighbour (he was a gurn)
he asked me if I would do him a turn.
I said I would that I didn't mind
for wee builders can be very kind.
Well I finished the jobs
sent in the bills for the turn and the wall
I got a cheque from the gurny man
but the wifie never paid me at all.

....

Sleep Time

I really get depressed at this time of year
I get to thinking, you're all pretty queer.
If only the fairies my wish would remember
that I would rather sleep
from October through December.

....

The Stag

Me and my lorry were working late one night
when I got a signal to stop
a blue light flashed behind me
yes it was a traffic cop.
His colleague was a woman
and she was a cracker
blonde blue eyed and slim
her hair kept in place with lacquer.
Well the policeman got quite angry
then he started gurning
about my two headlights
why only one was burning.
The lassie just looked on and smiled
so impersonal but still impressive
and that is why the big guy
was acting so aggressive.

....

Sweet Tongue

Twice I've had the experience
of being involved in a court of law
and twice I was astonished
at what I heard and saw.
I saw the wheel of justice
and a judge that looked so wise
but why did he ignore the truth
and believed a pack of lies.
Then I thought how easily we are deceived
because it's always the sweetest tongue
that's the one that is believed.

....

Boys

I met a man I knew sixty years ago
when we had few toys for fun
but he remembered when we were boys
I gave him a wee cap gun.
Yet honestly didn't remember
the getting or the giving
but just remembering the good times
that is the art of living.

....

One Answer

If you are going through a bad patch
and the light is not in sight
you think it is never going to end
you know, you could be right.
And then you reach the stage
when you think you are under a curse
everything is up hill
and every day is getting worse.
The answer to this problem
is not to go outside
go back to your bed for a day or two
and sob and swear and hide.

....

Another Turn

I feel another one of my turns coming on
for I have this terrible disease
it flares up so suddenly
and takes me to my knees.
In fact if I get a severe attack
it takes me right to the floor
my legs and hands go all shaky
Oh I better tell you no more.

So I'll just prepare myself with a wee dram
or maybe even a gin and ton
and hope by the time I have one or two
the terrible turn will be gone.

....

Setting out a Rig

Last night I had a nightmare
I dreamed I worked at Nigg
sweeping the floor of that big shed
and trying to set out a rig.
You may rightly ask, what's wrong with that
it's better than the dole or pensions
but you see the thing that frightened me
I just didn't know the dimensions.

....

Old Habits Die Hard

If ever I have an affair
it will be with twenty fags
well do I remember
the pleasure of these drags.
The joy of slowly sooking
and then the quick inhale
right down to my toes
the smoke just seemed to sail.
I remember too the panic
when I couldn't find a light
lying in bed just thinking
I'd be waken half the night.
Then in the morning
that glorious ring of fire
that electric cooker
gave me my heart's desire.
My eyes would shine
my lips would pout
and I would take an oath
never to be without.
If a choice had to be made
between cigs and food
I'd take the cigs
yes I know I would.

....

Taxes

The price of cement is really grave
but us wee builders will have to be brave
especially when it's a pound for a brick
when I see the invoice I'm really sick.
And just when you think everything is fine
up goes the price of lime

and of course the dreaded V.A.T.
that's seventeen and a half per cent
and that is added on to the bill
after all the money my client has spent.
Don't worry about me I claim it back
but it could give some old woman a heart attack.
Some poor pensioners keeping a roof over their head
not one complaint, nothing said.
Surely there's no need to tax O.A.Ps
or charge them licences and things like these.

....

Lesson From Bone

I was digging near the foundation
at the tower at old Kilmuir
when I unearthed a bone
it was human I was pretty sure.
Soft and brown some man's forearm
no good to anyone but could do no harm
so I picked it up and couldn't help but wonder
why's it here, a gravediggers blunder?
And then I thought, does it matter today
whether in crypt, abbey, or cathedral lay.
Nobody knows that he fills this spot
alas my friend you are quite forgot.
Time has passed while you slept
there's no one left with any regret.
Only I think of you now
whether you held sceptre, sword or plough
you clearly speak and tell me
that my worries aren't worth a thou'.

....

Complex

Reality really is a mystery
if you are honest you're bound to agree
that all the good things happen to you
and the bad things happen to me.
I've never won a raffle or even a game of pool
every time I speak at a meeting I feel a fool
my mother once told me I was a waste of skin
that I took after my father
and his kith and kin.
Now you must admit
what I've said is true
but the funny thing is
I don't feel inferior to you

....

Sex Manual

I think I'll write a book about sex

to tell you how to make a baby
well the first lesson for all young men is
it's not 'no' but 'yes' that means 'maybe'.
The next step is so simple
you just watch the rooster and hen
and mind chaps don't peck the back of her neck
or she won't you let you do it again.
Now that's all there is, now you know the lot
but don't bother trying it if you take the shot.
And just one word of warning
before you leap in the sack
that bed is the commonest place
to have a heart attack.

....

Idea Shared

A businessman once told me
of a great idea he had
he described it all in detail
and I said I was glad.
Now I just think I am an ordinary chap
and probably most likely are you
so I rushed through and was sick in the toilet
and slammed the door of the loo.
On my return I was composed
and said 'Oh John that's great'
(mind you I never liked that guy much)
but my dislike now turned into 'hate'.

....

Young Love

I fell in love for the first time
when I was about nine or ten
and I can picture that girl so clearly
when I think of her now and then.
But the social structure was against us
the whispers a nod and a wink
and both of us got a broken heart
just because she was called a tink.

....

The Aging Teddy Boy

The youngsters in Easter Ross have changed
we, were never like that
they are dancing to records in 'Discos' now
when we used to think that was kat.
But why should I judge them unfairly
when I don't know all of the crack
so I put on my drainpipes and Brylcream
to see if I still had the knack.

Then I went to a disco in Dingwall
Oh the noise and the heat
and the English accent of that D.J.
with patter like sweaty feet.
The manashees order up pernod
the gadgies buy pints of lager
the damsels take drink for drink with them
with only a little stagger.
They jump up and down
with all the lights flashing
while in the corner
an Alness guy is getting a bashing.
A dame is sick under a table
and the young bucks are peeing
against the gable.
Young gadgies as usual are getting rejected
and there are broken hearted dames
just as expected.
Falling in love is the preoccupation
God, I thought
I can hardly mind the sensation.
The beat was familiar
but there were no smoke
the smell in the gents toilets
would make you boke.
The barmaid as usual is just about blind
when I was nineteen they were all very kind.
Well that's it I thought
times are not just the same
and I thought of Chuck Berry
which was a bit of a shame.
So I buttoned my shirt up
and said 'I'll be dekeing ya' coffe'
for the bouncer was eyeballing me
so I'd better screw the loaf.
And then I thought of the great times
we had in the old town hall
and do you know apart from the records and smoke
I don't think things have changed much at all.
....

A Complete Blank

I got a phone call from a wifie one morning
and do you know, I got a bit of a fright
because I had a few drams the evening before
and I forgot what I said last night.
I kidded on the best I could
and pretended I knew the lot
oh it's a terrible thing to happen to a man
when he takes the shot.
By now the charm was oozing
the silver tongue really in gear

382

I would have crawled down the telephone
if that would make things clear.
And then the revelation
my answered prayer for salvation
the wifie said sorry, she was up at the quarry
and didn't get home last night.
....

Fallen Angel

Why is the sun warm
why is the sea blue
why was I born at all
well I haven't a clue.
Maybe I was an angel
and made some horrendous mistake
or I might have been a greedy cherub
and ate the whole of the cake.
But I know it's more than likely
I got drunk with some of these old kings
now that is a logical reason
why I lost my wings.
....

Effects

I once saw life as it is
and I said 'pass'
so I see it now
through the bottom of a glass.
Blessed oblivion from cruelty and greed
where love is weakness
and weakness seed.
....

Insurance Excess

I put on a chimney can for a wifie once
and the insurance said they would pay
so I threw on some cement and the ladders
and did it without delay.
The cost of the can was forty-eight pounds
and eighteen pounds for my time
I gave her the bill right away
and she said that was fine.
A week or two later, the poor old crater
into my hands did press
the envelope from the insurance
inside marked twenty pounds excess.
Well you might think I'm soft
for being out of pocket by twenty quid
but I thanked her and walked away
and that is what I did.
But you know sometimes I wonder

is it me that is getting feeble
because she has a mind like a razor
and a brain as sharp as a needle.
....

Rain

Look at the rain
does it not make your heart sink
mind you it cleans the place up
and gets rid of all the stink.
It washes down the pavements
the trees and inaccessible places
and if we stick our heads outside
it will even wash our faces.
It gives us our drinking water
and the bottles of Irn-Bru
and it's awful handy
if you take a dram or two.
But when it dries we get the flies
and they are the proverbial pain
so I'll keep on hoping
we don't get rain again.
....

Over the Top Again

You know I got a complaint once
about a job I did
well I rushed through to the bedroom
threw myself on the bed and hid.
You may laugh but I cried for an hour and a half
bawled abuse at the wife, threatened to take my life.
Jumped up and down like a crazy man
and generally made a commotion
but that is the kind of guy I am
I get things a bit out of proportion.
....

Just to Be Sure

An old wifie phoned me one day
and she sounded pretty sad
and she asked me how I was
and I replied 'not bad'.
She told me she hadn't a kindler
not one to light the fire
could I help her out
she'd even pay my hire.
Well I am not a miserable man
so I organised some sticks
and she was so grateful
I took her out of a fix.
Well some months later

the old lady went and expired
that really was quite sad
because she was much admired.
Anyway I got the job of demolishing the sheds
for every one was a total wreck
when opening the doors, they were all full of kindlers
yes, right to the very neck.

....

All Is Done

I lived I loved I laughed I cried
pleasured insulted was truthful and lied
got drunk stayed sober to make jokes I tried
and when I did all this I sighed and died.

....

The Impressionist

I was doing my Danny La Rue impression
and I had all the brickies in stitches
the labourers too were going 'hoo hoo'
and cackling like a heap of witches.
I was really quite delighted
as along the scaffold I wiggled
I must have looked pretty good
because even the joiners giggled.
Then along came that big foreman
he was either a German or a Pole
but his nationality doesn't matter
for in an hour I was signing the Dole.
I told the clerkess the circumstances
and she got hysterical as well
anyway how was I supposed to know
that the gaffer was as bent as hell.

....

Escape

My life revolves round a glass of wine
where my wits and senses slow
moments lost in winters frost
and my wickedness lays me low.
To be free of law in numb retreat
from a twisted world of vain conceit
the power and pecking on every street
unhappiness the child of the man.

....

Hard

You'll never see a Scotsman cry
except maybe when he's full of drink

are we shallow and not so sensitive
you know sometimes I stop and think.
....

Violence

I have never wanted to hurt anyone
except maybe once or twice
because I thought all that fighting
really wasn't nice.
That punching and kicking
would make me feel sick
I got far more pleasure
from laying facing brick.
In fact to be honest
I thought I was a different breed
and that violent feelings
came from different seed.
But now I'm older and wiser now
I realise we all come from the same dirt
for it will astonish you what you will do
if ever you really get hurt.
....

Guild Outing

My wife went down to Edinburgh
to a meeting of the Guild
and she was really pleased
the assembly rooms were filled.
She went with her friends Wilma and Betty
Margaret couldn't go
and neither could Nettie.
They travelled by train from Inverness
a four hour journey
well, more or less
They attended the meeting
and they were delighted
I think the singing got them excited.
But on the way home, I think it a disgrace
three old majors thought they'd give chase.
And us three husbands were horror filled
that any man would chat up the ladies,
and members of the Guild.
....

The Highland Seer

Who can tell what's going to happen in life
I don't think anybody knows
not even the gypsy in the caravan
who attends the Black Isle Shows.
There is Swein Macdonald of course
I went to see him twice

386

the first time it was semi-grand
but the second time wasn't so nice.
In fact to be honest, I'm afraid now
that's why never again will I go
if more bad things are going to happen to me
I really don't want to know.
....

The Attraction

She asked me why I was attracted
was it her hair or was it her eyes
but I couldn't tell her the truth
so I told her a pack of lies.
I told her all the usual things
without her I'd go down the tubes
but I never told her what attracted me
because it was her big boobs.
....

Lies

Donald James is a good boy
and he likes to have some fun
he kept nine of God's commandments
can you guess the other one.
Oh I'll not wait, I'll just tell you
although you're smart and wise
the one commandment I did not keep
is the one about the lies.
....

Hidden Truth

Yes, I walked the streets of London
like the lyrics in the song
and I wondered about the old man
how he lived so long.
Bent and crippled with a walking stick
it was so pathetic it made me sick.
I looked at his shaky limbs
and thought he should be in his bed
then he told me he wasn't old
he was a forty year old brickie instead.
....

White Settlers

They talk about the white settlers
how they buy up all the land
but they are spending money
and to me I think that grand.
They build their houses

when they get a plot
and the ones that employed me
they all paid on the dot.
In fact I quite liked working for them
I wouldn't even think twice
apart from maybe one or two
the rest are very nice.

....

Justice

Now I am just an average chap
and like to see the good defeat the bad
and when the criminal is caught
I cheer because I'm glad.
Yet now and again when watching T.V.
I get a funny feeling coming over me
and if I'm honest I'd have to say
'Oh I wish the robbers would get clean away'.

....

Sent Off

I was slow in learning this lesson
well, it's actually more of a fact
another of life's little mysteries
a wee bit of wisdom that I lacked.
The world is bound to stop I thought
that is, if I have an early demise
but it won't even slow down a bit
I believed a pack of lies.
And me thinking I was the centre pin
it really is a shame
that in the contest of living
I was off for most of the game.

....

Guaranteed Behaviour

My wife is going with her class to Paris
and I wondered if I should go
mind you I trust her explicitly
but on the other hand, you never know.
Of course it's out of my hands anyway
because I was never asked
and I didn't even try to learn French
while all her exams she passed.
Oh how suspicious is the mind of a man
I'm sure all men would agree
that if we had a week in Paris
our behaviour we'd guarantee.

....

The Quality

He was brought up to be a happy chap
to think fair play and honour was good
consideration and understanding
these virtues he understood.
But life can be rotten
when you start at the bottom
yet it teaches the way to succeed
virtue is fine but way down the line
when the quality you need could be greed.

....

A Bit Over The Top

When Moses conquered one country
he made a law and decree
that his troops were not to fornicate
with any women they see.
Unfortunately one young soldier
no doubt overcome by lust
thought that grossly unfair
and not really human or even just.
So he coaxed a bonny lassie
and she went into his tent
but she was seen by the high priest
and his anger he did vent.
He rushed into the shelter
his intentions were all too clear
and he impaled the two lovers together
on the end of his bloody spear.

....

Hidden Factor

The human brain is a wonderful thing
it's got trillions of electrical connections
the way it works nobody knows
it defies all know inspections.
They tried by X-ray, surgery and hypnosis
they used all known drugs in various doses
a computer was wired to do a calculation
but it couldn't work out the crazy equation.
A miserable failure by logic and knife
because the thing they were looking for
is invisible, it's life.

....

Symptoms

How the unemployed survive
this knowledge I now know
they walk up and down a useless hill

for there is nowhere else to go.
Everyone stares at the unemployed
nobody asks their advice
we are not women or men anymore
but a statistic, and that's not nice.
....

Explained Maybe

I always think it so strange
when I visit a city or town
why there are so many people
walking up and down.
Surely they can't all be unemployed
maybe there is a few on the sick
or perhaps there are some on holiday
but why are they all walking so quick.
They look so smart and really quite healthy
and by the look of their clothes they must be wealthy.
But how could they possibly have money
we all need cash to pay
the only thing I can think of
is they just all sneaked off work for the day.
....

Different Rules

Are we so smart and civilized
when we contemplate our inevitable end
the joy of eternal bliss
now that I can't comprehend.
A life of comparative plenty
then dignity in demise
and then a glorious future
appears before our eyes.
So where are the souls of the killing fields
and the millions of women and men
who never got a chance to be a Christian
or are there different rules for them.
....

The Alternative

I feel a relapse coming on
so I'll probably take the shot
but the wife gets home at six o'clock
and I don't want to get caught.
Maybe she wouldn't smell a vodka
but gin would be a disaster
oh maybe the cupboard is locked anyway
I wouldn't put it past her.
I've still got some pride so I won't even look
I'll go down to the pub instead
and by the time I stagger home
she'll be in her bed.
....

The Effective Tool

Politicians are the cream of debaters
with an audience they're at their best
they could put up a good argument
that 'east' is really the 'west'.
Yes, it must be great to be clever
I've thought of it time and again
but they should have a shot of hard graft
before being in charge of working men.
Union leaders too have a mouthful
but of course they speak from the heart
and that is far better than working
now that's what I call pretty smart.
So vote us in, their plea is clear
put on a boiler suit, no bloody fear
the voice is all the tools I'll ever need
I told you I'm a martyr and you agreed.
So I'll get you better conditions
and I will do it later, not now
for before we do anything, we'll debate
the age old question of 'how'.
....

The Two She Bears

I've never understood the story
of Elija and the two she bears
when the kids of the village were laughing
at his beard and long grey hairs.
Then out of the woods came the two bears
and killed every little brat
well I thought many a time
what on earth was the reason for that.
....

Near

When I was in Bethlehem
I went to the Nave
It wasn't really a stable at all
in fact we would call it a cave.
And there was the spot where Jesus was born
yes, I know some of you will scorn
the exact spot, how can that be
but I didn't care I was delighted
because it was near enough for me.
....

Ambitions

I've realised all of my ambitions now
except maybe one or two

mind, I had no great aspirations
in fact they were very few.
I rode a horse, I flew a plane
the wife is selling frocks in Tain.
I'm now a wee builder on my own
and in my car I have a phone.
But before you think I'm boasting
and I am being affected
I must confess about the phone
it's really not connected.
Well that is most of my ambitions done
and when you think of it, it's not a lot
I should have set my sights higher
now that I see what I could have got.
But now alas it's all too late
yes, misgivings I have a few
but do you think I'm bitter and regret
well I am, and of course I do.

....

Animal Farm

I must have been slaving away on a building site
the day this young doctor was born
he looks at me now so quizzical
'Are you sure your back is torn'.
'Yes' I said, 'I'm just out of bed'
and I'm not a man to swing the lead
but on your judgement I will rely
if you think I'm fit, I'll give it a try.
Then suddenly I thought of 'Boxer' the horse
going off to the knackers yard
and all the other animals
and the farm they were to guard.
So I stood up shakily and said no, no, no
I have done my share
now you all have a go.

....

A Dull Life

A life time of hard labour
that is the sentence I got
all because I wasn't smart enough
to learn the lessons they taught.
The clever ones were whisked away
taught the ways to serve the queen
loyalty and courage were paramount
and must be clearly seen.
Mind you I really can't complain
there are thousands more than me
but life can be pretty dull at times
when you're only a bee.

....

Outlook

Is it only in the Highlands
that you have to be nearly dead
before people will believe you
that you do not swing the lead.
Brought up to be brave and strong
or could the word be 'hard'
deny your heart compassion
when it's as soft as lard.
If understanding is weakness
and love is just a song
kindness is a foreign act
then there's something wrong.

....

Revenge of the Robin

I knew an apprentice once, who killed a Robin
while along the wall the wee bird was bobbin.
He took a small slate and with a flick of the wrist
spun the slate skyward with a fatal twist
an old labourer was aghast at the deed he had done
buried the Robin, and said 'my son'.
Because you have done this terrible thing
sorrow and tragedy that act will bring.
Well many years have passed and many a dark night
and when I think of what happened
the old labourer was right.

....

Murdered

I've seen the spot where Jesus died
yes you can say he was crucified
sure enough he was nailed to the cross
the books were balanced the profit and loss
lots were caste to own his clothes
that is the story that everyone knows.
But as I stood near that awful spot
and fingered the little cross I had bought
I could see the scene as he cried for water
nothing majestic but pure manslaughter.

....

The Plan for a Renovation

You know an x-ray is just like a plan
it shows the elevation and the detail of man
shows the results of neglect and abuse
the damage by impact, the joints that are loose.
The rot caused by dampness
the effects of the cold

so study the plan carefully
and all will unfold.
Yet we are so hampered
for so much is not shown
because there is more to a man
than sections of bone.
If only we had a copy of the original plan
then it would be so easy
to renovate a man.
....

Adjust

Nothing is going the way that I planned
why that is so I don't understand
the logistics were good organised to the detail
the timing was perfect this plan couldn't fail.
But the whirlwind of circumstances
confused the whole chart
and taught me the great lesson
'don't be too smart'.
It's good to prepare
but prepare to adjust
in the science of living
that is a must.
....

The General

I was in school with a boy called Hector
and he was a wee skinny lad
yet his uncle was a general
the finest the army had.
Although this happened years ago
and we were just boys at the time
it just seems like yesterday
and I really mind it fine.
Hectors big brother was kind of sick
so the local bully thought on him he'd pick
but Hector jumped in between the pair
looked at the bully and began to stare.
It really looked bizarre
this wee protector
but that was the day
I saw a general in Hector.
....

The Builders

My house it is a beauty
built in eighteen eighty-three
the walls are stone the roof is slate
and that suits the likes of me.
The masons must have been proud of it

I can imagine their justified pride
and I can visualise them all
when I take a walk outside.
Then I think of the snow and the rain
the long walk home from here to Tain
sore backs and hands full of hacks
their worries and their pleasures
but none of them has a sore head now
and couldn't care less about treasures.

....

Compensation

Well that is it this time
I really think I'm done
the chances of me being fit again
are little, or else they are none.
And I was so willing and supple
with a back that was broad and strong
oh well, never mind
where is the reel and the rod.

....

Guilt

I wonder why I feel so guilty
when I am not at work
then I feel guilty on Sunday
if I don't go to the Kirk.
I dodge around the house a lot
if you see me I'll go and hide
I get my paper delivered
so I won't have to go outside.
And all of this for what?
a pure Highland upbringing
if I was born anywhere else
I would accept it and be singing.

....

Guardian Angel

Young man you have to be careful
and try and do the right
because you have a guardian angel
who watches you day and night.
He likes to see you happy
gets pleasure when you have fun
he is the angel of brightness
of summer and the sun.
His duty is to fight off all evil
and this he surely can do
he takes care of the spirit world
and leaves this world mostly to you.
So beware young man don't deceive him

stay on the narrow track
persistently sin, take evil in
he'll leave and he won't come back.

....

Give to the Rich

It's strange when you have plenty
everybody offers you cake
but when you're poor and downcast
everybody wants to take.

....

The Virus

Do you know about the computer virus
well it is a right clever thing
you put in a disc to get rid of it
and on the disc it'll hing.
It'll jink and hide around the box
also infect another machine
and the wee thing is so small
it is hardly ever seen
It takes out numbers and puts others in
you would swear it was alive
and I thought it was only us that did that
in order that we would survive.

....

Builder

I'm proud to be a brickie
and part of the building trade
for I know that God likes builders
because he answered when I prayed.
'God' I said 'should I be a brickie
an accountant or a clerk
a doctor or a tax man
where will I make my mark.
Should I go into politics
and argue red or blue
what is the most honourable thing
that a man like me can do.
Well God answered me so simply
he said 'Building is the best, bar none
for when I had a choice to make
I made a joiner of my son'.

....

Tell The Truth

I never thought I'd tell a lie
even when under pressure

I was taught to be virtuous
and the truth I was to treasure.
I was so sure of my principles
on the corner stone of honesty they sat
yet I told a blatant lie today
and I can hardly believe I did that.
....

White Man's Treasure

I sometimes dream of Tahiti
before the white man came
after that discovery
it was never quite the same.
No work, plenty food, naked not rude
laughter and love, pure pleasure
and then us white men came along
and told them about gold and treasure.
....

The Reason

Were we really born to work I wonder
is the object of life to succeed
to pile up as much money as we can
well frankly I don't see the need.
Surely this struggle for money
is no reason for our existence
because when you think of it
all we need is subsistence.
You can't drink gold or eat a diamond
a pound note, a piece of paper
but money decrees you bend the knees
to the diner if you are the waiter.
Were we all brainwashed from birth
to want and desire this curse
can anyone think of another motive
even one that is worse.
Our whole social structure
based on wealth and gold
the rank of a man a dollar sign
and the sign of success, 'just sold'.
....

A Good Idea

Surely there are some politicians
even one or two
we can believe what they say
surely there must be a few.
Will the day ever come
when the opposition leader will stand
walk across the floor
and offer out his hand.

'To the members of the government
we have no wish to placate'
but what the prime minister proposes
that idea is just great.
....

Manners

The Highlander is often quoted
as being pretty dour
but I think we always had manners
supposing that we were poor.
Well, one hot summer I built an extension
for two white settlers, a woman and man
one day he asked me if I was thirsty
and I replied 'Why yes I am'.
Ten minutes later he called me
and pointed to the garage door
there all alone a mug of tea sat
in the middle of the concrete floor.
....

Convenient

You know that wee discs in your back
well I think one of mine just burst
and like any good building worker
I screamed and swore and I cursed.
I bawled about the injustice
and prayed 'Oh God, why mine'
and God replied in his usual way
'Oh you were just handy, at the time.'
....

No Choice

It is amazing how the older we get
the changes that come over you
a few years ago it was a G.T. I.
now any old twelve hundred will do.
You can't 'mind the round at the bar
to the barmaid you're the invisible man
you used to order a ploughman's lunch
now you go home for a bowl of bran.
Your wardrobe has clothes that do not fit
your shirts are too slack or too tight
you try and be nice to everyone
because you're too old to fight.
But there is not even any compensation
no money, wild women or Rolls Royce
If it wasn't for the alternative, I wouldn't age
but I never even got the choice.
....

Enlightenment

I never really quite appreciated
how helpless some folk must feel
but now I stand in their shoes
in a situation so unreal.
I cannot clean the drains out
nor can I fix a slate
the garden is so untidy
and the sneck fell off the gate.
The mental pain of boredom
I've rarely felt before
the feeling of vulnerability
I even lock the door.
Yes we all must learn our lessons
and understand the best we can
but I sometimes I really wonder
does it make me a better man.

....

Seeing is Believing

I've never believed in Fairies
the ones that frolic in the wood
but the older I get the more I know
therefore maybe I should.
To some folk some colours look the same
and 'green' and 'brown' are just a name
to them that is reality
horses see us magnified
but who sees the actuality.

....

Feeling Good

I often thought if I won the pools
that I would immediately retire
and on a cold wet winters day
I'd sit right by the fire.
And if I ever got a bit fed up
I'd take a run in the Rolls
and park outside a building site
to watch the workers dig, and cut some holes.
Now I'm not a sadist or cruel chap
but one hard fact I know
'wellbeing' is a matter of where you stand
and not a matter of what you know.

....

The Shake

I didn't take a dram last night
and today I really could curse

because I don't feel any better
in fact I feel a bit worse.
I thought I'd feel like 'Pinky' or 'Perky'
but now my hand is just as jerky
my head is throbbing with all the fresh air
well I for one don't think it fair
to be without anaesthetic is not nice
so that is a mistake I won't make twice.

....

Be Prepared

It is all very well to be spiritually pure
have principals and the highest ideals
but sometimes you have to be practical
for negligence there are no appeals.
God doesn't like a stupid man
it tests his patience beyond endurance
if your house burned down tonight
do you have the proper insurance.

....

Knowing the Laws

There's nothing unnatural about 'magic'
I would call it 'spiritual science'
only we don't know the rules of the game
and on rules we place great reliance.
The staff was turned into a serpent we're told
then the serpent turned into a stick
yet even Pharaohs magicians all could do that trick.
So what is the conclusion is it all an illusion
can the event precede the cause
can anything be true and be believed by you
supposing you don't know all of the laws.

....

A Legend

I really liked the legend
of the disciples James and John
when Jesus said 'come to heaven'
'all the rest have gone'.
And they replied solemnly
'Lord please let us stay'
and we will go on saving souls
right up to the very last day.
Now when I speak to a beggar
or maybe an Oxford Don
you never know it could be true
it might be James or John.

....

The Elect

One fact that I'm sure of is that God is King
the intelligence that created our planet
but when he sees us all now
I'll bet he can't understand it.
We terrorise each other with tales of Hell
you're all going down below, aye you as well
now I can't see that, no matter how I try
that only a certain religion is saved
and all the rest will fry.
Millions of Muslims, Hindu and Jew
Baptists and brethren to name but a few
all will be lost except for their sect
while they will be saved, they're the elect.
Well according to the logic of a builder
I ponder it often as I sweat on a wall
why aren't you guys on a building site
and why did he make me at all.

....

Adding Up

I've just been adding up my outgoings
and do you know I can't afford to live
such a poor amount in my bank account
and a statement that looks like a sieve.
Well I better try harder to work it out
by doing some more of the sums
because I need a new set of teeth
so I won't have to smile with my gums.
I also need glasses costing a hundred pounds
to me that's a ridiculous sum
I think the optician is charging too much
and I am getting done.
Oh the worry of pension and poverty
I'm just about fit to tether
oh well you never know
the computer may have made an error.

....

Decreed

One more time I'll tell you
how I admire our queen
the way she does her job
must make the ambassadors green.
If by chance she was born a builder
she wouldn't be long on the hod
it would only be a week or two
and she's be in charge of a squad.
Such is life, is it all luck
or do gods make some decree
then decided to give the job to her

401

and not to give it to me.

....

Genesis

Do you really believe there was an explosion
which now they call the 'Big Bang'
and particles shot off at random
not to a thought out plan.
Then another miracle, water appeared
and animals stalked the world
the earth didn't crash into anything else
as through the skies it birled.
Then another pure accident
animals started turning into men
well if I saw an animal doing that
I'd ask him to do it again.
There is no proof of the pudding of course
and I can't tell you how
but if animals really turned into men
why aren't they doing it now.

....

Doubt

I might watch Bob Hope at two o'clock
then maybe Thomas the Tank
yes, for all this entertainment
I've got a sore back to thank.
A few weeks ago I thought it was great
to have a rest and be lazy
now after five weeks idleness
the rest is driving me crazy.
I walk up and down from here to there
look out the window and just sort o' stare
then do my exercises, down then up
make some tea, another cup.
Resist the pull of the devilish magnet
of course I mean the cocktail cabinet,
check the policies just once again
but all that jargon is beyond my ken.
Then I find myself on my knees
and asking God if this was a test
I didn't quite catch his answer
which was a bit of a pest,
but there was something
about me bawling for a rest.

....

Change of Heart

A rabbit was out in my garden
and I thought 'Oh how cute'
one of God's little creatures

not something to snare or shoot.
Well days went by and the mess got greater
and my heart got hardened to the wee crater
how diverse is human nature
I didn't see it now nice or funny
so I just went out and yes, I shot the bunny.

....

First Experience (nearly)

I received a note from a girl in school
that she would like to try 'hanky panky'
a prefect grabbed the note from me
he was big and lanky.
Well he gave me a lecture on morality
and told me to get on my bike
said that I was a dirty wee rat
and he'd never heard the like.
But he said he wouldn't tell the teacher
this being my first offence
mind you, I was just a lad
and hadn't very much sense.
Well many years later I discovered the traitor
and I remembered the date behind the bike shed
while I cycled home so gratefully
the rat took my place instead.

....

Planning

Are you one of the people
who find it hard to make a decision
you get blown from here to there
and don't quite know the position.
Do I go left or do I go right
I'll not do that, and then I might.
Yes the future is hard to comprehend
because most of the plans I made so far
very few worked out in the end.

....

Con Man

I knew a chap once who was told a sob story
so he gave the poor guy a hundred quid
you may not believe this
but I happen to know that he did.
And this young man was so grateful
'a godsend an saviour' he swore
but the funny thing was
he was back the next day for more.

....

D.I.Y.

I have plans for a brand new house
and others for a renovation
the chap who wants the new house
wants to do his own excavation.
Now I'm all for a bit of enterprise
on every building site
but when it comes to excavations
it's rarely or never done right.
And then when I start it is with a spade
and the client is still delighted
with the mess that he made
and how could I offend him
so I just say 'Oh that's fine'
but, really, you know to be honest
it was all a waste of time.
....

Wrong

I can't be bothered with explicit sex
that sometimes comes on the T.V.
and for entertainment in the evening
that's not what I want to see.
Now I am a normal healthy chap
with an average imagination
and to watch other people's acrobatics
I can live fine without the sensation.
Now I hope I don't sound too pompous
for to life's pleasures I sure belong
but in the pursuit of happiness
there are some ways we all know are wrong.
....

Big Odds

The risk of the operation is minimal
in fact it's ninety-nine percent sure
so you better take it
it is the only cure.
Well it was really quite easy
to work out that sum
ninety-nine from a hundred
that still leaves the one
....

Planning Department

The head of the planning department glared
and stared with an officious frown
'You never asked or paid attention to us
so we've come to knock your house down.'

He waved in the dozer and digger
but he never even heard the trigger
the bullet was sent in his heart it went
a victim of plans that were bigger.

....

Roused

The nature of man is simple at times
especially when it comes to sex
most of them are 'push overs'
after a few pints of Becks.
A moral upbringing in the beginning
surely that would stop their nonsense
but that's not true except for a few
a roused man just has no conscience.

....

Results

Hate is a creature of darkness
love is the pinnacle of light
truth is the pleasure of sunshine
and lies the delight of the night.
Contempt is the voice of evil
envy the destroyer of souls
contentment the reward of virtue
and kindness the giver of goals.

....

Circles

Young guys talk of lassies
Middle-aged men talk of drink
old men talk of women
we must be going round in circles
I think.

....

The Theory of Everything

They are trying to figure it out
how the world first began
personally I don't think they can do it
but the scientists reckon they can.
It's all to do with the equation, they say
algebra and mathematics
that's the key to the mystery
of that we're quite emphatic.
It may be me but I can't agree
that two and two sometimes makes three
a straight line isn't necessarily straight
and sometimes to multiply
you don't need a mate.

Yes, they know their sums alright
but they still can't see the trick
that there's a superior brain out there
and compared to it they're thick.
....

In Proportion

It really makes me depressed
when I think how ordinary I am
when I was always told I was special
right from my days in the pram.
It was the day I made my first million
that is the day that I suspect
I realised how many were like me
and better in many respect.
It could even be a law of nature
on me that day dawned
for rich or poor special or dour
it depends on the size of your pond.
....

Boomerang

Deeds are like boomerangs thrown in the sky
whether it be a good turn or even a lie
nobody knows the distance you threw
but rest assured they will return to you.
....

Tomorrow

Right, I have decided
I'll turn a complete new leaf
stop the smoke and drams
and cut down on the beef.
Get myself nice and slim
because my belly is like a pot
try and drink water or juice
and not to take the shot.
The fags and cigars they must go
deep down I know that right
I too should leave the women alone
well you never know I might.
Oh this new man will be so happy
no more guilt remorse or sorrow
but it's hardly worthwhile starting today
so I'll make the start tomorrow.
....

Experiences Teaches

When I was young I mind it fine
I happened to be speaking to an uncle of mine

well my uncle I confess would take the shot
beer and whisky he liked the lot.
And that night in particular too much beer
and a rake of nips it would appear
now me being young I had to grin
not intending for a moment to belittle him
he stared at me and growled 'Cheers'
'because you won't be laughing in twenty years!'
Now he was a very mild mannered man
so I got a wee bit of a fright
and now that the time has passed
I found out that he was right.

....

Hate

Hate's just a word, I know it's absurd
to say I 'hate' the word 'hate'
but to me it's a swear the same as a stare
negative not pleasant not great.

....

Scared

Now I'm old I do regret
that I didn't join in the game
I just stood back and watched
and now I feel that a shame.
I never took part in the scrimmage
just in case that I got hurt
I never ever scored a goal or try
or with any danger flirt.
I'm what you'd call a 'quiet man'
one of life's spectators
watching you getting hurt all the time
Oh you poor lucky craters.

....

Snapped

One thing fear the older I get
is that I'll turn into a dirty old man
the wife says I've been bad enough all my life
and I don't want to get worse than I am.
Now in the Daily Express in a court case I see
the advocate asked the judge if he would agree
that his client just snapped and that was the key.
Well that is what I fear the most
that that will happen to me.

....

Futility

The mystery of a miser

can never be understood
why they are all so miserable
when to their pound notes glued.
They scrimp and save right to the grave
and when they get to the other side of the wall
the currency is all in dollars
and not in pound notes at all.
....

The Start

If I knew then what I know now
I would have no regret
the mistakes we make in a lifetime
we have to try and forget.
forget about the bad times
that's natural and is good
forget about the hurts and pain
yes of course we should.
Futile is the words 'If only'
these words can break your heart
forget yesterday's sorrow, think of tomorrow
and that, will be a start.
....

The Way You Are

It's not easy to be humble and wealthy
not east to be confident and poor
not easy to be witty and charming
if your natural spirit is dour.
It's so easy for some folk to be a bully
and for some it's easy to give in
yet it's not easy to lose a race
if you really want to win.
....

A Happy Man

Some folk live their life in a craze
while others seem quite demented
some walk around in a dopey daze
and they seem quite contented.
Now you know too, this happy man
after all that's been done and said
the happy man hasn't a clue
and not nearly right in the head.
....

Superstud

I once knew a chap we called 'superstud'
I won't mention his name or mine will be mud

they said that his wife was pregnant
his girlfriend and the lass in his shop
and everyone in the town thought
'is this guy ever going to stop?'
Well it all turned out a vicious lie
as the truth became obvious by and by
we all knew the story sounded pretty tall
because it emerged
his wife wasn't pregnant at all.

....

The Seer Again

I went up to see Swein once
and do you know he was amazing
he told me of a hundred truths
and I just sat there gazing.
He told me of my past life
the present and future too
and all the things he told me
all came perfectly true.
But there is one little thing he told me
which I could hardly comprehend
he told me someone was wishing me harm
and was treating me just like a friend.
'They are plotting your downfall' he said
(but he didn't tell me the cause)
even now after all these years
I still don't know who it was.

....

Travel

Some folk travel and venture far
by aeroplane, train, and motor car
they go to France, Greece and Spain
but you know there is nothing much wrong
with a day in Inverness, or an hour or two in Tain.

....

Last Fling

Before the lights go out
I'd like to have one last fling
so if you're good looking and full of fun
please give me a ring.
Now I don't want replies from young ones
by that I mean any girl less than twenty
because you lot broke my heart as a loon
and the memories for me is plenty.
No, I want a mature woman
pretty, with a good sense of humour
because if she goes out with me
there is bound to be some rumour.

'Gosh' there's the phone ringing already
for the last fling of my life
and I can hardly believe the first to apply
yes, it was the wife.

....

Live and Learn

Have you ever reached the stage
when you think you can't go on
your youth is far behind you
and your better years have gone.
Opportunities lost to ambitions lust
your dreams of castles a pile of dust
that's when you'll see if you have what it takes
it is the time to learn by your own mistakes.

....

Late Learner

If I had my time again
I would prefer to be a nurd
forget about 'macho man'
they are quite absurd.
I'd stick in at school and do homework
wear flannels and forget about jeans
hang out at university or college
and wouldn't leave 'till out of my teens.
Then a career or profession
a wife and two and a half bairns
a mortgage and maybe a Mini
it's amazing how quick a fifty year old learns.

....

Tough

The birdies held a meeting
about the food they were fed
the Sparrows didn't like the nuts
and the Robins disliked the bread.
The Crows they were quite angry
and complained about the meat
didn't like the barley loaf
instead they wanted the wheat.
Well I am a patient fellow
but I had heard enough
so I shooed them all away
and if they are hungry, tough.

....

Regret

I must confess I punched a man once

into his face my fist just sunk
his eye swelled up and his nose turned red
his cheeks turned white and his teeth they bled.
And I stood aghast at this deed I had done
no compensation in the fact that I won
and then I thought, what started it
and did I then regret
No, not one bit.

....

Video

Memories are the strangest things
it's the videos in the head
we remember films of years ago
and stories that we read.
Yet stranger still, when seen again
they're some changes in the story line
our brains have updated the facts
and must be editing all of the time.

....

More Rules

Would there really be chaos
if we abolished all the rules
would the builders throw away their plans
and their working tools.
Would we mug and fight
and steal our clothes and food
no we all wouldn't do that
and only some of us would.

....

Realisation

I thought I was special when I was fifteen
by the time I was twenty
I was impatient and keen
then I reached thirty
there sneaked in a doubt
I started to wonder and figure it out.
Forty then fifty still building a wall
and then the penny dropped
I wasn't special at all.

....

A Bitch

I once knew a woman who was a pure bitch
she caused more rows than any old witch
no waiter or barman was safe from her tongue

if she lived last century she would be burnt or hung.
One time in town an alcoholic lay
some passed by whispering
well you know what they say,
then along came an angel
and raised him out of the ditch
who else would do it
but the pure little bitch.
....

Inherited

Do you ever notice the folk that are in power
go around with faces that look so sour
are they really happy, and it's all put on
do they do it to deceive us, is it all a con.
Perhaps it's like a drug this will to win
you never see a millionaire laugh
they just sort of grin.
Well I've figured it out at last
and I now see the true position
you're either just born good natured
or with a poor disposition.
....

No Satisfaction

Have you ever been stuck on a job
and you are expected just to doss
to hide for hours in the toilets
and generally not care a toss.
Trying to look busy doing nothing
and put in twelve hours a day
overseen by some ego maniac
and you have to do what they say.
Yes time stands still on these jobs
brain cells rot and fade
not even the satisfaction on Friday
when the wages of boredom are paid.
....

Being Poor

It's good to be poor somewhere I read
but I'm pretty sure that's what the rich man said.
There is nothing nice about a lack of food
or collecting hand-outs, that's not good.
Where is the dignity in waiting in a queue
and when you get to the chair
it's held down with a screw.
Filling in forms having to do it twice
feeling a failure, no that's not nice.
A smart man said once 'get on your bike'
but I wonder if he was me he would be like.

The endless hours at the vacancy section
the pangs of pain at every rejection
the monthly meeting with the obvious advice
no, to be poor, that's not nice.

....

Regret

I'm tired of working wonders
with concrete blocks and facing brick
and the thought of harling gables
makes me feel quite sick.
It nearly gives me a turn
when I think of sorting slates
and I don't have any patience left
to hang any iron gates.
There must be more to life
than all this physical pain
if I ever come back to this life
I would never live it the same.
No, I would be an aristocrat
with a big house and fancy car
a cellar full of whisky
and marry some superstar.
Never again would I mix cement
my days would be lazy and misspent
I'd be tall and straight, not wraxed and bent.
But I wouldn't have the satisfaction of saying
'Yes it was me who built that wall'
and do you think I would be sorry
No I wouldn't, no, not at all.

....

The Workers

we've had hundreds of years of parliament
passing thousands of laws
and hundreds of years of politicians
exercising their jaws.
Hundreds of years of councillors
advising us to go to the Kirk
and hundreds of years of yapping
I wonder who was doing all the work.

....

Time

The time will come when all dreams will come true
yes this will happen to me and it will happen to you.
Don't be impatient, you will be fine
you see it is all just a matter of time.
Time has no beginning no middle no end
I know it's hard for us mortals to comprehend
yet time will bring you your sweetest thoughts

and all your worries will come to naught.
Don't let this life beat you
remember your friend is time
just have a little patience
and you'll see, you'll be fine.

....

Sleeping

Gropey policemen groped
goofey politicians goofed
perverted judges judged
and parsons and priests were hoofed.
Small children cry out for a mother
and women regretfully wept
while knights of honour drank port and brandy
smoked cigars, talked, and slept.

....

Justice

Are we ever going to get justice right
not penalised for what you do
but rather for what you 'might'.
A right long sentence at one end of town
at the other end, the judge rebukes with a frown
an expensive lawyer can reduce your time
he'll impress and dazzle the judge so much
you'll probably get away with a fine
what do that lawyers do for justice, it's nil
but we all know what do they do for crime.

....

Loyalty

I once had a wee blue lorry
that all but broke my heart
the very moment I needed it most
the engine wouldn't start.
I could depend on it to let me down
some bit would fall off
in the middle of the town.
Just the mention of gutters and mud
and the back wheels started to spin
the cab was red with rust
and as thin as a syrup tin.
Then the D.O.E. got on to me
about this total wreck
how it contravened the regulations
and was really a pain in the neck.
Well I wrote them a stroppy letter
and contacted my M.P.
'I'll defend her to the death' I said
for she's mine and belongs to me.

....

Next Please

The goddess of love was Venus
her lover, Adonis the son of a king.
Yet he was killed by a wild pig
while the birds in the trees looked on
and waited for their turn to sing.

....

Day Dreaming

I looked out of the window
and started dreaming once again
of me chatting up beautiful women
and a film star now and then.
Being adored by my entourage
and all my many fans
that of course was normal
and was always in the plans.
And needless to say I was the hero
the tough guy of all the fights
giving the wrong doers a doing
and punching out their lights.
The mystery man at the casino
the one who would always win
when the losers saw my bulging wallet
they would exclaim 'Oh look at him'.
Well that's it, a red double decker just passed
and brought me back to reality, too fast
because one thing I like in this world
and you know what I mean
is to gaze out the window and just sit and dream.

....

Contempt

Of all sins that I know
'contempt' must rate high
it belittles God's creation
and holds hands with the lie
tells men they are nothing
the women we must despise
and the cross of salvation
to contempt, is a pack of lies.

....

Old Philosophy

When the salt has lost its savour
and the sun has lost its heat
when some men call you 'friend'
then twist and lie and cheat.
When the tide of life is against you

and everyone else is sailing
do what my mother told me
keep your chin up
though your arse is trailing.
....

Other Facts

Being smart and intelligent, that's superior
and if you're slow of mind, that's second class
the square root of ten, oh tell me again
and at sums I might get a pass.
Instead ask me about the passions of Caesar
or the war and siege of Rabat
the story of Troilus and Cressida
because everyone is bound to know that.
....

Tit for Tat

Before you knocked me flat, I was a cat
and I thought I was cuddly and fat
an hour before you pranged me, I killed a rat
do you think it's all a game, of tit for tat.
....

The Puncture

Did you ever wake up on Monday morning
and not a thing will go right
first of all a puncture
as I went to the building site.
The nuts were rusted solid
making my spanner slip
taking all the skin of my knuckles
with a pain that made me sick.
I screamed and punched my labourer wee Al
and told him he was sacked
I'm afraid the virtue of calmness
was the one I had always lacked.
I jumped up and down, cried a little
and cursed my rotten luck
then it started to snow
on me and my little truck.
Anyway I got the man from the garage up
after a long walk home
because all the miserable crofters about
hadn't put in the phone.
Well the man from the garage soon had the wheel off
he really had the knack
and me being impatient threw the wheel in the pick up
slipped and strained my back.
So now it's Monday afternoon
and I lie here in my bed

forty pounds the poorer
which pushes me into the red.
But I try and look at it philosophically
for just a mile down the hill
the police were breathalysing everyone
and I could be a border line case, for last night I took the fill.

....

Strength

Some peoples power
is being bad mannered and sour
others pretending they're dour
but it's not weak nice things to speak
and not nearly as bad as not sure.

....

Bombs

What a grand big factory I have
we employ ten thousand men
and we make bombs for the R.A.F.
and our enemies now and then.
We export to different countries
in fact we won an award
for quality production
and for a bomb that all can afford.
When it is dropped skilfully
it can maim a thousand yards away
I know because we tried it out
in tests the other day.
It creates a hole like the county tip
accurate enough to kill one child
or vaporize the whole crew of a ship.
If you ask 'Is our product a commercial success'
I would have to be honest and answer yes
we have cornered the whole market
and we have the monopoly more or less.
Our staff are all so happy too
mind you they're mostly young women and men
and if it wasn't us making the bombs
what would we do with them.

....

Old Soldiers

The young minister scornfully gazed
at the British Legion deputation, eyes half glazed
the smell of beer and whisky rose from the pews
comic old men in tartan trews.
A young little deacon rubbed his spectacles
and screwed up his face
I really think this is a terrible disgrace
Armistice Sunday when we should be deep in prayer

and we have to put up with that drunken rabble out there.
....

My Cat

I answered the phone, Oh what dreadful news
about my wee animal, the one that mews
killed by a Ford or perhaps a TR7
which propelled the beastie right into heaven.
So along the road solemnly clutching a poly bag
McGruther & Marshalls name was on it
which was a bit of a drag.
Then, there she lay at the bottom of the dyke
as stiff as a poker, I never saw the like.
Reverently I placed her into her polythene shroud
I shed a tear and my head was bowed.
Then at the slow march I returned home
dug a hole in the garden with a whimper and moan
placed there in the yellow plastic casket
regretted the times I called her a wee basket.
'What's done is done' I sobbed and finished my prayer
no Christian minister could have done mair.
Then with heavy heart I returned to my labour
I burned some rubbish to annoy the neighbour.
And what do you think came out of the smoke
my cat Suzzy, and I don't joke.
'My God' I thought, at last I've cracked
and I wondered if the drink had caught up with me
and that is a fact.
But no, the answer was so simple to any mouse or rat
I just made a mistake and buried a strange cat.
....

Depressed

I've fought depression with both drugs and booze
and between the two there is nothing to choose
one kids you on that you're not so bad
the other outfoxes the brain to make you glad.
And the level-headed doctor in whom you confide
you feel would rather have an ordinary suicide
yes you know it's an awful strange disease
to sob for no reason, then pray on your knees
to go around all day tripping over your chin
your face like a poultice your hair like a whin
you know I think the devil must grin
when he sees us lose and let him win.
But we depressives have to battle on
knowing well it's to the death we fight
glorious battles fought every day
and victories won each night.
....

The Fox

The fox lay crushed on the motorway
an end to a life time of guile
the tar stained red, the eternal bed
and rest at last for a while.
No snare around his white throat
or by rifle bullet did he die
but by a thoughtless young man
trying out his new G.T.I.
Sad sad fox, dishonoured in death
uncaring indifference
took your last breath
no fight to the finish
or any hunter to outwit
does it matter now, not one bit.
You lie there squashed
your body all wracked
and you are dead
and *that* is a fact.
....

Just Your Luck

I jumped into life and thought 'what fun'
learned to walk and then to run
laughed and danced I was really thrilled
then along came that bus
and I was killed.
....

Win

It's nice to be happy
but not to be smug
nice to have a carpet
and not just a rug.
It's good to have plenty
but is too much, sin
but if you are in the race anyway
you might as well win.
....

A Mistake

I sped over the bridge at Inverness
my lorry does fifty, well more or less
in the mirror I glimpsed a flash of blue
now you might think I'm joking
but this is all true.
I held my speed to forty-five
and cursed the drams of last night
the blue thing still weaved behind me

moving from the left and then to the right.
I prayed it would overtake
get a puncture or even break down
or chase some speeding maniac
coming out of the town.
But no, I glanced again
some people are really sick
like a leach it hung behind me
and was getting right on my wick.
I flashed my indicator
oh please, please overtake
or take the turn to Dingwall
or even Evanton, for pities sake.
But no such luck the blue shadow still clung there
at Alness it moved to the left then back to the right
which I thought very unfair.
They're toying with my feelings I knew
and not a moment too soon
when Delny came into view
and me hardly did a sin since weeks
and that was all lies about the wifies breeks.
Anyway I jumped out of my lorry with legs like jelly
and I tell you now I had one of those pains in the belly
but bravely I turned to face the boys in blue
you mightn't believe this but it's all true.
There were no police car there at all
and me ready to admit guilt and say I was sorry
there were just a blue barrel of waterproofer
rolling about in the back of my lorry.
…………………………………..

Is Rich The Best

I was once very rich you know
and I lived like a king
I always dined at Maxims
and in my swimming pool did swim.
Sailed down the west coast
in my brand new yacht
revved up the Ferrari
that's the latest red one that I got.
President of the bowling club
my mistress, the belle of the ball
but then I made a blunder
and I lost it all.
My big house all but crumbled
the garden ran to weeds
the pool is now a silage pit
where a hundred shorthorns feed.
My business empire's now a nightmare
unwelcome at golf club and gymkhana
my accountant reminds me of a shark
and my banker a sixteen stone piranha.
But philosophically speaking
when you are down you see things as they are

how good trusty friends can be
as the pass your bike in their car.
And then of course you realise
the worth of every man
and the moral of this story is
stay rich as long as you can.
....

My Desire

I dread you'll start a war
before the cup final game
do you know it's only you
who wants to kill and maim.
In fact the most of us here don't
and it's not that we don't care
we just want to go to the football
and cheer and gasp and stare.
....

Delayed Reaction

Did you know that some radio programmes
have a seven second delay
that means its seven seconds behind
in everything they say.
I suppose it gives the editor time
to cut out the odd wee swear
but that was on old fashioned idea
and now most don't even care.
Well I got to thinking
that's a bit like me
for every point that's made
I'm convinced and usually agree.
But given the chance of seven seconds
I would have time to contemplate
but seven secs is not so long
and maybe is leaving it late.
But then my theory wouldn't work
it doesn't work for two or three
when I am getting my seven seconds
everyone else gets the same as me.
....

Read and Write

I really thought I'd like a degree
maybe one for reading and writing
I don't think they'd give me one for drinking
and definitely not one for fighting.
A certificate, a diploma, a book, or a pen
in fact any prize will do
my mortar board is full of cement the now
and it's my nose that's called 'true blue'.

Obviously there has been a huge mistake
a mistake that can't be mended
instead of a genius I am a brickie
and that's not what nature intended.
But I'll just have to put up with it
no sense in bleating and whining
as long as I can afford a jotter
and do a bit of rhyming.
....

No Lies

Some folk think the advice from a builder
is a service and totally free
you just phone one up
and an appointment you both agree.
Then you take him round your property
and quiz him through and through
but when it comes to do the job
he gets some jobbers that's on the brue.
Well one fly chap picked my brains
and I could see his tongue in his cheek
when he asked me how long it would take
and I said 'An easy job, it'll take a week'.
But I never told him about the bearing wall
how careful you had to be in case that it would fall
and how to prop the gable which would be left unstable
and the importance of the needles
underneath it all.
Now to be perfectly true
I never told him a lie
he was just so keen to get rid of me
that he never thought me fly.
Now when I pass, nothing is said
I just look at the mess sympathetically
and I just shake my head.
....

Away From Home

I bought a goldfish,
the biggest in the shop
and this chap would amuse us
so much energy he couldn't stop.
Into a plastic bag
then into the garden pond
do you know he didn't swim very far
but I don't think I was conned.
You see he hid behind the weeds
and shook for days like a leaf
you see he was lost and miles from home
but that is only my belief.
....

The Test

I knew fine the day would come
when my character would get a test
all I could do was submit to it
and do my very best.
But what I never thought of
was to practice to improve the betting
the only trouble with that was
I didn't know what I would be getting.
So I never practiced
and left it all to luck
and when it was my turn to bat
I was out for a duck.
Yes it does pay to practice
even when unsure you are right
the chances are it won't be
but you never know you might.

....

Ramblings 9

Education

The white man went to the island
to save the natives from sin
he brought them beads and axes
and pots that were made of tin.
He preached the joy of worry
the virtue of being a slave
how wicked making love was
and how abstinence was really brave.
He taught them how to work and sweat
and clothe themselves in cotton
wear motifs on their T-shirts
and wear trousers on their bottom.
Cut their hair and shave their face
they had to join the human race
get their food from the Spar or Mace
now they must really be happy.

....

Invergordon Smelter

Oh wondrous giant of Inverbreakie and Ord
you were the best thing B.A. could afford
a gleaming conveyor right down to the sea
a grand canteen to take our tea
Alcan tried it but we got thee
but now you're closed.
Oh grand big chimneys belching smoke
it's an awful pity you all went broke
but we sympathise and don't think it right
to close you down because you couldn't pay the light.
What will become of your wide tarred road
and the fields around with barley sowed
turnip, tatties and sugar beet
it makes all us Invergordon folk greet
to think that once you were like a bustling city
and I'll say it now it's an awful pity.

....

Pensions

Pensions and insurance I think are great
if you can die soon you get a better percentage rate
they've worked it out with pencil and paper
survive until you're eighty your pension is greater.
When the policy matures in your old shaky hand
they'll place a cheque for several grand
just think of the things you'll be able to afford
a holiday in Spain, a Honda Accord.
A couple of suits, a pair of boots
but booze and women I have my doots
not black twist but real cheroots
oh praise the Lord.

Now you'll be rich when laid to rest
they even supply a woman to dress you
and pull down your vest
and to avoid further embarrassment
we have an agent in heaven, what fun
he's got an office at the Pearly gates
if you'll pardon the pun.
You're even covered if you go to Hell
you'll find that in the small print as well
no need to worry or be apprehensive
just remember you're fully comprehensive.
....

Young

When I was young, oh what fun
long summers days in the wood
our bows and arrows were fantastic
our catapults made out of knicker elastic
yes these innocent days were good.
Time went by I'm no longer a boy
that spark is gone that I now call joy
the leaves have fallen the sun gone cold
the supple sapling now knarled and old
but the sound of laughter still better than gold
and memories of days in the sun.
....

Holidays Again

She snapped her castanets
and I looked into her Spanish eyes
I clicked my high heeled boots
(yes it was me again in disguise)
raising my arms I trotted around her
with a right disdainful look
and the entire crowd applauded
at every step I took.
Her red bolero heaved with excitement
for I really looked a treat
we danced around in a circle
dodging each other's feet
back to back then front to front
up the floor then doon
yes I was quite magnificent
and me, just a loon.
She swished her long skirt behind her
her hair drooped over my cheek
well my knees went all wobbly
and I felt kind of weak.
But my Lotus Bucks still pounded
when in walked Manuel
Conchita gave a squeal
which put my dancing to hell.
It was her man, built like a bull

I tell you now I felt a fool
in one hand he held a bull whip
in the other a great big stick
but like a true Scot I pointed and said 'Sir'
it wasn't me, it was her.

....

True Story

A few years ago I worked on a job
and there were two foremen there
and both were a sod
the wife of one died and everyone cried
some even prayed to God.
A wee while later the other gave a yell
he was quite high up when he fell
no one would help they said 'Go to hell'
and wouldn't lift him onto a stretcher.

....

A Bird

I'm tired of being human
I'd rather be a bird
I know it sounds ridiculous
in fact it sounds absurd.
I want to perch on branches
and make a nest with sticks
because they are much lighter
than one made of bricks.
Fed every day with monkey nuts
my, they are tasty to eat
I would fly down from the tree
and hang on the net by my feet.
I'd gobble up the crumbs and things
while keeping an eye on the cat
but he is as slow as a snail now
and has grown too fat.
Mind you, I would be choosy
I wouldn't be a robin and definitely not a tit
and if I were a Jenny Wren
I'd feel a proper twit.
I have sort of decided now to be a hen
in fact I'd be a rooster
and be in charge of my own deep litter
then the thought occurs to me
at Christmas would I feel bitter.

....

Smart

I'm very clever with lots of degrees
but the sharks in the seas knows nothing of these
so they ate me up without a cough
I'm sure I tasted better because I was a Prof.

....

The Jones's

It's nice to keep up with the Jones's
but nicer to pass them by
you know it can be amazing
what you can do if you really try.
So you struggle up the hill
with many moans and groans
and then who do you meet
yes another Mr Jones.
So once again you take up the chase
live your life like one mad race
by now you see the finish line
and there is not one soul in sight
you and Jones are the only ones left running
both are wrong, it's the rest that is right.
……………………..

Hard Work

The virtue of hard work
I'm sure is overrated
yet idleness is not desired
in fact it's hated.
They tell me a spell on the dole
can cripple a soul
and depression is all that's created.
I wonder who decided that work was so great
and that the unemployed should crawl
I know a few propagators of this myth
and they never worked at all.
Oh what a good worker they say at the grave
all his life he would sweat and slave
never a day was he unemployed
somebody somewhere must be overjoyed.
Work hard if you like but remember, nobody fails
your coffin lid has only a few nails
strain at the plough, buck or rear
in just a few years we won't even be here.
……………………..

Getting Older

Would you believe that I'm over the top
and almost a total wreck
most of my hair has vanished or turned grey
and grows away down my neck.
My fingers went kind of curly
at times it's a strain to point
the whole body is racked with rheumatics
in every single joint.
But my teeth they're almost brand new
yet they still go clickety click
they could never crack a pan drop

God it makes me sick.
My eye for the women has waned a lot
but mother nature has been quite kind
for what I ever did with them
it's a struggle to even mind.
My handsome face yes it's sagged
a bit like a boiler badly lagged
my once proud chest also has sunk
my breath with the rum smells like a skunk
all that's left is to be a monk
and the wife wonders why I get drunk.

....

Death Duties

Would you believe I own my house
also a bit of land
when I bought it first I was pleased
I'm sure you'll understand.
Well the Coal Board has the mining rights
the County has some rights too
they can come in and dig with a rig
and there is nothing you can do.
You cannot build a house or shed
without their permission
alterations or improvements
they have the final decision.
To pay the rates of course your domain
and keep it painted to keep out the rain
and when you die they take a share again
I tell you they ain't no beauties
the guys who invented Death Duties.

....

Advice

Now here is some advice on marital bliss
you'll all be so happy after this
no more nagging or no more fights
no more worries or sleepless nights
no more squealing or throwing of plates
I tell you now you'll be the best of mates.
Now for a start all must get drunk
rarely wash so you'll smell like a skunk
increase your smoking to fifty a day
and always slip something out of the pay
always complain you don't like the food
then fart and burp and generally be rude
thrash the kids when they come in from school
I know at the start you will feel a fool
but keep it up, have a will of steel
and in a month it's great how you'll feel.
Never tidy the garden that is a must
the neighbours must look with pure disgust
and on no account plant any seeds

that might interfere with the growth of weeds.
Next, for the house, the fireplace must smoke
the sink and the toilet also must choke
the doors and windows all must be draughty
you know to be happy you have to be crafty
now in a year if she complains
just you go and hide and dodge her
because I made a mistake and listened to mine
and in a week she ran off with the lodger.
....

Ruined

I stood at the brink of ruination
and looked down into the pit
and when I saw what happened there
I damn near had a fit.
Solicitors, bankers the income tax
stern faces sheriffs men with humpy backs
auctioneers to collect arrears me and the wife near in tears
and a transit van in the lay-by trying to sell snacks.
Well I slowly moved away from that terrible hole
and thought to myself 'there's not one soul'
no one would help, they'd shovel in coal.
Then I awoke and glad was I to see the light of reality
but I'll never forget that fictitious dream
because some people just run off at the mouth
and they just don't say what they mean.
....

M.O.T.

This morning I took my wee lorry for the test
I wasn't worried for she's one of the best
and oh man I was really proud of her green doors
inscribed with my name 'Builder Macleod'
her sparkling headlights, a new spare wheel
I welded her body and her cab as weel
we knocked out her king pins
and it was hard to hit it
but now my wee truck can go like a whippet.
We tuned her engine and tightened her brakes
I thought that safer for all our sakes
checked her springs, saw her back end was good
but I didn't look for that would be rude
I polished her all over with a good clart of wax
I went as far to get a road tax
but I was keen and I was willing
by the time I reached Inverness
she was like a new shilling.
Now here comes the crunch, disaster struck
when I reached Inverness in my little truck
the diesel was low and so was the oil
the 'radweld' slipped, she began to boil
the gearbox I knew was about to seize

and the front wheel went down with a slow wheeze
the exhaust fell off and when it landed it broke
by now the whole thing was covered in smoke
she started to tremble then really to shake
it was all my fault I made a terrible mistake
I should never have taken her up for a test
she was going fine without one she was my best
besides, all that maintenance is unnecessary
and to a builder it's all just a pest.

....

Pleasure

What pleasure young things can bring
a kitten playing with a bit of string
the wagging of a puppies tail
wee birdies having a bath in a pail.
So I only hope and pray
that I give pleasure one day
for as you get older and not so new
somehow you give pleasure to very few.

....

Hit by a Kindler

Today I was attacked by a kindler
in the confines of my very own shed
that stick had a whole fiendish army
while I felt faint and I bled.
I bravely held a hankie to my eye
keeping the brutes off with my feet
my head was sort of swimming
and my face was white as a sheet.
I could see the leer on their wooden faces
as I stumbled out of reach
but one jumped on my wellie
and hung there like a leach.
I tried to reach my weapon
I had been hasty in throwing it away
through the blood and the tears
I now saw where it lay.
Quick as a flash I grabbed it
and circled the terrorists
though I had the courage of twenty
most of the swipes just missed.
But one cheeky devil jumped up and got me
and oh my nose was sore
then I thought of the better part of valour
so I rushed out and I slammed the door.

....

Inverness

I got so excited about a day in Inverness

but to me the ends of the earth
was the gigantic city of Perth
soon I learned of Glasgow
then of London town
but of all the cities I know
only Inverness never let me down.

....

Outlook

If my mother was 'her ladyship'
I'd be a lord today
I wouldn't be a builder
waiting for my pay.
I wouldn't be any smarter
in fact I'd be the same
the only difference being
the 'sir' before my name.
Then I thought am I really sure
a different upbringing and education
an outlook coming from another station
Einstein's theory is a revelation
it all depends where you are standing, at the time.

....

Be a Punk

I wasn't cut out to settle down and marry
maybe I should have been a punk rocker instead
bop about the nightclub and disco
and go completely off the head.
Dye my hair a shocking pink
and sew zips all over my jeans
hang a heap of beads about my neck
and in my nose stick safety peens.
Powder my face with self-raising flower
my lips I'd paint them blue
(mind you, with all the booze I drink)
they're like that the noo'.
Then I'd get a motorbike
and hang myself in chains
rev her down the high street
to impress all the dames.
And they would sigh as I clank on by
they would think I was just great
well you don't get many punk rockers
who's over fifty-eight.

....

Gladiator

I stood there strong and proud
in the centre of the ring
the arena filled with people

432

and I bowed before the king
he gave me a little wave
as he always did before
for I am the peoples champion
and me they all adore.
I've fought both lions and tigers
and Christians now and then
chariot raced with Ben Hur
and various other men.
Held the people in rapture
with nimble feet and flashing blade
the best of all the gladiators
I put the others in the shade.
My public oh my public
my picture is in every home
they cannot do enough for me
the most popular man in Rome.
Hear them cheer, 'Hail, Hail'
'Macleod, Macleod' they chant
I coolly look round the assembly
my eyes at a noble slant.
I do not smile or wave
that's not expected from a saint
for if I showed I cared for them
some are bound to faint.
So I just look with my penetrating eyes
the women throw their hankies
and some men they throw their pies.
Aha the time has come at last
the king motions to the door
in came a herd of elephants
(they hadn't been here before).
'Still' I said, I'll tire them out
and tore off round the ring
waving to the crowds as I passed
even taking the time to nod to the king.
But now I'm a wee bit suspicious
for as past the royal box I flew
the old fella stuck out his foot
and I tripped over his blue suede shoe.
....

The Mason

I have no desire to go to war
or fire rockets in the sky
I do not want to play with guns
I don't want anyone to die.
No desire to fly a jet
and drop my deadly cargo
I want to turn on the radio
and listen to Handel's Largo.
Why should I kill a fellow mason

433

it goes right against the grain
for the brickie building in Russia
him and I are the very same.
He gets sore fingers and sometimes his back
he has no thoughts of me to attack
his hands too in the winter hack
and if he could see me he would wave.
Now who are the men who start all the fuss
one thing certain they're not one of us
at the end of the day, they don't need a truss
frustrated they just want to kill.
They sit in their office surrounded by phones
and try and imagine the plight of the drones
half should be in old folks homes
and let us get on with our building.
They don't know how to act on the level
there must be an angle or else some bevel
and sit in their bomb shelter and they revel
that's after they give me a gun.
....

My Bolster

Of all my tools I like my bolster the best
I could use it for hours without a rest
yes a mason is really blest
if he has a good bolster.
Mine is made from the finest of steel
a nice long handle for you to feel
a mason may never be down at heal
as long as he has a bolster.
But cutting a stone yesterday, it slipped
that taught me never to boast
yes, it's always the tool you like the best
that's the one that hurts the most.
....

The Gala Queen

When I was a young lad I had a great desire
to impress the lassies with a brand new car
but my wee wages didn't go that far
so I ended up with a banger.
Well anyway off I flashed
actually more of a rumble
the Gala Queen behind me got a bit red
then she started to grumble
mind you I could understand a bit
for the starting handle fair makes you humble.
Anyway round the ring the maids in the boot
my old Ford Eight coughing out soot
when one of the crowd said 'Hey look oot'
the old black car's on fire.
Well that was it, the queen had enough
though I tried to be kind and tried to be tough

off she went home in the huff
lost was the Gala Queen.
Now twenty years later I have a new car
a Rolls Royce sleek and fine
and when I see the old Gala Queen
I give her the victory sign.

....

Working Horses

I remember when horses were used on the farms
and they also worked in the wood
dragging in trees weighing a ton
I tell you they earned their food.
Eager to work they took the strain
some frothed up white from shoulders to mane
flattened ears through wind and rain
not one complaint did they make.
Now most of the lads were good to their nags
fed, well watered and groomed
but there were a few I'm sure they now rue
their treatment and long heavy drags.
Well I believe at Saint Peters gate
a Clydesdale stands at the side
and the lads that were cruel
were kicked down for fuel
in the flames of Hell they'll bide.

....

Two Pheasants

Out in the snow two pheasants strutted
so I went and got my gun
the cock and the hen were pecking away
when I went and shot one.
A wee while later the other reappeared
and looked me straight in the eye
he cocked his head, I had killed his mate
and his wee chest rose in a sigh.
How sad he looked, really pathetic
and I felt apologetic but suddenly I shot him too
well if you had a family starving to death
you would do it too.

....

Sir Walter

I looked up at the statue of Walter Scott
and I thought to myself, what a strange deal he got
sitting there in Princess Street
looking awful worried and as white as a sheet.
Then I thought of life's intricate turns
for this was a man that actually spoke to Burns
now he faces the traffic and fumes so thick

no wonder poor Walter is looking sick.
So I wrote a letter to the powers that be
'Please Lord Provost do this little thing for me
turn Walter round and stand him up tall'
I'm sure he would smile
if he was facing, The Usher Hall.

....

Nice Flowers

I am a flower, you are a weed
I lie in a bed, you where the cat peed
'Here comes the weed killer, you'll be deed'
awful nice flowers us roses.

....

The Temptation

There is nothing like a wee temptation
to forget your worries and rise in inflation
sometimes it can be a great sensation
depending on what attracts you
now the joys of strange women do little for me
besides the wife would never agree
but things ain't the same when you're seventy-three
I'd much sooner have a dram.
Well all these temptations are all egotistic
we're tempted by things we do best
that is why I relent and go to the pub
because I can out-drink all the rest.

....

Diesel

I hate the noise of engines
and that horrible thick black fumes
poisoning all the flowers and trees
and spoiling all their blooms.
Bronchitis in us humans
red-eyed with heart attacks
but still we rev our engines
along the widened tracks.
But when I'm mixing concrete
our bodies bent like a weasel
I look to the sky and say a prayer
'Thank God that we have diesel'.

....

The Negative

Now there are bad news and good news
and I prefer the bad
I'm never quite so happy

than when I'm feeling sad.
All births are accidents I know
I'd rather hear about death
or about some dreadful new illness
leaving you short of breath.
I like to see fighting and trouble
and some woman on the street blazing
I can hardly believe how strange people are
and really find their behaviour amazing.

....

Lost tribe

The missionaries found the long lost tribe
and great was their delight
much wine was drunk and food was ate
and they slept deep that night.
In the darkest hour one woke up troubled
so he knelt on the ground to pray
he started 'Gracious God'
and this is the words he did say.
'Thank you Lord for choosing me
to find these people and set them free
and Lord, I'll do all this for thee
and blessed be thy name'.
Now in a clearing just across the river
an old tribesman awoke and gave a shiver
he stood tall and raised his arms to the sky
he shook again and gave a short cry.
'Mighty Moon, hear your son
over the river strangers come
oh great god of the night, send us light
for in the morning we are going to kill them'.

....

The Burglar

When I was young I was afraid of none
secretly I wished he'd come
for I was sure that he would run
because I was strong.
In middle years I still had no fears
though I kept the phone quite handy
and if I had a doubt it was soon put out
by a little nip of brandy.
But now I'm old I just can't be bold
too weak even to run I expect
but what I fear to me is dear
it's my own self-respect.

....

Bambi

I used to poach the stag, the roe and the hind

and the hill behind my house every day I climbed
I used my rifle and my dog was handy
but all this came to a sudden stop
when I saw the film 'Bambi'.
....

Sorry

When I was nine I mind it fine
I made a grand big catapult
then I broke a window
and admitted it was all my fault.
Soon things were forgot
so I went and bought
just for a bit of fun
and many a happy day I had
chasing rabbits with my air gun.
Well years rolled on
my childhood gone
blue eyes now pale in their sockets
and I am now a General
and I love to play with my rockets.
But I never forgot my childhood
now it's not windows or rabbits my quarry
and if I kill a thousand of folk by mistake
I can always say that I'm sorry.
....

The Creeper

I am a creeper and I like to cling
on the best of buildings you'll see me hing
in fact I can creep on anything
especially if it's tall and strong.
Everybody knows that I am there
my foliage spreads away up in the air
I enjoy my creeping, it's really rare
but I don't like too much string.
I have many colours most people I suit
plenty on show but hardly a root
everyone likes me, they think I'm cute
but to a few I just give the creeps.
....

The Brute

Long ago when the world was young
and you my friend were an ape
what fun we had swinging in the trees
or just to sit and scratch and gape.
We had no stress or worries then
only the constant search for food
making love three times a day
and also when we were in the mood.

We followed the sun all the year round
no need for houses or nests
never cold in paradise
no coats no trousers no vests.
Freedom perfect freedom
until we plucked that fruit
then that awful knowledge
that we were just a 'brute'.

....

Nice

I have built plenty houses
but just one hotel
I've built some extensions
and toilets as well
I've built them in brick
and I've build them in stone
some were a mortgage
and other a loan.
But what I like most
apart from the price
is when the client just smiles
and says, 'Isn't that nice'.

....

My Best Friend

Only yesterday you were my best friend
then you went and won the lottery
and what a change came over you
I saw your eyes go all watery.
No doubt you'll buy a fancy car
and cancel the weekend we have arranged
then you'll likely buy a big house
oh I hate you now, the way you've changed.

....

Paddy

Yes there was Paddy on that site
sure, you are bound to remember
he wore no warm clothes at all
only a vest from January to December
never took dinner never took tea
well I heard he died with pleurisy
oh it was terrible, they say he had piles
and on his neck grew a lot of biles
and the grass died around for many miles
every time he took a pee.
But the women cried and the men they sighed
when the heard about poor old Paddy
then someone spoke, 'He should have worn a coat
and stopped for his bloody tea'.

....

Old Legend

Many years ago in Tarbet Estate
Black Andrew was the Laird
they called him 'black' for his heinous deeds
the worst that was ever heard.
He built seven castles in Easter Ross
and spread them around his domain
he killed and slew his subjects
or sent them to jail in Tain.
He buried alive those who complained
he buried them up to the knee
only they were down head first
an example for all to see.
One day at the farm at Newmore
quite near his castle up there
Andrew laid down a decree
that the women in the fields worked bare.
Then he stood at the great front door
and gazed and lusted and leered
while the women tried to hide themselves
as over the fields he peered.
Yet nature can use a man's bad nature at times
some justice for the lives he did wreck
for he got so excited he tripped on the steps
fell down and broke his damn neck.

....

Near Perfection

Oh Jesus I must be near perfect
look how I bow my head
see how I clasp my fingers so tightly
that my fingernails go red.
The job I do is of great importance
and I wear clothes to suit my station
I am always courteous and well spoken
and took a course of smoking cessation.
I do not allow my children to mix with riff-raff
they all go to public school
that is where they'll learn to get on
and observe the golden rule.
Yes the first basic law of success in life
is not to mix with another grade
why, no one ever got anywhere
associating with any man in the building trade.

....

Donald's Tup

Get up get up Heather said
look at the tup I think it's dead
Donald got up and through the window did stare
and sure enough, there it was, wi' it's feet in the air.

It seemed to expire with a mighty sigh
while all the ewes looked on
wi' a tear in their eye
Donald went white and to the floor he slid
'You know that tup cost four hundred quid'.
What mental anguish as he ate his brose
he rent his hair and tore his clothes
he knelt and prayed 'Oh God save us sinners'
'and keep a watchful eye on the gimmers'.
But the prayer was too late for before his eye
two of them passed over to that great fank in the sky
well I tell you now I've never seen such pain
I was sure Donald would never be the same again.
Heather looked on as he squirmed in grief
looked up to heaven and grinded his teeth.
'That's it I'm finished, his eyes sore and red
'I can't take any more, I'm off back to bed'.
Well days went by in terrible torment
a piper from Culrain played a lament.
All the crofters from the strath came up
and they held a service for Donald's tup.
But nothing would console that demented man
for that tup to Donald was more than a ram
the doctor was sent for and gave him pills to sleep
'And if they don't work' he said, 'try counting sheep'.
....

Another hand

I've heard it now quite often
'Oh what might have been'
usually accompanied by a broken heart
or some deep unhappiness it would seem.
And yes, of course I sympathise
it's human to look back and regret
but really life is not what you remember
or even what you forget.
You get dealt your playing cards all right
always quite plenty to play the game
and everybody has a different hand
nobody gets the same.
Then of course it's up to you
whether you play or pack them in
remember that even a pair of two's
can very often win.
So don't look back to regret
we all have to understand
yesterday we may have not done so well
but today It's another hand.
....

Life

You can't forecast life you know
you just never know the minute

a bit like a sausage roll
you never know what's in it.
But of course you give it a try
not to be ignorant like some
but really you aren't so smart
in fact forecasting's pretty dumb.
You see tomorrow always comes
in one form or another
there's not a lot that you can change
and I was told that by my mother.
So if you're worried about pain or death
or just another creaking joint
if your actions of today won't count at all
then what's the bloody point.
....

The list

There's so many conspiracy theories about
behind every stone there's a spy
a bomber on every plane
as it hurtles about the sky.
All accountants are liars and crooks
all politicians are greedy and thick
all policemen bullies and corrupt
the list would make you sick.
Lazy workers and stupid bosses
the unemployed are skivers that's true
but just take a look at the list
and you are there somewhere too.
....

Lions

I dreamed of wild animals again last night
if you think they were lions then you would be right
now they weren't stalking the plains of Africa
or on the Serengeti lolled and lay
no it was Clyde Street in Invergordon
and would you believe it, in the YMCA.
Now I was some kind of sheriff in my dream
and I had to patrol the town
so I sauntered up the street
and then I sauntered down.
Then as I passed the YMCA on the corner
where the young folk used to dance
the door was open and I heard the roar
well you can imagine the state of my pants.
The doors were still ajar, so I closed them quick
of course I hadn't a gun but I had a walking stick
now I remember thinking I'll do some detection
but from lions a walking stick is not much protection.
So I remember then making a bit of a spurt
no sense in hanging around and maybe get hurt
well the lions still roared inside the hall

and I was lucky I didn't faint or fall
as I sped off, on someone's bike I hopped
and do you know I was in Alness before I got stopped.

....

Lorry again

Yes it seems to be dream time again
and once more I dreamed of my lorry
it wasn't the green or blue one this time
it was the yellow one I bought from Norrie.
Of course the wee truck wasn't insured
or even taxed or passed the test
and there I was as proud as punch
with a load of blocks like the rest.
Then as usual here comes the crunch
I could see the chequered hats come into view
skulking behind was the traffic commissioner
with a nose that begged a punch from me or you.
Needless to say I was stopped abruptly
in a very arrogant manner
then he started to hit my lorry
with his bloody little hammer.
This was to see if any nuts were slack
and of course there were always a few
but my lorry was ten years old
and really looked far from new.
I kept my cool and bit my lip
resisted the urge to give him a slap
I knew they were deliberately annoying me
but this was just an old trap.
So I sat there fretting and vulnerable
thirty years ago but I remember it well
yet I'm still awake with a knot in my stomach
and feel as guilty as hell.

....

No Dream

I didn't dream at all last night
so I thought what on earth's going on
not a lorry, a lion or film star
there must be something wrong.
I checked the bedroom
then the whole of the house
opened the cocktail cabinet
and checked the Grouse.
Then at last the penny dropped
and I began to realise
it was still the early morning
and I hadn't yet opened my eyes.

....

Lies

Why are lies so easily believed
no need for evidence or proof
while authentic reality is despised
and ignored is the virtue of truth.
The traitor is now called an 'anti-hero'
to steal and cheat is called human
ethics and morals are now so quaint
no hope for man or respect for woman.
....

Navy

I remember the days when I was young
when the navy came into port
the lassies came from miles around
the sailors for them to court.
I remember that brave young guys clearly
trying to make contact with home
queuing along the pavement
outside the red box that we called a phone.
Some got drunk admittedly
just across in the Royal Hotel
others got blitzed in the Caley bar
and some in the Commercial as well.
Yet when I think of it now, no wonder
they were conscripted to fight to the death
and it wasn't for fair play or justice they fought
but for power for some and for others wealth.
I still remember their raucous singing
their love of life, of dangers, no fuss
when there were no way to get to a dance in the Strath
they just went out and stole a bus.
Oh yes it might have been carefree days in a way
yet still I am proud I knew these men
but now that I'm old I sit in the cold, and ponder
why was our government so harsh with them.
....

Outside Craig Dunain Hospital

My wife went to visit in the hospital one night
her sister and mother as well
while I sat outside in the car park
or this story I couldn't tell.
Well I sat in the car for an hour or so
in that time I saw a drama unfold
the players, two policemen and a drunk old man
in a scene that left me quite cold.
I had just recovered my composure
when out my relatives trotted
gazing around the car park
until in the dark it was me they spotted.

Still chattering away they all piled in
each trying to tell the same tale
how a nice police sergeant arrested a man
and all the nasty drunk man did was wail.
They all admired the policemen's patience
their manners and how any annoyance they hid
but I was out in the car park
and I saw what they really did.

....

Big Bird

I went out in the garden yesterday morning
for my usual hour of exercise
I don't even know why I said that
because that is a pack of lies.
The only bit that is exercised now
seems to be my elbow and wrist
yet somebody once said I have a nice swallow
but three bits of me is hardly a list.
Anyway back to the story, I was out the back, as we say
and you can believe every word that I tell
in fact a sighting so far in the North
I can hardly believe it mysel'.
No I'm not going to enter the realms of fantasy
or make up a story that is so absurd
but honestly in the field beside the house
stalked a giant of a bird.
Now I quickly cleaned my glasses
and regretted the drams last night
I couldn't even call the wife and bairns out
in case they got a fright.
So I just crouched down and made for cover
like a commando doing the 'monkey run'
well I was afraid that I would startle it
and I don't like frightening big birds, like some.
Now as I lay parting the grass in front of me
I heard the wife start squealing
'Look at your grandpa he must have croaked'
and she said it with such feeling.
Of course the big bird heard her too
and took off just like a jet
then of course the neighbour appeared
with his damn mongrel he calls a pet.
It was obvious then that all was lost
never again would that big bird I'd see
but isn't nature so very astute
not to show the bird to anyone else
and only showed it to me.

....

Mouse trap

Every morning I open the shed
to inspect my new plastic trap

the instructions said it was painless
all would be extinct in just one snap.
Now every morning for about ten days
there was another lifeless mouse
no more the sounds of scratching
as they scurried around the house.
Yes I admit it was an efficient trap
it could have been created in Hell
but men are so inventive at killing
maiming and wounding as well.
Anyway one morning it was empty
and I hadn't got to think twice
as I slid to the floor intuition told me
I had wiped out a family of mice.

....

Wedding

One thing about life I'm certain
I won't be invited to the marriage
anyway the train fare from here is far too dear
and the car is in the garage.
So I won't bother brushing my suit
it's only the elite of the country who'll go
not one mason or carpenter will be there
but there again you never know.
Bishops and lords aplenty
aristocrats by the ton
but will there be a brickie or a plumber there?
no there won't, not one.
Now I know that may sound like sour grapes
but could mother nature have made such a blunder
bred special genes for the halls of fame
of course she didn't, but sometimes I wonder.

....

Greed

I knew if I was elected
that I was sure to succeed
I would introduce a new crime
and I would call it 'greed'.
The penalty for breaking this law
would be jail or else a fine
and if I get my way
the only option would be time.
But why should I be too hard on folk
the only sentence being detention
so why not take all their money away
and make them live on a pension.
Yes I think that's solved it
put most of the greedy ones in a home
then we could sell their houses
now that will make them moan.
Then of course their pension must stop

and we could call that 'clawing back'
our operatives won't even have to be trained
because it's not a trade but a knack.
Yes indeed I've cracked it
so I'll need to keep my nerve steady
in case the other party hears of it
and say it's been thought of already.
....

Memories

All our memories are still in our brains you know
but they are stored in pictures and not like a book
every taste, every smell, every touch and sound
every picture your eyes ever took.
Yes all is there in the subconscious mind
recorded at speeds supersonic
some memories carefully filed away like films
and others scattered about like comics.
Now you will have to edit and sort your stuff
or your brain will overflow and start leaking
and then every time you tell a tale or talk
It will be rubbish that you will be speaking.
Now nature has made this editing easy
and to evolution we are really indebted
to put the surplus in the recycle bin
it's so simple, we just forget it.
....

Guardian Angel

Gabri'elle' the arch angel is a lady I'm sure
not a man, like Gabriel the Jew
It's just what we were told many years ago
and you were probably told that too.
I had visions of Gabriel with a long grey beard
a toga and a dirty white turban
and not a beautiful young woman with a heart of gold
a spotless saint and a virgin.
Now I got to calling her my guardian angel
and to her I would constantly pray
that might be a bit of an exaggeration
but I made contact every other day.
I never asked her for much of course
for a start that would be bad manners and rude
and honestly I never mentioned the lottery at all
or anything that I normally would.
We just spoke about ordinary things
like the cost of living and dying
and we both kept a grip of our feelings
lest the two of us started crying.
Now to ingratiate myself I did not intend
but to be honest I did just a bit
well I'm only a weak old man you know
and I wasn't fancying the burning pit.

Anyway, Gabrielle soothed all my worries
my destination pretty much now secured
she told me how she pulled some strings
now that's better than being insured.
Only one thing left I still worry about
a wee niggling thing that I had always feared
when I present myself at the pearly gates
I'll see a grinning wee man with a long grey beard.

....

Too Late

It's never too late to learn anything
or to slim if you are fat
never too late to change your ways
I wonder who on earth said that.
Oh yes there is always a precocious smart arse about
like the 'scripture Union' girls at the school
answering all their Bible questions
making the rest of us feel a fool.
The leaders of the Cubs and Scouts
so power crazed it would make you sick
the aim in life is to get one more badge
It's no wonder we took the Mick.
But there it is, all gone forever
we thought that when we left the schools
but who did we meet on our first job
yes wee Nigel and his golden rules.
And of course smelly Johnnie his henchman
a sort of back up bodyguard for Nigie'
hanging around the bosses boots
thinking he was a right smart gadgie.
Yes the most important lesson you can ever learn
don't leave your future to luck or fate
because if you're not a prick right at the start
you might just be a bit too late.

....

Old Age Again

Do you ever think, it's just not fair
you get a pot belly and lose your hair
the teeth is next to disappear
your eyes are ornaments and so is an ear.
The famous wit is absent, gone A.W.O.L.
and every joint creaks and is knackered as well
all your muscles are flaccid in every member
and where your passion went, you can't remember.
Could it be I see my glass half empty, not full
am I thinking so negative and pessimistic too
no I'm not, you won't understand
until it happens to you.

....

Egyptians

I think the Egyptians had got it right
when it comes to the end of the day
all your deeds go onto the scales
then somebody has got to pay.
If not the books wouldn't balance
the world would be lopsided so to speak
and who would want a lopsided world
nobody, not even the meek.
So I wonder who knows the whole truth
are we all destined to wither and die
of course I sometimes wonder how
but mostly I wonder why.
Will we be obliterated entirely
or maybe allowed to look on
like watching a play in the theatre
until all the little Indians are gone.
I suppose that could be exciting
even some twisted compensation
and to witness our friends misdemeanours
might turn out to be a sensation.
But to be a 'mummy' doesn't seem right
bandaged from your head to your toes
all your guts stuffed in jam jars
and your brains pulled out of your nose.
No I can't see the sense in that idea
where did they ever learn that technique
I think I would rather a sad funeral in Kilmuir
preferably at the end of the week.
But where is your soul as you lie on the slab
are you clinging on the ceiling to watch
keeping an eye on the apprentices
in case some of them make a botch.
Now I don't mean to be flippant
because this is all very serious stuff
so stick with it a little longer
and don't go off in the huff.
If there is a superior intelligence
called Allah or some just call it God
but for peace healing and kindness
I probably would give Buddhists' the nod.
Now don't make a mistake and ignore the future
everyone must admit it will come
if this is true you have a choice of two
there is life hereafter or none.
....

Drivers

The next time you're out in the car
take a look at the drivers faces
then count how many look happy
and how many could kill at ten paces.
Yes it's a sad reflection on us British

the drivers look so angry and depressed
maybe I look like that too behind the wheel
my face in a lurk like the rest.
But seriously I think it an awful shame
to drive along with a gurn
shaking fists and rude gesticulations
and screaming insults at every turn.
But do you ever wonder why drivers do this
why so easily do they lose the plot
Is it because they are cowards
and know that they can't get caught.
Or perhaps it's just a release of emotion
to get rid of the daily stresses
to be honest I don't really know
though I do make one or two guesses.
But the cure is straight forward and simple
one or two adverts on the TV should do
no need to make a saga about it
but I'll leave that entirely to you.
Now this is how the advert should go
It would screened when the bairns are in bed
then it wouldn't matter a lot
what any of the actors said.
First of all a rusty old car and an ugly driver appears
then a caption below in bold type
and the ugly guy whispers 'Oh how I hate that lodger,
but I'm early so I'll catch the jolly roger'.
And now that you know the reason some drivers are angry
so next time you see one give the thumbs up in sympathy
your expression so understanding and kind
and after seeing the advert he will think you know the lot
and that everyone else knows too, what's on his mind.
....

More Angry Drivers

Now on the subject of angry drivers
there is always a few on the road to Inverness
sometimes there are four and sometimes three
but two on an average, well, more or less.
Now anger doesn't bring out the beauty in anyone
In fact it brings an evil look to a face
and it's pretty obvious what they are thinking
well I think it an outright disgrace.
No need for behaviour like that on the A9
and it gets progressively worse as you go south
then when you are on the dual carriageway at Tore
the women join in too and run off at the mouth.
Now I used to think we Highlanders were patient
understanding and on an occasion quite kind
I must have been half shot when I thought like that
or else out of my tiny mind.
Yes although it saddens me to think it now
when once I thought we were one of the best
well-mannered and kind of special too
and not angry like a lot of the rest.
....

The Jeep

I once had a four track Jeep for years
I tell you this just so you'll know
in all the years that I had that car
we never got a flake of snow.
Now I won't even tell you what happened
when I then bought a low slung GTI
ignoring completely 'Sods Law'
only my timing would make you cry.

....

Success

Success is a journey you know, not a destination
when you think of it, it's very akin to a cruise
you don't check the lifeboats all the time do you
or listen to the weather forecasts for storms and news.
No you don't, you enjoy the moment
the reality of enlightened undulating poetic rhyme
that precious moment when you can feel, hear, smell and see
and even taste the very presence of time.

....

Are You Happy

I can hardly believe what the government is doing
and the project is costing two million quid
they employed a consultant to see if we are happy
honestly, that is what they did.
I presume this consultant is an expert on happiness
and goes around Westminster grinning and singing too
but if you or I got two million pounds
I would be singing the same song as you.
Now I wonder how he collects his statistics
does he sneak up when we're in a good mood
or maybe waits for Monday morning
when we're not feeling quite so good.
Now the more I think of it the mind just boggles
a bit like Hercules cleaning out the Augean stable
but our government took that story to heart
and didn't realize the 'impossible' was only a fable.
No doubt the happiness consultant started on Monday
that's after a weekend of laughter and mirth
but his mother said he was always a comedian
right from the day of his birth.
No it's really strange how times have changed
but it's time these laughing guys got some luck
in my young day if you giggled all the time
they were likely to lock you up.

....

Jack the Lad

I knew a man that was so egocentric

451

whenever we stopped for a blether
he always finished the conversation
by saying that he would 'never'
never do this and never do that
always stay slim and never get fat
never get drunk smoke or swear
never get bald, he'd keep his hair
kept himself to himself never was bad
he would never be called 'Jack the Lad'.
But alas alas all that was stopped
and nature once more declared king
you see you only get points for doing
and none for not doing a thing.

....

The Solution to the Sparrow Hawk

A murderer flew into my garden
oh yes he was beautiful in flight
but he turned our long hot summer days
Into a screeching, killing, dark evil of night.
He murdered the doves as they loved and cooed
ripped nests out of hedge and tree.
Now can you guess who got his gun and shot it dead
well I'll tell you, that man was me.
Now you can philosophise all you like
about how nature has got to have balance
how some evolved feet and others' hooves
and some others grew claws and talons
now don't get me wrong I agree with you all
as any deep, serious thinker would
but a huge choir is singing in my garden right now
for in my little world *I* am dominant, and that is good.
Now I don't say all that to feel important and smug
because of the community already I'm a pillar
but I am quite honest about the man I am
I'm just another ruthless killer.

....

Hard Disc

My hard disc crashed the other day
that's what they call it in computer jargon
and when I bought the thing for twenty quid
I really thought I was getting a bargain.
I filled the files so quickly
the programs were so quick it was frightening
and there I was typing away
my wee fingers going like lightening.
And then it came, yes the crash
just when I was on the last chapter
I thought I'd finish my book wi' a bit of art
so I was on the scanner pressing 'capture'.
And here it is now, a frozen display
the screen saver, an old Christmas card
but now I know why they say it's frozen

and why they call the wee disc 'hard'.
Now I have been wise over the years
and left quite a lot to 'fate'
so I'll just make up another story
and this one will really be great.
Yes I regret a wee bit I didn't make a copy
even some notes in any old jotter
oh but nobody would read it anyway
with a name like Harry Potter.

....

Tesco

Who would ever write a rhyme about a shop
well I would like to write one about Tesco
not Morrison, Lidl or even Low's
or Sainsbury's, Aldi or Presto.
I better mention Somerfield for they are local
but I think they wavered and lost all hope
transferred all their stocks and shares
and sold the lot to the Co-op.
But that is the world of big business
never staying too long in one place
how simple it was years ago
when it was just the Spar and the Mace.
Yes it is a bit unsettling I suppose
to change your loyalties one more time
but I like Tesco because they're cheaper
and to say anything else would spoil the rhyme.

....

A Pipe Line

Have you ever wondered when you're having a bad time
what on earth is going to happen next
and of course the anticipation is always so negative
leaving you helpless worried and vexed.
Well I suppose this is not going to cheer you up much
so keep your head and nerves quite steady
because all the things that are going to happen to you
are on their way already.
You see situations are like a shower of rain or snow
a magician or saint can go out and shout 'Hold'
but there is half an hour on the way down
and that half an hour can't do what it's told.

....

Hate

I never really believed that I could hate
yes maybe a person, but not a nation
but when I read a wee story yesterday
I hated a hundred percent on that occasion.
There is no need to mention the country

to say they are backward is not to overstate
and if there is a heaven and a burning hell
most of that population will find out too late.
Well it took me ages to really calm down
and to think of all the wars that were fought
only to find out eventually
that progress was not what we got.
Is there any way to civilise people quickly
and not resort to the bomb, torture and gun
but we were like them two hundred years ago
like a pack of wolves when all's said and done.
Yes the wheel of progress turns relentlessly slowly
heartless cruelty and violence still far from dead
but in the end there is true justice for all
and I believe what that young man said.

....

Recipe for Happiness

Where did all the farm workers go
did they all die or just fade away
or did they go to the cities and towns
and learned to live another way.
I sometimes wonder when I see their cottages
built in a street in one long row
I wonder if they lived in happy times
for to be honest I do not know.
In these days money was very scarce for them
but they were told wanting more money was bad
hard labour was the way to happiness
to get more cash would just make them sad.
And do you know a lot of them believed that idea
knowing what I know now they might well be right
real contentment and happiness are so elusive
even the richest man can't find it, try as he might.
In fact I would say the rich are at a disadvantage
for having all that cash and are so wealthy
and no, I will not bore you
about how much better it is to be healthy.
You see happiness is not about material things
as they say, 'it is all in the mind'
you don't see a lot of millionaires laughing do you
but of course they don't seem to have the daily grind.
So what is the answer does anybody know
there is only one thing I'm certain is true
that nobody knows, and neither do I
and I am pretty sure neither do you.

....

Sense

To walk a few miles in someone else's shoes
shouldn't bring many surprises
nine out of ten they won't fit you anyway
because they come in so many sizes.
Most men can sort the other man's wife

and appease wild dogs with a bone
even other folks children he will understand
but can make no sense of his own.
Yes it would be nice, a different outlook of life
at will switch to other beliefs
but if we could do that there would be no Indians
and the country would be full of chiefs.
So the answer is, be content with yourself
and appreciate more what you've got
live your own life the best that you can
because you only get the one shot.
Don't even think about improving other men
by saying their behaviour is appalling
unless you are a politician or a minister
or have some other noble calling.
Leave everyone else to live their own life
you just can't appreciate the other man's thirst
but maybe you believe that you can do this
If you do then you are the first.

....

School Days

Do you remember when we were at school
spending most of the day in the class
sitting and scratching our heads all day
difficult exams and tests to pass.
Paying attention to the teachers
like pigs listening to thunder
realising just how clever they were
yet sometimes now I wonder.
I only wish that memories were true
and that we were studying and analysing
while all the time in the back row
most of us were dreaming and fantasising.
Writing so neatly without ever a smudge
forgiving the bullies not bearing a grudge
being terrified of religion scared of going blind
morphing into werewolves and tales of that kind.
Yes it would be nice to remember the teachers
with love and respect in our eyes
but if I ever tried to do that
it would all be a pack of lies.
In my day a lot of cruelty went on
by cane leather strap and lines
writing out all your mistakes of the day
and doing it hundreds of times.
Yet really us kids handled it all quite well
even when we were told we were stupid creatures
but there were always some you couldn't forgive
just one or two sadistic teachers.
Now you might think we all grew up twisted
and not at all well balanced
yet most of us forged ahead all right
because now they just call us challenged.
So did any of us turn out normal
maybe only a few or perhaps many

well I have to be truthful and tell you
honestly I don't think there were any.
....

Cold Winter

I really must try harder to figure it out
develop and devise some cunning plan
in order to lower the price of oil
for I'm down to my last Jerry can.
It's all right for them in the middle east
where they never get snow or frost
why did nature put a lot of the oil out there
without a thought of price or cost.
And there they are in their desert tents
trying to keep reasonably cool
while the wife and I are chattering
and feeling a bit of a fool.
Then I think of the lads in the North sea
working their fortnight off then on
but they must be doing some homers
because we're told most of the oil is gone.
Still I don't grudge them their perks at all
the rigs are not nice places to be
and it must be cold and dangerous
out there in the sea.
Now my cunning plan has hatched at last
so simple I would call it fair at any rate
if you feel the cold in Scotland
why not emigrate.
....

The Worst

The greatest leveller of humans
yes for both women and men
is a daily dose of pain
when it attacks you again and again.
Some say the worst is the pain of birth
it can drive some women crackers
but there again a man might say
it's not as sore as kick in the knackers.
Yet we all have our own Achilles heel
some are worse as we get older
but one thing that screws us all up
is when we get the cold shoulder.
....

Frustrated Builder

Did you ever fancy being a salesman
maybe to sell a car or some clothes
or even be a plastic surgeon
making bigger boobs and alterations to a nose.

In the trade we call that a 'chancer'
well known on the building site
I know you would never be one
but you never know you might.
I have often been drawn to the thrill
of impersonating a famous man
maybe doing a heart transplant
yup that's the kind of guy I am.
Perhaps negotiating deals worth millions
more exciting than pricing an extension
but I haven't given an estimate in ages
so I thought it would be worth a mention.
Yes I can see you and I being partners
a bit like the supermarkets Aldi and Lidl
spying on each other every day
wondering who was on the fiddle.
A pilot or priest would also do at a push
the list is just never ending
a solicitor too would equally do
then I could grin at the bills I'm sending.
Now isn't it a wonderful exciting world
but don't let it go to your head
the potential is there but you've got to be fair
so I'll stay a bricklayer instead.
....

Another Fact

Life is just a learning curve you know
you sometimes lose and sometimes gain
but the only thing you can be sure of
is that nothing stays the same.
The good times the bad, the happy the sad
all things get worse or gets better
the weather too can go all askew
and the dull day gets drier or wetter.
You may greet the morning with a smile
sing along with the birds in good voice
or else just look and glare at the sky
but that is your only choice.
....

Birds

Every bird in the north is in my garden now
this is due to the snow and the frost
me and the wife feed them twice every day
and we say 'forget the cost' (or words to that effect).
Now we are not reckless people really
mind you the wife can be a bit of a spender
though I don't suppose she is worse than most
of any other of the female gender.
So we buy the huge bags of seeds and nuts
we already have a big plastic jug
that is just to keep the back lobby tidy

and not to get seeds on the rug.
Then after all the wee creatures are fed
our chests swell up with pride
kick the snow off our boots
and then take them off inside.
Now many may think this is a simple act
not mercenary but a kind thing to do
but just think of this, in another life
that the two crows might be me and you.

....

Dog Brains

Have you ever looked at your dog
and wondered what she is thinking
because dogs can look quite vacant at times
with one paw in the air and both eyes blinking.
Yet when you really think about their intelligence
they have been on this planet longer than you
now do you think evolution forgot them
and ignored them as they developed and grew.
Well I get the funny feeling at times
and I also get the same feeling with my cat
in fact I get it with most creatures
yes even a weasel and a rat.
You see we have all been here millions of years
all the animals tried our way of life before
they went down the same road as us long ago
now they do not want to do it anymore.

....

Sense

I don't like the way our country is going now
what happens next I just don't know
but if we keep on going the way we are
we will be putting old folks out in the snow.
Young students are asked to go deep into debt
to pay for their advanced education
looking forward now to years in the red
now isn't that a great expectation.
More wars are planned that is for sure
a good time to scrap the Ark Royal!
entertainers are long since knights of the realm
still ignoring brave soldiers who are loyal.
Our politicians are bright and clever all right
but maybe they're a bit out of touch
paying pen pusher millions of pounds a year
when a penny on the pension's too much.
There are plenty of experts and consultants about
all with their snout in the trough
taking a year to ask one silly question
will somebody just say 'enough is enough'.
Do we really have to make all that rules
when half of them are just a pretence
how about a wee bit of wisdom

and a smattering of common sense.
The final blow of course is the new ploy
ministers say boldly they won't apologise
implying they are totally innocent
and never told a pack of lies.
Well is our country going to go down the tubes
not knowing what is wrong and what's right
when we can play ball in one field and kill in another
I sometimes think we might.

....

Sunday Morning

Do you ever take out the photo album
then just sit and reminisce
glance out the window at the snow
and think that this is bliss.
You are warm safe and cosy
don't have any bombs to ban
then in ten short minutes
everything hits the fan.
The cat crawls in she'd been in a fight
she went in heat and stayed out last night
and if you think a tom called Fluffy is bad
his alter ego would be a Brillo Pad.
Then the bairns come in from Sunday school
they had learnt about sin and another rule
of course at this the wife got excited
declaring her wee boys deserved to be knighted.
Of course now that I had time to think
she thought the new rule was about the drink
by now I had started sliding out the door
pretending I wasn't moving and looking at the floor.
And there the bairns were yapping about sinning
the cat by the fire dreaming and grinning
and me trying to escape out to the shed
regretting that I didn't stay in my bed.
But that is the way of Sunday mornings
all week you work hard and do the biz'
then somebody turns the stress tap on
and that's just the way it is.

....

The Final Curtain

It's amazing how a programme sticks
which were taught at our mothers knee
some of these truths are never forgot
and remembered since we were wee.
And now as I face the final batch of mortar
laying the last facing bricks in neat rows
I phoned the wife on my mobile
to get ready my clean underclothes.

....

Another Novel

Well I tried again to write a novel
and to be honest it wasn't very good
considering I can be so descriptive
without getting too rough or rude.
So I persisted with my epic story
and made my heroine an aristocratic cow
no idea why I did this and no idea how.
The hero of course was based on me
artistic intelligent and brave
but then I had to face the facts
he had no idea of how to behave.
In fact my hero was a proper lecher
fond of drink but happily not the drugs
might pass for quite good looking
if it wasn't for the big nose and lugs.
So here was my dilemma
would it be truth or lies I'd tell
too late to be a saint now
so to tell porkies I might as well.
But of course they call it fiction today
and I remember a sheriff using that word too
when I denied being drunk and disorderly
and swore it was all lies and untrue.
What do we need then for a real hero
would Spiderman be worth a mention
but there again he has been invented already
so he is probably out of the question.
Well there is too much stress in writing a novel
when I started I knew at the time
where never was a hero like me
so I'll stick to a short little rhyme.
....

Would You

Once again I had to stop reading the news
before I broke down and cried
bribery, fraud and corruption
and politicians admitting they lied.
Yes this is 'Rip Off Britain' all right
It would make any woman or man's blood boil
as soon as we get cold with frost and snow
up goes the price of heating oil.
It's all a matter of supply and demand they say
and we do make a bit more profit we admit
if you were in our shoes you would do the same
disappointing but true, when you think of it.
....

The Gala

Gala day at the swimming pool

for the parents was a real treat
but nine times out if ten it was pretty cold
unless the sun was shining to give some heat.
The freestyle under fifteens race
really had my granny grinning
because I was in the front for a while
which meant I might be winning.
Then the underwater race
which wasn't really a race at all
it was just who swam the furthest
and wasn't knocked out on the concrete wall.
Oh but it was good fun alright
I can still hear the cheering crowd
and they never ever got one complaint
that their voices were too loud.
Then later we all dived for pennies
that was always the talk of the town
because the provost in the middle seat
always threw in two bob or half a crown.
Then after that was the prize giving
silver cups and postal orders
then Jewkitt took a photo or two
of all the medal holders.
So what did become of the outdoor pool
the cold showers where we would freeze
the diving board and the concrete steps
where we would fall and skin our knees.
Well I can hardly believe it
no sense was ever showed
some even said it was progress
to knock it down and build a road.
I suppose the road was handy enough
but now tar Macadam fills that spot
where fair play and even cheating was learned
and also how not to get caught.
They say loads about the playing fields of Eton
Prime ministers left them and made a rule
one day when they get enough money
they'll restore our swimming pool.

....

Depression

I don't think Christmas helps a lot
and Jingle Bells is just another curse
the shaking of hands and happiness
makes all things ten times worse.
But depressives really can't help it
we would love to be one of the crowd
and not adjust the stereo to turn it down
because it was playing too loud.
We would love to start the 'sing-a-long'
to be a font of glee and joy
pull a Christmas cracker
and be delighted with our toy.

Tickle the wife underneath the mistletoe
overdoing the kiss by half
doing that to entertain the neighbours
and to give our relatives a laugh.
But we can't do any of these things
we are in a strange body with us inside
wishing that we were somewhere else
where we could go and hide.
It's mindless mirth at any soirée
where all the clocks are running slow
that jovial party tomorrow night
how I'll get out of it I just don't know.
But now I see there is an operation for us
it's supposed to be better than electric shocks
they take a drill and bore a hole in your head
and out of the hole depression pops.
I know that is a bit facetious and flippant
not a worthy description of the old black dog
if only a magician could find a way
to get rid of this dark relentless fog.

....

Another Rant

Do you ever feel like screaming out
that's not justice that's wrong not right
when a farmer shoots a burglar
in the middle of the night.
The farmer gets sent to prison
for hurting the poor thief
the way this country is going
is just beyond belief.
The criminal gets amnesty and succour
because he fathered a child
while his victim lies in her cold grave
does that not make you wild.
A traitor is not a traitor now
he just hates us and wishes us harm
I see them rubbing their hands with glee
when they see our troops disarm.
No more fighter planes for us
the prime minister declares
then we won't need aircraft carriers
because there won't be more warfare's.
So don't ask for armoured Land Rovers
when a nice wee Suzuki will suffice
my daughter has a new one
and she thinks it very nice.
There is no aliens in foreign countries
wanting to kill us and do other things
they are just ordinary folk like us
who happen to be waiting in the wings.
In fact it is well known in the west
that most of them are poor
where they get their cars and palaces from

well I'm not really very sure.
Don't mistake their religious passion
and confuse it with fanatical zeal
if you had only a bomb or two
think of how you'd feel.
So let's have more understanding
about all twisted people who are so sad
and us ordinary people can emigrate
and in another country we can all go barking mad.
....

Ramblings 10

Road Rage

This 'road rage' thing is a quite new craze here
I never 'mind it happening long ago
maybe it was a habit in other places then
but in all honesty I do not know.
Now these chaps who do it, maybe are young
or else old guys who never quite got the plot
for up in the North it's a personal insult
and to get away with rude gesticulations
sometimes you do and sometimes not.
Now I was told this story by a big woodman
who took offence at a stranger's middle digit
and like any man of his ilk he gave chase
his Land Rover screaming after the MG Midget.
Of course soon enough he ambushed the road rager
by taking a shortcut by the wood around the town
his Land Rover leaping out of the forest
turning the MG upside down.
Now the woodman was a big powerful man
eighteen stone and stood six feet four
he grabbed the wee car by the hood
and ripped off the driver's door.
Now the driver tried to defend himself
attempted to deny the visual abuse
but all the alibis fell on deaf ears
and every other feeble excuse.
Now seeing all escape was useless
and being a bit traumatised like normal men
he made a defiant brave final gesture
and stuck up his finger again.
Now this act incensed our man
so he gave the stranger a right good thrashing
by then a tourist had dialled nine nine nine
and very soon the blue light was flashing.
Name and address the policeman said
and be sure the reason makes sense
right away I can see it was gross provocation
or else a clear case of self-defence.
Now you can believe this tale if you like
but I'm sure you will agree
I just nodded my head in understanding
when this story was told to me.
....

Laughter

Laughing too much was once considered mad you know
then gradually the preserve of the weak minded
soon it was considered inappropriate at times
just a habit with no sense behind it.
And now all mirth is acceptable
smile, titter or raucous laughter
and the more people that joined in
It's quite nice to hear, but dafter.

Then of course science came in
and told us laughter produced drugs
which sailed around our bodies
and killed off all dangerous bugs.
So now I think we have it all sussed out
laughter is important for the health of you
It's also important for happiness
and for wealth it might be too.
So treat all your instincts with respect
by chance they did not appear
If laughter is not essential in life
I tell you now it's pretty near.
....

Gullible

The most frightening conversation I ever had
was with a man middle-aged and mature
I don't think it matters how old he was
a good job because I wasn't so sure.
Anyway he rattled on about the unbelievable
accepting the most incredible fiction
everything that he read was real and true
and all else was just an addiction.
Now this naivety struck a small chord in me
as simplicity can sometimes be charming
but deliberate ignorance and gullibility
Is tantamount to self-harming.
....

A Talent

I knew a man who was a member of a forum
this is a site where you can record your blog
I hope you noticed the internet jargon
but unlike the others I have nothing to flog.
Anyway I used to enjoy the crack on the site
It was always witty intelligent and clear
but anyway a self-appointed genius logged on
then the train of thought went all awry I fear.
Well this chap was a master of the good cop bad cop
and also at 'sarcasm, the lowest form of wit'
I always took those observations with a pinch of salt
but this was the first time I saw the real power of it.
The good cop bad cop was a bit of a revelation
I only really ever experienced it on TV
It is designed as a play on your emotions
and it does confuse your feelings I'm sure you'll agree.
Ah, but sarcasm is out ahead on its very own
you could describe it as the scum on the heap
we had all learned that years ago
as children it made a few of us weep.
To be an outcast in the middle of the herd
but never the less alone and unwanted
stupefied, stunned and bewildered

466

by our own obvious ignorance haunted.
So as we drown in this gross embarrassment
we come to the real tricky bit
was there an embedded inferior suggestion
so well encoded that we believed in it.
Or is sarcasm just a wonderful natural gift
the preserve of the brilliant and clever
to be expounded and delivered at will
whenever people are gathered together.
But no, sarcasm is a totally negative talent
It exposes our hates and what we hold dear
It strips us of all our esteem and self-worth
and leaves us all alone with, fear.

....

Lost

Oh how I miss the days of my youth
yet at the time I wasn't so keen
In fact I wasn't happy at all then
If you understand just what I mean.
My childhood too was akin to youth
I remember wishing I was more mature
and now that I have these things aplenty
right now I'm not very sure.
So here I am tottering into dotage
putting on a brave wrinkled face
and all the time remembering
that sometime long ago
for some reason I lost the place

....

Paranoid

Do you ever think there is a conspiracy against you
or am I the only paranoid man around
walking down the street I say 'Hello'
to one of the conspirators I'll be bound.
I notice in the checkout they're all watching me
and the manager behind the two way glass
I think he watches too much TV
which makes him a pain in the ass.
Out in the street the police car is crawling
I can see it's in my direction they stare
but I take a tighter grip of my poly bag
and pretend that I didn't even care.
Then the dogs out a walk give me a snarl
and I could have booted that yapping Yorky
as for that apology of a whippet
couldn't catch a cold he's so porky.
Then I start to think I'll go home and hide
maybe out in the shed if it's not too cold
but the wife will just give me some orders
and scream 'Do what you are bloody told!'
So what chance do us paranoias have
after all we are ordinary women and men

but don't go round telling everybody else
or I won't tell you anything, ever again,
....

Insight

Have you ever been confronted with your own mortality
that is so philosophical and poetic but that's what they say
well on Thursday I was at an old lady's funeral
and it happened to me on that day,
I was singing and praying in the church as usual
quite proud I put ten pounds in the collection
looking forward to the soup and sandwiches
and of the rake of drams I won't even mention.
Then when we arose to sing the last hymn
I must have looked the epitome of sadness and grief
hair neatly combed wrinkles suitably sagged
a man exuding faith hope and belief.
Yet underneath that pious exterior
lurked a self-centred man of dreams
at least when I look back on my act
that is what my performance seems.
Anyway getting back to the business
the last hymn and prayer was now finished
they wheeled the coffin down the isle
immediately I knew then I was diminished.
Instead of an old lady on her last journey
It was just so plain then to see
that inside that sad sombre box
was a small part of you and a small part of me.
....

Identical

Have you ever thought 'this is it'
I mean by that 'you've had your lot'
most people feel like that now and then
then make the most of what they got.
But that is just a bit of depression you know
It's not fatal, only a bit of a pest
you think why can't you be happy
and be stupid and flippant like all of the rest.
Of course you see now that attitude is so twisted
you can hardly believe that you thought that
but maybe you were right about your neighbour
and his wife too is still a wee twat.
So don't beat yourself up about your secret thoughts
treat life as more of a game of forfeit or true
because everyone else is human as well
and they are having the same thoughts as you.
....

The Induction

She asked me if I had the shakes before
or ever hallucinated at all

did I ever stagger around
and did I eventually fall.
Did I ever tell a lot of lies
or did I even start stealing
then she got quite personal
about the way that I was feeling.
By now I was hurt and insulted
which I didn't think very nice
In fact if a had the gun with me
I could have shot the wee cow twice.
So the interrogation went on relentless
did I wash and change my clothes
yet the only scent was the smell of her
that really got up my nose.
Eventually of course the grilling ended
as all good and bad things do
so don't look for respect in that place
because that won't happen to you.
Then just when you are at your lowest ebb
and things couldn't get any worse
you have to queue for your calming pills
dispensed by a grumpy big nurse.
Of course there is always the 'Coup de grâce'
the penalty for all your drunken capers
and this blow of scorn and contempt was delivered
by the man who came in to sell us papers.
....

First Book

I remember getting my first book in school
taking it home to show everyone after lunch
of course we called it 'dinner time' then
anyway there I was as pleased as punch.
Into the bakers shop next door to my house
flaunting my new acquisition
being quizzed by the ladies in the shop
about my future ambition.
Then they told me how clever I was
and none of them called me a little brat
I was so surprised and so pleased
now I know I'll not forget that.
....

Karma

I remember well a time long ago
that is before I lost the place
I thought I was the dogs bollocks
only with such a pretty face.
Everything I touched turned to gold
you are 'clarted' somebody said
but it didn't take very long
for the gold to turn into lead.
So I studied this phenomenon quite often

because I had nothing else to do
and do you know what I realised then
(if it hasn't happened already)
that this is going to happen to you.
Life is just a prelude for Karma
to ensure a true balance on the scales
then along comes the grim reaper
with his claw hammer and big bag of nails.
Now I don't say this to scare or alarm you
to do so would be appalling and base
no, I tell you all this to give you plenty of time
so revise and amend, then keep the smile on your face.
....

Men

I never took a drink since ages now
well... it's at least a day or two
but that is not a record for me
albeit it might be for you.
Now my life doesn't revolve round a dram
it's more like a drop of fresh air
awful nice to breathe it in
and a comfort to know it's just there.
But there again did you ever notice
that sometimes men act and don't think
their conversation is usually about women
football, fishing, work or drink.
That doesn't sound too complicated does it
not exactly straining or taxing
in fact you can do it lying in bed
or sitting in a chair relaxing.
But that is the way of the male gender
so different from the ladies that's sure
yet ladies would you want us more complex
like a disease that has no cure.
....

Last Chance

Have you ever looked at life
and wondered about your lot
loads of money and possessions
and you can't count how much you've got.
Then you realise disappointedly
that for a few more pounds you are wishing
so you work hard to get a bit more
and for another year or two you are missing.
You get to thinking just one more year
then you can enjoy your life
even go on a holiday or two
in fact you could afford a family and wife.
You could go and watch a football game
and scream along with the rest
even take a wee look at cricket

to see which of the two is the best.
Try out the ten pin bowling
and skating that looks great fun
go and see horses and dogs racing
and see the big buggers run.
Socialising and dancing every weekend
chatting up everything in a skirt
getting to grips with a different world
and forgetting about all that work.
So by now you are getting excited
the world is your oyster you think
pleased that you were astute and careful
as you avoided the drugs and the drink.
Then as you await for a divine answer
as you sit in your chair and you dream
and you dream the dream of an old man
about your life and what might have been.
But reflection can be a mistake at times
and can leave you heart sore and bereft
so do you go and join in the dance
and make the most of what is left.
You know in your wisdom it is a bit late
but you don't even ask why or how
you don't analyse it or figure it out
do you just change and do it right now.
Now all this could be a normal dilemma
and you could toil for years with this teaser
you see if I were in your particular shoes
I just wouldn't know what to do either.

....

Instinct

It's been said that life is a huge learning curve
that's more modern than saying it's a school
some even liken it to a college or university
that's so poetic and academic it's not cool.
Anyway most of us do learn as we go along
starting off with one and one then two
then rapidly the mysteries reveal themselves
not for everyone, but there are always a few.
Then eventually as we get older and mature
we try to come to terms with the works of the heart
and the more we contemplate and figure it out
instinctively we knew all this from the start.
Now I'm not saying we don't have to learn
to think along those lines would be absurd
but you really don't have to teach a fish to swim
or give lessons about flying to a bird.
But we are human and not a bird or a fish
some even say we have infinite potential
never the less keep your instincts clear and clean
for to advance *all* knowledge is essential.

....

Blind

Have you ever made a snap judgement
a 'first impression' would be more correct
you think that someone is a right twat
and a pain in the arse you suspect.
Then for some reason the very next day
you think, 'oh he's not so bad'
just a victim of his upbringing
not all nasty, just a little bit sad.
Then as the weeks and months roll by
when another thought comes into your mind
that that guy is a pure bastard
and not to see it you must have been blind.

....

Faux pas

Did you ever make a real faux pas
that's posh for an embarrassing blunder
when you slip up trying to be smart
and the ensuing silence is like thunder.
Well I did more than once you know
when I think of it now I still cringe
oh yes I admit I had a dram or two
but I wasn't out of control on the binge.
Now I didn't think of this before now
but there were two occasions much the same
both times I was trying to be so charming
the only difference being the lady's name.
I started off with my usual blog
trying to be a smoothy more or less
but it wasn't very long
before I was in a right mess
I silently pleaded with my wife
not to leave me with my howler alone
all she did was whisper to me
'you are all on your very own'.
At one time that would be punishment
but not comparable to what I was feeling
I know now what the electric chair feels like
when you pray to God in the ceiling.
They say when you are near life's end
your life flashes before your eyes
If anybody tell you that's not true
they don't really know and tell lies.
Now I can hardly bring myself to write this
I can't even say it was a mistaken tongue twister
because I said how pretty her daughter was
and she replied I was wrong, and that it was her older sister.

....

Unfair

Do you know for a man my age
I never tried a lot of crime or sin

472

never really fancied doing very much
apart from a little whisky and gin.
Now you may think that's not normal
or else I hadn't quite got the guts
and I can think of lots of reasons
but there is always a list of 'buts'.
Now all this abstinence doesn't matter a lot
before you start thinking I'm a saint
maybe the thought never entered your mind
so I'll make it clear I ain't.
You see if you think of anything at all
It gets recorded in your mind as a fact
If you are fancying your neighbours wife right now
It doesn't matter if it is courage you lacked.
All gets recorded as real as if you did it
I personally don't think that very fair
but if you could look in your memory banks
you will see the truth and that action is there.
Did you ever think of swindling the stock market
even robbing a bank or train
how about a post office or corner shop
or hijacking an aeroplane.
Are you jealous of your friend's financial success
maybe silently hate the little sod
all that thoughts gets down loaded and encrypted
and is more or less waiting on a disc for God.
Nothing is missed out not one thought
every desire you have ever had
I'm lucky I have forgotten most of mine
but they are still there and that is sad.
So nobody escapes, it's a justice I suppose
but I still don't think it very fair
the wee blonde down the road had a torrid romance
yes with me, and I get the blame and I wasn't even there.
....

Nature

We get lots of creatures round our house at night
and you may well ask how do I know
well it's all so very logical
I can see their tracks in the snow.
Roe deer, pheasants, and some kind of cat
foxes and badgers some mice and a rat
why do they come only in the moonlight to appear
do they leave their tracks so we know they were here.
Or is the reason far more simple than that
why they all come out of the wood
It's just because they are hungry
and we give them some food.
Now you would think by now
that we would know each other by name
for shouting out 'puss puss' and 'chook chook'
Is not really quite the same.
But nature has decreed a separation

that none of us should hold hands
why, even the mouse knows that too
and every fox quite understands.
....

Mild Fantasy

I used to think I don't want to be me
in fact at times I wanted to be you
but really I didn't think that all of the time
maybe you do this too.
But that is just a normal fantasy
as they say the grass is always greener
and the cows that stretch over the fence
they're not smarter at all just keener.
So yes I've begun to disagree already
now I don't want to be you or even Elvis at all
I was just wondering what a dance would be like
if I were the most famous man in the hall.
....

A Guard

I was watching a film about Auschwitz
and do you know it made me think
If I were a German guard and got orders
would I be a coward and swim or a hero and sink.
It's only human to think that I would be brave
not do the wrong but do the right
be positive brave and confident
and not even consider that you 'might'
Oh yes hindsight is a wonderful thing
It's a wisdom quite often felt and seen
It takes away the guesswork and questions
of what you might have done and been.
So now we can all be smug and cocky
with no doubts at all, no, none
but if you are as sure as all that
then you are the only one.
....

Brain Cells

They used to say that you can learn too much
and if you do your brain will snap
but I don't go along with that theory
in fact I think it is crap.
Your brain is not a receptacle
that can be damaged by overfill
it's more like a jug of water
when it's full it starts to spill.
And all the overflowed stuff
can flow at a terrible rate
and that doesn't matter at all

because all of it is out of date.
Then the brain starts to compress the rest
until the data's like the head of a pin
then you have an empty mind
and once more you can begin.
Now that is why a professor looks scary
you may even think his behaviour distressing
but when he is scratching his head and mumbling
he's not really mad but decompressing.

....

Gods

Your pin code has four little numbers
do you appreciate how many ways they can go
if you can't figure it out all by yourself
come clean and say you don't know.
If you pay attention maybe I'll tell you
right now I'll say there are tons
of course that is a measure of weight
and nothing to do with our sums.
Well before I lose the place I will tell you
there are ten thousand ways minus one
and if you think there is a short cut
I'll tell you now there are none.
Now think of that four wee numbers for a while
then add two billion more
and see how many ways they will go
you may even notice it is a lot more than four.
Now after that exercise you must feel drained
the configuration of near an infinite amount
that is an almost never ending sum
which is near enough for those who can count.
By now you must be getting excited
the enormity of natural truth
it all seems so unnaturally gigantic
but there again I have no proof.
Now where is this all leading you may ask
of course it's the number of cells in your brain
yes we have the potential to be gods
because the numbers are the very same.

....

The Shooting

Did you see the police shot dead the architect
who was raving and quite distressed
he was brandishing a shotgun out of the window
and displaying all the symptoms
that he was depressed.
Now the police had plenty of marksmen
and of their accuracy I have no doubt
they could shoot the head of a pin
yes, at a hundred yards or there-about.
Now they had the artist surrounded

a sniper behind every window and wall
and they all shot the man in the heart
for some reason, unknown to us all.
....

Rude on the Road

Oh my goodness I thought
that driver has lost the place
all because of a little gesture
he turned a wee run in to a chase.
I wish he didn't react like that
the gesticulations weren't really meant
just a little boyish prank
as down the road they went.
But now I see the devil in his eyes
hell bent on a confrontation
if he had a faster car
he could cause a big sensation.
But his old Ford is a donkey
and I have no wish to brag
but he hasn't a chance in Hades
of catching me in my Jag.
....

Rusty Cars

I remember the British cars years ago
were synonymous with Fridays and rust
then our motorcycle industry joined in too
and most of them went and got bust.
Now I wish I could be sorry for them
but their cars and bikes I couldn't afford
and really even the new ones were rusty
so eventually I bought a Honda Accord.
Yet our companies were so stubborn then
convinced the foreign ones wouldn't catch on
yet every park is full of them now
while most of ours have all gone.
Now of course I do have pangs of regret
as a true loyal Brit' that is just
until I was told it was the gospel truth
that they deliberately made cars that rust.
....

New Minister

The decorators are now in the manse next door
and doing their papering and painting
I hope the new ministers wife didn't hear about me
or else she'd be panicking and fainting.
But the stories about me were all an exaggeration
well most of them more or less
but I'm not going to rehash that old chestnut

because what I remember is only a guess.
Yes I only think that I kept them all young at heart
but there again it is only God that knows
only I do remember Roddy was getting jumpy
and poor Margaret was really kept on her toes.
Yes that is just a part of life that's now all over
but I'm not going to say that I'm finished
maybe just a wee bit tired out
or perhaps you could say, diminished.
Yet at the moment I have no intention of reverting
but if I don't give them a visit they might be offended
I just wonder if they ever got the sofa fixed
or the wee antique coffee table mended.
Now isn't all this so exciting for us all
new people to socialise with and befriend
and if they don't like my visits
do what everyone else does and just pretend.

....

Hero's

I never believed in Santa or Rudolph
or any other of Mister Claus's reindeer
never believed in the cabbage patch or stork
but with Oliver Twist shed many a tear.
Now mostly I believed in Robin Hood
although I knew the story was just a fable
the same as it was with Sir Arthur
and the other knights who sat round the table.
But I firmly believed in Morgan the Mighty
I knew him so well I just called him Mighty
and I was so enthralled with his story
I would read a wee bit nightly.
You see all wee boys need a hero
and little girls need a heroine too
maybe yours was Wonder Woman or John Wayne
so in times of trouble, ask them what they would do.

....

Have a Price

Do you ever get to thinking the country is cracking
there are so many people in the wrong jobs
millionaires pleading for charity money
and once respected policemen acting like yobs.
Politicians too seem so out of touch
they don't know the price of a loaf of bread
instead of research they read the papers
and take all that news as gospel instead.
A million pounds is just a trifle they say
yes when it's compared to a hundred and twenty
a semi-detached is just a hovel
if you are one of the landed gentry.
How can anyone know what it's like to be poor
especially the rich, even me and you
we just use a bit of imagination

and then we still only think that we do.
But poor men are rarely good leaders
and I do not wish to give insult or slight
not that they get much of a chance anyway
so you never know, they might.
Who do we trust then to lead us onward
now by that I don't mean who is bonny and nice
I am just so disappointed I remember the words
'That every man has his price'.
So does that mean that there is no hope for anybody
and we are all lost in some chaotic mess
will greedy men always succeed by craft and guile
like they are doing now, well more or less.
Anyway that does seem to be the way of the world
and that is the way that it always has been
you see the world hasn't changed very much at all
it all depends on the way that it's seen.

....

For Burning

I decided to burn some compositions
supposing to a publisher they were never sent
the text was quite understandable
even I knew what most of it meant.
But in the interest of economy of space
I had to let some chapters go
and how was I going to do that
in all honesty I didn't know.
Now to be truthful the script was total junk
and the meaning was minute or just some
in fact it contained such little sense
and if I were honest there were none.
So into the poly bag the chapters went
with hardly a second look
it never even entered my head
that it could be a damn good book.
But those thoughts were so presumptuous
because I knew it wasn't like 'War and Peace'
although I read it for many an hour
I always kept wishing that it would cease.
So I dragged the bag over to the furnace
actually it was an old oil drum
but that was better than a hole in the ground
and even the hole was better than none.
Now as you can imagine it was all so emotional
I almost wept as I emptied the bag
and as the papers fluttered in the drum
I gave a little whimper and my jaw gave a sag.
My chin was quivering with pent up grief
my knees went all wobbly
and I shook like a leaf.
Then alas alas, as I struck the match
gave a quick prayer and tossed it into the tin
I remembered what my granny told me
'There are times in life son when you just can't win'.

....

The Tattie

Do you ever use the word 'Tattie'
now that's what you call a real word
in a competition 'spud' would come in second
and 'potato' come a poor third.
Yes Tattie really has charisma and presence
especially when conjoined with milk
you just blend the two together
until the mixture is as smooth as silk.
And of course if you're feeling flush
you can mix the Tattie with butter
my granny said it could cure a cold
and it's said it could sort a stutter.
Oh yes Tattie has a wonderful sound
it has also a very good taste
and you can even feed pigs with the peelings
to avoid unnecessary waste.
Oh where would we be without a Tattie
the other staple diet would be pasta or rice
and quite honestly they are okay for puddings
but with beef I would have to think twice.
So let's make a toast to the Tattie
it can make a scone, soup or veggie dinner
can give you the vitality of a golf professional
while pasta and rice man is like a beginner.
....

Mood Swing

Do you ever sit and worry
about things you can't control
dig the hole of depression
and burrow away like a mole.
Then very soon you are so deep
that nobody's throws you a rope
you see you are out of sight by then
quite out of reach of even hope.
Now this bit of advice takes effort
just go and get your garden spade
and stop digging with your mind
instead you use the blade.
Now this technique is guaranteed
in one hours' time you will feel good
you see sweat and honest toil
always changes a mood.
....

Learning

Have you ever noticed a thing about learning
sometimes you don't have to even try
you just have to trust your unconscious mind
and don't even ask it how or why.
Just put yourself into a nice little trance
no need to wait for the concentration to begin

479

you just give your unconscious mind the nod
and it will rev up and take it all in.
Now this part of your brain never sleeps at all
in fact it is always twenty-four hours at the ready
sometimes it is so keen to get going
you might have to hold it back and say 'steady'.
I'm sure you remember when you were young
by rota you learned the tables
you also learned poetry by repetition
and maybe you still remember some fables.
Yet the strange thing about learning that way
when you think about it this is perfectly true
I remember learning lots of things perfectly
but what all the words meant, I hadn't a clue.
Then many years later for some unknown reason
a formula or a verse comes to mind
and right away you see the sense of it
you think for years you must have been blind.
The reason for this is quite simple really
your unconscious never forgets one letter or word
every figure symbol or number's still there
and it doesn't care if it's wise or absurd.
You see that is not the part of the brain that cares
all the information it contains could be right or wrong
the theory of relativity holds the same importance
as the words and tune of any old song.

....

Sparrow Hawk

I've taken a hand in the pecking order
and I have done it once or twice
I act when I see a predator dominate
and the results are always quite nice
I know it's not politically correct just now
in fact you may shout 'what are you doing'
but I have a hundred birds in my safe garden
whistling singing, loving and cooing.
Now you can sit in your stark cold yard
and stare hopefully at bare fence posts
waiting for a murdering monster to appear
all movement now are shadows and long gone ghosts.

....

Punishment

Another young woman murdered
dark deeds are still done at night
some perverts twisted reasoning
for evil ones to get some delight.
Now I know I've argued against it
and I've done so many a time
that we have to be more understanding
when dealing with punishment and crime.
But we should really be more practical

remembering that there are evil and sinning
because at this very moment in time
the wickedness in the world is winning.
Now I do not suggest mass hangings
or lots of shootings by firing squad
no priests or ministers or spiritual leaders
screaming for vengeance from God.
No, ignore the emotional radicals completely
and of course consider extenuating conditions
then do take that into consideration
as everyone makes their submissions.
Then with clear-headed common sense
and I don't say this for a reason to rhyme
do we really need a reminder from an old song
and make the punishment fit the crime.

....

Somewhere

I was very disappointed when I read a theory
or you could call it a hypothesis or a thought
yet it took two hundred pages to expound it
in a second handbook that I bought.
Now I won't write a big volume about it
because it really put me in a bad mood
the truth can sometimes be sickening
as of course nasty things really should.
Now the gist of the theory is quite simple
so for some imperfection you can allow
but no matter what you can think of and imagine
somebody somewhere is doing that right now.

....

Rules

Here in Britain we are horrified
and abhor our own mortality
while in the east it's seen as okay
and quite accept the odd fatality.
But did you wonder why this is so
are our characters a little bit weak
or do we hold life more precious
while in the east they see it as cheap.
So what then is the worth of a man
or a wife, mother, daughter or sister
does the value drop right away
if you're a female and not a mister.
By now we should have got it right
and in our judgement take some pride
surely we don't need a book of value
and call it 'The Human Glasses Guide'.
But we seem to need a written law
advice for every value and action
a volume of rules for a lot of fools
and a regulation for every distraction.

....

Fish

Lorries are passing my house every day
I was told they are exporting fish
some to France and some to Spain
to make some European dish.
Now has any firm that many trucks
every day I see two or three
and if I waken in the night
I'll see more I'll guarantee.
Well I got to thinking about the fish
in the north there were always plenty
but with all that lorries passing now
it's no wonder the seas are empty.
....

Government

I often wonder about the British people
our voting pattern can be a bit of a joke
we all seem to be doing quite well
until the opposition says they can do better
and do all this at a stroke.
Then we vote them in and 'oh disaster'
they never realized we were in such a mess
so they will have to raise our taxes
and everything else as well more or less.
Yes you can see the glee in their eyes
as they make a maiden speech
puffing up their chest like a peacock
and tell us that prosperity is just out of reach.
Then they give all the leaders a rise in pay
and that is so we can get and keep the best
only they go and make a cock up of things
and for the new prime minister that is a pest.
One poor man couldn't organise salt for winter
and to get the gritters out he quite forgot
the salt and grit was so dear to buy by then
so he just thought he had better not.
Another minister claimed too much expenses
when the speaker saw it he shouted 'Good grief'
'are you not remembering what we were told
that we all had to turn over a new leaf'.
So blundering on for five more years
the population appalled at their nerve
and of course some smart arse is always there
to tell us we get the government that we deserve.
....

The Slap

I told you I got slapped in the face by a teacher once
and of that incident I never forgot
then anytime I thought I would be cheeky

482

I knew that I better not.
As I grew up all was kind of forgiven
and honestly the slap I did forget
until I read a submission on a forum
or call it a blog on the internet.
The site was about my hometown and school
and the slapping teacher got a mention
after all these years the feeling was still there
the embarrassment, indignity and tension.
Now the man who wrote in was named William
and as boys we shortened his name to Billy
I don't quite know why we always do that
but I suppose it is better than Willie.
Anyway it transpired Billy was slapped also
and he told us all about the tears he hid
now I tell you justice can be truly blind
for Billy didn't deserve the slap while I really did.
....

Culloden Moor

I used to think I'd be awful brave in battle
charging about the field with my spear
of course I would have a sword as well
a gun a shield and the rest of the gear.
Then I went to visit Culloden Moor
that is a battlefield near Inverness
and after walking around for an hour or so
my bravery in battle grew less and less.
The noise of the guns, the screaming
panicking horses and terrified men
adrenaline pounding around bodies
giving horrified soldiers the strength of ten.
I hear, see, and feel the atmosphere so clearly
the smell of blood and the sweat
and I am so certain about my bravery now
that Culloden Moor I'll never forget.
....

The Economy

The world economy is all to hell they say
or 'We're all doomed' as someone once said
maybe it wasn't uttered like that at all
and it's just a little something that I read.
Anyway, pensioners are going bankrupt
and I for one believe that to be true
because I am experiencing retirement
but there again, you might be too.
Now I'm not going to bleat about money
in fact I'm not even going to moan
not going to mention the wars we are in
or when we can get our brave troops home.
The state of the roads is normal I suppose
anyway they are all covered with snow

because we didn't salt them at all this year
so to be truthful I really don't know.
All the regions have to review their budgets
and there will be massive pay offs and cuts
they we're told not to bother with excuses
or stupid alibis or their ifs and their buts.
Yet one little thing I have to say
I can't let it pass without a mention
what clever banker gave a fifty year loan
when you can't pay a mortgage on the pension.
Now that is hope gone barking mad
but I better stop before I totally digress
because unless you are not quite with us
you will appreciate we are all in a mess.
Now just to conclude, for what it's worth
about the bankers and city gents we've got
while they tell us that they are the dogs bollocks
I'd whistle them into the boardroom and sack the bloody lot.
....

The Sharpener

Children can be so perceptive you know
I remember it well when I was seven or eight
I noticed my teacher fancying my pencil sharpener
it was very unusual and I thought it was great.
On some pretext she confiscated the sharpener
and I just knew what was on her mind
she said it was for my own safety
but I knew well she was not that kind.
Now this all happened a very long time ago
and that incident now long lost in history
but when reminiscing about the fate of my sharpener
It is only me now who can explain the mystery.
....

Decisions

Well I must get up out of bed
and think of what I'll do then
the dream I had an hour ago
left me worried like other men.
I might have a fight with the wife
that's bound to change my mood
It doesn't work all of the time
but usually it is quite good.
Or else I could stalk her like a stag
with all my cunning and stealth
but that can make her quite jumpy
and maybe not too good for my health.
Of course I could kick the dog outside
and tell her to take a long walk
but the last time she was gone two days
and the neighbours began to talk.
Oh it's awful being a man of decisions
I'd be better off being a woman instead

so I'll have to think about that for a while
and in the meantime stay in my bed.
....

Instinct

I told you already of the last thought many men have
that is just before they are about to expire
and no, it's not a good book and a large dram
sitting on a cold day beside a warm fire.
As you probably know most men are not like that
to be blunt, they access the instinct to procreate
personally I don't really see the point
and I do think they are leaving things a little bit late.
Anyway it is a well-known statistic
that many men expire in this final act
of course I have no experience or data about this
but it seems to be a well-known fact.
Now I don't think the cause was the effort involved
in fact it is exactly the other way round
the mind knew what was going to happen quite shortly
and instructed the sex instinct as soon as it's found.
Now this final impulse seems to be part of all nature
all living things even flowers bushes and trees
threaten a non-productive plant with demise
and that makes the bush go weak at the knees.
For thousands of years people have known about this
that whenever confronted with danger and fear
men and women give reign to their instincts
and unleash a desire for what they hold dear.
Now getting away from the serious side a bit
and not to dwell on the odd heart attack
the same instinct raises its head quite often
I'll tell you one or two for the crack.
Did you notice when a man has a girl in his car
or on the back of his motorbike
he may drive like a demented maniac
you may never have seen the like.
Of course he doesn't know what he is doing
well you can't expect too much from a man
but he is trying to seduce her by fear
and doing the best that he can.
Much the same when a young man wants to brawl
hoping his girl will see him win the fight
this one is always is a bit risky, but worth it
if it changes the 'no' into a 'might'.
Yes instincts are a wonderful two edged sword
and I don't say that to be witty
you see if the young man gets a doing
he might get lucky with a bit of pity.
Now very few men are aware of such things
they don't even think they need to be shown
in fact they think they invented a new technique
yes, all on their very own.
....

A Tool

Now the last wee ditty reminded me of food
which is another instinctual tool
but you will have to use this one wisely
so you won't look an utter fool.
Now most of us have joined food together
with love affection and caring
so when you buy her a box of chocolates
you hope it's more than sweets you'll be sharing.
The most obvious one of all of course
is to take the lady out to dinner
already you know she's mixed up love and food
so this one could be a winner.
Now you've bound to have noticed on TV
or else you saw it in the pictures
how the hero teases his girl with delicacies
like grapes, pomegranates, and dolly mixtures.
Well I'm not going to tell you any more
except that most of the instincts are idiot-proof
if not psychologists would all be Casanova's
but they are not, and that is the truth.
. . . .

Reality

Nobody can really deceive you
you can only do that to yourself
but of course you can be misled
by cunning scheming and stealth.
Nobody can make a fool of you
and most of us know that's true
but that is just another state of mind
that is entirely up to you.
Yet all that wisdom may be a paradox
or only a rough description of reality
for if you feel a fool you are a fool
and that is the actuality. .
. . . .

The Internet Form

Well I filled in an official form today
and I did it on the internet
I spent three hours filling it in
It's an experience I won't forget.
Constantly having to go back all the time
to correct the page I had just completed
It looked like a 'just to be sure bit'
in case that I had deliberately cheated.
Well I slaved away dripping sweat
my nerves in absolute tatters

I was only lucky I remained conscious
as if that is all that matters.
Oh yes another confusing question again
in every two or three pages
well I didn't exactly time it to the second
but even reading the notes took me ages.
All the time the computer checked my work
like a teacher looking over my shoulder
I tell you now she was pushing her luck
and I am the very man that told her.
Grossly intimidated I kept plodding on
then the wife came in for some advice
of course I started screaming abuse
which I know now wasn't very nice.
But my nerves were like piano wires by then
so to keep the peace I explained it for her sake
then the two of us stared at the screen
and we both began to shake.
But eventually common sense did prevail
the only talent that we could boast
so I crammed it all in an envelope
and sent it all off in the post.

....

University Challenge

We were watching University Challenge
and we both got ten out of ten
not one question did we understand
I'll bet we couldn't do that again.
Well, honestly we tried the next round
and I thought we really did great
in fact I was very pleased with nine
but the wife did better with an eight.
Now you may think this is pathetic
but we got so angry we could cuss
so we talked to our friends and relations
and do you know, they are worse than us.

....

Sport

When I was an innocent boy
I never understood why I didn't ski
never played golf or tennis
these sports were just not for me.
Instead I played an odd game of football
but rugger and cricket was out
badminton too was taboo
and for sailing there was no doubt.
So I spent a lot of time with the girls
and many of them I did court
that was the best way to spend my time
and it is far better fun than sport.

....

Debt

I was thinking about lack of funding
that sounds a wee bit better than debt
and that is just not having the cash
to pay for the things that we get
Oh what a nightmare situation
to have absolutely less than nothing
the very worst feeling some men can have
and believe me now I am not bluffing.
Now I propose a fair solution
for the debtor and the indebted
and no, it's not a simple answer
when you can say 'don't borrow to get it'.
But all jokes aside I'm deadly serious
about the debt, how about enforcing fifty-fifty
that would make the lender more cautious
and the borrower a bit more thrifty.
Now there is always an alternative solution
this one's been tried out before more or less
It's still a learning curve all the same
as the firms come in and repossess.
Now this would be justice for all
give both a lesson in self-respect
but you know there is always an angle
and the two of them will find it, I suspect.

....